*The Wanderer in Nineteeth-Century German Literature*

*Studies in German Literature, Linguistics, and Culture*

# The Wanderer in Nineteeth-Century German Literature

## Intellectual History and Cultural Criticism

Andrew Cusack

CAMDEN HOUSE
Rochester, New York

First published 2008
by Camden House

Camden House is an imprint of Boydell & Brewer Inc.
668 Mt. Hope Avenue, Rochester, NY 14620, USA
www.camden-house.com
and of Boydell & Brewer Limited
PO Box 9, Woodbridge, Suffolk IP12 3DF, UK
www.boydellandbrewer.com

ISBN-13: 978-1-57113-386-1
ISBN-10: 1-57113-386-0

**Library of Congress Cataloging-in-Publication Data**

Cusack, Andrew, 1969—
The wanderer in nineteenth-century German literature : intellectual history and cultural criticism / Andrew Cusack.
p. cm. —
Includes bibliographical references and index.
ISBN-13: 978-1-57113-386-1 (hardcover : alk. paper)
ISBN-10: 1-57113-386-0 (hardcover : alk. paper)
1. German literature — 19th century — History and criticism.
2. Nomads in literature. I. Title.

PT363.N6C87 2008
830.9'3526918—dc22

2008009729

A catalogue record for this title is available from the British Library.

This publication is printed on acid-free paper.
Printed in the United States of America.

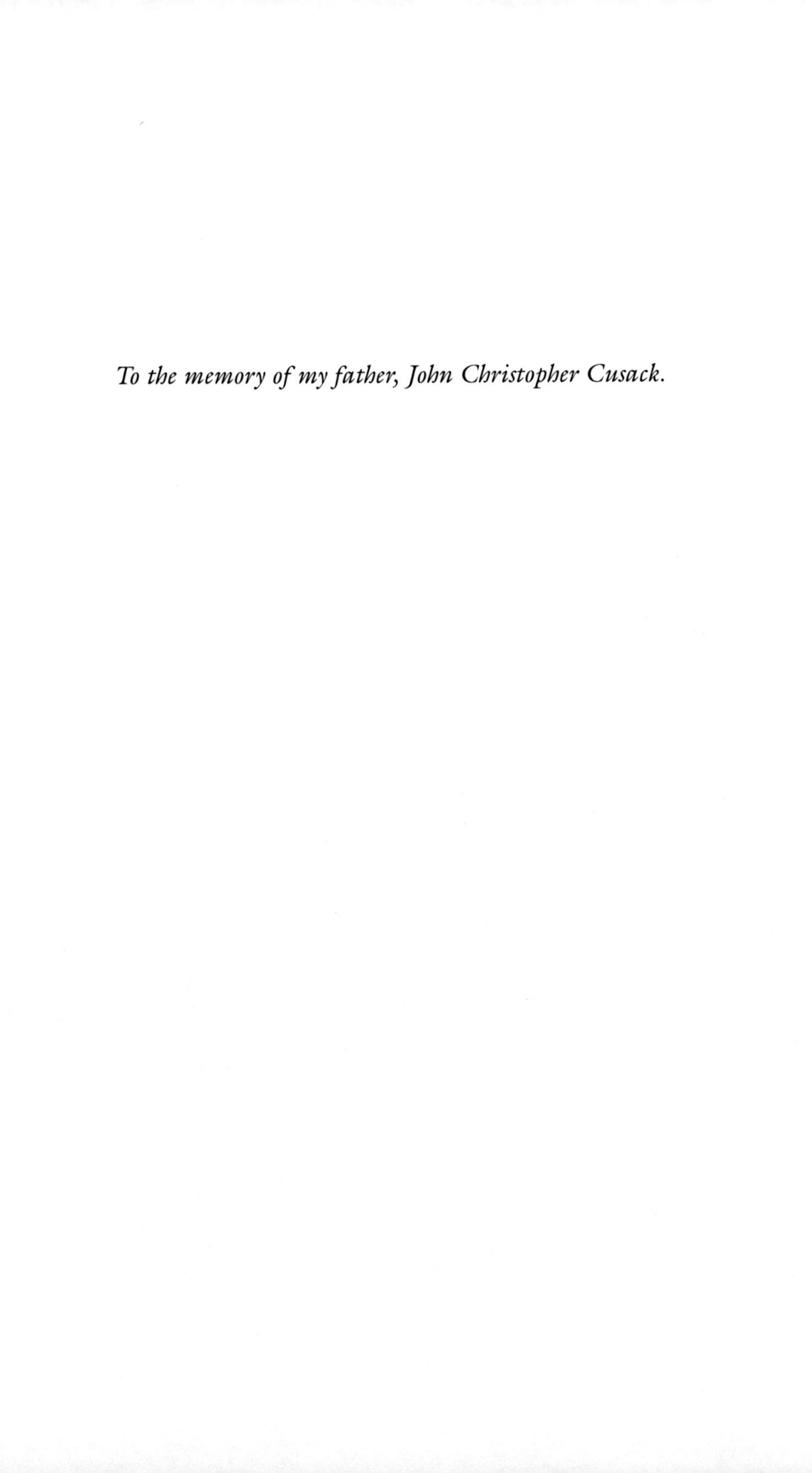

*To the memory of my father, John Christopher Cusack.*

Caminante, son tus huellas
el camino, y nada más;
caminante, no hay camino,
se hace camino al andar.
— Antonio Machado, *Proverbios y cantares*

[Wayfarer, it is your footprints
That are the road, and nothing besides;
Wayfarer, there is no road,
But that made in the traveling.]

# Contents

# Acknowledgments

THIS BOOK IS THE RESULT OF research conducted at Trinity College Dublin between October 2003 and October 2006. I am grateful to the Irish Research Council for the Humanities and Social Sciences, who provided the funding that made the research, including a three-month stay in Göttingen, possible. I would like also to thank the University of Dublin, whose scholarship included the privilege of rooms on Trinity's magnificent campus.

The staff and graduate students at the Department of Germanic Studies all provided encouragement and advice at various times. They are too numerous to name individually, but I hope they will accept this expression of thanks, which, though general, is heartfelt. The following individuals and groups all contributed materially to the project and I want therefore to make special mention of them.

Eda Sagarra put me in touch with colleagues and gave generously of her time and hospitality. Her dedication to teaching and scholarship, especially (but not exclusively) on the German nineteenth century, is a source of inspiration not only to this writer, but also to an international community of Germanists.

I am most grateful to Jürgen Barkhoff for sharing his expertise in Romanticism and the *Goethezeit* and for providing a wealth of suggestions on research literature and theoretical texts. But it was in his capacity as reader, and thus as the interlocutor I kept in mind during the writing of this work, that he gave me the greatest assistance. His scholarly interest and unhesitating willingness to accompany the work through numerous drafts are greatly appreciated.

Gilbert Carr offered valuable help, and spurred me on to completion. In Cologne, Heide Streiter-Buscher responded generously to my enquiries about Fontane. The friendly and knowledgeable staff of the Staats- und Universitätsbibliothek Göttingen and of the Library of Trinity College Dublin were always willing to answer my questions. For three years I was perhaps the best-known customer of Trinity's Inter-Library Loans office: their team tracked down German monographs and secondary literature with commendable efficiency.

At Camden House I had another learned reader and advisor in Jim Walker, the Editorial Director; he made me feel that his knowledge and experience were constantly at my disposal. His colleagues Katie Hurley (Managing Editor), Sue Smith (Production Manager), and Jane Best

(Production Editor) showed similarly impressive creative finesse and skill. Sue Innes was simply indispensable as a sharp-eyed and meticulous copy editor. At TCD, Tim Keefe helped prepare the illustrations for publication.

The Conference of University Teachers of German in Britain and Ireland generously provided financial assistance toward the costs of publishing the book.

Brenda Cusack and Brian Cusack, my mother and brother, were the source of essential moral support and encouragement throughout the various phases of research and writing. Their assistance has been no less valuable than that of my mentors. Brenda Cusack suggested Machado's lines as the epigraph to this book. And Brian Cusack provided a living example of a Romantic scientist of the kind I've tried to describe in chapter 2.

Dublin, February 2008

# Introduction

THE AIMS OF THE FOLLOWING STUDY are threefold: to identify a range of works of nineteenth-century German literature in which the wanderer motif is a significant element of composition, to enquire into the semantic function of the motif in those works, and to demonstrate how the motif creates links between literary and non-literary discourses. The focus will be on prose genres, and especially on the novel, since this can act as a highly effective integrator of elements from literary and non-literary discourses, lending it an unrivalled capacity to interpret the discursive totality of its own era.[1] Of course, it should be borne in mind that the novel is not restricted to an interpretive function but can itself participate in cultural change by acting as a vehicle for ideology.

The German nineteenth century that forms the frame of reference for this study is not as long as that proposed by David Blackbourn.[2] Its scope is defined by the discernible presence of the motif itself. Our century opens in 1795, the year in which the first three of the four volumes of Goethe's *Wilhelm Meisters Lehrjahre* appeared; and it closes in 1895, with the publication of Wilhelm Raabe's *Die Akten des Vogelsangs.* However, it soon becomes apparent that the wanderer motif is far more prevalent in the early part of the century, especially in what is often referred to as the *Goethezeit*, and indeed its prevalence in that era must in part be due to the influence of Goethe, in whose fictions the motif attains a unique functional range. By contrast, German literature in the latter part of the century, particularly from around 1850 onward, appears strikingly barren of what hitherto had been an important motif, a circumstance that this study will attempt to explain.

It is necessary to provide a definition of what we are to understand as a wanderer in the specific frame of reference of German literature. The English word is used throughout to stand for the German *Wanderer* as a convenience, though the English and German words have a different semantic range, as the definitions of the verbs *wandern / to wander* should clarify. First the Duden definition of the German verb:

> wandern: 1. eine Wanderung (längerer Weg durch die Natur, den man zu Fuß zurücklegt), Wanderungen machen [. . .]. 2. ohne ein Ziel anzusteuern, gemächlich gehen; sich irgendwo ergehen [. . .]. 3. (nicht seßhaft, ohne festen Aufenthaltsort) umher-, von Ort zu Ort, zu einem entfernten Ziel ziehen [. . .].[3]

Compare the corresponding definition of the English cognate:

> wander I. Intransitive senses. [. . .]. 1.a. Of persons or animals: To move hither and thither without fixed course or certain aim; to be (in motion) without control or direction; to roam, ramble, go idly or restlessly about; to have no fixed abode or station. [. . .]. II. Transitive senses. [. . .]. 5. To roam over, in, through (a place), to traverse in wandering.[4]

The sense of aimlessness or undirectedness, which is dominant in the intransitive senses of the English verb, is facultative in its German equivalent. The German verb *wandern* denotes traveling, primarily the action of walking, which may or may not be directed at a particular goal. In this respect it is closer to the transitive senses of its English cognate.

When I refer to wandering in the following, the word should be understood in all the senses conveyed by the German verb *wandern*, a semantic range covered by the transitive uses of the English verb *to wander*. That is to say, wandering will be used throughout to denote travel, frequently (but not exclusively) in the sense of a journey undertaken on foot, which may or may not be directed toward a particular goal, but also to refer to nomadism, those forms of existence distinct from the settled life. The wanderers that I have in mind are therefore the itinerant players, peddlers, journeymen, gypsies, and migrants who thronged the roads throughout the eighteenth and nineteenth centuries, as well as the artists, scientists, explorers, and students who, from the early phase of Romanticism onward, also identified themselves as wanderers.

We now need to attempt to clarify the status of that literary element, the motif, that forms the object of this study. The French word *motif* was first used as an aesthetic term in the *Encylopédie* of 1765, where it was used in musicology to denote a minimal melodic element. It came to be applied to the visual arts in the late eighteenth century. Goethe is credited with being the first to employ the term with regard to literature,[5] in which field it signifies a minimal unit of content: "Im Deutschen bezeichnet das Wort Motiv eine kleinere stoffliche Einheit, die zwar noch nicht einen ganzen Plot, eine Fabel umfaßt, aber doch bereits ein inhaltliches, situationsmäßiges Element darstellt."[6] The following definition is, however, more revealing of the functional role of the literary motif, specifying it as: "[das] kleinste selbständige Inhalts-Einheit oder tradierbares intertextuelles Element eines literarischen Werkes."[7] On this definition, the motif is not merely a minimal element of content; it is an element that is highly amenable to being transmitted from one literary work to another.

It is precisely the intertextual status of the literary motif and its ability to be transmitted diachronically that are of particular interest in this study, which is concerned with the ways in which the motif of the wanderer is implemented by different authors in their particular historical settings. The aim is not to replicate the collecting and inventorying of motifs, familiar to us from folk-literature studies from the Grimm brothers to Stith Thompson, or to revive the scientistic positivism of Wilhelm Scherer, but to attempt to relate concrete realizations of the motif to historical, aesthetic, and genre factors.

Remarkably few studies of the wanderer motif have been undertaken in the German literature of the nineteenth century, and the few that exist exhibit various shortcomings.[8] As late as 1999 Wolfgang Albrecht could remark of such efforts "Diese Ansätze sind weder für die sogenannte Goethezeit noch für spätere Perioden fortgeführt worden," concluding: "Nähere Beachtung verlangen ebenfalls die Motive des Wanderns in Literatur und bildender Kunst."[9] Both of the studies mentioned by Albrecht, to my knowledge the only surveys of the motif of the wanderer (more precisely, of wandering) in German literature, are hampered by their methodological approaches. Neither study seeks to relate the realization of the motif in the literary works to the extra-literary context, grounded as they are in a work-immanent approach. As a result, the manner in which the motif contributes to the historical specificity of the works goes unconsidered. Moreover, the studies are vitiated by their proneness to unsupported affirmations of the works discussed or of authorial genius.

The following study, by contrast, seeks to situate the motif of the wanderer in its historical specificity. This requires viewing the motif in a much wider context than previously. Skorna restricts his enquiry to a particular genre (the novel) and period (*Goethezeit*); Schmidlin is content to trace the motif of wandering in the oeuvre of a single author (Goethe). In principle, this study is interested in all literary works in a given period in which the wanderer motif is a significant element of composition. However, since some restriction of the field is necessary, the focus will be on prose narratives, especially the novel, for the reason given above.

It should have become clear from the foregoing that the study is interested in the historicity of the various realizations of the motif of the wanderer. The study is based on two guiding assumptions: first, that the motif is widely used, that it is in some way characteristic of a significant body of literary works in the nineteenth century. Second, I shall assume that the prominence of the motif can be explained with reference to changes in the material and intellectual conditions occurring during that period. To clarify what is meant by changes in material conditions one need only point to the new technologies of travel, especially the railway. These innovations, together with the new phenomenon of mass migration, undoubtedly changed the view of man and his possibilities. But the period also witnessed the emergence of a new episteme, what Foucault has identified as the advent of "man" as an object of such new disciplines as anthropology.[10] This turn of scientific attention to the processes of life gave rise to new cultural practices aimed at molding the human body. Among these we find a new form of pedestrianism, which Hans-Joachim Althaus terms "bürgerliches Freizeitwandern."[11] This practice is a product of the late Enlightenment, but it is the literature of Romanticism that is primarily responsible for popularizing it. What is significant about it is that it rests on a new understanding of the self as the object of knowledge and of ameliorative action. The political implications of the practice are clear: the technique of bourgeois wandering was aimed at maintaining the physical and mental condition, and hence the productivity, of the individual bourgeois subject.

A concern with the historicity of literary texts is characteristic of two closely related interpretive approaches: new historicism and cultural materialism. This study will draw on the hermeneutic resources of these models while trying to avoid some of their pitfalls, which I will discuss below. What these two approaches have in common is that they regard the culture in which literary texts are situated as a context. That is to say, they treat culture itself as a text, a paradigm associated in the field of cultural anthropology with its leading proponent, the ethnographer, Clifford Geertz. Geertz credits Max Weber, who sees man as inhabiting self-spun webs of significance, as his source; but French post-structuralism — Derrida's work on semiotics, Kristeva's on intertextuality — is the true fount of the current idea of culture as *texte général.*[12] For Geertz the only way for the ethnographer to get to grips with the complexities of a foreign (or any) culture is to employ the method that he calls "thick description." What this involves is a dense, layered hermeneutic writing that seeks to unravel the "structures of signification" in the cultural object under study. The key to this approach is acknowledging the distance that separates the interpreter, in his or her particular historical moment, from that object. This is, of course, an essentially literary mode of interpretation applied to new cultural objects. With the adoption of "thick description" as a method for the analysis of literary texts by new historicists and others, the wheel has turned full circle: a literary hermeneutic that had been appropriated by ethnographers has been rediscovered by literary scholars. This reimportation has transformed literary studies by expanding the range of objects to which its hermeneutic could be applied. Indeed, Neumann and Weigel claim that the semiotic model of culture — which implies that culture is readable — has gone some way to overcoming the crisis of confidence in literary studies, which can, after all, claim the skills of close reading as its stock-in-trade.[13]

The advantage of the culture-as-text model is that it puts texts (in the traditional sense) on the same footing for the purpose of interpretation as the cultural practices in which they are enmeshed. Because this model requires us to view all forms of cultural practice as bearing significance, we can show how they transmit meaning to, and receive meaning from, other cultural texts, such as literary works. We can show, for instance, how cultural "texts," such as the ritualized practices of journeymen, are appropriated and transformed in literature. Another advantage of this paradigm is that it allows us to view the human subject as a cultural construct, thereby acknowledging that subjectivity is to some degree the product of a particular historical moment. To this extent the model represents an improvement on humanist essentialism, which appeals to some notionally invariant human nature. Oddly enough, some new historicists have claimed to experience the concept of man-as-artifact as oppressive. Stephen Greenblatt, for instance, once seemed to contemplate this revelation with a sense of despair. Near the end of his influential work *Renaissance Self-Fashioning* he writes: "In all my texts and documents there were, so far as I could tell, no moments of pure, unfettered subjectivity; indeed the human subject itself came to seem remarkably unfree, the ideological product of the relations of power in a particular society."[14] But the news that we are culturally determined beings does not imply our essential unfreedom. Nor does it require that we renounce completely the notion of human universals, since what makes us human is arguably our very ability to assimilate culture — and our utter inability to survive without it.[15]

The value of new historicism and cultural materialism as critical methods lies in their recognition of the interpenetration of literary and non-literary discourses, an insight that has enabled critics to set up productive exchanges between literary and non-literary texts. There are, however, problems associated with both methods, problems that I will now seek to address. First, in their insistence on the textuality of culture, both new historicism and cultural materialism deny that the literary text has a privileged status; it is seen as just one more text among a plethora of others. It is a key tenet of new historicism that literary and non-literary texts "circulate inseparably."[16] Similarly, cultural materialists take the view that the literary text cannot be considered in isolation from other social practices.[17] The problem with the refusal to differentiate literary works from other texts lies in the failure to take account of the aesthetic moment in such texts. I will want to assert here that literary texts, as aesthetically formed artifacts, differ from others in respect of the multiplicity of meanings they are capable of bearing within them, a potential that accounts for such texts' resistance to paraphrase. This hard-to-define aesthetic quality is, moreover, one of the reasons why certain literary works prove very durable, surviving in very different historical conditions from the ones in which they were composed. (Canonical texts do not achieve their status merely because they have been selected by an authority, but also through selection by large numbers of readers.) Yet it is precisely the aesthetic dimension that practitioners of the new historically grounded methods have shied away from, perhaps out of a desire to distance themselves from the legacy and the methods of formalist criticism.[18]

One criticism that has been leveled at new historicism specifically is that, while its practitioners stress the textuality of culture, they are less keen to acknowledge the historicity of texts. Such criticism grew more intense with Greenblatt's decision to abandon the term "new historicism" in favor of "cultural poetics" as a label for his own critical praxis.[19] This perception is due no doubt to the undeniable fact that most new historicist studies operate with a synchronic perspective. Their aim is generally to probe the texture of a particular historical period — the English Renaissance, for example — by reading those literary and non-literary texts that coexist in it and constitute its discourse. At the same time, new historicists emphasize the uniqueness of the period under study, its distinctness from the present. In this they follow the founding father of nineteenth-century historicism, Herder, who insists that each age must be understood on its own terms.[20] Taken to extremes, this emphasis on distinctiveness and separateness can make each historical age appear like a backwater, cut off from the flux of history, "out of the swing of the sea," as it were. Yet there is nothing specific to new historicism, which is in any case a loose bundle of practices, that requires the interpreter to become mired in synchronicity. I will not want to take such a perspective here, where the task is to link changes in the function of the motif to historical change. Indeed, the study of a literary motif positively demands attention to the diachronic aspect, a point to which I will return presently.

This tendency toward synchronicity is connected with a prevailing view in new historicism, namely that literary works function in every historical period as instantiations of power. Although new historicists admit the possibility of subversion in literature, they maintain that it is inevitably co-opted by dominant power structures. They go so far as to claim that the dominant power structures of a society require the production of subversion in literature since this provides a justification for the exercise of power. Subversive moments in literature are seen as reinforcing the categories of the society by reproducing them. Here, too, I will part company with most new historicist critics and assert that aesthetic works can indeed form reservoirs of heterodox ideas, if only because their capacity for harboring multiple meanings means that, even if they are produced with the intention of validating dominant belief systems, they cannot always succeed in doing so. Cultural materialists, of course, maintain that literature can provide an effective locus of subversion and resistance to hegemonic ideologies. This latter view is to be preferred, not least because it is less dogmatic to claim that literature can, in certain circumstances, function as a locus of resistance than it is to insist that all manifestations of subversion in literature are contained as soon as they appear. Does rejecting the containment hypothesis[21] so characteristic of much new historicist writing then entail a turn to a cultural materialist approach? Not necessarily. Embracing cultural materialism comes at the price of opting in to a particular political program: the job of the cultural materialist critic is to unearth subversive moments in literature so that these can be applied in contemporary political practice. This commitment to producing subversive readings of literary texts seems unduly restrictive as an interpretive practice.

New historicism is a broad enough church to allow us to adopt its best features without reproducing some of its more questionable tendencies. This is clear enough from the looseness of Greenblatt's early definition of new historicism as a critical practice that "challenges the assumptions that guarantee a secure distinction between 'literary foreground' and 'political background,' or, more generally, between artistic production and other kinds of social production"[22] a definition with which the founder of cultural materialism, Greenblatt's sometime mentor, Raymond Williams, would surely have concurred.

The study of motifs is preeminently suited to demonstrating the historicity of literature. Because the motif is a schema, a semantic framework, it is capable of acquiring new meaning at different historical moments, while at the same time carrying over residual meanings from earlier periods. In this respect the literary motif is a trans-historical element that acts to bind distinct periods together. The motif is therefore not just a site of innovation but a vehicle for "cultural memory."[23] Its intertextuality is not confined to a particular synchronic space but operates along the time–axis, so motifs play a key part in transmitting meaning from the literature (and culture) of a particular age to another. As the motif undergoes successive reinterpretations, it accumulates potential significances, which then become available to the next generation of authors. In the *Lehrjahre*, for example, Goethe provides a new interpretation of the figure of the wanderer as a man who undergoes a particular kind of education, one that prepares him to become a functioning member of a modern society. This new association of the figure of the wanderer with the discourse of education proved highly productive, spawning other literary wanderers also embarked on the *Bildungsweg*. One thinks of the protagonists of *Franz Sternbalds Wanderungen* and *Heinrich von Ofterdingen* as well as those of later variations on the theme of *Bildung*, such as Keller's *Der grüne Heinrich*.

On the face of it, the adoption of the culture-as-text paradigm is problematical, for it commits us to one of two available models of intertextuality, namely the global model of poststructuralism, which regards each and every text as forming part of a global intertext. The problem with this model, which effectively equates intertextuality with textuality plain and simple, is that it lacks the heuristic usefulness of the more restricted structuralist or hermeneutic model. This latter model restricts the term "intertextuality" to conscious, intentional, and marked references within a text to other texts. But, as Manfred Pfister argues, committing to one of these models does not require us to discard the other; rather, the phenomena that the restricted model seeks to grasp may be seen as striking instances of global intertextuality.[24] In an effort to mediate between these two models Pfister proposes a number of criteria for determining the intensity of intertextual references.[25] Pfister does not say so, but this scaling of intertextuality enables us also to assert the privileged status of literary texts vis-à-vis other texts, for literary texts are capable of a degree of intertextual intensity not attainable by other text types.[26] Consider the criterion of auto-reflexivity: literary texts have a unique capacity not only to refer explicitly to pre-texts but also to reflect upon their own intertextuality and, more generally, on their own mode of representation. The same holds for the criterion of dialogicity: literary texts are unrivalled in their ability to isolate mythemes (significant elements of myth) and other ideological elements from their original contexts, to subject them to scrutiny, and to place them in dialogue with new contexts, thereby relativizing them.

At this point I will rehearse those aspects of the critical practices of new historicism and cultural materialism by which this study will be guided, and the tendencies it will seek to avoid:

— "thick description," the use of a hermeneutic mode of writing that draws on a range of discursive sources in an effort to feel its way into a past era and evoke its texture.

— the idea that literary texts are embedded in wider discursive ensembles within which they can act as storehouses of social significance. They receive contemporary meaning from the discursive context but can also act as transmitters of uncontemporary meaning into that context. Motifs play an important part in keeping such uncontemporary meanings alive in literary discourse.

— the idea that subjectivity is to some degree constituted by the discursive ensemble of a given epoch.

— dissent from the new-historicist assertion that literary and non-literary texts "circulate inseparably" and the tendency to ignore the specific qualities of aesthetically formed texts.

— dissent from the new-historicist view that literature creates world-views and cements power relations rather than interrogating and reflecting critically upon them.

In conclusion it will be necessary to make a few remarks concerning the selection of the texts upon which this study is based. Apart from the matter of genre, two general principles guided this selection. First, it was considered desirable to get as even a distribution of materials across the nineteenth century as possible, in order to judge whether the motif underwent changes in function in this period. Second, the aim was to locate the motif in the broadest possible discursive context: to this end works were selected on the basis of their apparent affinity for certain discourses, among them Romantic aesthetics and *Naturphilosophie*, education/anthropology, nationality/cosmopolitanism, and social marginality. These categories have a purely heuristic status, the intention being to draw out and amplify as many different functional aspects of the motif as possible, and not to imply that individual poetic works need to be seen as belonging to one sphere of discourse or another.

Perhaps something needs to be said about the selection of the works themselves. The inclusion of Goethe's *Wilhelm Meisters Lehrjahre* (1796) and *Wilhelm Meisters Wanderjahre oder die Entsagenden* (1821/29) needs no justification in a study of this nature: these two novels influenced as none other what has been called the "German tradition of self-cultivation,"[27] and in both the wanderer motif is intimately bound up with the theme of *Bildung*. The complex of wandering and education recurs in Tieck's *Franz Sternbalds Wanderungen* (1798) and Novalis's *Heinrich von Ofterdingen* (1802), which deserve to be recognized as foundational texts for a generation of Romantic artists and scientists. Heine's *Harzreise* (1826) and Fontane's *Wanderungen durch die Mark Brandenburg* (1861–81) are each in their own way concerned with the matter of "Vaterländische Wanderungen,"[28] domestic tourism used in the constitution of national identity. Heine ironizes the practice, questioning its complicity in a chauvinist strain of nationalism; Fontane affirms it as a means of recovering the values of the past. Büchner's *Lenz* (1839) contributes to political discourse in a more oblique manner, attacking the aesthetic norms that underpin bourgeois ideology. Four novels form the basis of the final chapter: the context for the first, Gotthelf's *Jakobs Wanderungen* (1846–47) is the pauperization crisis in the turbulent years prior to the March 1848 revolution. Like Heine's and (to some extent) Fontane's works, this novel represents an attempt to intervene directly in the contemporary political situation. Gotthelf's target readership is made up of politicized artisans, a highly mobile group, which the conservative author fears as a potential source of social revolution. Holtei's *Vagabunden* (1851) is torn between the desire to embrace the actor's life and an acute awareness of the stigma of its unbourgeois character: against its author's intentions the work reveals the normative pressures bearing down on those whose lives were at odds with a nascent ideology of the settled life. Finally, Raabe's *Abu Telfan* (1867) and *Die Akten des Vogelsangs* (1895) are included for their exemplary use of the wanderer motif as an intertextual element in narratives that question the prevailing ideologies of their day.

## Notes

1 Although the wanderer motif is a prominent element in lyric genres (one has only to think of Eichendorff or of Wilhelm Müller's *Winterreise*), its function in those genres arguably merits a separate study, one capable of doing justice to the specificities of lyric form. Nevertheless, instantiations of the motif in lyric poetry are occasionally referred to here in order to illustrate the motif's general literary value in a given period.

2 David Blackbourn, *History of Germany, 1780–1918: The Long Nineteenth Century* (Oxford: Blackwell, 2003).

[3] *Duden: Das große Wörterbuch der deutschen Sprache*, 6 vols. (Mannheim: Bibliographisches Institut, 1976–81), 6:2838.

[4] *Oxford English Dictionary*, 2nd ed., 20 vols. (Oxford: Oxford UP, 1989), 19:868–69.

[5] In *Wilhelm Meisters Lehrjahre* (1796). See Harald Fricke et al., eds., *Reallexikon der deutschen Literaturwissenschaft*, 3rd ed., 3 vols. (Berlin: Walter de Gruyter, 1997–2003), 2:638–43; here, 639; According to the *Oxford English Dictionary* the earliest attested use of the term "motif" in English to refer to a literary work occurs in 1851.

[6] Elisabeth Frenzel, *Stoff- Motiv- und Symbolforschung*, 3rd ed. (Stuttgart: Metzler, 1970), 28.

[7] Fricke, *Reallexikon*, 2:638.

[8] Bruno Schmidlin, *Das Motiv des Wanderns bei Goethe* (Ph.D. diss., University of Bern, 1953; repr., Winterthur, Switzerland: Keller, 1963). Hans-Jürgen Skorna, *Das Wandermotiv im Roman der Goethezeit* (Ph.D. diss., University of Cologne, 1961).

[9] Wolfgang Albrecht, "Kultur und Physiologie des Wanderns: Einleitende Vorüberlegungen eines Germanisten zur interdisziplinären Erforschung der deutschsprachigen Wanderliteratur," in *Wanderzwang — Wanderlust: Formen der Raum und Sozialerfahrung zwischen Aufklärung und Frühindustrialisierung*, ed. Wolfgang Albrecht and Hans-Joachim Kertscher (Tübingen: Niemeyer, 1999), 1–12; here, 11).

[10] Michel Foucault, *The Order of Things* (London: Routledge, 1994), 308–9.

[11] Hans-Joachim Althaus, "Bürgerliche Wanderlust: Anmerkungen zur Entstehung eines Kultur- und Bewegungsmusters," in Albrecht and Kertscher, *Wanderzwang*, 25–43.

[12] Clifford Geertz, *The Interpretation of Cultures* (New York: Basic Books, 2000), 5. Julia Kristeva, *Sémeoitiké: Recherches pour une sémanalyse* (Paris: Éditions du Seuil, 1969). The term *texte général* from Jacques Derrida, "Avoir l'oreille de la philosophie," in *Écarts: Quatre essais à propos de Jacques Derrida*, ed. Lucette Finas et al. (Paris: Fayard, 1973), 301–12; here, 310.

[13] Gerhard Neumann and Sigrid Weigel, eds., *Lesbarkeit der Kultur: Literaturwissenschaften zwischen Kulturtechnik und Ethnographie* (Munich: Fink, 2000), 9–16 (introduction).

[14] Stephen Greenblatt, *Renaissance Self-Fashioning* (Chicago and London: U of Chicago P, 1980), 256.

[15] This is an argument made by Geertz, who asserts that the internalization of a particular culture (understood as a semiotic system) is the essential prerequisite for thought itself: "Human thinking is primarily an overt act conducted in terms of the objective materials of the common culture, and only secondarily a private matter" (*The Interpretation of Cultures*, 83).

[16] Harold Aram Veeser, *The New Historicism Reader* (New York and London: Routledge, 1994), 2.

[17] The view of Raymond Williams has defined the cultural materialist position: "We cannot separate literature and art from other kinds of social practice, in such

a way as to make them subject to quite special and distinct laws." *Problems in Materialism and Culture* (London: Verso, 1980), 44.

[18] Both new historicism and cultural materialism have been taken to task for getting away from the close reading of texts. For example, J. Hillis Miller has complained that new historicism is "an exhilarating experience of liberation from the obligation to read." *Theory Now and Then* (Hemel Hempstead, UK: Harvester Wheatsheaf, 1991), 309–27; here, 313.

[19] See Richard Wilson and Richard Dutton, eds., *New Historicism and Renaissance Drama* (Harlow: Longman, 1992), 228, for their discussion of the concept of cultural poetics. Cultural poetics is the name given to New Historicist practice by Greenblatt after 1988. Many critics have seen this relabeling of the critical praxis as signaling a move toward formalism, a new tendency to hypostatize culture as an autonomous semiotic system. For Kiernan Ryan, editor of *New Historicism and Cultural Materialism: A Reader* (London: Arnold, 1996), xiv, this move "exchanges a stress on the historicity of texts for a concern with the textuality of culture." John Brannigan, however, maintains that the change of name is not accompanied by any identifiable shifts in the critical praxis, thereby implying that a tendency to downplay the historicity of texts has always been a part of new historicist criticism. See *New Historicism and Cultural Materialism* (London: Macmillan, 1998), "Cultural Poetics: After the New Historicism?" 83–93.

[20] See Isaiah Berlin, "Herder and the Enlightenment," in *The Proper Study of Mankind: An Anthology of Essays*, ed. Henry Hardy and Roger Hausheer (London: Pimlico, 1998), 359–435. From Herder, too, comes the gesture of "feeling oneself into" (*sich einfühlen*) a foreign culture or remote historical epoch by the act of interpretive empathy so characteristic of Geertz and other ethnographers (Berlin, "Herder and the Enlightenment," 389).

[21] A hypothesis first formulated in Stephen Greenblatt's 1981 essay "Invisible Bullets: Renaissance Authority and Its Subversion; Henry IV and Henry V," in *Political Shakespeare: Essays in Cultural Materialism*, ed. Jonathon Dollimore and Alan Sinfield, 2nd ed. (1985; repr., Manchester, UK: Manchester UP, 1994), 18–47.

[22] Stephen Greenblatt, "Introduction: The Forms of Power," *Genre* 7 (1982): 3–6; here, 6.

[23] This term from Jan Assmann, *Das kulturelle Gedächtnis: Schrift, Erinnerung und politische Identität in frühen Hochkulturen*, 5th ed. (Munich: C. H. Beck, 2005). Assmann's concept "cultural memory" is derived from Maurice Halbwachs's theory of "mémoire collective," which has as its main thesis that no memory is possible without recourse to those external frames of reference (Halbwachs: "cadres sociaux") by which we fix and retrieve our remembrances (Assmann, *Das kulturelle Gedächtnis*, 34–48). Assmann builds on this thesis to assert the primacy of writing among these frames of reference as a source of social meaning.

[24] Manfred Pfister, "Konzepte der Intertextualität," in *Intertextualität: Formen, Funktionen, anglistische Fallstudien*, ed. Ulrich Broich and Manfred Pfister (Tübingen: Niemeyer, 1985), 1–30. Cautious adoption of the global model of intertextuality need not imply acceptance of poststructuralist theorems concerning the demise of the subject. For a rebuttal of postmodern attempts to deconstruct individual subjectivity see Manfred Frank, *Die Unhintergehbarkeit von*

*Individualität: Reflexionen über Subjekt, Person und Individuum aus Anlaß ihrer "postmodernen" Toterklärung* (Frankfurt am Main: Suhrkamp, 1986).

[25] The six criteria are: *referentiality:* the degree to which a text refers to and quotes from its pre-text and elaborates or comments upon it; *communicativity:* the degree of intentionality of the intertextual reference; *autoreflexivity:* the extent to which a text thematizes its own intertextuality; *structurality:* the extent to which a pre-text serves as the structural basis for a whole text; *selectivity:* the pointedness with which an element from the pre-text is referred to, and *dialogicity*, the semantic or ideological tension between the original and new contexts (Pfister, "Konzepte der Intertextualität," 25–30).

[26] Wolfgang Riedel warns of the dangers inherent in the "culture as text" paradigm, which tends to underestimate the autonomy of the literary text, reducing it to the level of a mere "document." Deploring the use of this metaphor, Riedel argues that literature is better regarded as a "commentary" on its proper culture, a role that its characteristic aesthetic and reflexive distance enables it to fulfill. Riedel, "Literarische Anthropologie: Eine Unterscheidung," in *Wahrnehmen und Handeln: Perspektiven einer Literaturanthropologie*, ed. Wolfgang Braungart, Klaus Ridder, and Friedmar Apel (Bielefeld, Germany: Aisthesis, 2004), 337–66, esp. 350–52.

[27] Walter Horace Bruford, *The German Tradition of Self-Cultivation: "Bildung" from Humboldt to Thomas Mann* (Cambridge: Cambridge UP, 1975).

[28] Friedrich Ludwig Jahn, *Deutsches Volkstum* (1810; repr. Leipzig: Reclam, n.d.), 249–53.

# 1: The Wanderer as the Subject of Education

## "Steile Gegenden" and "Umwege": Goethe's *Wilhelm Meisters Lehrjahre* (1795–96)

### The Bildungsroman: An Obsolete Interpretive Model?

In 1984 Hans-Jürgen Schings proposed reading *Wilhelm Meisters Lehrjahre* using the category of "Heilung" or "Genesung," offering this as an alternative to what he called the "erstarrte[s] Modell *Bildung*."[1] Indeed, the energies of Germanists in the post-1945 period were for a long time consumed in an inconclusive debate as to whether Goethe's novel should really be called a *Bildungsroman*. The *Lehrjahre* has been regarded as the archetype of that genre since the term was first applied to it by the academic Karl Morgenstern.[2] It was to be expected that dissenting voices would make themselves heard just when the German tradition of self-cultivation appeared irreparably tarnished by the recent experience of totalitarianism. *Bildung* was seen as an institution deeply implicated in the beginnings of a modernity that had so recently come to a catastrophic end. Thus commentators like Karl Schlechta felt the need to separate Goethe from a compromised tradition and to portray him as a farseeing critic of the destructive tendencies within it. Similarly, in the 1970s a new generation of critics felt compelled to disavow the link between Wilhelm Meister and *Bildung*. Stefan Blessin's reading of the novel as a document of bourgeois false-consciousness whose protagonist has "nichts gelernt" is characteristic of the ideology-driven criticism then prevalent.[3]

Doubtless the new readings helped to overcome the discipline's one-sided fixation on the theme of education and cast new light on "die erstaunliche und unerhörte Mannigfaltigkeit"[4] of a work that had exerted an unparalleled influence on the German novel in the nineteenth century. They did not, however, succeed in overturning the dominant interpretive paradigm: rather, they enriched it. There remain compelling grounds for retaining that model. In the first place, many of the earliest and most incisive interpreters of the *Lehrjahre* — Schiller, Wilhelm von Humboldt, Christian Gottfried Körner — invoke the category of *Bildung* in reference to it, either explicitly or implicitly. Second, and this is significant for the following discussion, both the motif of a wandering protagonist and the major theme of education are taken up by those contemporary authors who had studied the work closely and were receptive to its influences: Ludwig Tieck and Friedrich von Hardenberg. Moreover, the "anthropological turn" in the criticism of the work ushered in by Schings, with his emphasis on the themes of melancholia, suffering, and healing, by no means represents a break with the interpretive term *Bildung* but is eminently compatible with it. Schings's most recent work has drawn on insights from the study of late Enlightenment anthropology to arrive at a fuller understanding of the discourse on education as it appears in the novel.[5]

It is this approach — reading *Wilhelm Meisters Lehrjahre* in the context of the contemporary discourse on anthropology — that will be taken here in an effort to shed light on the function of the wanderer motif and its connection with the theme of *Bildung*. The guiding concept of the reading, "anthropology," should be understood as that philosophical discipline which came to prominence in a late phase of the Enlightenment — partly as an attempt to rehabilitate man's sensual nature in the face of the earlier deification of reason by speculative philosophy. This was a discipline that sought to comprehend man as unity of body and soul, of nature and reason; that is to say, its primary focus was on man as a natural being.[6] It differs from idealistic or transcendental philosophy in that it regards both of these poles — however they are described — as equally important aspects of what it means to be human. As such it is concerned with human nature, with the physical being. We may take our warrant for such a reading from the words given to Wilhelm Meister — "der Mensch ist dem Menschen das Interessanteste und sollte ihn vielleicht ganz allein interessieren" — a paraphrase of Alexander Pope's dictum: "The proper study of mankind is man."[7]

## Wilhelm Meister as Pedestrian: The Body Language of Autonomy

In chapter 10 of the first book we hear for the first time that Wilhelm Meister, whom up to then we have known only as a "jungen, zärtlichen, unbefiederten Kaufmannssohn" (10), unremarkable save for his unrestrained enthusiasm for the theater, intends to set out on a "Wanderung in die Welt" (35). Although the journey relates to the pursuit of what he sees as his "Bestimmung zum Theater" — at the side of his actress lover Mariane — it is evident that no clear purpose is in view; instead of a plan of action we have a jumble of ideas, "ein Gemälde auf Nebelgrund." Indeed the intention to depart seems to derive at least as much from a negative impulse — to escape — as it does from any will to self-realization. The youth desires "sich aus dem stockenden, schleppenden bürgerlichen Leben herauszureißen" (the note struck here recalls Thomas Mann's remark about the *Lehrjahre* being the "Sublimierung des Abenteuer-Romans"): he wants to be rid, not only of the stuffy atmosphere of his father's house, but also "von jeder angenehmen Erinnerung."[8] This recurring desire to make a decisive break, to begin afresh, unencumbered by memories, will finally be revealed as folly by the Abbé.

At the outset, then, we have a youth on the verge of breaking with his past and casting off the pressures and responsibilities of his social station. A little later we learn something that puts a different complexion on the intended departure, namely that the initial impetus comes not from Wilhelm but from his father, who seeks to prepare his son for commercial life by sending him on a business trip. Because the youth sets out with an agenda that, however ill-defined, is radically different from that of his father, his journey carries within it the seeds of conflict. The unapproved pursuit of a theatrical career is a tacit rebellion ("unterlassene Revolte"); the son avoids confrontation with his father, pursuing his own ends by subterfuge.[9] For Stadler, the causes of the rebellion lie in the thwarted aesthetic ambitions of the youth: first Meister Senior deprives his son of an educational resource by selling off his own father's collection of *objets d'art*, and later he communicates his disapproval both of the puppet theater and of the stage proper. Stadler's reading is compelling because it establishes a link between the psychological dimension of the father-son conflict and the wider rebellion against patriarchy, including the French Revolution. It was against the backdrop of that trauma that the work to transform the fragmentary *Theatralische Sendung* into the *Lehrjahre* took place (1794–96). Although its setting in the previous decade allows it to avoid having to treat the trauma directly, the work is preoccupied with the consequences of that rupture.[10] We will return to that theme later, but for the moment it is necessary only to note that Wilhelm Meister's surreptitious rebellion manifests itself not only in his inappropriate choice of career but also in the nomadic existence that this entails: the journey becomes a substitute for revolt: because he dare not change his circumstances by tackling his father, the youth opts for a change of place.[11] The option for an existence in the company of vagabond players is, in part, a flouting of bourgeois norms.

Wilhelm's tacit rebellion is in part a refusal of behaviors appropriate to his social standing, a refusal that extends to the mode of travel itself. Resuming his travels after his separation from Mariane, Wilhelm sets out on horseback. As a member of Melina's troupe, however, he becomes a pedestrian. The symbolic aspect of this new — and, for the 1780s, socially marked — mode of travel is apparent from the hero's musings on the appropriate garb for a walker early in book 4:

> Er fing nun an, über seine Kleidung nachzudenken. Er fand, daß ein Westchen, über das man im Notfall einen kurzen Mantel würfe, für einen Wanderer eine sehr angemessene Tracht sei. Lange gestrickte Beinkleider und ein Paar Schnürstiefeln schienen die wahre Tracht des Fußgängers. Dann verschaffte er sich eine schöne seidene Schärpe, die er zuerst unter dem Vorwande, den Leib warm zu halten, umband; dagegen befreite er seinen Hals von der Knechtschaft einer Binde. . . . Ein runder Hut mit einem bunten Bande und einer großen Feder machte die Maskerade vollkommen. (210)

These reflections reveal a newly fledged actor's exaggerated concern with appearances, but, beyond this, the choice of clothing signals a rejection of traditional bourgeois forms. Both his mode of travel and his clothing are imbued with revolutionary symbolism, registered by the narrator: thus the wanderer frees his neck "von der Knechtschaft einer Binde." Naturally, his appearance and behavior are here presented in thoroughly ironical terms: the whole exercise is a "Maskerade," a form of playacting founded on self-deception. Pedestrianism had, however, in the context of the Enlightenment project, acquired a symbolic aspect. The upright bearing and independence of the walker were themselves emblems of the process of self-emancipation. For this reason, walking — a travel mode formerly regarded as inappropriate for the bourgeois — was then undergoing a revaluation, becoming a key symbolic activity of that social class. In the essay *Beantwortung der Frage: Was ist Aufklärung?* (1784), Kant makes use of the metaphor of pedestrian progress to signify the process of emancipation: "Aufklärung ist der Ausgang des Menschen aus seiner selbst verschuldeten Unmündigkeit."[12] Elsewhere in the same essay, Kant makes reference to the fetters of dependency ("Fußschellen einer immerwährenden Unmündigkeit"). In the hands of Kant, the self-directed physical act of locomotion becomes a powerful symbol of the self-directed activity of thought and hence of the dictum "Bestimme dich aus dir selbst."[13]

For Herder (who had studied under Kant at Königsberg) the connection between man's upright stance and gait and his vocation to reason was more than merely symbolic: it was material. In the first volume of the *Ideen zur Philosophie der Geschichte der Menschheit* (also published in 1784), Herder derives man's possession of reason from the anatomical fact of his upright gait. In doing so, he accepts a thesis first proposed by the French materialist philosopher Claude Adrien Helvétius in his *De l'esprit* (1758). Herder writes:

> Mit dem aufgerichteten Gange wurde der Mensch ein Kunstgeschöpf; denn durch ihn, die erste und schwerste Kunst, die ein Mensch lernet, wird er eingeweihet, alle zu lernen und gleichsam eine lebendige Kunst zu werden. Siehe das Tier! Es hat zum Teil schon Finger wie der Mensch; nur sind sie hier in einen Huf, dort in eine Klaue oder ein ander Gebilde eingeschlossen und durch Schwielen verderbet. Durch die Bildung zum aufrechten Gange bekam der Mensch freie und künstliche Hände, Werkzeuge der feinsten Hantierungen und eines immerwährenden Tastens nach neuen klaren Ideen. Helvétius hat sofern recht, daß die Hand dem Menschen ein großes Hülfsmittel seiner Vernunft gewesen.[14]

Man is distinguished from the animals, according to the above, by his upright gait, an essential precondition for possessing hands capable of grasping and manipulating tools, but also for the free gaze with which he surveys his surroundings. Herder believes that this structural disposition to use tools is the source of man's superior intelligence. Of course, the theological implications of such a materialist account of the origins of human reason were potentially scandalous, especially when uttered by an official of the Lutheran church, and Herder later toned these remarks down by setting them in the context of divine providence. But what is most interesting about this account is its derivation of reason from physical principles, of the spirit from the human body in action. It is an explanation in the mode of the empirical anthropology of the day; and it is worth recalling that the first two parts of Herder's *Ideen* (1784, 1785) were developed in conversation with Goethe at Weimar, with the third part being forwarded to him in Italy (1787).[15]

The above-mentioned episode in the *Lehrjahre* would be of marginal interest were it not for the recurring metaphors of gait in that work. The unnamed stranger with whom Wilhelm converses about his grandfather's art collection takes those who live unreflectingly to task in the following terms: "Wir bilden uns ein, fromm zu sein, indem wir ohne Überlegung hinschlendern, uns durch angenehme Zufälle determinieren lassen und endlich dem Resultate eines solchen schwankenden Lebens den Namen einer göttlichen Führung geben" (71). Following his introduction to the works of Shakespeare, Wilhelm expresses to Jarno the intention henceforth "in der wirklichen Welt schnellere Fortschritte vorwärts zu tun" (192). Moreover, it is striking how frequently body language and especially gait are used to characterize individual figures. By focusing on nuances of physical appearance and bearing, Goethe evokes the essence of a character, or of a mental state, in a few brush strokes. In the first book, Wilhelm's slackness, his hangdog attitude is made visible to us in the adolescent slouch, which, we feel, he should by now have outgrown. Thus, when Mariane, unhappily preoccupied with thoughts of Norberg's arrival, turns him away at her door, he "slinks" ("schlich") away (68). Later we see him straying hither and thither with wavering steps, half in a dream, unable to decide whether to go home or not. Pusillanimity, indecision, and vapid sensuality: all are indicated by the verb "schleichen." So it is with the sentimental *promeneur solitaire*, whom Philine makes fun of, and who comes "mit einem Buche durch den Wald geschlichen" (101). The gait of the Abbé is eloquent, but in the opposite sense; it bespeaks his emancipated and enlightened status. Striding along "mit starkem Schritte" (421) on the way to Lothario's residence, he is able to keep pace with Wilhelm, who is *on horseback*.

In the episode cited the motley wanderer is ironized; the sense we get is not of a man striding resolutely toward his eventual enlightenment but of a youth who has succumbed to delusions of grandeur. (He is at this point still thoroughly infatuated with the aristocratic ideal.) Nevertheless, his playacting is evidence of his struggle to create a role for himself;[16] indeed, since his career in the company of strolling players is a surreptitious rebellion, it is also an attempt at self-determination, however misguided.

Although Wilhelm's wandering does not fulfill the Kantian "sapere aude!" ("have the courage to use your own intelligence") at this stage, it does comply with the injunction "Bestimme dich aus dir selbst!" if we accept that self-determination can entail determination by instinct as well as by reason. Wilhelm believes that he represents an ideal of active purposeful behavior — the Enlightenment ideal —in terms of metaphors of gait and movement. For him an ethical ideal is represented in terms of an image of corporeal self-expression: the free man striving purposefully toward his goal. From time to time he measures himself against this image — and finds himself wanting. So it is in the aforementioned conversation with Jarno, and again following the ambush of the theater company: "Er wollte nicht etwa planlos ein schlenderndes Leben fortsetzten, sondern zweckmäßige Schritte sollten künftig seine Bahn bezeichnen" (238).

## Travel as New Educational Norm: "Die beste Bildung findet ein gescheiter Mensch auf Reisen"

Wilhelm is interrupted in his preparations for departure on the journey that he hopes will bring him closer to Mariane and the theater by the arrival of Werner. The two friends discuss one of the incomplete poetic works of Wilhelm's adolescence, the verse allegory "Der Jüngling am Scheidewege," in which two female figures, one personifying commerce, and the other (though this is not made explicit) art or the theater, vie for the attentions of a youth. We may suppose that the genii of the two paths represent two alternative forms of educational journey, the bourgeois *Bildungsreise* and something resembling the aristocratic grand tour.[17] Werner, Wilhelm's pragmatic antipode, struggles to convince his dreamy friend of the merits of the former, enthusing for an itinerary centered on major sites of commercial activity:

> Besuche nur erst ein paar große Handelsstädte, ein paar Häfen und du wirst gewiß mit fortgerissen werden. Wenn du siehst, wie viele Menschen beschäftiget sind; wenn du siehst, wo so manches herkommt, wo es hingeht, so wirst du es gewiß auch mit Vergnügen durch deine Hände gehen sehen. Die geringste Ware siehst du im Zusammenhange mit dem ganzen Handel, und eben darum hältst du nichts für gering, weil alles die Zirkulation vermehrt, von welcher dein Leben seine Nahrung zieht. (38)

For Werner, travel is only of value insofar as it enables the methodical gathering of professionally useful knowledge. In his view education has to serve the ends of a society dominated by the principle of the division of labor. Despite this, it is indicative of the productive nature of dialectic between them that Werner echoes his friend's holistic arguments. The young capitalist sees his friend's journey as a timely initiation into the commercial world, the only field in which a young man of his background can hope to make a name for himself, for: "Der kleinste Raum unsers Weltteils ist schon in Besitz genommen, jeder Besitz befestigt, Ämter und andere bürgerliche Geschäfte tragen wenig ein; wo gibt es nun noch einen rechtmäßigeren Erwerb, eine billigere Eroberung als den Handel?" (39).

Of the two figures in his friend's allegory Werner prefers the "goddess" of trade: "Sie führt freilich lieber den Ölzweig als das Schwert; Dolch und Ketten kennt sie gar nicht; aber Kronen teilt sie auch ihren Lieblingen aus." In doing so he appeals to a common topos in eighteenth-century thought, the ideal of *le doux commerce*, commerce as a civilizing force, a notion that was then supplanting the older military-honor ethic.[18] This aristocratic ethic is obsolete, so Werner's argument goes, since no new lands are available for conquest; the only opportunities for self-enrichment and fulfillment lie in trade, an economic reality that can be exploited only by specialists. Werner thus concurs with the views held by the "Society of the Tower," the cooperative and educationally minded society whose doings — as we shall see — are central to the *Lehrjahre*, on the possibilities of education.

In a letter following his announcement of the death of Wilhelm's father, Werner remarks: "Die beste Bildung findet ein gescheiter Mensch auf Reisen" (289), recalling his earlier comments where he had contrasted art as mere diversion with travel as educational process. Werner's observation indicates the new emphasis on travel in the bourgeois model of education. In his reply — the *Bildungsbrief* — which contains the oft-cited declaration "mich selbst, ganz wie ich da bin, auszubilden, das war dunkel von Jugend auf mein Wunsch und meine Absicht" (290), Wilhelm strongly asserts the ideal of a rounded education, which he claims to be seeking in the theater; he is thus enunciating an uncontemporary vision of education, holding out for more than the development of a limited set of faculties to utilitarian ends. The classical ideal of education is present in Wilhelm's childhood in the form of his grandfather's art collection, comprising paintings (that of the "kranke Königssohn" has especial significance for the youth) and other *objets d'art.* Even at this point, for the older Meister this collection — whose sale is a source of latent tension between father and son — represents not an educational resource but a commodity. For the Werners, father and son, as for the old Meister, learning is not to be had from the perusal of collections of artworks, one of the principal activities of the aristocratic grand tour. Indeed, the collection was by this time becoming outmoded as an educational instrument. This is especially true of the natural history collection, a resource based on an essentially static view of nature. In this older view, the natural world was seen as a vast space, a plenitude of forms that had coexisted since Creation, the so-called "great chain of being." Now, toward the end of the eighteenth century, the natural world came increasingly to be viewed under the aspect of time, in terms of the temporal processes of development and metamorphosis. The cultural historian Arthur Oncken Lovejoy has coined the term "temporalization" to characterize this shift in the understanding of the natural world, a change reflected in the rise of the new discipline of physiology at the expense of natural history.[19] The reframing of nature as a time-determined entity brought with it a dynamization of the worldview, which in turn required the development of new educational strategies. If a world now conceived of in terms of dynamic processes was to be understood adequately, the learning subject itself had to be set in motion, moving through the world in search of useful empirical data. The new bourgeois practice of the *Bildungsreise*, advocated by Werner, grows in part out of this dynamization of the worldview: the acquisition of data in travel supersedes the static study of collections.

Shortly after his arrival in the lively trading city where Serlo's company is located, Wilhelm receives a letter from his father, urging him to send the journal he was supposed to have been keeping as a record of the statistical, geographical, and commercial knowledge gained in the course of his journey, for which purpose Meister Senior had provided a "tabellarisches Schema" (266). Naturally, no such document has been kept, but — mindful of the dereliction of his filial duties — Wilhelm hastens to put together a plausible travelogue for his father's benefit. Reviewing his career, he notices for the first time how little impression external objects had made on him, compared with ideas and emotional impressions. This self-evaluation is a crucial juncture in Wilhelm's acquisition of what Ilse Graham has called "an eye for the world."[20] The discipline of composing a narrative at once reveals to him the deficiencies in his attention to the fabric of the world, for although he has seen "vieles," he is at a loss to know what to say about it. He is obliged to enlist the aid of his friend, Laertes, who proves an ideal partner in such an undertaking, with his melancholic restlessness that is the wellspring of a striking productivity.[21] Laertes's avid consumption of travelogues (which he uses to alleviate the symptoms of his depression) gives him a keen sense of what is required. Using the resources of the city's large lending library, he sets about assembling a mass of data. It is simply a matter of compiling information from other travelers' journals since, as Laertes observes: "Ist nicht ganz Deutschland von einem Ende zum andern durchreist, durchkreuzt, durchzogen, durchkrochen und durchflogen? Und hat nicht jeder deutsche Reisende den herrlichen Vorteil, sich seine großen und kleinen Ausgaben vom Publikum wiedererstatten zu lassen?" (267).

The fictional journey corresponds to the itinerary suggested by Werner, and the practical insights in the report meet with his wholehearted approval. On one level, the fact that the recipient is so easily beguiled into accepting the authenticity of the document reveals the superficial nature of the *Bildungsreise* as it is understood by Werner. The knowledge supposedly gained on the journey has, in fact, been culled from archival sources: to this extent the journey itself appears superfluous. But the work on the travelogue represents a significant shift in the protagonist's view of the world, heralding a move toward a more practical orientation: Wilhelm has become more attentive to "die Zustände und das tägliche Leben der wirklichen Welt" (276), the sense of his father's exhortation to keep a journal dawns upon him, and his old prejudice against the sphere of commerce is diminished. What had appeared as the fundamental dilemma of his youth, the either-or choice between the poles of commerce and art, is viewed with more circumspection: "Da steh' ich nun, sagte er zu sich selbst, abermals am Scheideweg zwischen den beiden Frauen, die mir in meiner Jugend erschienen. Die eine sieht nicht mehr so kümmerlich aus wie damals, und die andere nicht so prächtig" (276). Even if Wilhelm Meister cannot be said to have had anything as clear as a program of self-education in mind when setting out for the theater, he represents his wanderings in precisely those terms in his reply to a letter from Werner, who seeks to persuade him to end his travels. Yet again the sparring with his antagonist, Werner, has borne fruit, because it has compelled the wanderer to reflect upon and articulate clearly what he had hoped for from such a course. What previously had been "ein Gemälde auf Nebelgrund," an impulse toward *Bildung* as ill-defined as it was keenly felt, now becomes a fairly lucid manifesto, and one that envisages the harmonious development of his physical and mental powers.[22] Of course, what the reply leaves unsaid is the degree to which Wilhelm's worldview has shifted in the direction of the position represented by Werner. That Werner never actually receives this reply, the *Bildungsbrief*, does not lessen its importance for its author as a form of reckoning with his theatrical career.[23]

Given the convergence between the paths of the two friends, and the fact that at the beginning of book 8 they embark on a joint commercial venture, are we not compelled to see Wilhelm as a slow learner and the novel, with Novalis, as an "Evangelium der Oeconomie"?[24] Certainly it appears that the two paths of Wilhelm's allegory, apparently representing irreconcilable educational standpoints, have in the end converged in a thoroughly prosaic reality. Indeed, viewed from the perspective of the provisional end point, the "Society of the Tower," Werner's pragmatic course would have to be preferred, since it has evidently been the more direct route. But the narrator's determination to show us the painful inequalities between the two figures indicates that Wilhelm's wanderings are not to be assessed solely with regard to the end result of his initiation into that society. If the two paths of Wilhelm's allegory may be considered to stand for two conceptions of the possibilities of the *Bildungsreise*, and, by extension, for two distinct models of education, then it is clear that the pragmatic bourgeois model has taken its toll of Werner. Indeed, "Der gute Mann schien eher zurück als vorwärts gegangen zu sein" (498). Werner, who has taken on the appearance of "ein arbeitsamer Hypochondrist," is astonished by his friend's robust health, exclaiming: "Wie doch das Faulenzen gedeiht!" Wilhelm's good physical condition, which he attributes to "Leibesübung" (291), part of his theatrical training, throws his own "eingedrückte Brust," "vorfallende Schultern," and "farblose Wangen" into sharp relief (498). In these symptoms are manifest the hazards of subordinating human education to a one-sided instrumental rationality; Werner's material success has been purchased at the excessive price of his physical integrity, and thus of his capacity to enjoy the fruits of his labors. Small wonder that Schiller was filled with enthusiasm for this scene, which accorded so closely with his own observations on the deforming effects of contemporary bourgeois education.[25]

Wilhelm's allegory is reminiscent of a common motif in contemporary prints and engravings, that of Heracles at the crossroads, beckoned to by the female personifications of virtue and vice. By playing on this motif the novel sets up the expectation of a straightforward dichotomy between the path of "virtue" (or reason) and the path of "vice" (or sensuality) of the kind that had been constitutive for the didactic novels of a previous generation, for example, Christoph Martin Wieland's *Geschichte des Agathon* (1766–67). The apparent erring of Goethe's protagonist, however, thoroughly confounds such paradigmatic expectations, and with them the notion that education requires the subordination of sensuality to reason.

## The "Society of the Tower" and the Pedagogy of Error

In the final chapter of the first book, Wilhelm, having been turned away from her door by a fretful Mariane, strays irresolutely about the streets of his own town. Eventually he is stopped by a stranger, who, on the pretext of seeking directions, draws the youth into a conversation about his personal circumstances. It emerges that the stranger is well acquainted with those circumstances, having acted as an agent for the purchaser of Meister Senior's art collection, when Wilhelm was ten years old. What had transpired then, unbeknown to Wilhelm, was his first meeting with a member of the "Society of the Tower," an agency that makes its presence felt at various intervals of his theater years, but of which he remains unaware until meeting Lothario in book 7. Some attention to this society will be necessary to justify my claim that Wilhelm's odyssey involves some kind of education, especially since those critics who have disputed this see the "tower" as the crucial point in the novel.

Building on the solid foundations laid by Rosemarie Haas — who has explored the connections between the novel, Goethe's own contact with Freemasonry and the Illuminati,[26] and the secret-society novel — Schings has recently sharpened the historical perspective on the tower by recalling that secret societies were very much a phenomenon of the prerevolutionary decade in which the *Lehrjahre* is set.[27] More importantly, his study casts light on the pioneering role played by numerous members of the League of

Illuminati in developing the discipline of empirical anthropology. Among the most eminent of these pioneers was Jacob Friedrich Abel, Schiller's favorite teacher at the Stuttgart *Karlsschule*. Schiller, though avowedly "weder Illuminat noch Maurer," would go on to write the first German secret-society novel, *Der Geisterseher* (1787–89), a work that spawned a host of imitations in the 1790s. For our purposes it is important to realize that "Bildung," the principle that the Illuminati championed above all others, was the object and end of their anthropological studies.

Given Goethe's involvement both with Freemasonry and with the Illuminati, it is impossible to escape the conclusion that the fictional society — the introduction of which dramatically alters the character of the *Lehrjahre* vis-à-vis the *Theatralische Sendung* — had definite personal and historical roots. Significantly, Haas has shown that Goethe owned the second edition of Adam Weishaupt's *Pythagoras oder Betrachtungen über die geheime Welt- und Regierungs- Kunst* (1795), evidence of his engagement with a key text of the Illuminati at the very time that the theater-novel torso was being reconstructed as a *Bildungsroman*. How does Goethe transform the Illuminati? In an effort to answer this question, Schings applies a triad of terms, "Geheimnis — Bildung — Endzweck,"[28] which sums up the essence of the pedagogy of the Illuminati, to the "Society of the Tower." Examining the initiation scene in the *Lehrjahre*, Schings notes that the *Lehrbrief* handed to Wilhelm closely resembles the key practice of presenting the initiate with a biographical report compiled by members of that league. By contrast, the intimidating and mystifying elements present in the league's initiation ceremonies, blindfolding, the ritual use of daggers or other weapons, the swearing of oaths, or the use of arcane formulae, are all eschewed, or else dramatically toned-down, in the version imagined by Goethe. Objective mysteries, Schings remarks, have no part in the tower's scheme of things. At most they make use of petty mystifications to divert credulous undesirables, or as part of their sometimes gauche attempts to persuade impressionable youths: one thinks here of the veil with its stitched-in message "Flieh! Jüngling, flieh!" (328), by means of which the tower seeks to end Wilhelm's association with the theater. Nor, significantly, does Goethe reproduce the hierarchy of knowledge characteristic of the Illuminati. Gone from his tower is the internal segregation into degrees, the lowest of which could have knowledge only of the order's public purposes (education, philanthropy), while the secret and final purposes were known only to their superiors (political revolution, war on despotism). Indeed — and here we arrive at the third of Schings's terms — the society gathered around Lothario knows nothing of final purposes: it has no revolutionary plans, nor does it aspire to world government. It is a society shorn of the grand designs and mystifications common to Freemasonry and the Illuminati; the sole concept that Goethe imports from that sphere is the idea of *Bildung*. But the conception of *Bildung* that finds its articulation in the *Lehrjahre* is not that of the secret societies, who studied anthropology with the object of governing men, of directing them in the pursuit of hidden ends. Rather, what is imagined is a form of human cultivation that takes full cognizance of the worth of the individual, refusing to subordinate that individual to external ends. It is a form of development, in short, that virtually requires the person undergoing it to be represented as a wanderer.

The use of the motif of the wanderer in an educational context is, naturally, not unique to Goethe. Such usage has a number of historical precedents and contemporary parallels, both in literature and in the ritual structures of the secret societies. It is worth reviewing these briefly in order to see what is innovative about Goethe's handling of the motif. Most obvious, perhaps, are the parallels with the masonic tradition: the three degrees of the masonic "craft" being a symbolic appropriation of the three stages of the artisan's progress: apprenticeship, journeying, and mastership. Accordingly, the motif of the wanderer plays a considerable role in the ceremonial and occasional literature of the lodges. We get a sense of this function from the *Lied zur Gesellenreise*, written by Wolfgang Amadeus Mozart to celebrate his father's elevation to the second degree (*Geselle*) at the Viennese lodge "Zur Wohltätigkeit" on 26 March 1785. The song sets words by Joseph Franz von Ratschky (1757–1810), a member of the other prominent lodge in Vienna "Zur wahren Eintracht":

> Die ihr einem neuen Grade
> Der Erkenntnis nun sich naht,
> Wandert fest auf eurem Pfade,
> Wißt, es ist der Wahrheit Pfad.
> Nur der unverdrossne Mann,
> Mag dem Quell des Lichts sich nahn.

In this song the aspirant to knowledge is addressed as "Pilger," and the wish expressed that "Wißgier" will guide his steps on the "Lebensreise." For the freemasons, wandering is an abstraction, a metaphor for individual and collective progress toward enlightenment; it does not refer to a material practice specific to the order, unlike the guild practice of the *Wanderschaft*. In view of this it is interesting that Goethe introduces the device of the *Lehrbrief* (the journeyman's indentures), a feature absent from the initiation procedures of the Freemasons and the Illuminati (whose biographical reports are not so named). As Haas rightly notes, the introduction of the *Lehrbrief* and the solemn act of *Lossprechung* — releasing the journeyman from his indentures — links the tower's ritual more closely to its roots in guild tradition than was the case in masonic rites.[29] This is significant because it shows that, while jettisoning the pompous trappings of such rituals in an effort to render the tower more natural ("jene Maschinerie von dem Verdacht eines kalten Romanbedürfnisses zu retten und ihr einen ästhetischen Wert zu geben," Goethe says in a different context to Schiller, 9 July 1796),[30] Goethe moves that agency closer to the artisanal tradition of the *Wanderschaft*.

The other important source for the motif of the wanderer in quest of knowledge is literary: early eighteenth-century French novels of education, especially Fénelon's enduringly influential *Aventures de Télémaque, fils d'Ulysse* (1699) and Jean Terrasson's *Séthos* (1731).[31] Such works are the sources of the key motifs of the secret-society novels of the eighteenth century: a wandering hero, a journey to the Orient, or in a subterranean realm (in the case of *Séthos*), combined with the elements of testing and of initiation into arcane knowledge. The protagonists of these novels are young noblemen possessed by an insatiable wanderlust (we think of Tieck's parodies of aristocratic vagabonds in *William Lovell* and *Sternbald*). In this regard, and in the sense that their protagonists' arcane education is intended to prepare them for a ruling role, novels of this kind are a kind of literary pendant to the grand tour, not least because their milieu is usually the Near East of classical antiquity.

The ways in which *Wilhelm Meisters Lehrjahre* breaks with the pattern established by this genre and represents a new departure in the handling of the wanderer motif are significant for the handling of the theme of *Bildung*. First, and most obviously, in Goethe's work the protagonist is bourgeois. What the novel retains from secret society novels like *Séthos* and from the mythologies of the societies themselves is the figure of a wanderer in quest of knowledge. But Wilhelm's wandering is of a fundamentally different character from that of Terrasson's or Fénelon's heroes, both of whom are accompanied every step of the way by an enlightened tutor (the "Mentor" of Fénelon's novel) whose edifying discourse is a constant source of guidance. The use of the motif in these and later secret-society novels thus reflects a paradox at the heart of illuminist and masonic models of education, namely the assumption that one could *lead* individuals to the independent exercise of their reason. By contrast, the *Lehrjahre* fully exploits the symbolic potential of the wanderer motif by depicting an individual who, for good or ill, sets his own course. The place of the ever-present mentor is taken by the non-dogmatic and self-effacing emissaries of the tower, who make only occasional appearances.

The depiction of Wilhelm as a wanderer is essential to the representation of a process of self-development, that is, of *Bildung* proceeding according to an internal principle. As we have seen, *Bildung* as it was understood by freemasons and illuminists entailed the subordination of the individual to external and inscrutable ends. This was a conception of education which, moreover, made a fetish of knowledge and control, and, as a consequence, was profoundly intolerant of error. Herein lies the crucial distinction between the illuminist model and the "Pädagogik des Irrens" espoused by the Abbé in Goethe's novel.[32] This pedagogy derives from

Goethe's critical engagement with the educational program of the Illuminati, as outlined in Weishaupt's *Pythagoras.* It is a reaction against the directive and hierarchical nature of that program. The Abbé holds that the individual must be allowed to err, and through erring learn ultimately to legislate for him or herself. During the initiation scene Wilhelm hears the following: "Nicht vor Irrtum zu bewahren, ist die Pflicht des Menschenerziehers, sondern den Irrenden zu leiten, ja ihn seinen Irrtum aus vollen Bechern ausschlürfen zu lassen, das ist Weisheit der Lehrer" (494–95).[33] The first intimation of the pedagogy of minimal intervention comes in book 3, chapter 8, following Jarno's suggestion to Wilhelm that he study the works of Shakespeare. Here the narrator addresses the reader apothegmatically:

> Der Mensch kommt manchmal, indem er sich einer Entwicklung seiner Kräfte, Fähigkeiten und Begriffe nähert, in eine Verlegenheit, aus der ihm ein guter Freund leicht helfen könnte. Er gleicht einem Wanderer, der nicht weit von der Herberge ins Wasser fällt; griffe jemand sogleich zu, risse ihn ans Land, so wäre es um einmal naß werden getan, anstatt daß er sich auch wohl selbst, aber am jenseitigen Ufer, heraushilft und einen beschwerlichen weiten Umweg nach seinem bestimmten Ziele zu machen hat. (180)

Here, a directive form of education is implicitly contrasted with a *laissez-faire* approach. Although the merits of the helping hand are not weighed explicitly against those of self-help, the narrator here provides the key term—"Umweg"—that characterizes Wilhelm's educational journey. The value of this circuitous mode of self-education is finally ratified in the initiation scene in words given to the "ghost": "Steile Gegenden lassen sich nur durch Umwege erklimmen, auf der Ebene führen gerade Wege von einem Ort zum andern" (495), a phrase which, though opaque, suggests that, while learning by erring may be appropriate to the "steile Gegenden" of youth, a more direct approach is required in the more settled phase of maturity. The metaphor of the path is prominent in the account given by Natalie of the Abbé's pedagogy (which she and her siblings, Lothario, the Countess, and Friedrich, have experienced at first hand). Natalie reports the Abbé's words as follows:

> Ein Kind, ein junger Mensch, die auf ihrem eigenen Wege irregehen, sind mir lieber als manche, die auf fremdem Wege recht wandeln. Finden jene, entweder durch sich selbst oder durch Anleitung, den rechten Weg, das ist den, der ihrer Natur gemäß ist, so werden sie ihn nie verlassen, anstatt daß diese jeden Augenblick in Gefahr sind, ein fremdes Joch abzuschütteln und sich einer unbedingten Freiheit zu übergeben. (520–21)

The correct path is the one appropriate to the individual's nature, that is, the unique set of faculties and dispositions with which every human individual is born. Such attention to the claims of human nature marks a signal departure from illuminist assumptions about the primacy of education and the perfectibility of man. Schings has shown that a key text for illuminist anthropology is Helvétius's *De l'homme:* it is from this work that Weishaupt derives the theory of man as *tabula rasa*, infinitely amenable to rational molding.[34] This was a philosophical position that Goethe could not embrace, not least because his own observations in the field of plant biology taught him the importance of innate principles (what we now know as genetic factors) in the development of individuals. Instead, Goethe holds that the human faculties are *essential*, and that, accordingly, they can only be helped to unfold. What is imagined in the *Lehrjahre* is a pedagogy that will make this possible, that will allow the full exfoliation of the individual character without doing violence to it. So, what is envisaged is a *natural* pedagogy, the logical model of which is the unfettered journey. Wandering, in its narrow sense of walking, is the characteristic *self-directed activity* of humans; it is the analogue of growth, the self-development of plants.

"Wo die Illuminaten 'ausrotten,' 'zustutzen' und 'abrichten,' vertraut der Turm (und mit ihm Goethe) der Gunst der Natur und läßt wachsen."[35] Or, to select a contemporary analogy, the Illuminati's metaphors of uprooting, pruning, and cutting into shape the human individual recall nothing so much as the coercive techniques of the French garden with its geometric formalism. Such formalism, far from being accidental, was a direct aesthetic expression of the mechanistic rationalism of the *philosophes.* (It is perhaps worth recalling that the forms created by the classical French garden could only be enjoyed fully from an elevated vantage, a God-like perspective, as it were.) The tower, for its part, favors a pedagogy more akin to the aesthetics of the English garden, which married natural and man-made forms. Essential to imagining this *laissez-faire* approach to personal development is the model of the journey, the course of which is determined by the individual in accordance with his needs and desires as he sees them — rightly or wrongly — at each successive stage of his development.

Naturally, such a pedagogy, which aims to bring an individual from an initial position of longing for the full and unconditional realization of personality to the knowledge of the necessity of assuming a restricted role carries within it the risk that the person so educated will be overpowered by regret at the contemplation of a past life that he has come to see as wasted. Something of the sort happens to Wilhelm when he describes his theatrical existence to the Abbé as "ein unendliches Leere" (422). He is dissuaded from such a negation of his past by the latter, who moves quickly to reassure him that "alles, was uns begegnet, . . . Spuren zurück [läßt], alles trägt unmerklich zu unserer Bildung bei" (422). The tower makes use of the devices of a theatrical initiation ceremony and of biographical narrative to overcome this problem and to reconcile Wilhelm to his past. Both of these devices work by narrating the candidate's life in the form of a journey. Individual episodes from the past are isolated and presented in the initiation ceremony as a series of scenes, the various encounters with the emissaries of the tower: the art connoisseur, the country pastor who so closely resembles the Abbé, the young officer seen in Jarno's company at the count's residence, and the "ghost" from Hamlet. "Sonderbar!" Wilhelm exclaims, "sollten zufällige Ereignisse einen Zusammenhang haben? Und das, was wir Schicksal nennen, sollte es bloß Zufall sein?" (494). The answer to the question is, naturally, that the contingent events of a life may indeed cohere, but only insofar as they are made to do so by imposing order on them in retrospect. This is the function of the initiation ceremony and of the biographies that the tower compiles of its members, the parchment rolls called *Lehrjahre* that make up its archive. The *Lehrjahre* abstract from reality, presenting the postulant's past in "großen, scharfen Zügen" (505): indeed, more than this, they make past, present, and future cohere, thereby acting as what Kermode has called "fictions of concord."[36] The selection of scenes for review from Wilhelm's past is arbitrary; it is, however, useful, since it allows him to conceive of these events as conforming to a moral pattern, as a progression. To narrate a life as if it were a journey means to impose a symbolic order on contingency, to ratify the past (and rob it of its power to accuse and hence to paralyze) by interpreting it with regard to a moral goal.[37] The tower presents itself to Wilhelm as the goal toward which his long career of erring has, without his knowing, been directed; but it is only an interim goal, since the ultimate end of the process of *Bildung* is not specified, a fact that has fed critics' doubts as to whether the *Lehrjahre* can be grasped with reference to that category.[38]

There is another crucial respect in which Wilhelm's wanderings differ from those of the heroes of the secret-society novels, namely in the absence of mystification concerning the ends of the journey. Unlike Terrasson, or Johann Heinrich (Jung) Stilling, whose *Heimweh* (1794–97) features a protagonist whose journey to the Orient is an initiation into arcane knowledge at the hands of the *Felsenmänner*, Goethe has no use for the situational motif of the esoteric journey. On the contrary, the wanderings of his protagonist take him outwards to the world, acquainting him with social spheres to which he would have had limited access had he remained within the confines of his allotted role. Not an esoteric journey, then, but an exoteric one, and one in which the half-stated object is the garnering of anthropological knowledge. That at any rate is what Wilhelm expects to gain from his association with the aristocratic *grand monde:* "Unser Freund, der auf Menschenkenntnis ausging, wollte die Gelegenheit nicht versäumen, die große Welt näher kennen zu lernen, in der er viele Aufschlüsse über das Leben, über sich selbst und die Kunst zu erlangen hoffte" (154). "Menschenkenntnis" is sought not merely for its own sake but also for the insights it gives into the practice of art, including the art of living. The meandering journey, Wilhelm's "Umweg," is the means by which it is pursued. In the world of Goethe's novel the knowledge of man is equated simply with knowledge of the world. The principal and unchallenged object of interest is always man; in the novel's perspective all other objects pale into insignificance. Of non-human nature the work appears to say with the uncle of the *Bekenntnisse:* "Alles außer uns ist nur Element" (405). This tacit identification of "Menschenkenntnis" with "Weltkenntnis" would later be made explicitly in Kant's *Anthropologie in pragmatischer Hinsicht* (1798), where it is justified with the argument that of all creatures man alone is "sein eigener letzter Zweck." Prominent among the means to such knowledge cited in that essay are "Reisen" and even "das Lesen der Reisebeschreibungen," though Kant, that most sedentary of philosophers, is quick to add that living in a large city, a seaport and commercial hub like his native Königsberg, and studying the people in it, is an acceptable substitute.[39]

Wilhelm's *Bildungsreise* is an incomparably richer source of anthropological knowledge for having been undertaken in the company of Melina's "wanderndes Reich," culminating in Serlo's more sophisticated urban theater, which represents the summit of the medium. If Jarno is correct when he mockingly suggests that the failings of actors faithfully reproduce those of the wider society, then the theater has been a microcosm of the world, and the sojourn in it not squandered time but an object lesson in the way social ensembles operate. In Serlo's theater a kind of perfection — if a fragile one — is attained in the production of *Hamlet:* the parts are harmonized into an efficient, smoothly functioning, and aesthetically pleasing whole, which foreshadows the cooperative spirit of the "Society of the Tower."

## "Die Sache ist, daß ich wieder Interesse an der Welt nehme": The Italian Journey as Origin of Goethe's Practical Anthropology

Between the theater novel and the *Lehrjahre* lies the Italian journey, the damascene experience of Goethe's maturity after which, among other results, he finally renounced his dream of becoming a landscape painter and reconciled himself to his existence at Weimar. Although he did not begin work on the revised version until more than five years after his return, this period was a long fermentation of accumulated impressions, an essential prelude to the new opus. The greatly increased scope of the *Lehrjahre*, which formally and thematically breaches the bounds of the theater world, derives to a great extent from the slow assimilation of this experiential mass.[40] Goethe had long intended an Italian journey in his father's footsteps; but the moment of decision, when it arrived, was not a sanguine one. His departure for Italy in September 1786 was an act prompted by a threefold crisis that had afflicted him that summer. In the first place he had gnawing doubts about the role of minister that he had played for a decade. Second, there was the crisis in his relationship with Charlotte von Stein. Finally, his sense of creative frustration, long growing, had finally come to a head: the Weimar decade had been littered with poetical fragments, one of which was the *Theatralische Sendung*. The journey was not, however, solely an act of flight ("hegira" is the term Goethe uses for episodes of this kind in his biography), but the realization of a plan of education: a *Bildungsreise*. His ostensible goal was to train as a "Landschaftszeichner," but what he clearly intended was a schooling of the senses. In this there was also a therapeutic aspect, a will to restore the sensuous side of being that had atrophied in the confines of Weimar, to bring the faculties of the senses and the intelligence back into balance. If we accept this, then it is hardly too large a claim to assert that anthropological learning is the unstated object of the *Bildungsreise*, understood as empirical knowledge about the perennial problem of the *commercium mentis et corporis*, the interaction of mind and body. The impulse for this learning comes from Goethe's need to gather his scattered powers and to gain mastery over his own circumstances, which were then in crisis.

What I wish to propose here is that the *Lehrjahre* seeks to embody and communicate the anthropological knowledge garnered in the course of the Italian journey, and I will seek support for that thesis in the relationship between the novel and the *Italienische Reise* (1816/17). In doing so it is necessary to bear in mind that the latter relates only indirectly to the historical journey (undertaken between September 1786 and April 1788), being the highly formed product of a later phase in Goethe's life, although it is entirely derived from contemporaneous material (letters and the diary kept for Frau von Stein). If the *Lehrjahre* is Goethe's first venture into the thematic territory of *Bildung*, then we may say that with the *Italienische Reise* he writes "einen Erziehungsroman über sich."[41]

The first and most obvious similarity between Goethe's anabasis and Wilhelm's journey is that the shadow of the father bulks large over both. But although Goethe, far from undertaking a "surrogate rebellion" against the shade of Johann Caspar, is retracing his father's footsteps, the moment of conflict is arguably present in an unvoiced desire to surpass his achievements. More importantly for our purposes, both journeys involve some form of "aesthetic education" in a sense not unlike that intended by Schiller, although the outcome of the *Lehrjahre* was rather different from what Schiller hoped for. In addition, both have something of the eclecticism of the aristocratic grand tour. At the level of motivation we find in both an aspiration to some notion of wholeness of personality, either to be developed or to be restored.

An aesthetic education entails an education under the twin auspices of nature and art, which are invoked repeatedly in the *Italienische Reise*, most strikingly in the programmatic statement: "Ich wandle starken Schrittes in den Gefilden der Natur und Kunst herum"(*HA* 11:388). "Natur" in the sense of instinct and sensory perception is to be complemented by "Kunst," understood as the exercise of the intelligence and artistic production. The *Italienische Reise* documents an unrelenting sensory activity. On the road from the Brenner Pass to Verona Goethe notes: "Mir ist jetzt nur um die sinnlichen Eindrücke zu tun, die kein Buch, kein Bild gibt"(*HA* 11:25). The therapeutic dimension to this program of observation is then hinted at: "Die Sache ist, das ich wieder Interesse an der Welt nehme." This idea is elaborated fully in the reference to Rousseau's "hypochondrischen Jammer" against which the prophylactic of "Anteil an den natürlichen Dingen" is specified (*HA* 11:211). In keeping with this prescription, much of the *Italienische Reise* is taken with Italy as it impresses itself on Goethe's senses. The dominant mode of description is pictorial and ecphrastic rather than interpretive or exegetic. We are not treated to historical disquisitions, and even the descriptions of artworks are restricted to surface appearance; at all times the main interest is in that which offers itself immediately to the senses.

Nature and art are the authorities that rule over Wilhelm Meister's aesthetic education, too. The lure of art and the pull of instinct are the two forces that propel him toward the theater. These two forces are so profoundly intertwined that Wilhelm at one point finds it difficult to decide whether it is his love for Mariane that gave rise to his attraction to the theater or vice versa. For the first five books nature, in the form of instinct, what Boyle terms "motivation by mood and chance"[42] predominates. The protagonist is drawn to the theater by a dream of erotic fulfillment with Mariane. After the breach with her it is Philine's charms that draw him back into that orbit, where other natural affections — friendship for Laertes, sympathy for Mignon and the harpist — combine to hold him fast. Wilhelm, in short, is a protagonist "der durch sich selbst handelt, der liebt und haßt, wenn es ihm sein Herz gebietet" (254). While instinctual nature remains a powerfully molding influence on the youth throughout, the role of art for his formation grows in significance as he moves from Melina's troupe to Serlo's theater. Serlo's aim is to exploit the talents slumbering in Melina's players: in order to do this he must lick the "Naturalisten und Pfuscher" (275) into shape. His theater is therefore an educational institution with aims not unlike those of the tower, namely to bring its members to the fullest possible realization of their potential as members of a collective body, overcoming "Eigendünkel, Dummheit oder Hypochondrie" in the process. In Serlo's biography an early striving to unconditional freedom is replaced by a growing insight into the need for self-restraint, learned, as it were, in play. "Selbst das tolle Handwerk, das er trieb, nötigte ihn bald, mit einer gewissen Mäßigung zu verfahren" (272). Similarly, Wilhelm's "wandering," understood as the instinctually led and playful theatrical phase of his youth provides him with dispositions that pave the way toward his integration into the "Society of the Tower," namely with "Gemeinschaftsfähigkeit," the ability to renounce his claims to autonomy and to an integral personality in the interests of the cooperative society with which he has entered freely into association.[43] It is thus a paradox of the *Lehrjahre* that the wandering subject, who seeks nothing beyond the greatest possible realization of his own individuality, must come at last to the recognition of the need for self-restriction, for renunciation.

The term "play" suggests another significant moment common to the *Lehrjahre* and the *Italienische Reise:* the performative aspect. As is evident from Moritz's theater novel *Anton Reiser* (1785–90), travel and performance were inextricably linked in the contemporary imagination, not least because of the ample opportunities for role-playing, including imposture, that existed at a time when there was relatively little onus on the traveler to provide documentary evidence of identity. In Italy Goethe traveled under the alias Philippo Miller, *pittore tedesco.* Although the alias was initially adopted to prevent his whereabouts becoming known by Carl August before he had reached Rome, the fact that he kept it up suggests that the assumed identity had acquired an importance beyond that of concealment. With his Italian journey Goethe stages his own social death and rebirth; the alias permits a temporary dissociation from the author of Werther and the Weimar minister. This sloughing off of the appurtenances of his Weimar identity was a necessary preliminary to an aesthetic education by means of which Goethe sought rebirth as an artist. Rebirth or renewal is an abiding theme in the *Italienische Reise*,[44] as the following letter to the Herders written in June 1787 attests:

> Ich habe mich in eine zu große Schule begeben, als daß ich geschwind wieder aus der Lehre gehen dürfte. Meine Kunstkenntnisse, meine kleinen Talente müssen hier ganz durchgearbeitet, ganz reif werden, sonst bring' ich wieder euch einen halben Freund zurück, und das Sehnen, Bemühen, Krabbeln und Schleichen geht von neuem an.(*HA* 11:354)

Not only the reference to apprenticeship ("Lehre") but the metaphors of gait also put us in mind of Wilhelm Meister. What they imply is a will to recast the self in the image of the upright man, striding through the "Gefilden der Natur und Kunst," gathering in sense impressions along the way, and out of that mass of material fashioning works of art. In this way the unrelenting sensory activity is matched by an equally unstinting productivity, mainly of drawings and sketches, by means of which Goethe sought to capture the plethora of natural and artistic forms surrounding him, but also of poetical works, *Tasso, Iphigenia*, and the diaries and epistles that made up the main yield of the journey. The receptive and productive, the sensory and the intellectual sides of his personality are strained to the utmost; it appears as if he sought a balance between body and soul by maximizing the activity of both.

Wilhelm Meister is also concerned to achieve such an equilibrium: it is this he hopes for from the theater. In his *Bildungsbrief* he makes the following demand: "Geist und Körper müssen bei jeder Bemühung gleichen Schritt gehen" (292). But the *Italienische Reise* attests to the possibility of such equilibrium outside the theater, namely at those instants when body and mind are at a high pitch of activity. In other words, the "semblance" of the integral personality in which all the faculties appear to be in balance can be achieved in performance, and not only in the theater.[45] This investment of energy in the present moment recalls what Schings has identified as the salient anthropological principle of the *Lehrjahre:* "das Prinzip der Gegenwärtigkeit."[46]

In a letter to Zelter, a long-standing correspondent and friend in Berlin, Goethe uses the term "Gesundheit des Moments" to characterize the ancients' attitude to time, neither brooding on the past nor longing for the future: "Der Augenblick müsse prägnant und sich selbst genug sein um ein würdiger Einschnitt in Zeit und Ewigkeit zu werden."[47] This attitude to time, according to which each moment of existence must be treated as sufficient unto itself, is the kernel of Stoic and Epicurean anthropological thinking: Goethe sees it as being championed in his own age by Winckelmann. The "Prinzip der Gegenwärtigkeit" is, equally, a central precept of the "Society of the Tower" and its successor body in the *Wanderjahre*, the "League of Wanderers." It is implied in Lothario's "Hier oder nirgend ist Amerika!" (431), a demonstrative assertion of acceptance of one's circumstances as the raw material for productive activity. It is proclaimed overtly in the motto inscribed in the "Hall of the Past": "Gedenke zu leben!" an obvious inversion of the Christian *memento mori*, a readjustment in favor of the classical *art de vivre*. This hall, though a burial place, awakens in the viewer feelings of "die reinste Heiterkeit"; it is an architecturally harmonious space constructed in such a way as to banish all thoughts of death and thereby to suggest the fullness of the moment and of the individual existence. In addition, the frescoes with their depictions of archetypal human activities gesture toward the measure of eternity available to man in the succession of generations.[48]

The possibility of attaining a measure of eternity by regarding one's existence under the aspect of species being and by attending to the present moment: that is one way of formulating the collectivist and activist ethos of the "Society of the Tower," which makes up the content of Wilhelm's *Bildung*. Action at the service of a collective is the remedy proffered by Jarno for the alienation that is an inevitable consequence of the division of labor. Under such conditions the individual's only hope of fulfillment is to learn "um anderer willen zu leben und seiner selbst in einer pflichtmäßigen Tätigkeit zu vergessen" (493).

If the necessity of attention to the present is intimated in the *Lehrjahre* — and that work provides its own requited moments in which past, present, and future coalesce in a "fullness of time," the encounter with the "beautiful Amazon," and the restoration to Wilhelm of his grandfather's art collection being the two most significant — then that necessity is articulated more emphatically in *Wilhelm Meisters Wanderjahre* in the practices of the "League of Wanderers." This association of individuals, who are linked primarily by an ethic of circumspection, seeks to instill in its members the greatest possible respect for time as "die höchste Gabe Gottes und der Natur"(*HA* 8:405). Respect for time is the essential prerequisite for creative activity: "Etwas muß getan sein in jedem Moment, und wie wollt' es geschehen, achtete man nicht auf das Werk wie auf die Stunde?" The league takes this principle to the extreme of calling for the mass production and distribution of timepieces in the new society that it intends to set up overseas.

What does the neo-classicistic principle of attention to the present moment have to do with the wanderer motif? The pendant to the tower's *memento vivere* in the *Wanderjahre* is Lenardo's "Gedenke zu wandern!"(*HA* 8:318), an admonition whose suggested equivalence between life and wandering has a significance exceeding that of the originally Christian metaphor of the life journey. Instead "wandern" as it appears here indicates a particular stance to be adopted toward the world, a posture of alertness whose iconic symbol is the figure of the wanderer, a man on the qui vive, whose upright stance indicates both a maximum receptivity to his surroundings and a readiness to reach out and grasp the material of which they are made. The stance entails renunciation too; but that is a matter I will address in my discussion of the *Wanderjahre*.

## "Dauer im Wechsel": *Wilhelm Meisters Wanderjahre oder die Entsagenden* (1829)

> Der Wanderer. — Wer nur einigermaassen zur Freiheit der Vernunft gekommen ist, kann sich auf Erden nicht anders fühlen, denn als Wanderer, — wenn auch nicht als Reisender nach einem letzten Ziele: denn dieses giebt es nicht. Wohl aber will er zusehen und die Augen dafür offen haben, was alles in der Welt eigentlich vorgeht; desshalb [sic] darf er sein Herz nicht allzufest an alles Einzelne an hängen; es muss in ihm selber etwas Wanderndes sein, das seine Freude an dem Wechsel und der Vergänglichkeit habe.
>
> Friedrich Nietzsche, *Menschliches: Allzumenschliches*[49]

### The Nature of Renunciation in the Wanderjahre

The earliest reference to a projected sequel to the *Lehrjahre* is in a letter written by Goethe to his publisher Johann Friedrich Cotta in May 1798, which contained a list of planned projects, one of which was noted as: "Briefe eines Reisenden und seines Zöglings, unter romantischen Nahmen, sich an Wilhelm Meister anschließend."[50] The note reveals that the nexus of travel and education we find in the *Lehrjahre* was already intended at this early stage to form the thematic core of the sequel. Indeed, the very concept of *Lehrjahre* would have stimulated public expectation of a trilogy in which the *Wanderjahre* would be succeeded by *Meisterjahre*, according to the logic of the artisan's progression from apprentice (*Lehrling*) through journeyman (*Geselle*) to the position of master craftsman (*Meister*).

The renunciation theme, already incipient in the last two books of the *Lehrjahre*, is now dominant, proclaimed in the double title *Wilhelm Meisters Wanderjahre oder die Entsagenden:* the dilation of being that characterizes so much of the earlier work is seemingly replaced by a sense of contraction. The following discussion will attempt to discover what part the wanderer motif plays in elaborating that theme. When last we encountered Wilhelm Meister we had thought him securely berthed in the safe haven of the Society of the Tower. At the outset of the sequel we find him once again on his travels, for reasons that are not immediately apparent. He remains connected to the Tower, but only loosely, by the letters and his diary, which taken together form a sort of *Rechenschaftsbericht*, and by a number of arcane rules, administered by the Abbé, that Wilhelm has agreed to observe in the course of his wanderings. These rules are as follows: the wanderer (and Wilhelm is repeatedly identified as such) may spend no more than three nights under any one roof; on leaving he must put a (presumably Prussian) mile between him and his last station, which he may not revisit for at least a year; and, finally, he is permitted no companion other than Felix.[51] The similarity between these rules and the ascetic strictures imposed on itinerant members of religious orders is unmistakable. They may have been suggested to Goethe by two experiences during his (first) Swiss journey in 1779. Shortly before dictating the opening chapters of the *Wanderjahre*, comprising *Die Flucht nach Egyptien* and *Sankt Joseph der Zweite* in May 1807, Goethe had been editing his letters from Switzerland for publication (an Alpine landscape is evoked in the opening chapters of the *Wanderjahre*). Schmidlin takes the view that this activity would have recalled two experiences of the journey to Goethe.[52] One of these was an encounter with a peasant woman on the road from Brig to Münster on 11 November 1779. She recounted for Goethe the legend of St Alexius, said to have abandoned his new bride to begin a life of wandering as a pious mendicant.[53] Renunciation appears to have preoccupied Goethe at that time, for on the following day, he made notes on a sermon he had heard in the Swiss town of Realp on the self-denial demanded of Catholic clergy, whose vocation requires a readiness to move from place to place providing pastoral care wherever the need is greatest.[54]

The harshest condition imposed on Wilhelm by the journey is perhaps the early separation from Natalie. This lends the journey a rather darker quality than the sentimental pilgrimage to Mignon's homeland anticipated in the *Lehrjahre*. The purpose of the rules governing the wanderer is obscure, but a process of testing and purification is evidently involved: "Sonderbare Pflichten des Wanderers habe ich auszuüben und ganz eigene Prüfungen zu bestehen" (12). Observance of the vow is intended as a corrective to what Wilhelm calls "meine Fehler," faults that — in a manner consistent with the narratorial tendency to keep the reader in the dark — are not specified further. Apart from these references the reader must at this point be content with a cryptic comment in the letter to Natalie: "Diese Gebote sind wahrhaft geeignet, meine Jahre zu Wanderjahren zu machen und zu verhindern, daß auch nicht die geringste Versuchung des Ansiedelns bei mir sich finde." A protracted journey is indicated; indeed Wilhelm avers: "Mein Leben soll eine Wanderschaft werden" (11–12). No final goal is mentioned, but the purpose of the journey has at least been intimated. The intention is to wean the traveler from undue attachments, in the first instance to places, but also, by implication, to material possessions and to individual persons.[55]

This is the sense of Jarno's pronouncement, which Wilhelm reports in a subsequent letter to Natalie: "Du bist von der Menschenart, die sich leicht an einen Ort, nicht leicht an eine Bestimmung gewöhnen. Allen solchen wird die unstäte Lebensart vorgeschrieben, damit sie vielleicht zu einer sicheren Lebensweise gelangen" (282). This prescription of a nomadic, indeed unsettled, existence as a means to a more secure way of life is only apparently paradoxical. Jarno's pedagogical point concerns the dangers inherent in allowing oneself to be seduced by the illusion of fixity, rather than keeping a destination or purpose in view.

Wilhelm's journey is an exercise in twofold renunciation. I have already named one of its aspects: the deliberate abandonment of the settled life. On the other hand, the protagonist is to be brought to the exercise of a specialized activity. This entails renouncing a measure of personal autonomy, since acknowledging the need for specialization within a social ensemble requires recognition of the restricted capacity of the individual. Striving toward development of the whole person of the kind we observe in the *Lehrjahre* thus proves to be the prelude to a more restrictive phase of training adequate to the conditions of modernity. If the *Lehrjahre* had imagined education as growth, as the blossoming of the whole personality, in the *Wanderjahre* we get a pruning of the faculties, an at-times-painful curtailment.

The decisive move toward adopting a profession comes when Wilhelm encounters Jarno in the unnamed mountainous territory evoked in the opening chapters. This saturnine emissary of the Tower has embraced the principle of specialization, having become a geologist, assuming the name Montan. His new role as a wandering renunciant who has shunned society for the mineral world is in keeping with the misanthropic character we recall from the *Lehrjahre*. Montan characterizes Wilhelm as "einen Wanderstab, der die wunderliche Eigenschaft hat, in jeder Ecke zu grünen, wo man ihn hinstellt, nirgends aber Wurzel zu fassen" (40). This observation moves Wilhelm to produce the medical bag that he has carried about as "eine Art von Fetisch" and provokes the conversation in which he asserts his desire to be trained as a surgeon, asking that Jarno intervene to release him from the constraints of his journey. Jarno, who had earlier announced, "Ja, es ist jetzo die Zeit der Einseitigkeiten; wohl dem, der es begreift, für sich und andere in diesem Sinne wirkt. . . . Mach' ein Organ aus dir und erwarte, was für eine Stelle dir die Menschheit im allgemeinen Leben wohlmeinend zugestehen werde" (37), agrees to intercede for him with the Abbé. Thus, even at the outset of the journey, the prospect of the removal of the binding strictures — voluntarily entered into by Wilhelm — is anticipated at the point where an appropriate vocation is found.

This leads us to the question of the philosophical character of the renunciation required of the members of the League of Wanderers, the successor body to the Tower. Jarno's jocular remark: "Wandre nur hin, du zweiter Diogenes! Laß dein Lämpchen am hellen Tage nicht verlöschen!" (33) might be taken to as an indication that what is involved is an exercise in stoicism. Although the members of the League do indeed strive to be governed by reason rather than emotion, abstaining from impatience, longing, and from velleities of all kinds, not all of what they renounce is necessarily superfluous or undesirable, so the theory of the stoa does not seem exactly to fit. Nor does renunciation of a Christian kind in which that which is valued is sacrificed in the expectation of an ultimate restitution of the good,[56] since it is not clear quite what restitution is anticipated. Bahr points out that the note that Wilhelm gives to Susanne defines the stance of renunciation in terms of the restricted status of the individual.[57] This restriction is defined in three ways: existentially, cognitively, and ethically. Each person is "immerfort bedingt, begrenzt in seiner Stellung," and "gelangt . . . im allgemeinen zu keiner Klarheit," and is called upon to observe "die Pflicht des Tages" (426). But renunciation as thematized in the *Wanderjahre* involves insight, not only into restricted human capabilities, but also into the limited field of action available to each individual. We owe this insight to Rahel Varnhagen von Ense, whose incisive criticism of the *Lehrjahre* provided the theoretical basis for her husband's essay "Im Sinne der Wanderer" (1832). For Rahel the *Lehrjahre* is "ein Gewächs, um den Kern als Text herumgewachsen."[58] This "kernel" comprises two key passages, Werner's encomium of commerce: "Der kleinste Raum ist schon in Besitz genommen, jeder Besitz befestigt, Ämter und andere bürgerliche Geschäfte tragen wenig ein; wo gibt es nun noch einen rechtmäßigeren Erwerb, eine billigere Eroberung als den Handel"(*HA* 7:39) and Wilhelm's exclamation to Aurelie: "O wie sonderbar ist es, daß dem Menschen nicht allein so manches Unmögliche, sondern auch so manches Mögliche versagt ist!"(*HA* 7:280). Rahel's reading initiates a tendency, taken up by Karl, of viewing the restrictions to which renunciation is a response partly in terms of human essentials but primarily as emanations of the material and political conditions of the age. For Karl this reading of the *Lehrjahre* offered an interpretive key to the *Wanderjahre*. As early as 1821, in his review of the first edition, published in that year, he draws attention to the reprised theme of a densely settled world in Lenardo's *Wanderrede*, a world all of whose lands have been taken into possession. In his path-breaking 1832 essay, Karl August Varnhagen von Ense sees his earlier suspicion concerning the importance of this theme for the *Wanderjahre* confirmed by the fact that the second edition returns to it twice, in both Lenardo's and Odoardo's speeches to their respective bands of wanderers (385 and 408). These two passages are crucial to understanding the Goethean nexus of renunciation and wandering. Fundamental to it is the perception that the age is "settled," in the broad sense of presenting to the individual a thicket of preexisting institutions denser than that of any previous time and denying him a space he might truly call his own. Such a perception entails a transvaluation of values. Lenardo opens his *Wanderrede* by calling for just such an adjustment, which would result in a greater value being placed on work and on human productivity than that attributed to property, a theme seized upon by the *Linkshegelianer*, who were the only early partisans of Goethe's misunderstood and unloved last prose work:[59]

> Wenn das, was der Mensch besitzt, von großem Wert ist, so muß man demjenigen, was er tut und leistet, noch einen größern zuschreiben. Wir mögen daher bei völligem Überschauen den Grundbesitz als einen kleinen Teil der uns verliehenen Güter betrachten. Die meisten und höchsten derselben bestehen aber eigentlich im Beweglichen und in demjenigen, was durchs bewegte Leben gewonnen wird. (385)

In his speech Lenardo unfolds a strategy for managing a contemporary situation in which the majority are, as it were, dispossessed *a priori* and have little prospect of securing their existences by acquiring fixed assets. Lenardo's remedy for the effects of mass dispossession — a process driven in part by the unprecedented population growth in Goethe's lifetime — is to renounce aspirations to fixed assets and land in favor of more mobile forms of production. He has in mind the intellectual capital of craft knowledge. Lenardo's plans thus represent the culmination of a tendency already present in the Society of the Tower, which is the nucleus of "eine arbeitszentrierte, mobile Gesellschaft."[60] In the light of this ethos Wilhelm's position at the end of the *Lehrjahre* requires a new journey that would bring him to productive activity. His ascetic wanderings prepare him for this by fostering psychic mobility, a stance toward the world that allows him to free himself from undue attachments to places and possessions. Wandering of this kind is more than the external manifestation of the stance of renunciation,[61] it is identical with the *practice of renunciation*. Taking up the surgeon's vocation does not spell the end of this practice for

Wilhelm. It will merely spell the end of the disciplinary strictures, changing the character of "die auferlegte Wanderschaft" from one organized "nach Tagen und Stunden" to one directed toward "dem wahren Zweck einer vollständigen Ausbildung" (264). Wilhelm may well relinquish his nomadic existence, but he will continue to view the world as a wanderer; that is to say with a degree of circumspection, an awareness of the finitude of his own capacities. Such a view also entails alertness and a respect for the resource of time, a key principle of the League of Wanderers.

## The Archival Novel and the Reader as Wanderer

The *Wanderjahre* contains a number of interpolated narratives that make it a considerably more complex, variegated, and — by the standards of contemporary novelistic practice — unconventional work than its forerunner, which contains only one large heterogeneous element embedded in an authorial narrative, the *Bekenntnisse einer schönen Seele.* In the *Wanderjahre,* Goethe makes use of a fictional editor, the compiler of a range of disparate archived materials, who takes the place of the authorial narrator of the *Lehrjahre.* This strategy makes new demands on the reader, who remains unaware of the fictional editor until an intervention in book 1, chapter 10, where the decision to withhold an essay by Makarie is announced. Elsewhere the reader is confronted with conundrums and unannounced shifts of narratorial perspective. For example, the opening Saint Joseph sequence at first seems to be presented by an omniscient narrator but soon turns out to be an edited version of Wilhelm's diary. Similarly irritating are the references to the unidentified fetish carried by Wilhelm, which is not identified as the surgeon's bag from the *Lehrjahre* until the end of book 2, and the tantalizing mystery of the casket discovered by Felix, the contents of which are never revealed. As Volker Neuhaus has pointed out, the use of the fictional editor makes it impossible directly to identify any position articulated in the novel with Goethe.[62] This narrative strategy, in which the novel appears as the product of the redaction of a collection of very diverse texts, has prompted the use of the term "archival novel."[63] Although the novellas were already present in the first edition, the archival fiction was an innovation of the 1829 edition. The dispersed and heterogeneous structure of the novel was the cause of considerable irritation to Goethe's contemporaries as well as to later generations of critics. Theodor Mundt's incomprehension is typical: "Es ist zusammengetragenes Material, mitunter treffliches Bauholz zu einem didaktischen Roman."[64] However, a few perceptive critics concluded that the structure was intended as an adequate reflection of a complex reality. Among the first to do so was the monk Joseph Stanislaus Zauper, who interpreted the 1821 edition in the light of the venerable metaphor of the *navigatio vitae.* He saw the novel as a series of unconnected encounters that mirror the individual's progress through a fragmented modern existence.[65] Hermann Broch took a similar line in his 1936 essay *James Joyce und die Gegenwart*, asserting that the work is characterized by a striving for totality characteristic of twentieth-century modernist fictions, and that Goethe had created a sort of "book of the world" in the Joycean mode. Broch saw the formal innovation as an attempt to overcome a crisis of representation taking place in Goethe's time.[66]

Although the original distinction made by Trunz between framing narrative (*Rahmenerzählung*) and the internal narratives (*Binnenerzählung*) has been undermined by the recognition that what appear initially as two separate narrative levels are in fact interlinked (characters from the novellas turn up in the "framing" narrative) and has been supplanted by the archive model, some researchers still cleave to the notion of a double structure to the novel. Henriette Herwig, for instance, argues that the novellas form a space in which the claims of individual subjectivity are preserved, while the framing narrative is more concerned with collective processes.[67] This observation is relevant for our approach to the representation of wandering in the novel, for the novellas present not only individuals but also individual instantiations of the theme of renunciation and of the wanderer motif.

The decentering that is a consequence of the archival fiction also has implications for the wanderings of the protagonist, whose dominance is lessened by the appearance of new figures, especially Lenardo. The narrative focus is no longer on the tribulations of the hero's consciousness to the extent that it had been in the *Lehrjahre*. Accordingly, the reader is not granted the same degree of access to Wilhelm's reflections: almost the only time these are glimpsed is in the sparse letters to Natalie. As a result Wilhelm Meister appears conspicuously pale and bereft of individuality when contrasted with the hero of the *Lehrjahre*.

The loss of individuality is also reflected in the fact Wilhelm's peregrinations are no longer open to moments of chance, arbitrariness, and instinct as they were in the *Lehrjahre*. The new journey is neither aimless nor ever undertaken for its own sake; the itinerary is determined largely by the interests of others. This change in the dynamic of the journey as compared with the *Lehrjahre* is perhaps the main reason for the striking pallor of the protagonist, whose interests are seemingly indistinguishable from those of the groups with which he aligns himself along the way. Thus, Wilhelm seizes the opportunity to reunite Lenardo with his family, going to Makarie in order to find the reason for his mysterious reluctance to return home at the conclusion of a three-year-long grand tour. Having learned that Lenardo is concerned about the fate of Susanne, daughter of one of his uncle's tenants, Wilhelm then undertakes to find her in order to allay Lenardo's concerns. In the sense that he is effectively sent from one station to the next, Wilhelm again appears essentially passive in the course of his wandering. This apparent passivity is, however, effectively belied by his active engagement on behalf of those whom he meets. His intervention to reconcile Lenardo with his family allows us to concur with Schmidlin, who observes: "Es ist ein von helfender Liebe, von der Tat erfülltes Dasein, welches Wilhelm lebt."[68] On the whole, he appears to have assumed a role similar to that of the self-effacing emissaries we recall from the *Lehrjahre*, going about at times under an assumed name and acting less on his own behalf than as an intermediary.[69]

As had been the case in the *Lehrjahre*, the emphasis in Wilhelm's journey is less on the process of travel than on the individual stages reached, the characteristic domains of the novel: the mountainous environs of the village of Saint Joseph, the rational colony of the "Oheim," Makarie and her circle, the collector's patrician townhouse, the pedagogical province, Mignon's home on the shores of Lake Maggiore, and finally the valley in which the League of Wanderers hold their conference.[70] For Maierhofer, the emphasis on these distinct domains, which she regards as representing different social forms, corresponds with the a loss of individuality in the protagonist, a figure effectively relegated to a narrative function: "Eine wandernde Zentralfigur ist vor allem nötig, um die verschiedenen Bereiche zu verbinden."[71] This reading views Wilhelm's journey as the narrative thread that allows the different elements of the totality that Goethe wishes to evoke to be linked together.

What is characteristic of the individual stages and the figures encountered is the ambiguity of their rendition. The fictional narrator remains in the background, concealed by the *pluralis majestatis*, providing few clues as to what value should be ascribed to them. This is the case where the Saint Joseph episode is concerned: what appears initially as an idyllic, religiously defined existence, seems on closer inspection to be an empty exercise in imitation, devoid of any real religious content.[72] Similar uncertainty attaches to the figure of the *Oheim*, who simultaneously embodies traits of an enlightened despot and of an entrepreneur. Another trait of the archival fiction is the looseness with which the scenes are connected: the reader is unprepared for the appearance of the widow and Hilarie at Lake Maggiore. On meeting the two women, Wilhelm produces a letter from them inscribed with the symbol of an arrow. Neither the significance of the symbol nor the contents of the letter are revealed: it is left to the reader to surmise that the meeting is due to Makarie's intervention. This lack of preparation of events, the withholding of information, the use of blind motifs (the casket found by Felix, the unexplained sounds heard in the first chapter of book 3), and the existence of a plurality of perspectives make considerable demands on the reader's attention. Vaget has called the novel a "Leseexerzitium" that forces the reader to reflect on the processes whereby information is acquired in the act of reading.[73] Such views are close to those of a line of *Wanderjahre* research stretching from Zauper to, say, Maierhofer, which understands the complexity and multi-perspectival nature of the work in terms of an attempt to provide an adequate representation of what Goethe experienced as an increasingly complex and fragmented age. Bahr paraphrases Vaget's thesis succinctly:

> Durch den Verzicht auf Deutungsvorgaben wird eine realistische Form der Textaneignung gewonnen, die der empirischen Wirklichkeitserfahrung des Lesers entspricht. Die verschiedenen Textsorten konfrontieren den Leser mit Fakten und Bewußtseinsvorgängen, über die er sich Gewißheit verschaffen muß, um zum Verständnis des Romans zu gelangen.[74]

Adolf Muschg, noting the non sequiturs in the work referred to above, has remarked of the *Wanderjahre* that it is not only the figures of the novel that wander but also the narrator:

> Der Autor wandert selbst. Sein Diskurs ist überall bereit zum Exkurs. Er gibt zu erkennen, daß er nicht für seine Figuren haftet, ihre Wege nach eigenem Belieben mitgeht und sie stehenläßt, wenn er ihrer im Augenblick nicht bedarf oder keine Lust mehr zu ihnen hat. Der Vertrag, der ihn an sie bindet, gehört nicht mehr den Regeln und Fiktionen des klassischen Romans.[75]

We might turn this perspective around and assert that it is the reader who is effectively compelled to assume the role of wanderer, a traveler who strives to impose sense on the diversity of impressions encountered on his or her progress through the novel. Maierhofer has used the term "Roman des Nebeneinander" to characterize the loose, dispersed structure of the *Wanderjahre*. That label was first applied by Karl Gutzkow to his own novel *Die Ritter vom Geiste* (1850–51), which is identifiable as a contrafactum of the *Wilhelm Meister* novels. In the foreword to his novel Gutzkow explicitly casts his *reader* in the role of wanderer, a point not mentioned by Maierhofer. Anticipating resistance on the part of his readers to such features as the absence of an authorial narrator and the use of a simultaneous rather than serial narrative, Gutzkow appeals to his readers to treat their reading as a journey through difficult terrain in which the lay of the land will not always be apparent.[76] Gutzkow likely had the *Wanderjahre* in mind here; indeed, the metaphor of reader as wanderer is equally applicable to Goethe's novel: in progressing through the archival fiction the reader to an extent reenacts the learning process of the fictional protagonist with its confusions and lacunae. And, inasmuch as the reader is obliged to make do with incomplete information in interpreting the world evoked in the novel, he or she is also forced into the role of a renunciant. However, the dispersed structure and the rigorous perspectivism can also be experienced as emancipating the reader from the imposition of the narrator's will. From this point of view, the two collections of aphorisms "Betrachtungen im Sinne der Wanderer" and "Aus Makariens Archiv" represent a maximum of reader independence by dispensing entirely with a linear narrative.

### Wandering as Theme in the Internal Narratives

Interwoven with the main narrative thread of the *Wanderjahre* are a number of subsidiary narratives that, while highly self-sufficient, form integral parts of the whole. Although some of these texts are novelistic — *Die pilgernde Törin, Wer ist der Verräter? Der Mann von fünfzig Jahren* — the others cannot satisfactorily be classified as novellas. One thinks especially of Lenardo's prosaic travel journal, with its minute recording of work processes, but also of the fairy tale *Die neue Melusine*, the short story *Nicht zu weit!* and the *Schwank: Die gefährliche Wette*. The *Sankt Joseph der Zweite* story is also sometimes considered a novella, but it might better be regarded as a reworking of Wilhelm's diary. What the stories have in common is not genre but a definite didactic intent; that is to say, their purpose is to exemplify certain typical constellations of motivations and actions. A quick glance at their titles reveals that they are typological; they refer to specific personal or behavioral types, and they carry an admonitory charge. One is reminded of medieval *exemplae*, of the fatal hubris of *Der arme Heinrich*, of Erec's *sich verligen;* it seems all the more plausible that the stories have an instructive function when we consider that they form part of the archive available to the League of Wanderers. The wanderer motif is a significant element in many of these stories, all of which revolve around the central thematic complex of right acting and renunciation, of doing and leaving undone. In them the motif is used to exemplify various possibilities of behavior, usually defective ones, inviting the reader to reflect on the balance between renunciation and action.

In *Die pilgernde Törin* a mysterious and beautiful female vagrant is offered sanctuary by a landowner, Herr von Revanne. First, however, the woman is compelled to give assurances concerning her good character: solitary female pedestrians were apt to be taken for prostitutes. Accepting Revanne's offer, the woman is accommodated in his home, where her genteel behavior shows her to be "ein Frauenzimmer von Stande" (55). She refuses, however, to provide any further information concerning her plight. A mysterious song that she performs, a "burleske Romanze," appears to shed some light on the cause of her peripatetic existence. The theme of the song is betrayal: it initially appears that the man wandering barefoot through a winter landscape has been betrayed by the miller-girl. In the final verse, however, a dramatic reversal occurs: the voice of the girl herself is heard, mocking the man's distress and labeling him as the offender: "So geh' es jedem, der am Tage / Sein edles Liebchen frech belügt." When she has given her song the woman asks to be allowed to continue her wanderings. However, she allows herself to be persuaded to prolong her stay and soon becomes the object of the unwanted affections of both Herr von Revanne and his son. From this predicament she is able to extricate herself by convincing each man that she is pregnant by the other. Before she disappears, she asserts her loyalty to the "Freund[ ] von der Mühle" (64), expressing the hope that she might one day be reunited with him, when he realizes the value of what he has lost. It is this misplaced sense of loyalty to her faithless lover that has made the woman mad and caused her restless wandering. The figure of the *pilgernde Törin* exemplifies a hazardous life of wandering and inconstancy arising from the inability to renounce a ruined life plan and begin anew. If Wilhelm's wanderings can be seen as an induction into renunciation, then this novella presents the inverse of this situation: the unsettled life is the result of the inability to renounce.

*Wer ist der Verräter?* is the title of a second French novella that Hersilie makes available to Wilhelm during his stay at the residence of the *Oheim*. This is a narrative of the confusions — ultimately resolved — arising from the courtship of two sisters by two men. It is intended that Lucidor will marry Julie, thereby cementing the ties between their two families. With this object in mind the young student is sent by his father to spend time at the home of his intended bride, the daughter of a senior official. However, the dutiful Lucidor is soon agonized by the discovery of his apparent incompatibility with Julie, "neckisch, lieblich, unstät, höchst unterhaltend" (87), feeling himself attracted to the more tranquil temperament of her sister. Soon the discord between natural affection and duty threatens to undermine the plan devised by the two fathers, a plan vitiated by the fact that less thought is given to the individuals concerned than to strategic interests. An otherwise viable alliance between two families is threatened because the two widowed patriarchs orchestrating it are not acting out of pure motives: indeed Lucidor's father, a lecturer in geography, is drawn to Julie partly because of her interest in his subject.

Maierhofer has noted of the *Wanderjahre* as a whole: "Positionen der Ruhe und Tradition stehen neben Maximen der Beweglichkeit und des Fortschritts."[77] Such an opposition is especially manifest in this novella, where the figures of Lucidor and Lucinde can be said to belong to a less dynamic and more traditional world than the other, modern pair: Julie and Antoni, a seasoned man of the world. Lucidor's account of his wanderings through Switzerland "mit dem Bündelchen auf'm Rücken" (90) interests the impetuous Julie far less than Antoni's traveler's tales of Genoa, Naples, and Constantinople. The contradiction between modernity and tradition embodied by these figures is overcome at the end of the novella, when Lucidor is reconciled with Julie, from whom he had initially been alienated.

Julie and Lucinde represent fundamentally different attitudes to mobility. While Julie is defined by her desire to know the world and her delight in motion ("Pfui übers Hocken!" 95), Lucinde espouses a different form of wandering. She and Lucidor agree on a kind of pedestrianism whose merit lies in its boundedness, in the repeated revisiting of familiar objects:

> Abwechselnd einfache natürliche Gegenstände zu durchwandern, mit Ruhe zu betrachten, wie der verständige kluge Mensch ihnen etwas abzugewinnen weiß, wie die Einsicht ins Vorhandene, zum Gefühl seiner Bedürfnisse sich gesellend, Wunder tut, um die Welt erst bewohnbar zu

> machen, dann zu bevölkern und endlich zu übervölkern, das alles konnte hier im einzelnen zur Sprache kommen. (95)

The contrast between the measured pace allied to cultivation, a mode of wandering that is georgic, and the self-regarding haste of an upcoming generation exemplified by Julie and Antoni could scarcely be greater. For the latter pair, what counts is not "Einsicht ins Vorhandene," but the restless pursuit of new experiences. Julie eschews the practice of walking in favor of a swift vehicle; her allegiance is not to the earth but to the "kleinem beweglichen Himmel" (108): the two-seater chaise in which she will take her place at Antoni's side. Speaking of the *Weltmann* Antoni, Julie notes appreciatively: "Das gestehen Sie doch, der ewige Jude, der unruhige Anton Reiser, weiß noch seine Wallfahrten bequem genug einzurichten, für sich und seine Genossen: es ist ein sehr schöner, bequemer Wagen" (110). There is an ambivalence about Julie's affectionate application of the name Anton Reiser in reference to her beloved. For a contemporary readership, Anton Reiser, the hero of Karl Philipp Moritz's celebrated psychological novel, is a byword for a restlessness that leads ultimately to madness and self-destruction.

Julie and Antoni are not the only representatives of a modernity characterized by impetuous haste: the high-ranking official also has a son. On their tour of the park, which the official has laid out in separate areas reflecting the tastes of his children, this "lustige Junker" leads his sisters and Lucidor to his own particular corner. To get there they must cross uneven paths, rocks, and boggy ground to a place where they see "allerlei Maschinenwerk verworren aufgetürmt" (95). This fairground, a jumble of ill-assorted machinery, is the son's pet project. In this comic vignette we are presented with a disastrous vision of an irrational modernity: not only do the "holprichte Pfade" that lead to the Junker's domain contrast with the "breiter, fahrbarer Weg" laid out by his father through the park, but the fairground itself appears as a blasted heath beyond the tilled fields. The dominant impression is one of infertility, and the "lustige Junker" has indeed provided neither the original concept of his project, which he has from a "gescheiterter Kerl," nor the capital, which he has from his father. This vision of a landscape disfigured by ill-conceived development also anticipates Susanne's later fearful remarks on the "überhandnehmende Maschinenwesen" (429) that threatens "das hübsche frohe Leben" of the valleys.

Although the characters of *Der Mann von fünfzig Jahren* are not presented as wanderers, the novella is worth citing, if only for one scene that presents mobility as the appropriate stance toward a mutable world. The theme here is, as in *Wer ist der Verräter?* the hazardous negotiation of sexual relations, and the potential for injury and disturbance when such negotiations go awry. The central motif is that of the woman between two suitors, father and son, a situation that reflects that of Hersilie, who for a long time seems undecided as to whether she should bestow her affections on Wilhelm or on Felix. Not only does the novella sketch a wintry landscape imbued with an atmosphere of renunciation, but it also provides a memorable image of two persons on the move in that landscape. As was the case in *Wer ist der Verräter*, the novella presents two false pairings (the old major and his niece Hilarie, Flavio and the "schöne Witwe") that need to be dissolved and rearranged in order for equilibrium to be restored. Before this can occur, however, Hilarie and the widow must themselves undergo a spell of renunciative wandering.

What brings Hersilie and Flavio together is the disastrous winter flooding, an event that unites them in beneficent action, bringing vital supplies to inundated neighbors by boat. Cold weather follows and the flood waters freeze over, but the distress of the neighbors must still be alleviated: the young pair continue their mission, using sleighs to traverse the ice. The frozen lake is a striking symbol of precariousness, illustrating both the futility of attachment to a particular place and the necessity of urgent action, key tenets of the League of Wanderers: "Eilig war jeder im Sprechen und Handeln, Kommen und Gehen, denn es blieb immer die Gefahr, ein plötzliches Tauwetter möchte den ganzen schönen Kreis glücklichen Wechselwirkens zerstören, die Wirte bedrohen und die Gäste vom Hause abschneiden" (212). Implicit in this symbol is the recognition of the potential for contingent events to take the ground from under one's feet. But the frozen surface is not just a plane of charitable action; it is also the space of a rather grave courtship in which the pair, skating on the ice, enact a sort of ballet of renunciation: "Man bewegte sich lustig und lustiger, bald zusammen, bald einzeln, bald getrennt, bald vereint. Scheiden und Meiden, was sonst so schwer aufs Herz fällt, ward hier zum kleinen, scherzhaften Frevel, man floh sich, um sich einander augenblicks wieder zu finden." This game anticipates the rhythm of meetings and partings on Lake Maggiore, where Wilhelm and the artist occupy one boat with Hilarie and the beautiful widow in the other.[78]

In the milieu of the League of Wanderers Wilhelm hears three further stories that reflect on the dialectic of renunciation and action. The first of these, the fairy tale *Die neue Melusine* has as its narrator a wanderer, an opportunist who desires only to live for the moment. In his opening remarks he sketches out in advance the entire futile arc of the tale:

> Einst nahm ich mir eine Reise vor, die mir guten Gewinn verschaffen sollte; aber ich machte meinen Zuschnitt ein wenig zu groß, und nachdem ich sie mit Extrapost angefangen und sodann auf der ordinären eine Zeitlang fortgesetzt hatte, fand ich mich zuletzt genötigt dem Ende derselben zu Fuße entgegenzugehen. (354)

The journey in question is undertaken in the company of Melusine, not the sea nymph of the original French tale, but a dwarf princess in search of a human suitor. She succeeds in kindling the desire of the narrator, who after the first kiss is "ihr ganz leibeigen." The woman hints that his desire may be requited if he faithfully carries out the tasks she sets him. These center on a mysterious casket that the hero is instructed to transport from place to place, making special provisions for its handling and safe-keeping. Despite the dubious nature of a mission that requires unquestioning adherence to obscure instructions, the narrator acquiesces. There begins a spell of journeying and testing, in which the suitor's susceptibility to distraction repeatedly gets the better of him. Bored and unable to withstand the lure of the bottomless purse entrusted to him, he abandons himself to wild carousing. On each occasion the woman reappears: remorse is expressed and forgiveness granted. A more serious infraction occurs when the suitor's curiosity impels him to peer into the casket during one of his beloved's periodic absences, glimpsing her in her diminutive form. Even then the pair are reconciled, when the man undertakes "dieser Entdeckung niemals vorwurfsweise zu gedenken" (363). However, he breaks this promise too, in a fit of drunken choler, whereupon the princess reveals the secret of her origins and threatens to return to her world. Again the hapless lover pleads with her, and again she relents, agreeing to let him accompany her. The fairy tale reflects on the theme of renunciation by presenting its opposite: a chronic inability to master desires and impulses. As Henkel has pointed out, it is necessary to attend to the demonic moment in the tale in order to fully understand the curious nature of the testing to which the hero is subjected.[79] What qualifies the hero to become the consort of the princess is his very susceptibility to temptation, his inability to defer fulfillment. Paradoxically, this changeability is a proof of loyalty, but only to unconditional desire, manifested in an unending journey with no goal other than self-gratification, funded from a bottomless purse. Not even in the magical domain of the beloved is this longing stilled; the flight from this domain is less an "eminent sittlicher Akt" (Henkel) of self-liberation than a new expression of discontentment, an inability, as it were, to sit still. Nothing is learned, nothing is gained: the tale completes its circular trajectory, depositing its hero at the point from which he had set out, empty-handed.

The short story *Nicht zu weit!* forms a pendant to the exposition in the following chapter of the attitude taken by the League of Wanderers to the resource of time ("Der größte Respekt wird allen eingeprägt für die Zeit"; 405). In it some light is shed on the biography of Odoardo, the author of the European settlement program. This "vorzüglicher Mann" (397) is the victim of a court intrigue that puts an end to his brilliant career and results in his banishment to a remote province. Although Odoardo is able to resign himself to his new role, his wife, accustomed to the splendor of court, chafes at her provincial existence. It is she who is the wanderer, seeking compensation in empty social activity, and straying beyond the confines of her social role to the extent of entertaining a lover. On the evening of her birthday she has failed to return from one of these excursions; as the hours pass her husband and children become worked up to a fever of impatience. Finally, in an access of despair Odoardo himself flees the house, leaving the housekeeper to pass the following remark on her mistress's behavior: "Sie kann es nicht lassen. Wenn sie nicht immer Menschen, Männer um sich sieht, wenn sie nicht hin und wieder fährt, sich an- und aus- und umziehen kann, ist es, als wenn ihr der Atem ausginge" (395). The theme is the potential of impatience — insufficient respect for time, the failure fully to inhabit the present moment — to undermine the precarious foundations of contentment. Impatience, manifested initially in an insatiable need for distraction, restlessness to the point of hyperactivity, infects the woman before communicating itself to husband and children ("Leidenschaft erzeugt Leidenschaft"; 400) with fatally destabilizing results. The story is in part a piece of cultural criticism, the diagnosis of a contemporary malaise, an inability to *refrain* from acting when the occasion demands it ("sie kann es nicht lassen"). Here the wanderer motif illustrates the consequences of unthinkingly straying beyond limits in an access of impatience, a straying that prompts the admonition "Nicht zu weit!"

*Die gefährliche Wette* evokes student wandering as an example of a carefree and irresponsible life. As in *Die neue Melusine* the moral point is brought into focus in the opening sentences:

> Es ist bekannt, daß die Menschen, sobald es ihnen einigermaßen wohl und nach ihrem Sinne geht, alsobald nicht wissen, was sie vor Übermut anfangen sollen; und so hatten denn auch mutwillige Studenten die Gewohnheit wahrend der Ferien scharenweis das Land zu durchziehen und nach ihrer Art Suiten zu reißen, welche freilich nicht immer die besten Folgen hatten. (378)

That the story is intended as a corrective is apparent: it is told by the courier Saint Christopher, a giant of a man, something of a patron of the League of Wanderers, to "einem Kreise versammelter lustiger Gesellen." In it a practical joke, planned and executed in haste, has lifelong repercussions for victim and perpetrators. The story invites reflection on the dialectic of thought and action by showing the unforeseen results flowing from a single inconsequential deed.[80] It is a humorous reformulation of the proverb "Übermut tut selten gut," revealing the dangers resulting from arbitrary and spontaneous conduct.

## Lenardo's "Wanderrede": Wandering as Ethos and Political Program

In his introduction to the 1949 Gedenkausgabe edition of the *Wanderjahre*, Gerhard Küntzel refers to the work's "Doppelantlitz," which reflects both "die Goethesche Existenz in ihrem Innersten und in ihren Verschwiegenheiten" and "das Bild der Epoche." This Janus-faced quality characterizes Lenardo's "Wanderrede," the speech in which he sets out the emigration plans of the League of Wanderers (book 3, chapter 9). This speech is a great conspectus of contemporary and historical wanderers: desert nomads, students, explorers, sentimental travelers, journeymen, traders, robbers, Jews (who, in an inversion of the Ahasver myth, possess "den Segen des ewigen Wanderns"; 387), artists, musicians, actors, pedagogues, missionaries, pilgrims — all categories whose "Tun und Lassen ohne Wandern meist nicht denkbar wäre" (388), but also farmers, in so far as they are engaged in cultivating new lands.

Before considering the political dimensions of the *Wanderrede*, let us first examine its ethical content, the level closest to "die Goethesche Existenz." In Lenardo's speech, wandering is affirmed primarily as a metaphor for an ethical or existential stance on the part of the individual, involving adaptability and flexibility. Survival for an individual amid the instability of dissolving institutions in Post-Napoleonic Europe requires seeking out a niche, securing one's existence by fulfilling some need arising in the social whole:

> Man hat gesagt und wiederholt: "Wo mir's wohl geht, ist mein Vaterland!"; doch wäre dieser tröstliche Spruch noch besser ausgedrückt, wenn es hieße: "Wo ich nütze, ist mein Vaterland!" Zu Hause kann einer unnütz sein, ohne daß es eben sogleich bemerkt wird; außen in der Welt ist der Unnütze gar bald offenbar. Wenn ich nun sage: "Trachte jeder, überall sich und anderen zu nutzen!," so ist dies nicht etwa Lehre oder Rat, sondern der Ausspruch des Lebens selbst. (386)

The implications of this survival strategy are worked out still more fully in one of Goethe's "Allgemeine Betrachtungen zur Weltliteratur," written not long after the publication of the *Wanderjahre:*

> Die Frage, ob diese oder jene Beschäftigung, welcher sich der Mensch widmet, auch nützlich sei? wiederholt sich oft genug im Laufe der Zeit und muß jetzt besonders wieder hervortreten, wo es niemanden mehr erlaubt ist, nach Belieben ruhig, zufrieden, mäßig und ohne Anforderung zu leben. Die Außenwelt bewegt sich so heftig, daß ein jeder einzelne bedroht ist, in den Strudel mit fortgerissen zu werden; hier sieht er sich nun genötigt, um seine eigenen Bedürfnisse zu befriedigen, unmittelbar und augenblicklich für die Bedürfnisse anderer zu sorgen, und da fragt sich denn freilich, ob er irgendeine Fertigkeit habe, diesen aufdringlichen Pflichten genugzutun.[81]

It is significant that these remarks appear in a discussion of the topic of "Weltliteratur," for what they gesture toward is a pragmatic cosmopolitanism. Not the political creed of world government, virulent since the French Revolution, but cosmopolitanism as an individual survival strategy is what Goethe has in mind. Such a strategy requires that the individual define himself less in terms of allegiance to the native soil or patrimony than with respect to a functional role. This entails mobility, a willingness to move to wherever that role can best be fulfilled to the advantage of the individual and the host community, to which he is then bound by a relation of reciprocity.

Unlike its Enlightenment equivalent (see my discussion of *Die Harzreise*) this idea of cosmopolitanism is founded not on altruism but on egoism, a concern for private interests tempered by the attitude of "Weltfrömmigkeit."[82] It renounces the bonds of origin in favor of relations of mutual benefit. Only these are capable of offering some kind of stability in a thoroughly dynamized world: the "Dauer im Wechsel" referred to in Goethe's 1803 poem of that name. The wanderer motif allows the concise expression of this ethical stance, which involves sustained activity in which self-interest and the interests of others coincide and a willingness to regard the entire world as the sphere of such activity. Moreover, it allows the renunciation required by that stance to be grasped as active and productive.

Now let us consider the speech in its political aspect, as "Bild der Epoche." In it Lenardo unfolds the plan to establish a quasi-democratic society in the New World. Crucial to Lenardo's advocacy of emigration is the understanding that constructing a sustainable social order capable of embracing the changes registered in the novel (overpopulation, mechanization) is impossible in the Old World. Such changes can only be met by beginning anew ("von vorn anfangen"; 142) as Lenardo puts it, that is, by social and political reorganization aimed at liberating the productive capacities of individuals and groups. The remedy that the *Wanderjahre* proposes for a modernity in which "die Bande sind zerissen, / Das Vertrauen ist verletzt" (317), that is to say, in which the institutions of feudal agriculture and guild manufacture that had until then provided some degree of shelter for individuals, are "melting into air,"[83] is primarily an ethical one. Individuals are called upon to find a niche by fulfilling the material needs of their neighbors, thereby creating bonds of reciprocity that can take the place of outmoded and crumbling institutions. But how feasible is such a remedy in an Old World where "alles Schlendrian [ist], wo man das Neue immer auf die alte, das Wachsende nach starrer Weise behandeln will"? (332). How, given rapid population growth and the advance of machinery capable of abolishing whole areas of productive activity at a stroke, could each and every individual be sure of finding a place in a social ensemble governed by the principle of the mutual fulfillment of needs? The reactionary atmosphere of the 1820s with its curbs on personal freedoms and its economic pressures was hardly conducive to the innovation needed if new functional roles were to be found for the many.

It is the author's guilty conscience about the adequacy of the ethical program that makes the political program of emigration a structural necessity. However, Goethe is unwilling to have the *Wanderjahre* read as a wholehearted affirmation of emigration, and so he is obliged to come up with an alternative. Hence the inclusion of Odoardo, whose sole function is apparently to mitigate the implied disaffection with the contemporary situation by keeping alive the idea that the necessary reforms are possible in the European setting. Perhaps this is why the European settlement plan feels like something of an afterthought. Nor is Odoardo's solution an entirely convincing one: like Lenardo he envisages a society founded on craft manufacture, but while the League of Wanderers is prepared to take ship to offset "das überhandnehmende Maschinenwesen," it is unclear how Odoardo's artisans are to evade the same threat.

Perhaps the main symbolic function of the wanderer motif in the literature of the nineteenth century has been as a figure for desiring man. In the works of the early Romantics (see my discussion of Tieck and Novalis) the claims of desire find very full expression. The figures of Heinrich von Ofterdingen and Franz Sternbald, for example, can be seen as embodiments of a longing for the untrammeled extension of body and mind. Their yearning for corporeal and psychic emancipation has something of the spirit of the Age of Revolution. Since these works set the tone for later Romantic narratives of wandering, it is easy to imagine that the denial of desire inherent in Goethe's interpretation of the motif would have had an alienating effect on contemporary readers, who had grown accustomed to the wanderer as man-at-liberty, as one of Eichendorff's or Jean Paul's youths roaming freely through Nature.

By contrast, the *Wanderjahre* provides a bleak prognosis of a society in the thrall of an ethic of renunciation and unrelenting activity. It is, moreover, a society for which the ultimate act of renunciation, that of emigration, appears as the only viable political option. However the novel does not merely lay bare a modern condition in which mobility is synonymous with productivity; it also affirms the praxis of renunciation as a stance that is adequate to the new realities. One should approach life as a wanderer, the work appears to be saying. This entails inhabiting the present rather than yielding to longings for that which is distant. In Nietzsche's words, quoted as the epigraph to this chapter, the wanderer — the person who has come to the "Freiheit der Vernunft" — may not set his or her heart on minutiae, but must delight in the endless flux of things.

## Notes

[1] Hans-Jürgen Schings, "Agathon — Anton Reiser — Wilhelm Meister: Zur Pathogenese des modernen Subjekts im Bildungsroman," in *Goethe im Kontext: Kunst und Humanität, Naturwissenschaft und Politik von der Aufklärung bis zur Restauration*, ed. Wolfgang Wittkowski (Tübingen: Niemeyer, 1984), 42–68; here, 43.

[2] Morgenstern's lecture "Über das Wesen des Bildungsromans" (given December 1819 and published in *Inländisches Museum* 1 (1820), no. 3, 13–27) explicitly identifies Goethe's novel as a paragon of the genre. Fritz Martini's study of the history of the term *Bildungsroman* remains unsurpassed: "Bildungsroman: Zur Geschichte des Wortes und der Theorie," *Deutsche Vierteljahresschrift* 35 (1961): 44–63.

[3] Karl Schlechta and Kurt May are the most eminent of the first wave of critics to question the applicability of the category *Bildungsroman* to the *Lehrjahre*. Karl Schlechta, *Goethes Wilhelm Meister* (1953; repr., Frankfurt am Main: Suhrkamp, 1985; Kurt May: " 'Wilhelm Meisters Lehrjahre,' ein Bildungsroman?" *Deutsche Vierteljahresschrift* 31 (1957): 1–37; Heinz Schlaffer, "Exoterik und Esoterik in Goethes Romanen," *Goethe-Jahrbuch* 95 (1978): 212–17; Stefan Blessin, *Die Romane Goethes* (Königstein im Taunus: Athenäum, 1979), 41.

[4] Schiller, in a letter to Goethe 2 July 1796. *Briefe an Goethe*, ed. Karl Robert Mandelkow, 2 vols. (Hamburg: Wegner, 1982), 1:231.

[5] Hans-Jürgen Schings, " 'Wilhelm Meister' und das Erbe der Illuminaten," in *Die Weimarer Klassik und ihre Geheimbünde*, ed. Walter Müller-Seidel and Wolfgang Riedel (Würzburg: Königshausen & Neumann, 2003), 177–203.

[6] "Anthropology" should be understood as the theory of man as natural being, that is, in a sense consistent with the evolution of the term in the German-speaking lands. It is thus used here to denote a *philosophical* discourse and not as a synonym for the *social sciences* of "ethnography" or "ethnology," as it commonly is in English-language contexts. See Wolfgang Riedel, "Anthropologie und Literatur in der deutschen Spätaufklärung: Skizze einer Forschungslandschaft," *Internationales Archiv für Sozialgeschichte der deutschen Literatur* 6 (1994): 93–157, esp. 94–95. On the history of the term see Odo Marquard's article "Anthropologie" in *Historisches Wörterbuch der Philosophie*, ed. Joachim Ritter and Karlfried Gründer, 12 vols. (Basel: Schwabe, 1971–2004), vol. 1 (1971), cols. 362–74.

[7] Johann Wolfgang Goethe, *Werke*, ed. Erich Trunz (Hamburg: Wegner, 1948–60), vol. 7 (6th ed., 1965), 101. Further references to volume 7 will be made in the main body of the text using page numbers alone. References to other volumes of the edition will be indicated by the abbreviation *HA* followed by the volume and page numbers.

[8] Thomas Mann's 1939 lecture "Die Kunst des Romans," in *Gesammelte Werke*, 13 vols., 2nd ed. (Frankfurt am Main: S. Fischer, 1974), 10:348–62, here 357.

[9] Ulrich Stadler, "Wilhelm Meisters unterlassene Revolte: Individuelle Geschichte und Gesellschaftsgeschichte in Goethes *Lehrjahren*," *Euphorion* 74 (1980): 360–74.

[10] Thus Dieter Borchmeyer, *Höfische Gesellschaft und französische Revolution: Adliges und bürgerliches Wertsystem im Urteil der Weimarer Klassik* (Kronberg im Taunus: Athenäum, 1977).

[11] Looking back on the decade of the Revolution in the *Tag und Jahreshefte* for 1803 Goethe remarks that the general unrest in the wake of the Revolution frequently manifested itself in the form of a desire for mobility (*HA* 10:459).

[12] Immanuel Kant, *Beantwortung der Frage: Was ist Aufklärung?* in Kant, *Werke*, 10 vols. (Darmstadt: Wissenschaftliche Buchgesellschaft, 1975), 9:53 and 54.

[13] The declaration by Johann Gottfried Seume, the author of the popular travelogue *Der Spaziergang nach Syrakuse im Jahre 1802*, is characteristic: "Ich halte den Gang für das Ehrenvollste und Selbstständigste in dem Manne und bin der Meinung, daß alles besser gehen würde, wenn man mehr ginge." *Werke in zwei Bänden*, ed. Jörg Drews (Frankfurt am Main: Deutscher Klassiker-Verlag, 1993), 2:543–44.

[14] Kurt Bayertz, "Der aufrechte Gang: Ursprung der Kultur und des Denkens; eine anthropologische Debatte im Anschluß an Helvétius' *De l'esprit*," in *Zwischen Empirisierung und Konstruktionsleistung: Anthropologie im 18. Jahrhundert*, ed. Jörn Garber and Heinz Thoma (Tübingen: Niemeyer, 2004), 59–75. The Herder quotation appears on 67–68. It is taken from Johann Gottfried Herder, *Ausgewählte Werke in Einzelausgaben*, ed. Heinz Stolpe (Berlin, Weimar: Aufbau 1965–), vol. 1: *Ideen zu einer Philosophie der Geschichte der Menschheit*, 113. Herder's justification of man's position at the summit of creation on the basis of his upright gait derives ultimately from Ovid's *Metamorphoses.*

[15] Nicholas Boyle, *Goethe: The Poet and the Age* (Oxford: Oxford UP, 1992–), 2:345–47.

[16] On the role of performance in Wilhelm Meister's attempts to constitute his own identity, see Jürgen Barkhoff, "Theatricality in Goethe's *Wilhelm Meisters Lehrjahre*," in *Goethe and Schubert: Across the Divide* (Proceedings of the Conference "Goethe and Schubert in Perspective and Performance," Trinity College Dublin, 4–5 April 2003), ed. Lorraine Byrne and Dan Farrelly (Dublin: Carysfort, 2004), 90–102. Analyzing the *Bildungsbrief*, Barkhoff argues that Wilhelm Meister aspires not so much to the Renaissance ideal of the integral personality in which all the faculties are balanced, as to the "semblance of balance" (96) and of poise that he sees embodied in the aristocracy.

[17] The new cultural practice of the *Bildungsreise* resembled the aristocratic grand tour insofar as both were directed toward the accumulation of knowledge. What made the *Bildungsreise* a new and specifically bourgeois practice is both the type of data collected and the ends to which this was put. While the purpose of the grand tour was the collection of *symbolic capital*, to use Bourdieu's term (the right to be listened to, social prestige), the *Bildungsreise* was geared to the accumulation of *cultural capital*, that is, commercially or technically usable knowledge and competencies. The grand tour thus served the aristocratic function of *representation*, whereas the *Bildungsreise* served the bourgeois function of *production*. On the grand tour see Winfried Siebers, "Ungleiche Lehrfahrten: Kavaliere und Gelehrten," in *Reisekultur: Von der Pilgerfahrt zum modernen Tourismus*, ed. Hermann Bausinger, Klaus Beyrer, and Wolfgang Griep (Munich: C. H. Beck, 1991), 47–57.

[18] Charles Taylor, *Sources of the Self: The Making of the Modern Identity.* (Cambridge: Cambridge UP, 1989), 214. An encomium of trade similar to Werner's can be found in Georg Forsters *Ansichten vom Niederrhein* (1791), a representative Enlightenment travelogue: "Aus diesem Gesichtpunkte betrachtet, ist also der große Kaufmann, dessen Spekulationen das ganze Rund der Erde umfassen und Kontinente an einander knüpfen, in seiner Thätigkeit des Geistes und in seinem Einfluß auf das allgemeine Regen der Menschheit nicht nur einer der glücklichsten, sondern durch die Masse von praktischen Erfahrungen . . .

zugleich einer der aufgeklärtesten Menschen." Georg Forster, *Werke in vier Bänden*, ed. Gerhard Steiner (Frankfurt am Main: Insel, 1967–70), 2:429. Both Forster's and Werner's praise of the commercial vocation turn on the idea of the businessman as the anti-type of the despot ("Dolch und Ketten kennt sie gar nicht").

[19] Arthur Oncken Lovejoy, *The Great Chain of Being: A Study of the History of an Idea* (1936; repr., Cambridge, MA: Harvard UP, 1998); Peter Matussek, ed., *Goethe und die Verzeitlichung der Natur* (Munich: Beck, 1998), esp. the introduction, 7–14; Hugh Barr Nisbet, "Naturgeschichte und Humangeschichte bei Goethe, Herder und Kant," in Matussek, *Goethe und die Verzeitlichung der Natur*, 15–43; Wolf Lepenies, *Das Ende der Naturgeschichte: Wandel kultureller Selbstverständlichkeiten in den Wissenschaften des 18. und 19. Jahrhunderts* (Munich and Vienna: Hanser, 1976).

[20] Ilse Graham, *Goethe: Portrait of the Artist* (Berlin and New York: Walter de Gruyter, 1977), 182–226.

[21] See Franziska Schößler, *Goethes Lehr- und Wanderjahre: Eine Kulturgeschichte der Moderne* (Tübingen and Basel: Francke, 2002), 119–21.

[22] "Dein innerstes Bedürfnis erzeugt und nährt den Wunsch, die Anlagen, die in dir zum Guten und Schönen ruhen mögen, sie seien körperlich oder geistig, immer mehr zu entwickeln und auszubilden"(276).

[23] Rolf Selbmann sees this fact as diminishing the importance of the *Bildungsbrief*, "Damit ist gezeigt, daß man die 'Lehrjahre' falsch liest, wenn man diesem Brief eine zu grundsätzliche Bedeutung beimißt." Selbmann, *Der deutsche Bildungsroman* (Stuttgart: Metzler, 1984), 71. On the contrary, it may be argued that the reference to Werner's non-receipt of the letter highlights its importance for its *author*.

[24] Novalis, *Schriften: Die Werke Friedrich von Hardenbergs*, ed. Paul Kluckhohn and Richard Samuel (Stuttgart: Kohlhammer, 1977–), 3:647.

[25] Schiller to Goethe, 9 July 1796: "Was Sie über Wilhelms Äußeres Wernern in den Mund gelegt, ist von ungemein guter Wirkung für das Ganze." Schiller takes up the theme of one-sided contemporary education in the sixth of his *Ästhetische Briefe*. Mandelkow, *Briefe an Goethe*, 1:251.

[26] The League of Illuminati was founded in Ingolstadt in 1776 by Adam Weishaupt (1748–1830), who had grown dissatisfied with Freemasonry. Following the suppression of the league in Bavaria in 1784, Weishaupt moved to Gotha at the invitation of Duke Ernst. For the purposes of this discussion the Illuminati and the Freemasons may be considered to have been sister organizations, and indeed they were to a considerable degree congruent in terms of membership and ideology.

[27] Rosemarie Haas, *Die Turmgesellschaft in "Wilhelm Meisters Lehrjahren": Zur Geschichte des Geheimbundromans und der Romantheorie im 18. Jahrhundert* (Frankfurt am Main: Lang, 1975); Hans-Jürgen Schings, "'Wilhelm Meister' und das Erbe der Illuminaten," 177–203.

[28] Hans-Jürgen Schings, "'Wilhelm Meister' und das Erbe der Illuminaten," 186.

[29] Haas, *Die Turmgesellschaft in "Wilhelm Meisters Lehrjahren,"* 28.

[30] *Goethes Briefe*, ed. Karl Robert Mandelkow, 4 vols. (Hamburg: Wegner, 1962–76), 2:230.

[31] This work is of interest since it was a prime source for Mozart's and Schickaneder's *Die Zauberflöte*, which was performed under Goethe's direction at Weimar on 16 January 1794. Goethe's composition of the *Zauberflöte Zweiter Theil* in December 1795 is evidence of the extent to which the themes of wandering and *Bildung* are interlinked in his imagination at the very time that he was intensely preoccupied with Wilhelm Meister. In Goethe's fragmentary libretto Tamino and Pamina are set wandering in search of their son, whom the Queen of the Night has locked away in a golden casket. There, as in the *Lehrjahre* (the third volume of which had appeared in autumn 1795), we have the motif of a journey toward an ideal that is never attained.

[32] Schings, "'Wilhelm Meister' und das Erbe der Illuminaten," 197; Schings is indebted to Haas for the "Pädagogik des Irrens" thesis. Haas regards the Abbé as an "Ideenträger" introduced into the second version of the novel "um die Art, wie Wilhelm irrend sich bildet, als theoretisches Prinzip zu vertreten und zu legitimieren" (58).

[33] The Abbé's educational theory is first mentioned by the canoness, the author of the "Bekenntnisse einer schönen Seele" (419).

[34] Schings, "'Wilhelm Meister' und das Erbe der Illuminaten," 194–95.

[35] Schings, "'Wilhelm Meister' und das Erbe der Illuminaten," 196.

[36] Frank Kermode, *The Sense of an Ending: Studies in the Theory of Fiction* (New York: Oxford UP, 1967), 59, 62, 71, and 80.

[37] Thus also Nicholas Boyle, who interprets the tower in the light of Kant's *Kritik der teleologischen Urteilskraft*, "There can, according to Kant, be no *objective* grounds for believing that our past life, whether individual or collective, has a particular moral pattern. That depends on the moral goal we freely set ourselves for the future: once we know where we are going we can read that pattern back into the past and have a reasonable confidence that it is a story of gradual improvement." *Goethe: The Poet and the Age*, vol 2 [2000]: *Revolution and Renunciation*, 375–76. Boyle rightly alludes to the comic aspects in the presentation of the tower; these are necessary since "no external authority could *seriously* claim to dictate to our self-understanding" (375).

[38] Kurt May, "Das Endziel der Bildung ist also im Unendlichen der Zeit gelegen und nur im Ganzen der Menschheit in einer zu gründenden idealen Gemeinschaft zu verwirklichen." "'Wilhelm Meisters Lehrjahre,'" 33 The apparently indeterminacy of the end of *Bildung* leads May mistakenly to attribute a utopian perspective to the novel. By contrast Schings argues that the "offenes Geheimnis" of *Bildung* is an end in itself.

[39] Immanuel Kant, *Werke*, 10:400.

[40] In a circular letter written to his correspondents in Weimar (2 Oct. 1787), Goethe indicates his intention to utilize the material of the Italian journey in the completion of the Wilhelm Meister project: "Zuletzt wird alles im 'Wilhelm' gefaßt und geschlossen" (*HA* 11:411).

[41] Norbert Miller, *Der Wanderer: Goethe in Italien* (Munich: Hanser, 2002), 57.

[42] Boyle, *Goethe: The Poet and the Age*, 2:244.

[43] Schößler sees Wilhelm's promise to make good the losses of Melina's troupe arising from the ambush as an essential prelude to his eventual incorporation into the "Society of the Tower" with its bourgeois ethic of performance: "Die Gemeinschaftsfähigkeit Wilhelms vollzieht sich im Kontext des sich etablierenden Leistungsgedankens" (*Goethes Lehr- und Wanderjahre*, 90).

[44] "ein neues Leben"; "ich zähle einen zweiten Geburtstag, eine wahre Wiedergeburt, von dem Tage, da ich Rom betrat."; "Die Wiedergeburt, die mich von innen heraus umarbeitet, wirkt immer fort" (*HA* 11:126, 147, 150). "Wiedergeburt" also connotes Renaissance in the sense of a cultural rebirth, specifically the rebirth of the culture of classical antiquity in the modern age.

[45] See Barkhoff, "Theatricality in Goethe's *Wilhelm Meisters Lehrjahre*," 96–97.

[46] Hans-Jürgen Schings, "'Gedenke zu leben': Goethes Lebenskunst," in Fuhrmann, ed. *Wilhelm Meister und seine Nachfahren: Vorträge des 4. Kasseler Goetheseminars* (Kassel: Wenderoth, 2000), 33–52; here, 47.

[47] Johann Wolfgang von Goethe, *Werke*, ed. Gustav von Loeper, Erich Schmidt, et al., 4 parts, 133 vols. (Weimar: Böhlau, 1887–1919), 4 46:110–11.

[48] Schings draws our attention to the resemblances between the "Hall of the Past" and classical funerary monuments viewed by Goethe in Verona ("Gedenke zu leben," 50; *HA* 11:42).

[49] Friedrich Nietzsche, *Menschliches: Allzumenschliches I*, no. 638, in Friedrich Nietzsche, *Kritische Studienausgabe*, ed. Giorgio Colli and Mazzino Montinari, 15 vols. (Munich: Deutscher Taschenbuch Verlag, 1999), 2:362–63.

[50] Erhard Bahr, "Wilhelm Meisters Wanderjahre oder die Entsagenden," in *Goethe-Handbuch*, ed. Bernd Witte et al., 4 vols. (Stuttgart: Metzler, 1996–98), 3:186–231; here, 187.

[51] *HA* 8:11–12. The page numbers of subsequent references to volume 8 will be supplied in parentheses in the main body of the text. Although the *Hamburger Ausgabe* is used here for reasons of convenience, it should be noted that other editions such as the *Artemis-Gedenkausgabe* or the more recent *Münchner* and *Frankfurter Ausgaben* are to be preferred because of their fidelity to the text as it appears in the *Ausgabe letzter Hand.*

[52] See Bruno Schmidlin, *Das Motiv des Wanderns bei Goethe* (Winterthur, Switzerland: Keller, 1963), 135–36.

[53] Goethe, *Werke*, ed. Gustav von Loeper, 1 19:280–81.

[54] Gerhard Küntzel speculates on a connection between the Realp sermon, which links "das Thema von Wanderschaft und Prüfung mit der christkatholischen Forderung von regula und disciplina" and the content of Wilhelm's first letter to Natalie. See his introduction to Goethe, *Gedenkausgabe der Werke, Briefe und Gespräche*, ed. Ernst Beutler, 24 vols. (Zurich: Artemis, 1948–54), 8:885–958; here, 929. This edition is known as the Artemis Gedenkausgabe.

[55] Arthur Henkel has pointed to the parallel between Wilhelm's relationship to Natalie and Goethe's to Charlotte von Stein. Henkel, *Entsagung: Eine Studie zu Goethes Altersroman*, 2nd ed. (1954; repr., Tübingen: Niemeyer, 1964), 114. The

travel diary kept by Wilhelm for Natalie — which resembles the diary kept by Goethe for Charlotte von Stein on his Italian journey — is an exercise in unpossessive love, "Liebe ohne Besitz," the formula Henkel uses to define Goethean renunciation.

[56] "For the stoic what is renounced is, if rightly renounced, ipso facto not part of the good. For the Christian what is renounced is thereby affirmed as good. Paradoxically, Christian renunciation is an affirmation of the goodness of what is renounced." (Charles Taylor, *Sources of the Self*, 219). The consensus in the research is that the concept of renunciation in the *Wanderjahre* is not stoical in character. See Bahr, "Wilhelm Meisters Wanderjahre," 203–6.

[57] Bahr, "Wilhelm Meisters Wanderjahre," 206.

[58] Karl August Varnhagen von Ense, "Im Sinne der Wanderer," in *Goethe im Urteil seiner Kritiker*, ed. Karl Robert Mandelkow, 4 vols. (Munich: C. H. Beck, 1977–84), 2:26–31. Rahel to Karl Varnhagen von Ense, 17 December 1808 (quoted from *Goethe im Urteil*, 2:508).

[59] Heinrich Gustav Hotho, Review of Goethe's *Wanderjahre*, 2nd ed., in *Jahrbücher für wissenschaftliche Kritik*, Dec. 1829 and Mar. 1830 (quoted from *Goethes Wilhelm Meister: Zur Rezeptionsgeschichte der Lehr- und Wanderjahre*, ed. Klaus F. Gille [Königstein im Taunus: Athenäum, 1979], 118–28). Also Karl Rosenkranz, *Göthe und seine Werke* (Königsberg, 1847) (quoted from Mandelkow, *Goethe im Urteil*, 2:310–13). Also Ferdinand Gregorovius, *Göthe's Wilhelm Meister in seinen socialistischen Elementen entwickelt* (Königsberg: n.p., 1849) (quoted from Mandelkow, *Goethe im Urteil*, 2:318–27). This line of criticism received its most important stimulus from Karl August Varnhagen von Ense. Among the correspondence on the *Wanderjahre* published by Varnhagen in *Der Gesellschafter* we find the following remarks: "Zur Besiegung des nächsten größten europäischen Weltübels . . . muß aller materielle Besitz verhältnismäßig leiden. Grund und Boden, rohe Produkte, müssen übermäßig tief im Preise fallen. . . . Das Reale hingegen, welches man auch das Ideale nennt, Fleiß, Regsamkeit, Industrie, Talent, Erfindungskraft, bewegliche Geistigkeit, müssen für lange Zeit ein unverhältnismäßiges und alles Bestehende störendes Übergewicht über Grund und Boden, rohe Produkte und Kapitale gewinnen." Oscar Fambach, *Goethe und seine Kritiker* (Düsseldorf: Ehlermann, 1953), 256.

[60] Schößler, *Goethes Lehr- und Wanderjahre*, 155.

[61] "Die Wanderschaft ist ein äußerer Ausdruck dieser Stellung [der Entsagung] zur Welt. Sie zerreißt jede geknüpfte Verbindung und legt dem Wanderer ein Entbehren jedes gewonnenen Gutes auf." Max Wundt, *Goethes Wilhelm Meister und die Entwicklung des modernen Lebensideals* (Berlin and Leipzig: Göschen, 1913), 476.

[62] Volker Neuhaus, "Die Archivfiktion in *Wilhelm Meisters Wanderjahren*," *Euphorion* 62 (1968): 13–27.

[63] See Erhard Bahr, *The Novel as Archive: The Genesis, Reception, and Criticism of Goethe's* Wilhelm Meisters Wanderjahre (Columbia, SC: Camden House, 1998), 28. The "Novel as Archive" concept originates with Volker Neuhaus.

[64] Theodor Mundt, Review of the *Wanderjahre*, 2nd ed., *Blätter für literarische Unterhaltung*, 1830, no. 266 (quoted from Gille, *Goethes Wilhelm Meister*, 135).

[65] Bahr, *The Novel as Archive*, 60.

[66] Bahr, *The Novel as Archive*, 67–68.

[67] Henriette Herwig, *Das ewig Männliche zieht uns hinab: Wilhelm Meisters Wanderjahre; Geschlechterdifferenz, Sozialer Wandel, Historische Anthropologie* (Tübingen and Basel: Francke, 1997).

[68] Schmidlin, *Das Motiv des Wanderns bei Goethe*, 152.

[69] Elsewhere in Goethe's works the wanderer motif appears in the context of charitable activity. Goethe recalls making a diversion during his Harz journey in the winter of 1777 to visit a young man, Friedrich Plessing, who had written to the author of *Werther*, seeking advice on how to rid himself of chronic depression. Concealing his identity, Goethe sought Plessing out and provided him with encouragement, enduring the awkwardness of having to refer to himself in the third person in answering Plessing's questions. See *HA* 10:324–35. Compare also the retrospective in *Dichtung und Wahrheit:* "Aber der Mensch will leben; daher nahm ich aufrichtigen Anteil an andern, ich suchte ihre Verlegenheiten zu entwirren, und, was sich trennen wollte, zu verbinden, damit es ihnen nicht ergehen möchte wie mir. Man pflegte mich daher den *Vertrauten* zu nennen, auch, wegen meines Umherschweifens in der Gegend, den *Wanderer*" (*HA* 9:520–21).

[70] As Waltraud Maierhofer notes: "Einen wesentlichen Teil des Inhalts macht zwar das Wandern aus, aber nicht als Handlung und Aktivität im herkömmlichen Sinn, sondern als theoretisches Thema." Maierhofer, *"Wilhelm Meisters Wanderjahre" und der Roman des Nebeneinander* (Bielefeld: Aisthesis, 1990), 119.

[71] Maierhofer, *"Wilhelm Meisters Wanderjahre,"* 121.

[72] Schößler puts this episode in the context of Goethe's criticism of a Romantic appropriation of Christian symbolism, characterizing Joseph's *imitatio* as a "kontingenter Lebensentwurf" and drawing attention to details such as the ruinous state of the cloister, which contains the depictions of the saint's life, as an indication of the superficiality of a Romantic turn to Christianity that embraces the iconography of that religion while ignoring its doctrines. Schößler, *Goethes Lehr- und Wanderjahre*, 205–13; here, 205.

[73] Hans Rudolf Vaget, "Johann Wolfgang Goethe: Wilhelm Meisters Wanderjahre (1829)," in *Romane und Erzählungen zwischen Romantik und Realismus: Neue Interpretationen*, ed. Paul Michael Lützeler (Stuttgart: Reclam, 1983), 136–64.

[74] Bahr, "Wilhelm Meisters Wanderjahre," 208.

[75] Adolf Muschg, "'Bis zum Durchsichtigen gebildet': 'Wilhelm Meisters Wanderjahre,'" in *Goethe als Emigrant: Auf der Suche nach dem Grünem bei einem alten Dichter* (Frankfurt am Main: Suhrkamp, 1986), 105–43; here, 117. More recently, Karin Schutjer has also interpreted wandering as a poetological principle: "Wandering, as a complex, variegated, existential condition functions as a meta-ideal in the novel. That is, even the novel's irony, its semiotic indeterminacy, its narrative perspectivism, anti-essentialism and cosmopolitanism fall under the trope of the wanderer." Schutjer, "Beyond the Wandering Jew: Anti-Semitism und Narrative Supersession in Goethe's *Wilhelm Meisters Wanderjahre*," *German Quarterly* 77 (2004): 389–407; here, 390.

[76] "Es wird eine lange, weite Wanderung werden, lieber Leser, zu der ich Dich auffordere! Rüste Dich mit Geduld, mit geschäftlosen Sonntagsvormittagen und einem guten aushaltenden Gedächtniß! Vergiß mir nicht morgen, was ich Dir heute erzählt habe! Werde nicht müde, wenn Du unabsehbare Ebenen erblickst, sich der Weg zwischen gefahrvolle, nicht endende Gebirgspässe zwängt oder die Landstraße plötzlich sich wie in die Wolken zu verlieren scheint!" Karl Gutzkow, *Die Ritter vom Geiste* (1850). http://gutenberg.spiegel.de/gutzkow/ritter/ritt0011.htm (para. 1 of 14). Accessed 18 Aug. 2006.

[77] Maierhofer, *"Wilhelm Meisters Wanderjahre,"* 124.

[78] "Einige Tage wurden so auf diese Weise zwischen Begegnen und Scheiden, zwischen Trennen und Zusammensein hingebracht; im Genuß vergnüglichster Geselligkeit schwebte immer Entfernen und Entbehren vor der bewegten Seele" (*HA* 8:233).

[79] "Geht es im Märchen nicht um die Vereinigung mit einem dämonischen Wesen? Und wirkt nicht die Anwesenheit des Dämonischen nach Goethes Meinung eine seltsame Aufhebung des moralischen Systems? Wie steht es mit der Moralität der Prüfungen, die dem Helden zugemutet werden?" Henkel, *Entsagung*, 85–93 (quoted from *HA* 8:695, "Anmerkungen").

[80] In doing so it complements Jarno's remarks: "Denken und Tun, Tun und Denken, das ist die Summe aller Weisheit, von jeher anerkannt, von jeher geübt, nicht eingesehen von einem jeden. Beides muß wie Aus- und Einatmen sich im Leben ewig fort hin und wider bewegen; wie Frage und Antwort sollte eins ohne das andere nicht stattfinden. Wer sich zum Gesetz macht, was einem jeden Neugebornen der Genius des Menschenverstandes heimlich ins Ohr flüstert, das Tun am Denken, das Denken am Tun zu prüfen, der kann nicht irren, und irrt er, so wird er sich bald auf den rechten Weg zurückfinden" (*HA* 8:263).

[81] Goethe, *Gedenkausgabe der Werke, Briefe und Gespräche*, 14:915, "Allegemeine Betrachtungen zur Weltliteratur," 30 Mar. 1830.

[82] The term originates with the Abbé: "Wir wollen der Hausfrömmigkeit das gebührende Lob nicht entziehen: auf ihr gründet die Sicherheit des einzelnen, worauf zuletzt denn auch die Festigkeit und Würde des Ganzen beruhen mag; aber sie reicht nicht mehr hin, wir müssen den Begriff einer Weltfrömmigkeit fassen, unsre redlich menschlichen Gesinnungen in einen praktischen Bezug ins Weite setzen, und nicht nur unsre Nächsten fördern, sondern zugleich die ganze Menschheit mitnehmen" (243).

[83] Marshall Berman's phrase, *All That is Solid Melts into Air: The Experience of Modernity* (New York: Simon & Schuster, 1982), is a translation of Marx and Engels's "Alles Ständische und Stehende verdampft" from the *Communist Manifesto.* Karl Marx and Friedrich Engels, *Manifest der Kommunistischen Partei*, in *Frühe Schriften*, ed. Hans-Joachim Lieber and Peter Furth, 6 vols. (Darmstadt: Wissenschaftliche. Buchgesellschaft, 1975–81), 2:813–58; here, 821.

# 2: The Wanderer in the Romantic Imagination

## The Artist Unbound: Tieck's *Franz Sternbalds Wanderungen* (1798)

### The Literary Appropriation of the Wanderschaft

IN *FRANZ STERNBALDS WANDERUNGEN* WE ENCOUNTER a narrative of wandering that resembles *Wilhelm Meisters Lehrjahre* in its adoption of the paradigm of the *Gesellenreise.* In Franz Sternbald, Tieck imagines a pupil of Albrecht Dürer who sets out from Nuremberg "um in der Fremde seine Kenntnis zu erweitern und nach einer mühseligen Wanderschaft dann als ein vollendeter Meister zurückzukehren."[1] The protagonist is therefore a traveling artisan, whose journey, it appears, will be determined by the requirements of his guild. The keywords "Wanderschaft" (which still had the dominant sense of the regulated artisan's journey) and "Meister" (which specifically denotes the status aspired to by the journeyman) suffice to set up these expectations.[2] This is an important departure from Goethe's novel, which — while alluding to the practices of journeymen in certain details, such as the *Lehrbriefe* conferred upon initiates into the Society of the Tower — is not actually about a journey of this sort. Indeed, Wilhelm Meister's travels (and travails) are as far removed from those of a journeyman as the Tower is from a tradesman's guild. Nevertheless, Goethe's novel undoubtedly played a part in suggesting the narrative framework of the *Wanderschaft* to Tieck. *Wilhelm Meisters Lehrjahre* could not have failed to have influenced Tieck, not least because of the possibilities for identification that Goethe's protagonist afforded the young author, with his passion for the theater, his lifelong engagement with Shakespeare, and his own extended wanderings in the company of his friends. It was in the course of these journeys, undertaken during and after Tieck's university career, that he began to develop his own aesthetic positions.

The first of these journeys, a tour of the Harz in July 1792, was Tieck's first experience of a mountainous landscape, held by his biographer Köpke to have had the force of a revelation for him. The second significant experience followed his move from Berlin to the University of Erlangen in the summer semester of 1793; this formed the base for excursions to Nuremberg, Bamberg and Pommersfelden, and a walking tour of the Fichtelgebirge: on all of these journeys Wilhelm Heinrich Wackenroder accompanied him. Finally, Tieck and Wackenroder both traveled to Dresden in the summer of 1796, where they viewed works by Correggio and Rafael in the city's *Gemäldegalerie.* The ecstatic experience of wilderness in the Harz was crucial to Tieck's development of an aesthetics of the sublime: his essay *Über das Erhabene* appeared later in the same year, 1792. Of even greater importance for the nascent aesthetics of these two young men, pioneers of the Romantic movement in the arts, were the impulses received from the journeys of 1793 and 1796. In the towns of Catholic Franconia, Tieck and Wackenroder came face to face for the first time with what seemed to them an intact German Middle Ages. Their sojourn in Dresden was the occasion of their awestruck first encounter with the art of the Italian Renaissance. These influences would leave an indelible mark on the aesthetic ideal worked out by both men in the early Romantic manifesto *Herzensergießungen eines kunstliebenden Klosterbruders* and popularized in Tieck's *Franz Sternbald*, a work that played a decisive part in communicating enthusiasm for Gothic and Renaissance art to a subsequent generation of Romantics, notably the Nazerene school.

That *Sternbald* relates to the *Wanderschaft* in a more immediate way than Goethe's novel is evident from the opening scene, in which the friends, Sebastian and Sternbald, take leave of one another amid tears and avowals of friendship. The emotional tenor is entirely in keeping with the few available biographical accounts by artisans. Accompanying the departing journeyman part of the way formed part of the procedure surrounding the commencement of the *Wanderschaft*, as the following extract from the seventeenth-century biography of a Saxon barber makes clear:

> Endlich wurde ich losgesprochen. Des andern Tages, umb elf Uhr, so zog ich in Gottes Namen aus, und ging der Vater mit mir bis in die Hausthüre mit diesem Spruch: "Dein Lebelang habe Gott vor Augen und im Herzen und hüte dich, daß du in keine Sünde willigest noch wider Gottes Gebot thust, so wird dir's wohl gehen" — die seelige Mutter und Schwestern aber gingen mit mir bis an'n "Grünen Hof." Unter vielem Weinen nahmen sie auch Abschied und gingen nach Haus, ich aber in die weite Welt.[3]

The emotional content of such leave-takings — and we may assume that Tieck, whose father was an artisan, a master ropemaker, had witnessed such scenes at first hand — must have had a particular suggestive power for a generation of artists committed to an ethics of friendship. The moment of departure is viewed more with dread than anticipation; indeed, Sternbald characterizes it as an expulsion. At this point the moment of longing for distant horizons is less evident than what the friends experience as "den Druck des Abschieds" (13). The intensity of the experience of impending separation is signaled by the tone of the dialogue and by the non-verbal language of tears and embraces — "Sie gaben sich die Hände" (11), "Sie hielten sich beide fest umschlossen" (18) — in which we recognize gestural elements of the cult of friendship revived by the Romantics, who esteemed that institution alongside the family as one of the original forms of human sociability.[4] The importance attributed by the Romantics to ties of friendship in the psycho-social development and aesthetic training of the artistic subject becomes apparent in the course of the narrative.

Tieck's decision to pattern his novel on the *Wanderschaft* was doubtless motivated in part by his experience of rapid social change: the lives of artisans represented a traditional way of life to the Romantics in an age where such forms appeared threatened by the dissolution of class boundaries, and by the abolition of the guilds in revolutionary France. In thematizing the journey of a young artisan, Tieck is connecting directly with the traditional social ritual of the *Wanderschaft* with its defined forms and specific aims.[5] Specifically, the *Wanderschaft* is a ritual of initiation into the practice of a trade. As a transitional ritual (*rite de passage*) it consists, according to the schema devised by the ethnologist Arnold van Gennep, of a separation, a threshold, and a reincorporation phase. Transitional rituals operate by separating the novice from his accustomed environment, placing him in a threshold or liminal state. This state is characterized by insecurity of identity and confusion, which the novice must overcome before successful reintegration into his social setting at a higher level of status (*Meister*) can take place.[6] Thus by selecting the paradigm of the *Wanderschaft*, Tieck is setting the stage for a journey through a liminal phase of uncertainty to the point of the hero's successful reintegration as a functioning artist.

The precise nature of the dangers that the liminal state holds for the apprentice is apparent from his first letter to Sebastian, which falls into two parts. The first part reprises Rousseau's demand for a return to nature; artistic and individual freedom is construed as a lost birthright: "die himmlische Freiheit, die uns eigentlich angeboren ist" (32).

The note of disillusionment is more pronounced in the second part of the letter, written on reaching the town: "Kaum habe ich nun die Stadt, diese Mauern und die Emsigkeit der Menschen gesehen, so ist alles in meinem Gemüte wieder wie zugeschüttet" (35), but it is not a consequence of changed circumstances of production: German towns were, as yet, untouched by industrialization. Rather it is the increasing pace of life, most acutely experienced in the urban setting, that distresses the wanderer. In the second part of the letter a process of self-reflection is initiated; Sternbald ruefully takes stock of his shortcomings, which include an excitability that has been intensified by the experience of travel: "Wenn nur das ewige Auf- und Abtreiben meiner Gedanken nicht wäre! Wenn die Ruhe doch, die mich manchmal wie im Vorüberfliegen küßt, bei mir einheimisch würde, dann könnt' ich von Glück sagen, und es würde vielleicht mit der Zeit ein Künstler aus mir" (34).

Tieck deploys the metaphor of a raging torrent to describe the excess of emotional impressions that threaten to overwhelm his protagonist. The problematic disposition thereby revealed raises the reader's expectations that the journey will take the form of future trials leading to an ultimate correction of Sternbald's excessive emotionality, consistent with the pattern established by *Wilhelm Meisters Lehrjahre*. However, the narrative does not develop in accordance with such expectations, for reasons I will outline presently.

## Sehnsucht: Creative Drive and Destructive Force

In his second letter to Sebastian, Sternbald describes the emotional agitation that has taken possession of him following a fleeting encounter with his childhood beloved, Marie; in his ecstasy the artist refers to himself as "einen Berauschten," possessed by a form of madness: "dieser schöne Wahnsinn" (79). With the appearance of Marie the journey has acquired a new goal, separate from that of the *Wanderschaft*. At this point the novel has deviated from the narrative model of the *Bildungsroman* by introducing a key plot device of the Hellenistic romance: the separation and eventual reunion of two lovers. The introduction of this device is governed by the need to supply a more powerful emotional impetus to the journey. Accordingly, in the letter cited above Sternbald defines himself no longer as a journeyman artist but as a searcher, consumed by the search for his Platonic other ("Bruder seiner Seele") and ascribes this motivation to every other traveler he sees:

> Ich denke mir alle die mannigfaltigen Wege durch Wälder, über Berge, an Strömen vorüber, wie jeder Reisende sich umsieht und in des andern Heimat sich in der Fremde fühlt, wie jeder umherschaut und nach dem Bruder seiner Seele sucht, und so wenige ihn finden, und immer wieder durch Wälder und Städte, bergüber an Strömen vorbei weiterreisen und ihn immer nicht finden. Viele suchen schon gar nicht mehr, und diese sind die Unglücklichsten, denn sie haben die Kunst zu Leben verlernt, da das Leben nur darin besteht, immer wieder zu hoffen, immer zu suchen, der Augenblick, wo wir dies aufgeben, sollte der Augenblick unsers Todes sein. (78–79)

As the end of the journey recedes and its object becomes more nebulous, the anticipated reunion displaces all thoughts of structured, planned progress toward a vocational goal. Through Sternbald, Tieck is articulating a specifically Romantic conception of wandering. In contrast to the Enlightenment ideal of purposeful travel directed toward finite goals, Sternbald describes a non-systematic form of wandering, presented as an end in itself ("die Kunst zu leben") and as an unending process ("immer zu suchen"). The ideal form of the Romantic journey is the circle, the completion of which brings the protagonist both to his origins and to a higher existential level. However, given that this circularity is rarely achieved in Romantic texts — and *Sternbald* is no exception — generalizing references to the "zyklische Struktur der romantischen Reise"[7] fail to describe adequately the dynamics of the Romantic journey. Rather it appears that the Romantic journey is determined by two separate and (usually) conflicting moments: a tendency to circularity and a tendency to infinity — centripetal and centrifugal moments respectively.

The tendency to circularity is provided by the goal of the return to origins, and the tendency to infinity — the centrifugal moment — is manifest in the longing for distant horizons and for transcendence in the widest sense. It is this latter moment that Korff emphasizes when he characterizes Romantic longing as "säkularisierte Himmelssehnsucht."[8] The two moments *can* be reconciled in an unending circularity — Kremer cites the example of Eichendorff's *Ahnung und Gegenwart* to show that his definition of Romanticism as "freies unendliches Reisen"[9] does not contradict the achieved cyclical form, but he does not explain why such syntheses are so rarely achieved. In view of this, it seems more reasonable to construe the Romantic journey as the function of two potentially contending moments, rather than asserting without qualification its cyclical structure. Sternbald's journey tends from the outset to conform to the ideal: both his platonic journey and his *Wanderschaft* have goals that indicate a return to origins. But the tendency is not sustained.

It is apparent that the journey is driven not by rational calculation but by feeling — specifically, the feeling of longing (*Sehnsucht*), whose object is the mysterious beloved, Marie. Thus, with respect to motivation, the journey appears as an analogue of the creative process itself as understood by the Romantics. In common with the earlier *Sturm und Drang* generation they repudiated the widely held Enlightenment view that art comprised a set of techniques that could be studied and taught. For the exemplary artist's journey, as for the act of creation itself, it is of axiomatic importance for Tieck that motivation should be governed by mood and spontaneity rather than calculation and planning. But Sternbald's reference to his "schöne Wahnsinn" makes it clear than *Sehnsucht* as a non-rational motor of wandering and of creativity harbors a pathological potential. That Tieck understood *Sehnsucht* as a potentially hazardous psychological state as well as a source of creative impulses is apparent from the plight of William Lovell, whose longing is associated with restlessness and indecisiveness. The link between *Sehnsucht* and pathological states was well established in contemporary literature — and especially in the context of the Enlightenment critique of religious fanaticism. Nowhere is this pathological aspect of *Sehnsucht* more clearly articulated than in *Wilhelm Meisters Lehrjahre*, in which Mignon and the harpist are driven to their destruction by what Grimm defines as "schmachtendes verlangen . . . krankheit des schmerzlichen verlangens."[10]

The gulf that separates Sternbald, with his susceptibility to emotional overstimulation, from Dürer, who represents an ethic of controlled sentimentality, is apparent from the letter cited above. Here we find a description of an engraving that depicts St. Jerome as an exemplary artist, working in hermetic seclusion in an attitude of piety. This image is juxtaposed with the following *Wanderlied* with its theme of longing for the breaking of all restrictions on the subject:

> Alle Ketten sind gesprungen,
> Frei sind alle Geister dann,
> Jeder Knechtschaft kühn entschwungen
> In dem Wollustozean. (85)[11]

Both Dürer and Lukas van Leyden conform exactly to the ideal of St. Jerome; their productivity is grounded in their settled status as respected members of a community. They are confronted by no problems of self-definition, and they fill their roles without self-consciousness. For Sternbald, however, who includes the description of the St. Jerome engraving as a fond reminiscence of Dürer's workshop — "Wie ich da wieder unter euch war!" (83) — identification with such a paragon is not possible for as long as he is under the influence of an enthusiasm that drives him to wander. This peripatetic existence, now primarily driven by the platonic search, stands in a relation of tension with the traditional practice of art, in which technical mastery is born of diligent studio-bound practice, as in Lukas van Leyden's case: "Es ist eine seltsame Sache mit dem Fleiße . . . so treibt es auch mich Tag und Nacht zur Arbeit, so daß mich manchmal jede Stunde, ja jede Minute gereut, die ich nicht in dieser Stube zubringen darf" (96).

The strong emotions triggered by the encounter with Marie and declared with lyrical intensity in the letter to Sebastian correspond with an intensification of imaginative activity. Lying in the grass outside the city of Leiden, Sternbald visualizes himself as a figure in the foreground of one of the many paintings of Leiden he has seen. Later, a moment spent looking at the moon from the window of his lodgings in Leiden gives rise to a succession of progressively more fantastic images. Instead of perceiving the object as a single image, the act of seeing triggers the projection of a plethora of unrelated images generated by the imagination onto the object. Sternbald views the moon not with a painterly eye to the possibilities of representation but with "sehnsüchtigen Augen" (92). He is aware that his oversensitivity and unfettered imaginative activity threaten his artistic perception and complains of his predicament to Lukas:

> Meine innerlichen Bilder vermehren sich bei jedem Schritte, den ich tue, jeder Baum, jede Landschaft, jeder Wandersmann, Aufgang der Sonne und Untergang, die Kirchen, die ich besuche, jeder Gesang, den ich höre, alles wirkt mit quälender und schöner Geschäftigkeit in meinem Busen, und bald möcht' ich Landschaften, bald heilige Geschichten, bald einzelne Gestalten darstellen, die Farben genügen mir nun nicht, die Abwechslung ist mir nun nicht mannigfaltig genug, ich fühle das Edle in den Werken

> andrer Meister, aber mein Gemüt ist nunmehr so verwirrt, daß ich mich durchaus nicht unterstehen darf, selber an die Arbeit zu gehn. (99)

Far from correcting the initial problem, the journey has thus far exacerbated it by confronting the unformed and unstable artist with a proliferation of images. The abundance of sense impressions gathered in traveling threatens the creative subject with paralysis; taking Sternbald out of the stability of familiar surroundings, in which his hypersensitivity was constrained, has apparently done more harm than good. Among the artist's problems is his inability to select a genre or to impose an order on these impressions of the kind that Christianity as a teleological worldview with its integrating schemata offers to the traditional artists Lukas van Leyden and Dürer. Lukas promptly diagnoses "[eine] zu große Verehrung des Gegenstandes" (99) and tries to dissuade the pupil from continuing his journey, since further stimulation of this kind could only be invidious in view of his "Reizbarkeit" (100). Lukas, convinced of the ahistorical and nationally bounded nature of art, questions the value of a journey to Italy, suggesting that the youth would be better off applying himself to the study of "wahre nordische Natur" (101). This questioning of his guiding assumptions has a disillusioning effect on the young artist. The pupil has also become distanced from his masters in his tendency to view art as an end in itself; while the latter view their art solely as a profession and as a means to the end of worship, Sternbald holds art itself to be worthy of veneration.[12] The contradiction that prevents the young artist from fitting seamlessly into the tradition is apparent from his dismissal of Lukas as "nur ein Handwerker" (105): Sternbald is himself an artisan, one at least nominally engaged in the completion of his *Wanderschaft* in accordance with the rules of his guild.

In the dialogue between Dürer and Lukas the two old masters agree on a mimetic conception of art consistent with Enlightenment aesthetics: "Die Natur ist also die einzige Erfinderin, sie leiht allen Künsten von ihrem großen Schatz; wir ahmen immer nur die Natur nach, unsre Begeisterung, unser Ersinnen, unser Trachten nach dem Neuen und Vortrefflichen ist nur wie das Achtgeben eines Säuglings, der keine Bewegung seiner Mutter aus den Augen läßt" (115).

But Dürer, unlike Lukas, possesses a historical understanding of art and allows the possibility of technical progress. He therefore dissents from Lukas's pessimistic assessment of the implications of the journey for the impressionable Sternbald. While Lukas represents the uncontrollable proliferation of impressions as a hazard for the untried youth, Dürer asserts the value of a period of confusion and interrupted work from which he believes his pupil will ultimately benefit, thereby upholding the value of the transitional ritual of *Wanderschaft* and of the threshold conditions associated with it: the exposure of the apprentice to new and confusing impressions, and to a period of emotional uprootedness: "Wenn Franz auch eine

Zeitlang in Verwirrung lebt und durch sein Lernen in der eigentlichen Arbeit gestört wird, und ich glaube wohl, daß sein sanftes Gemüt dem ausgesetzt ist; so wird er doch gewiß dergleichen überleben und nachher aus diesem Zeitpunkte einen desto größern Nutzen ziehn" (122).

The end of Sternbald's sojourn in Leyden is marked by another leave-taking, mirroring his departure from Nuremberg. Once again the parting is accompanied by the gestural language of tears and embraces. Dürer expresses his affection for his pupil: "Denn du bist mein Freund; der einzige, der mich aus recht voller Seele liebt, der einzige, den ich ganz so wiederlieben kann" (132). Despite these avowals of friendship, however, the parting is another step on Sternbald's journey away from his artistic origins and out of the confines of a religious aesthetic. With each step on that path the ties linking him to Nuremberg grow weaker, and Dürer and Sebastian diminish in importance as points of aesthetic and moral reference.

### The Artist's Journey as Liminal State

We have already remarked that the defining characteristic of the artisan's journey, viewed as ritual process, is the experience of liminality. Following his departure from Leyden, Sternbald enters into a new and more intense liminal phase in which the friendship ties that had previously sustained him are loosened and new companions take the place of Sebastian and Dürer. The most significant of these for Sternbald's future development is Rudoph Florestan, the German-Italian "Zwittergestalt,"[13] a vagabond poet, whose wandering is as much a condition of his worldview and aesthetic practice as seclusion and immobility are for the ideal painter, St. Jerome:

> Mein unruhiger Geist treibt mich immer umher, und wenn ich einer Weile in meiner Heimat gesessen habe, muß ich wieder reisen, wenn ich nicht krank werden will. Wenn ich auf der Reise bin, geschieht es mir wohl, daß ich mich nach meinem Haus sehne, und mir vornehme, nie wieder in der Ferne herumzustreifen; indessen dauern dergleiche Vorsätze niemals lange, ich darf nur von fremden Ländern hören oder lesen, gleich ist die alte Lust in mir wieder aufgewacht. (143–44)

Florestan's "unruhiger Geist" is an aspect of his disposition that he shares with Sternbald, but which, in his case, proves to be no obstacle to the practice of his art. The vagabond poet is a successful autonomous artist, unencumbered by traditional poetic models. Utterly devoid of the religious sentimentality of Sternbald, he is committed to a hedonistic sensualism, to which he seeks to convert his companion during their subsequent wanderings together.

The new liminal phase referred to above corresponds with the protagonist's wanderings through a forest near Strasbourg, a kind of *selva oscura*, an enchanted space that bears the hallmarks of Tieck's studies of Dante, Ariosto, and Shakespeare.[14] The suspension of causality, the foregrounding of the magical, and the blurred distinction between dream and reality in this sphere mark its as a place apart from the rest of the world of the novel. Hunting horns sounding in the distance create the impression in Sternbald that he is crossing into the spirit world, just as if he were a neophyte entering a liminal space in a ritual: "Franz glaubte, die Geisterwelt habe sich plötzlich aufgeschlossen, weil sie vielleicht, ohne es zu wissen, das große zaubernde Wort gefunden hätten" (222).

The spirits turn out to be the members of a noble hunting party led by a countess, a willful Diana-like figure. In her household the practice of art is bound up with the hedonistic ethos of the nobility: the Dionysian revelry surrounding the contest of the poets sets the tone for a series of *fêtes galantes*, in which Florestan plays the principal role. This charmed circle resembles what Turner has called a *communitas*, a counter-society of the kind simulated in rituals, a society in which social norms and conventions are temporarily suspended.[15] Here social barriers are abolished: the journeyman becomes the confidant of the countess and later he will find himself on comradely terms with the aristocratic adventurers Roderigo and Ludoviko. This dissolution of formal constraints on behavior extends to relations between the sexes; the forest is a place of erotic license, symbolized by the countess's favored pastime, the hunt. In a way that resembles the function of the *communitas* in rituals, the sojourn in this company opens up a field of play in which new ethical and aesthetic perspectives can be tried out. Under these conditions, Florestan, the agent of Sternbald's initiation, succeeds to a degree in freeing him of his "unschlüssige Ängstlichkeit" (200).

Apart from being a period of sensual awakening and growing self-confidence, the period in the forest also proves to be a testing time for Sternbald. The most significant challenge to his aesthetic assumptions arises from his solitary excursion to seek out an artist said to be mad and living in hermetic seclusion in the forest. Reaching an elevated point in the path that affords him a view of the landscape, Sternbald experiences an emotional epiphany of nature that resembles Tieck's own "Offenbarung"[16] in the Harz. Instead of being a moment of inspiration, however, the synesthetic vision — the emotional impact on the observer is indicated in musical metaphors — has an unsettling effect on him, revealing the inadequacy of art to the task of representing nature: "O unmächtige Kunst! . . . wie lallend und kindisch sind deine Töne gegen den vollen, harmonischen Orgelgesang" (249).

The encounter with the hermit, Anselm, further shakes the young artist's belief in the possibility of mimesis and confronts him with the possibility of failure: "Er war durch die Erzählung des alten Malers wehmütig geworden, es leuchtete ihm ein, daß es ihm möglich sei, sich auch über seine Bestimmung zu irren" (265). Anselm is a strayed artist, "ein verunglückter Künstler" (254), despite possessing a natural inclination toward art. His failure casts a shadow on Sternbald's own conviction that natural aptitude is a sufficient guarantee of success as an artist. This disillusionment is mitigated only by the discovery of a portrait in which Sternbald recognizes Marie's face, confirming that he is on the right course where the platonic journey is concerned.

Anselm's description of the requirements of a great artist correspond closely to the aesthetics of unrestrained emotionality so characteristic of the young Tieck: "Sein Gemüt muß wie ein Strom bewegt sein, so daß sich seine innere Welt bis auf den tiefsten Grund erschüttert, dann ordnen sich aus der bunten Verwirrung die großen Gestalten, die er seinen Brüdern offenbart" (256). However, in view of Anselm's failure, his outsider status, and his obvious misanthropy, the value of his understanding of the disposition from which art emerges appears questionable. His use of the metaphor of the raging torrent echoes Sternbald's earlier reflections on his own excitability and hypersensitivity, providing an uncomfortable reminder of the self-destructive potential of the artistic disposition.

The process of testing in the liminal space of the forest continues when Sternbald and Florestan resume their journey to Italy. They are soon joined by a series of improbable figures: a pilgrim and the noblemen Roderigo and Ludoviko; as a result the journey becomes a companionable wandering. It is probable that Tieck's university career forms the biographical substrate for this episode in the novel, which bears the hallmarks of the vacation wanderings then becoming popular among students at German universities. Such excursions were encouraged by late Enlightenment educationalists as a valuable adjunct to the taught curriculum — as such they were regarded as a productive way to make use of the vacations. Highly reminiscent of student wandering are the easygoing sociability (the artisan Sternbald blends easily with the mainly aristocratic company), the airy discourses on philosophy and aesthetics, and the music-making that takes place underway. Especially notable are the *Wanderlieder*, a lyric genre whose emergence, according to Heinrich Bosse, coincides with the advent of the social practice of vacation wanderings.[17] The making and singing of *Wanderlieder* by students, evoked here in Florestan's contributions, call to mind the fact that student wandering was a pursuit closely associated with literature: even if such journeys were only infrequently occasions of literary production, lyric texts were used to reflect individual experiences and to produce an appropriate group atmosphere.

Roderigo and Ludoviko resemble Florestan in inclination and social origin: all three are noblemen and dilatory wanderers (Ludoviko's nobility is implied by his mysterious origins). Roderigo had been drawn to Ludoviko by a shared restlessness: "die Reisesucht, das Verlangen, fremde Gegenden zu sehn, das in uns beiden fast gleich stark war, hatte uns zuerst aneinandergeknüpft" (291). Ludoviko is — in Florestan's approving words — "ein wahrer Teufelskerl" (295) whose wanderlust is tinged with recklessness, a willingness to endanger himself and his companions, a toying with self-annihilation. The abrogation of responsibility that their unreserved commitment to adventurous play entails is evident in the friends' propensity for going about in disguise: they present themselves by turns as beggars, peasants, and artists. In the willful transgression of boundaries the addiction to travel reveals itself in these figures as the symptom of a constitutional unwillingness to restrict oneself to a single social role. Their adventures are a travesty of the *Bildungsreise:* instead of the consolidation of a single stable identity the aim is the dissolution of self in a multiplicity of guises.[18]

The picaresque wandering of Florestan and the others has a distinctly libidinous aspect to it, which comes to light in Roderigo's account of his solitary journey and his meeting with the countess. He describes how he was ready to renounce his impetuous enthusiasm, his mad travels, and the erotic adventures that formed a part of them for her sake.

> O, süße Reiselust! . . . geheimnisreiche Ferne, ich werde nun von euch Abschied nehmen und eine Heimat dafür besitzen! Lockt mich nicht mehr weit weg, denn alle eure Töne sind vergeblich, ihr ziehenden Vögel, du Schwalbe mit deinen lieblichen Gesängen, du Lerche mit deinen Reiseliedern! Keine Städte, keine Dörfer werden mir mehr mit ihren glänzenden Fenstern entgegenblicken, und ich werde nun nicht mehr denken: Welche weibliche Gestalt steht dort hinter den Vorhängen und sieht mir den Berg herauf entgegen? (297–98)

But neither the habit of vagrancy nor the libido that is its mainspring is readily tamed: "Sehnsüchtig sah ich jedem Wandersmann nach, der auf der Landstraße vorüberzog; 'wie wohl ist dir,' sagte ich, 'das du dein ungewisses Glück noch suchst! ich habe es gefunden!'" (298).

Ludoviko, in whom the urge to travel manifests itself as a form of mania (witness the repeated self-identification as "Tor"), exhibits signs of dilettantism. Despite asserting that he has dreamed of becoming a painter, it is apparent that he views art primarily as an outlet for his taste for the drastic and extreme:

> Dann würde ich einsame, schauerliche Gegenden abschildern, morsche zerbrochene Brücken über zwei schroffen Felsen, einem Abgrunde hinüber, durch den sich ein Waldstrom schäumend drängt: verirrte Wandersleute, deren Gewänder im feuchten Winde flattern, furchtbare Räubergestalten aus dem Hohlwege heraus, angefallene und geplünderte Wägen, Kampf mit den Reisenden. (314)

The landscapes produced by Ludoviko's febrile imagination are not translated into artistic creation; his art is entirely performative, expressed in the reckless pursuit of adventure. His restless pleasure-seeking barely conceals a nihilism in which neither a religious nor an anthropological worldview has any validity. He praises Luther only for destroying the edifice of religion; and he ridicules the centering of man in Enlightenment discourse.

This nihilism informs his self-analysis, his diagnosis of the futility of his wanderlust:

> Oft faßte ich aber auch eine Handvoll Sand, und dachte: Warum bist du nun so mühsam, mit so mancher Gefahr, so weit gereist, um dies Teilchen Erde zu sehn, das Sage und Geschichte dir nun so lange nennt. Ist denn die übrige Erde jünger? Darfst du dich in deiner Heimat nicht verwundern? (311)

The image of the handful of sand evokes associations with the *vanitas mundi* motif. Such musings are suggestive of a melancholy disposition and, together with his dilettantism, place Ludoviko squarely in the contemporary category of the *Schwärmer*:[19] there is an echo here of Moritz's Andreas Hartknopf, who disconsolately sketches figures in the sand.

Despite the *esprit de corps* among the wanderers, these figures all represent an ethical and aesthetic hazard for Sternbald. Ludoviko, in particular, represents a dissolute and ultimately unproductive vagrancy. If the cessation of contact with Dürer and Sebastian had deprived Sternbald of the guiding authorities that had hitherto accompanied him on his way, his new friends have nothing to offer in the way of a coherent alternative model. The sensualist Florestan, the exponent of an autonomous art, provides contradictory advice, enthusing one moment for an aesthetic of the senses and then appearing to advocate religious allegorical art. The mercurial poet is also ambivalent in his friendship, readily abandoning Sternbald for Ludoviko, who enthralls him. This affinity taints Florestan's sensualism by making it seem a species of Ludoviko's nihilism.

Sternbald's optimistic assessment of his new companions in his letter to Sebastian — "Ich fühle es jetzt wie glücklich ich bin! Mein Leben spinnt sich wie ein goldener Faden auseinander: ich bin auf der Reise, ich finde Freunde, die sich meiner annehmen, die mich lieben, meine Kunst hat mir wider erwarten fortgeholfen, was will ich denn mehr?" (335) — is belied by his experience of estrangement from them. Even while still in the seemingly idyllic forest sphere he had remarked: "Alle diese Menschen sind mir doch fremd" (321). This sense of isolation experienced following his emergence from the poetic sphere is accompanied by a new crisis of artistic confidence. Commissioned to renovate an image of St. Genevieve in a convent, Sternbald is alienated by both the religious subject matter and the naïve presentation. Again he is overcome by a sense of a rupture separating him from the artistic tradition: "In Dämmerung gingen die Gestalten der großen Meister an ihm vorüber, er mochte nach keinem mehr die Arme ausstrecken; alles war schon vorüber und geendigt, wovon er noch erst den Anfang erwartete" (356). In an attempt to reconcile himself to the work, Sternbald seeks out the portrait, acquired from Anselm, in which he had recognized the lineaments of his beloved. To his shock, however, the portrait summons up the image, not of the platonic Marie, but of his profane love, Emma. The violence of the emotional response that drives Sternbald out into the crowded streets is disproportionate to the event triggering it, an indication that his hypersensitivity is in no way diminished. The cognitive problem with which the artist was confronted at the beginning of his journey — the quantitative mismatch between perception and emotion — remains: this is indicated by the reprise of the metaphor of the raging torrent.

> Wenn er so in sein bewegtes Gemüt sah, so war es, als wenn er in einen unergründlichen Strudel hinabschaute, wo Woge Woge drängt und schäumt, und man doch keine Welle sondern kann, wo alle Fluten sich verwirren und trennen und immer wieder durcheinanderwirbeln, ohne Stillstand, ohne Ruhe, wo dieselbe Melodie sich immer wiederholt, und doch immer neue Abwechslung ertönt: kein Stillstand, keine Bewegung, ein rauschendes, tosendes Rätsel, eine endlose, endlose Wut des erzürnten, stürzenden Elements. (357–58)

Measuring by the standards of the popular contemporary genre of the *Schwärmerroman*, we can see that the wandering artist has learned nothing, at least as far as governing his predisposition to emotional excitement is concerned. But *Franz Sternbalds Wanderungen* is not a novel of disenchantment in the sense of *Wilhelm Meisters Lehrjahre:* his labile, hypersensitive disposition is not a "falsche Tendenz"[20] to be overcome: it is rather an integral part of the artistic constitution. The process of artistic becoming that we find in Tieck's novel has less to do with learning than with undergoing an arduous initiation, in the course of which the artist comes to terms with the ambivalence and destructive potential of his disposition. So it is with Sternbald, for whom the passage through the liminal phase of the forest involves an induction into sensuality rather than the acquisition of concrete technical and aesthetic knowledge. This process of initiation is completed in Italy: "Franz war jetzt in der blühendsten Periode seines Lebens, sein Ansehn war munter, sein Auge feurig, seine Wangen rot, sein Schritt und Gang edel, beinahe stolz. Er hatte die Demut und Schüchternheit abgelegt, die ihn bis dahin immer noch als einen Fremden kennbar machte" (376).

The development undergone by Tieck's protagonist is *Bildung* in the strictly Romantic sense of growth in accordance with an inner essence. (The roots of this Romantic idea in contemporary *Naturphilosophie* will be discussed further in connection with *Heinrich von Ofterdingen*). Sternbald's triumph consists in his fidelity to this essence — his problematic artistic disposition — through all the trials of the liminal phase. His wandering, his refusal of stable commitments (marriage to the daughter of the art patron, Vansen) instead of accompanying maturation in the sense of the *Bildungsroman*, serves the prolongation of youth, of immaturity as a creative state — in the words of the Klosterbruder: "In ewiger Erneuerung gibt es kein Alter" (198). At the same time, however, the artist in his travels cannot avoid the loss of self-identity, "das Anderswerden" (309–10), since an artistic disposition of the specifically modern kind entails always being at odds with oneself. The enduring youth of the artist is no idyll, since it brings no resolution of the dilemma of a consciousness that, ever longing for distant horizons, cannot be at one with itself in the present.

Given Sternbald's development beyond his origins in Nürnberg — already indicated by his temperament and made more profound by the hedonistic experiences in the forest sphere and in Italy — his sudden longing to return to the restricted moral and aesthetic horizons of Dürer's world seems implausible. The turning point comes when Sternbald views Michelangelo's works in the Sistine Chapel, an experience that instantaneously cures him of his recent doubts concerning his separation from the old masters and reawakens the memory of Dürer: "Eine neue Liebe zur Kunst erwachte in ihm. . . . Er machte sich Vorwürfe, daß er bisher so oft Dürer und Sebastian aus seinem Gedächtnisse verloren" (397). The psychological improbability of this "plötzliche Rückverwandlung"[21] reveals the relatively superficial characterization that is a feature of the work, an aspect that Meuthen has emphasized: "Die entworfenen Figuren sind nicht als Abbild autonom handelnder und in der Auseinandersetzung mit der Umwelt heranreifender Personen zu verstehen. Sie sind "Marionetten," deren einzelne Züge bestimmten Darstellungszwecken entsprechen; sie sind (zum Teil) lebensfremde Projektionen eines konstruktiv artifiziellen Kunstwollens."[22]

Meuthen is entirely correct to emphasize the construct character of the figure, and the fact that the text is not an "Abbild" of a maturation process. Despite the undeniable flatness of its characterization, the enthusiasm with which *Franz Sternbalds Wanderungen* was received by Romantic artists such as Philipp Otto Runge suggests that Tieck succeeded in providing a congenial representation of the psychology of inspiration and creative paralysis.

Toward the end, the structural deficiencies in the narrative take their toll: the long-anticipated reunion with Marie abolishes the longing that had been the prime motor of Sternbald's wanderings. Motivating the return to Nuremberg would require imposing a new telos, further encumbering an already labyrinthine narrative. Tieck avoids forcing a solution: there is no return to Nuremberg, and the novel remains a fragment. Judged by the standards of the social ritual of the *Wanderschaft* with its ultimate reintegration of the artisan, Sternbald's journey would have to be accounted a failure.

## Sternbald's Wandering Considered as Ritual Process

What I referred to above as the centrifugal moment of the Romantic journey dominates Sternbald's wanderings, in which progress is marked by an increasing sense of separation from an artistic tradition and by the severing and weakening of friendship ties. This striving to infinity corresponds with the dynamic of Romantic art as "progressive Universalpoesie"[23] and with the historical self-awareness of the Romantics, who believed themselves to be on the cusp of a new era.

In adopting the formal schema of the artisan's journey, Tieck uses an established social ritual as a metaphor both for the initiation into the artistic vocation and for the struggle of the Romantic artist to free himself from the prevailing classical models of the Enlightenment. In this context the choice of the sixteenth century as historical setting is significant: it provides the paradigm of an age of intellectual innovation, one in which artists were beginning to free themselves from the constraints of religious narratives. The parallels between the historical setting and the sense of upheaval and transition experienced by Tieck's contemporaries are evident.

In its ritualistic character the practice of the *Wanderschaft* also gestures toward a desired remystification of art. However, the text deconstructs the ritual process upon which it is based, turning Sternbald's *Wanderschaft* from a ritual of integration into something that resembles a ritual of separation. Referring Sternbald's career to Gennep's triadic structure of transitional rituals it is evident that, while the first two phases, the separation and the threshold phases, are present, the reincorporation step is not realized.

Using Gennep's structure is useful in pointing up the incompleteness of Sternbald's ritual journey as opposed to the traditional pattern of the *Wanderschaft*, but it is to another theory of ritual behavior, that of Pierre Bourdieu,[24] that we must turn in order to grasp how the literary appropriation of the artisan's journey works in constructing a particular idea of what it meant to be a Romantic artist. Bourdieu notes that Gennep and Turner, while providing useful structural descriptions of the phenomenon of ritual, fail to account for its actual social function. Reviewing Gennep's work on rites of passage, Bourdieu argues that what such rites are meant to draw attention to is not so much the passage as the boundary crossed. Their purpose, Bourdieu holds, is to mark a distinction held to be significant in a particular society. Bourdieu thus prefers the term "rites of institution" to "rites of passage," arguing that the function of rituals is to consecrate or to confer authority on individuals undergoing them. Applying Bourdieu's analysis to Tieck's text enables us to conclude that the narrative of a ritual journey is intended to mark the distinction between artists and non-artists, to consecrate the artistic vocation. Sternbald achieves the standing of artist not so much by a process of learning as by enduring a liminal phase characterized by emotional confusion and sensual awakening.

If the ritual journey of the traditional artisan restores him to the aesthetic horizons of his society, the ritual journey of the modern artist — who no longer shares those horizons — is, in contrast, an initiation into a permanent threshold state, the proper domain of the autonomous artist, Sternbald. It is a domain that can only be occupied at the cost of sacrificing all forms of human sociability, including friendships: in this respect

Sternbald stands in a tradition that reaches from Joseph Berglinger to Adrian Leverkühn. The unstinting service of art demanded of the Romantic artist is exposed by the text as a threat to the very institution — friendship — needed to sustain it. In Ludoviko's words: "Wer sich der Kunst ergibt . . . muß das, was er als Mensch ist und sein könnte, aufopfern" (313).

Friendship represents one of the fundamental forms of sociability to the Romantics, and it is a central institution of Romantic art, a surrogate for the *atelier*, enabling the exchange of views and providing the psychological stability essential to the artist in view of his status as an outsider.[25] Indeed, Romantic art was frequently envisaged as a collaborative enterprise in the spirit of Friedrich Schlegel's ideal of "Symphilosophie und Sympoesie."[26] *Franz Sternbalds Wanderungen* was itself originally planned as a joint project before Wackenroder's failing health made collaboration impossible. In it, the narrated journey has a number of implications for the maintenance and formation of friendship ties. On the one hand, the trauma of parting leads to a temporary intensification of friendship, maintained during the journey by the exchange of correspondence. Furthermore, the journey gives rise to new friendships, and companionable wandering functions as a technique of friendship by providing a setting in which the joint contemplation of nature can take place, mirroring the social practices of the sentimentals.[27] On the other hand, the extended separation strains the existing ties to Sebastian and Dürer to breaking point, while the new friendships offer rather less security than the old. Thus, while the text affirms the unbounded existence of the Romantic artist, it simultaneously uncovers the dilemma threatening that existence: the conflict between the creative imperative of autonomy and the need for sustaining personal relationships.

Romantic artists and scientists conceived of themselves as an intellectual elite. However, this elite status exacted a high price in terms of separation from traditional institutions and forms. As a result they required a foundational myth, a self-conception capable of reconciling them to their social destiny and sustaining their morale. It is in this sense that Ludwig Tieck, then just beginning an independent literary career, imagines an exemplary artist's journey. His intention was to mark the distinctiveness of the artistic vocation and to ennoble it, and it was in this affirmative sense that the work was received by the majority of his artist contemporaries.

## Sanctifying Science: Novalis's *Heinrich von Ofterdingen*(1802)

On the face of it, Friedrich von Hardenberg's fragmentary novel, *Heinrich von Ofterdingen*, published posthumously in 1802 by his friend, Ludwig

Tieck, is not a promising work on which to base a discussion of the function of the wanderer motif in Romantic thought. The narrative barely thematizes wandering considered as a material practice, and the text in its esoteric nature contains little that can be deciphered in the way of references to the historical context. It is a novel of ideas, and the ideas embodied in it are its most contemporary aspect. Nevertheless, I will argue that in providing an affirmative myth of the artistic vocation the work relies on the presentation of the artist as wanderer, and that this presentation is fundamental to the self-conception of the Romantics, artists and scientists alike.

When Hardenberg (1772–1801) — whom I will subsequently identify by his better-known nom de plume, Novalis — began work on the novel in December 1799, Goethe's *Wilhelm Meisters Lehrjahre* (1796) and Tieck's *Franz Sternbalds Wanderungen* (1798) were significant background influences. The work was to a great extent the outcome of a long critical engagement with *Wilhelm Meisters Lehrjahre:* Novalis's detailed studies attest both to his admiration for that work and to a painstaking struggle to separate his own literary production from it. In time, unreserved admiration gave way to a more skeptical stance. While Novalis never ceased to wonder at Goethe's technique, he eventually came to deplore what he saw as that novel's affirmation of rational, instrumental control over nature, complaining: "Das Romantische geht darinn [*sic*] zu Grunde — auch die Naturpoësie, das Wunderbare . . . die Natur und der Mystizism sind ganz vergessen."[28] That *Heinrich von Ofterdingen* was conceived as a counterblast to Goethe's "Evangelium der Oeconomie" (3:647) is probable, given that Novalis intended to have his novel published in precisely the same format as the *Lehrjahre*, and by the same publisher, Unger of Berlin. In referring to the parallels between Novalis's and Goethe's novels my intention is not to tread the well-worn path of reading Novalis's novel as an "Anti-Meister"[29] but to draw attention to the most significant element the two works have in common, namely the situational motif of a youth's journey of formation. Novalis chooses to retain the portrayal of the protagonist as wanderer, and in this respect he also stays close to Tieck's *Franz Sternbalds Wanderungen. Heinrich von Ofterdingen* resembles the latter work most closely in the use of the journey to describe the process of initiation of a young artist, an initiation in which mystical and sacral elements are more apparent than in Tieck's treatment.

Novalis's summary of the plot in his letter to Tieck of 23 February 1800, in which, incidentally, he acknowledges the influence of *Sternbald*, suggests a journey of two phases: "Das Ganze soll eine Apotheose der Poësie seyn. Heinrich von Afterdingen wird im 1sten Theile zum Dichter reif — und im Zweyten, als Dichter verklärt" (4:322). The first part of the novel, *Die Erwartung*, is taken up with the business of the poet's initiation, just as the second, incomplete part, *Die Erfüllung*, was to have presented him in the exercise of his art. In the titles of the two parts the dialectic of anticipation and fulfillment upon which the work is built announces itself. The initiation into the poetic vocation is prefigured by the dream of travel and unfettered movement that opens the novel. Heinrich, the twenty-year-old hero, the son of an Eisenach goldsmith, is stimulated by the tales of a visiting stranger into a dream of the "blaue Blume" (later the archetypal symbol of Romantic longing), whose blueness is the color of the distant horizons toward which the wanderer strives. It is this eidetic image that continues to beckon to the youth on his subsequent journey, leading him ever onward. The dream foreshadows not only his journey from Eisenach to Augsburg and his meeting with Mathilde, whose "himmlisches Gesicht" is first glimpsed in the flower, but it also points toward the intended harmonious conclusion of the novel, the *unio mystica* between Heinrich and Mathilde after the latter's death. While on the biographical level this reunion is a way for Novalis to deal with his grief for the young Sophie von Kühn, it also functions as the allegory of a longed-for reconciliation between spirit and nature.

The moment of contingency, which plays such a significant part in structuring the plot of *Wilhelm Meisters Lehrjahre*, is strikingly absent; instead, Heinrich's progress appears as the unfolding of a predetermined plan.[30] The underlying teleology of the journey is revealed at various junctures in correspondences between individual figures (for example, the parallel between Heinrich and Zulima's poet brother), and in the fulfillment of presentiment (the miner's words seem familiar to Heinrich). That the journey is the fulfillment of a preordained plan is indicated definitively by the Provençal manuscript, in which Heinrich finds depictions of his own past and future life. On meeting Mathilde, the daughter of the poet Klingsohr, Heinrich recalls that it was her "himmlisches Gesicht" that he had beheld in the flower of which he had dreamed and observes: "Es war kein Zufall, daß ich sie am Ende meiner Reise sah" (277).

Nowhere does the claim of Romantic literature to the status of "progressive Universalpoesie" find fuller expression than in the presentation of its protagonists as wanderers striving for infinity. *Heinrich von Ofterdingen*, evidently conceived as a universal journey through a range of domains of human experience, can be considered as archetypal in this respect. The first phase, the journey to Augsburg, which Heinrich undertakes in the company of his mother and a group of merchants, is narrated as a series of conversations — topographical detail and elements of dramatic action are broadly excluded. The setting, indicated by the historical Heinrich von Ofterdingen's status as *Minnesänger*, is a chiaroscuro Middle Ages, between the darkness of antiquity and the light of an anticipated Golden Age. In the Arion and Atlantis fables retold by the merchants, Heinrich receives his initial instruction in the power that poetic art possessed in former times. At the crusader castle he gets a further intimation of his predetermined poetic vocation from the Oriental captive, Zulima, who sees a resemblance between Heinrich and her poet brother. But the most significant stage in the initiation phase is the encounter with the miner and the subterranean expedition that Heinrich undertakes in his company. The allegorical nature of the stages passed through and their function in the context of Heinrich's formation as a poet is underlined by Klingsohr, who provides a summary of the journey:

> In der Nähe des Dichters bricht die Poesie überall aus. Das Land der Poesie, das romantische Morgenland, hat euch mit seiner süßen Wehmuth begrüßt; der Krieg hat euch in seiner wilden Herrlichkeit angeredet, und die Natur und Geschichte sind euch unter der Gestalt eines Bergmanns und eines Einsiedlers begegnet. (283)

In the reference to the poet's capacity to act as a force for harmony a further intimation of Heinrich's preordained role is supplied. Already, in the encounter with the miner and the hermit, the hero had been presented with two fields of knowledge, nature and history, which were to be reconciled as part of a unified body of knowledge.

What I have referred to as the dialectic of anticipation and fulfillment structuring the work unfolds as the journey progresses. At each point in the journey the external events, the meetings with the various subsidiary characters, trigger the development in the hero of latent inner faculties. For example, the conversation with the miner produces in Heinrich "neue Entwickelungen seines ahndungsvollen Innern" (263). The movement through space, from Eisenach to Augsburg, is thus matched by an inward movement that gives rise to a fuller awareness on the part of the wanderer of the creative potential he bears within him. Heinrich's progress displays the characteristic doubleness of the Romantic journey in that the outward movement is, at the same time, a movement back to origins. In its essential harmoniousness and inwardness the journey differs markedly from those of Wilhelm Meister and Franz Sternbald. The sense of a "Bildungsreise nach Innen,"[31] most apparent in the encounter with the subterranean world of nature, is reinforced by the exclusion of conflict and of moments of psychological tension. It is on this episode, the descent into the earth, that I will now concentrate in order to draw out the characteristically Romantic idea of nature as a source of the self as articulated by Novalis.

The descent into the earth is a highly prominent episode; the fifth chapter, in which it occurs, is by far the longest in the novel. It is also here that the work comes closest to the material practice of pedestrian tourism as the early Romantics knew it. Wandering students frequently included a mine descent in their itineraries, partly because such objects were held to be interesting in themselves, but also because descents of this kind were viewed as morally bracing.[32] The mine's obscurity, the hiddenness of its depths, and its occult associations made it a locus of the sublime, and the aesthetics of the sublime played a crucial part in the self-finding and self-enlargement that the Romantics sought in nature generally. In the mine, as on the slopes of the mountain, the wanderer was confronted with those moments of danger (actual and imagined) to his physical person that — according to Kant and Schiller — could awaken a properly receptive individual to awareness of his moral autonomy.[33]

On the final stage of his journey to Augsburg, Heinrich's party pauses for a time in a mountainous area. Heinrich falls into conversation with a Bohemian miner, who proposes an excursion to a series of caverns nearby. By naming the miner Werner, Novalis pays tribute to Abraham Gottlob Werner (1749–1817), his mentor at the Freiberg mining academy in Saxony, where he had studied from December 1797 until the early summer of 1799. The fictional miner is a wanderer whose scientific curiosity has taken him far afield in his quest to understand the "wunderliche Baukunst" of nature:

> Unsere Kunst macht es fast nöthig, daß man sich weit auf dem Erdboden umsieht, und es ist als triebe den Bergmann ein unterirdisches Feuer umher. Ein Berg schickt ihn dem andern. Er wird nie mit sehen fertig, und hat seine ganze Lebenszeit an jener wunderlichen Baukunst zu lernen, die unsern Fußboden so seltsam gegründet und ausgetäfelt hat. (260)

This figure is driven by a powerful longing, akin to that experienced by Heinrich at the beginning of his journey in the dream of the blue flower: "Von Jugend auf habe er eine heftige Neugierde gehabt zu wissen, was in den Bergen verborgen seyn müsse, wo das Wasser in den Quellen herkomme, und wo das Gold und Silber und die köstlichen Steine gefunden würden, die den Menschen so unwiderstehlich an sich zögen" (239).

The miner, like Heinrich, is an idealized figure of Romantic longing, and the longings of both are directed toward the knowledge of that which is hidden. Significantly, this longing is "ein unterirdisches Feuer," a metaphor that emphasizes the role not of sober, rational interest but of unconscious drives in scientific curiosity, a moment very much present in Tieck's *Der Runenberg*, as we shall see presently. In Werner's desire to know the inner laws of nature, the true nature of Heinrich's longing for the blue flower is revealed. Heinrich's descent into the caverns in the company of the miner and his encounter there with the hermit bear all the hallmarks of a conception of nature indebted to Schelling's *Naturphilosophie*. Novalis had met Friedrich Wilhelm Joseph Schelling (1775–1854) in Jena and had studied his younger contemporary's most important writings on the philosophy of nature: *Ideen zu einer Philosophie der Natur* (1797) and *Von der Weltseele* (1798).[34] The title of the latter work points to Schelling's conviction that the natural world is endowed with a mind or logos of its own, a conviction evidently influenced by Spinoza's pantheism. Schelling, in common with other proponents of a Romantic philosophy of nature (for example, Herder and Goethe), viewed nature as undergoing an unconscious process of self-production: that is to say, they viewed nature itself as subject. In this respect Schelling and Novalis part company with the transcendental idealisms of Kant and Fichte, who effectively regard nature as the inanimate other of the human subject — the "Not-I" in Fichte's formulation.

Schelling's conception of nature as transcendental subject had two important epistemological consequences. First, it indicated an essential correspondence between the self and nature, in that both are seen as endowed with mind (*Seele*), and second, it ushered in the temporalization of nature. This latter change in the perception of nature accompanies a major paradigm shift in the natural sciences in the latter part of the eighteenth century.[35] In the course of this shift, natural history, with its synchronic representation of nature as an essentially static domain encompassing all possible forms of life, began to lose ground. Once nature began to be understood as an entity that was constantly producing itself, moving under its own volition from a simple, unorganized state to ever more complex and highly organized states, it had acquired a history of its own; that is to say, it came to be regarded under the aspect of time. With this new insight there came a demand for new approaches capable of grasping nature in terms of functions rather than structures — in the field of medicine, for example, the new discipline of physiology began to make headway against the structure-bound methods of anatomy. I have already alluded to this new dynamic view of nature in the discussion of *Wilhelm Meisters Lehrjahre*, arguing that it is a factor in the growing importance of the *Bildungreise*.

This understanding of the historicity of nature, as articulated by Schelling in his *Naturphilosophie*, is obviously present in Novalis's novel. On their way into the caves the explorers stumble upon fossils, relics of an unimaginably distant prehistory. The alliance between the miner, who represents the field of nature, and the hermit, who is a historian, further underscores the link between nature and history. Novalis evidently also concurs with Schelling's view that, in the course of its development, nature gave rise to the conditions of its own self-representation by bringing forth mankind: "Die Natur will selbst auch einen Genuß von ihrer großen Künstlichkeit haben, und darum hat sie sich in Menschen verwandelt, wo sie nun selber sich über ihre Herrlichkeit freut" (209).

By introducing the dimension of time to the representation of nature the *Naturphilosophen* effectively set nature in motion, representing it as being in progress through a series of historical stages. The term "progress" is key here, for nature's development in the course of time was seen as directed toward a goal, as teleological. In *Von der Weltseele*, Schelling holds that all living creatures are characterized by teleological structures; in other words, they are thought to carry the seeds of their own development within them.[36] Moreover, it was Schelling's belief that teleological structures were characteristic not just of individual creatures but of organic life and thus of nature as a whole.[37] It is a view articulated by Novalis's miner:

> Mag es seyn, daß die Natur nicht mehr so fruchtbar ist, daß heut zu Tage keine Metalle und Edelsteine, keine Felsen und Berge mehr entstehn, daß Pflanzen und Thiere nicht mehr zu so erstaunlichen Größen und Kräften aufquellen; je mehr sich ihre erzeugende Kraft erschöpft hat, desto mehr haben ihre bildenden, veredelnden und geselligen Kräfte zugenommen, ihr Gemüth ist empfänglicher und zarter, ihre Fantasie mannichfaltiger und sinnbildlicher, ihre Hand leichter und kunstreicher geworden. Sie nähert sich dem Menschen, und wenn sie ehmals ein wildgebährender Fels war, so ist sie jetzt eine stille treibende Pflanze, eine stumme menschliche Künstlerinn. (262)

Novalis deploys the anthropomorphic metaphor of the "stumme menschliche Künstlerin" to evoke the idea of nature's progression from initial disorder and antagonism to human needs toward a final state of harmony with man. Revealed in the metaphor is an organic view of nature that contrasts starkly with that mechanistic strand in Enlightenment thought that originates with Newton and Descartes. In the miner's account of the history of nature the affinities with Schelling's precepts are obvious: nature is presented as a force engaged in constant self-generation directed toward a goal of final perfection. In this respect the logic of nature's development mirrors the dynamic of Heinrich's own progress, which is shown to be teleological both by the dream of the blue flower, which represents the goal of his journey, and by the Provençal manuscript, in which the stages of the hero's life are mapped out in pictorial form.

Let us return to the first consequence of the view held by the *Naturphilosophen* of nature as subject: namely, the assumed identity or homology between the self and nature that flowed from that view. Novalis explores this idea of equivalence in the fragmentary and unpublished novel *Die Lehrlinge zu Saïs.* He had already started on that novel during the Freiberg period, but he put it aside in late 1799 in an effort to complete the thematically related *Heinrich von Ofterdingen.* To judge from the paralipomena to the *Lehrlinge*, the culmination of the novel would have seen its apprentice protagonist lifting the veil of the Egyptian goddess of nature, Isis, to behold his own countenance.[38] Both the self and nature were held by the *Naturphilosophen* to be imbued with mind, the *logos* of the self corresponding to the *cosmos* of nature. I have already suggested that the novel describes an inner journey: the descent into the depths is the symbolic equivalent of the inward movements of dream and introspection, which the novel portrays as the characteristic paths of the poet. This inward movement involves the experience of inner nature in the form of hidden strata of the personality, especially the faculty of the imagination, which, the Romantics believed, had been devalued by the exaltation of reason in the Enlightenment.[39] But the "Reise in die eigene Innenwelt"[40] is at the same time accompanied by revelations about the outer world, the historical progress of nature toward a final harmonic state: "das allmächtige Streben nach freyer, einträchtiger Verfassung" (262). Heinrich's own career, the future course of which is revealed in the Provençal manuscript, is intimately connected with this progress, since he is destined to bring about the establishment of the anticipated Golden Age. This he is to achieve in his capacity as poet, by healing the rifts and divisions among the various branches of human knowledge and enabling a new and fuller understanding of the relations between man and nature. In common with other Romantics, Novalis is convinced that poetic discourse alone has the power to bring about the integration of the plethora of discourses into which knowledge has been dispersed by the rise of intellectual specialization. Heinrich's mission of reconciliation is prefigured in those images contained in the Provençal manuscript that show him not only in amicable conversation with Moors and Saracens but also communing with plants and animals.

The figure of the miner, in which the new (work dominated by rational principles and advanced technology) fuses seamlessly with the old (piety, theistic worldview) embodies the Romantic project, with its projected reconciliation of the metaphysical-religious and empirical perspectives. This integrative project was a reaction to the proliferation of scientific discourses in the Enlightenment and their increasingly autonomous models, which were beginning to displace metaphysical worldviews. In the conversation between the miner and the hermit we find a questioning of the boundaries between different fields of knowledge that is characteristic of the totalizing aspirations of Romantic philosophy. It is in this sense that the hermit, hearing the miner characterize his studies as a search for original states, remarks "Ihr seyd beynah verkehrte Astrologen" (260), thereby postulating a link between the geology practiced by the miner in unearthing the past and astrology as a science of the future (using the word "astrology," as it could be at the time, in the present meaning of "astronomy"). Here we detect an echo of Novalis's vision of achieving the unity of all spheres of knowledge, his *Enzyklopädistik*, a project that he was unable to formulate in coherent philosophical terms and which he instead attempted to adumbrate in literary form.[41] From the miner Heinrich learns the value of the close observation of nature; from the hermit he learns that the poet is the ideal historiographer, who by instructing humanity in the history of the world's development can hasten the coming of the Golden Age: "Wenn ich das alles recht bedenke, so scheint es mir, als wenn ein Geschichtschreiber nothwendig auch ein Dichter seyn müßte" (259).

While the figures of the miner and the hermit anticipate the achievement of the Golden Age of reconciled discourses within a unified philosophical frame, they are themselves unable to bring it about. This power is granted not to these figures, who each possess a partial worldview, but to the poetic subject, the wanderer who takes the path that leads to the integration and reconciliation of these perspectives.[42] We recall that the two parts of the novel appear to correspond to a journey of two parts. The inner journey of poetic formation, the "Bildungsreise nach Innen,"[43] outlined in the first part of the novel, was to have had its pendant in an outward journey of poetic action directed toward the transformation of the world.[44] The mission of the poet is to move through the world healing the rift between nature and history, the worlds symbolized by the figures of the miner and the hermit.

It was Novalis's view that the literary form was the optimal one in which to formulate his ideas concerning the integration of the separated spheres of knowledge. He writes of the novel as the ideal theoretical form: "Der Roman, als solcher, enthält kein bestimmtes Resultat — er ist nicht Bild und Faktum eines Satzes. Er ist anschauliche Ausführung — Realisierung einer Idee. Aber eine Idee läßt sich nicht in einen Satz fassen. Eine Idee ist eine unendliche Reihe von Sätzen" (2:570). This formulation also offers a glimpse of the ontological status of the Golden Age envisaged by Novalis as philosophical goal. This is seen not in terms of some sort of ultimate stasis but as an ongoing process of realization governed by what Mähl, following Novalis, has termed a "principle of approximation."[45] As Mähl observes, the teleology is open-ended: the missing final pages of the Provençal manuscript show that the Romantic project of reestablishing harmonious relations between man and nature is understood as an ongoing process.

To Novalis the scientist, the idea of a progression toward a thoroughly integrated science by means of which it would be possible to know the natural world more fully was a highly desirable notion. In his professional capacity as inspector of salt mines (*Salinenassessor*) he found himself confronted with a bewildering range of sciences and technical disciplines over which he had to gain mastery. He was therefore particularly well placed to see the fragmentation of the field of science set in train by the bourgeoning of new technologies and methodologies. His technical notes, the so-called *Salinenschriften*, attest to Herculean efforts to stay abreast of developments in all the fields relevant to his career: there are references to planned studies in mathematics, chemistry, meteorology, and even of the legislation concerning land ownership.[46] But there is also a moral dimension to Novalis's attraction to a holistic philosophy in which the pursuit of knowledge and the technical control of nature might be tempered by a sense of piety. The destructive impact on the natural environment and on human health of the drive to make Saxony self-sufficient in salt and other minerals was all too apparent to the diligent inspector, whose reports detail the appalling conditions faced by mine workers. His report to Werner on conditions in the coal mines near Weißenfels, dated 28 April 1800 (3:773–90), is typical in this respect: "auch ist die Arbeit äuserst [*sic*] beschwerlich, schmuzig und ungesund. Hautschäden und Gichtübel sind unter diesen Leuten sehr häufig" (787).

With the rise of *Naturphilosophie* in the closing years of the eighteenth century, both nature and the self were increasingly perceived as time-determined entities governed by internal principles of development.[47] Accordingly, man's essence came to be seen as consisting in development (*Bildung* is the key term here) and hence in movement toward a goal. Given this change in perception of the essence of life, it is not surprising that those writers and philosophers who aligned themselves with Romantic philosophy began to cast about for metaphors adequate to the new understanding. The metaphor or figure that suggested itself most readily was that of the wanderer. This motif had the advantage of carrying a certain sacral content via its associations with the historical categories of the pilgrim and the journeyman: as such it was ideally suited to appropriation by the Romantics, whose aesthetics aimed to achieve a reconsecration of life in the face of the expansion of what they saw as the profanities of utilitarianism and technical control. For the Romantics, by whom I mean a predominantly urban intellectual group, artists and scientists alike (and many were simultaneously active in the aesthetic and scientific fields), the figure of the wanderer became a potent collective symbol embodying what Ernst Bloch has called "Weg- und Prozesspathos."[48] The dominant self-conception as wanderer became the basis of a shared myth that validated the intellectual labors of this group by allowing those labors to be understood in terms of a process of realizing innate potential.

In the hands of the Romantics, the motif of the wanderer in literary and visual artworks lends expression to a particular kind of teleological thinking that originates with the new philosophy of nature. We recall that this philosophy assumes that both nature and the self develop in accordance with their own internal logic, and that these processes are intimately connected — nature's progress toward an ever more ordered state being matched by man's progress in knowledge. Anticipated is a point at which the laws of nature become transparent to man. This narrative of development in accordance with an internal principle can be regarded as the foundational myth of Romantic science. It formed the basis of the assumption that both man and nature are endowed with mind (Schelling's *Weltseele*), out of which grew the idea of the intelligibility of nature as cosmos, as an ordered system. Apart from opening up the prospect of a fuller comprehension of the natural world, the notion of an essential correspondence between man as logos and nature as cosmos allowed the Romantics to represent their advances in the study of nature as promoting some sort of reconciliation between man and nature — this is the utopian dimension of Romantic natural science. Scientific investigation of nature appeared in this utopian perspective not as instrumental subjugation but as a morally irreproachable endeavor to reestablish lost unity.

Of course, *Naturphilosophie* encouraged the Romantics to view themselves as wanderers, not just because the teleological idea is most readily apprehended in terms of that metaphor, but also because the use of the metaphor was justified by the practices of natural science, as well as by the postulated unity between man and nature. If the former required the scientist to become a wanderer in the pursuit of empirical knowledge of the outer world, the latter encouraged him to explore nature as a means of gaining self-knowledge. Both types of motivation underpinned the explorations of Alexander von Humboldt (1769–1859) in the Orinoco basin, the Cordilleras, and other parts of the Americas. During these, Humboldt, an adherent of Schelling's philosophy, undertook botanical, geological, chemical, and anthropological studies aimed at developing an understanding of the natural world as a dynamic yet unified whole,[49] for which he introduced the term *Kosmos.* At the same time, Humboldt engaged in these explorations as part of a program of self-development.[50] In this respect his explorations can be construed as the mirror image of the inner journey of Novalis's novel. Heinrich von Ofterdingen takes the "Weg der innern Betrachtung" (208), plumbing the depths of the microcosmos of self in order to learn about the laws governing the macrocosmos of nature; Humboldt, himself a former pupil of Werner at Freiberg, takes the opposite approach, the arduous "Weg der Erfahrung" (208) into the primeval forests of the Americas, which were for him a locus of the sublime. What unites both approaches is the conviction that microcosmos and macrocosmos are linked by profound correspondences. The specific gain in knowledge to be had from wandering is the recognition of these correspondences — and of the fact that the self stands in a relation of dependency to the whole order, the "Weltgegend." This sense is conveyed by Heinrich's remarks to Sylvester in the incomplete second part of the novel:

> Ich lerne . . . meine Gegend erst recht kennen, seit ich weg bin und viele andre Gegenden gesehn habe. Jede Pflanze, jeder Baum, jeder Hügel und Berg hat seinen besonderen Gesichtskreis, seine eigenthümliche Gegend. Sie gehört zu ihm und sein Bau, seine ganze Beschaffenheit wird durch sie erklärt. Nur das Thier und der Mensch können zu allen Gegenden kommen; Alle Gegenden sind die Ihrigen. So machen alle zusammen eine große Weltgegend, einen unendlichen Gesichtskreis aus, dessen Einfluß auf den Menschen und das Thier eben so sichtbar ist, wie der Einfluß der engeren Umgebung auf die Pflanze. Daher Menchen [sic], die viel gereißt sind, Zugvögel und Raubthiere, unter den Übrigen sich durch besondern Verstand und andre wunderbare Gaben und Arten auszeichnen. (328)

Despite its fragmentary status, Novalis's novel provides a very clear indication of the philosophical implications of the Romantics' tendency to conceive of themselves as wanderers. Central to a specifically Romantic self-consciousness was the concept of becoming (*werden*), in the sense of development toward a life-goal, which, by virtue of its assumed immanence, provided a point of orientation and served as compensation for the demise of belief in a providential order. The importance of the concept of becoming to the Romantic mind gets perhaps its fullest articulation at the hands of Friedrich Schlegel in the *Athenäum:* "Die romantische Dichtart ist noch im Werden; ja, das ist ihr eigentliches Wesen, daß sie ewig nur werden, nie vollendet seyn kann."[51] Bearing this definition in mind allows us to understand the conception of the self as wanderer as an enabling fiction that allowed those who subscribed to it to believe in the idea of progress, of an eternal becoming. For many in the vanguard of Romantic science this self-conception was not only a fiction but was grounded in lived experience: something of this sense of becoming through striving is conveyed by the *nom de plume* Novalis, the cultivator of new ground.

The association between the conception of oneself as wanderer and a belief in the progressive nature of scientific work was especially strong in the case of Alexander von Humboldt, who describes his own investigative travels in *Kosmos* as a contribution to the perfection of human knowledge, "eine künftige Vervollkommnung des menschlichen Wissens."[52] A brief anecdote about an heirloom of Humboldt's should serve to illustrate the reality of this self-conception to one of the most eminent scientists of the nineteenth century. At the Freiberg mining academy Humboldt made the acquaintance of a fellow student, the geologist Christian Leopold von Buch (1774–1855). In the summer of 1797 the two men undertook a walking tour in the Tyrolean Alps, an undertaking that laid the foundations for a lifelong friendship. The tour marked the beginning of a fruitful collaboration between the two scientists, which ended only with Buch's death. In his testament the geologist stipulated that his walking stick be given to his friend Humboldt. That Humboldt numbered Buch's *Wanderstab* among his most treasured possessions is clear from the precise instructions concerning the object in his own testament: he ordered that it was to be passed to Julius Ewald, Buch's successor in the work on the geological part of *Kosmos.*[53]

As should be clear from the foregoing, the reason that Novalis and his co-partisans of Romantic thought favor the concept of "becoming" in describing themselves and their artistic practice is fundamentally bound up with the conviction that the universe itself is in constant motion. In this respect they differ from the prevailing Enlightenment view, according to which it is possible to arrive at some final description of the universe, provided that a sufficient number of laws are formulated by induction from empirical evidence. This to the Romantics is nonsense, since for them nature is constantly destroying and creating forms anew, with the result that it can never be fully apprehended. Nonetheless they remain true to the idea that nature is intelligible — as the frequent occurrences of the originally christological *liber naturae* topos in their writings indicates — but not completely, not exhaustively. This commitment to the study of nature and the realization that such study can never be brought to a conclusion gives rise to a peculiar sort of actionism that is characteristic of the scientific arm of Romanticism, that finds its theoretical expression in Fichte's doctrine of the will. It is a hallmark of Novalis's biography: his diaries with their constant exhortations to greater effort testify to a punishing work-schedule. The goal of a comprehensive understanding of nature and of a reconciliation with it can only be approached — asymptotically, as it were — but not finally and permanently reached. Isaiah Berlin sums up the Romantics' view of the universe and of their own place in it succinctly:

> The brute fact about the universe is that it is not fully expressible, it is not fully exhaustible, it is not at rest, it is in motion; this is the basic datum. . . . Effort is action, action is movement, movement is unfinishable — perpetual movement. That is the fundamental romantic image.[54]

It is this awareness of the infinitude of the object that one seeks to understand and to embrace that gives Romantic *Sehnsucht* its particular unfulfillable character: the object, the *blaue Blume*, recedes even as it draws the wanderer ever onward. While the goal cannot ultimately be attained, the pursuit of it generates its own creative energy.

What was Novalis's legacy to Romantic science? It is true that his contemporaries and immediate successors in the field make scarcely any reference to his scientific writings. Instead it was through his literary work, and especially through *Heinrich von Ofterdingen*, that he managed to exert an influence on scientific posterity. To judge from the memoirs of Gotthilf Heinrich Schubert (1780–1860), a pioneer in the field of psychology, as well as a natural scientist and alumnus of the Freiberg academy, who recalls having the book in his knapsack on a summer hike, the novel seems to have been a sort of vade mecum for students and scientists alike.[55]

Carl Gustav Carus (1789–1869), physician, anatomist, natural scientist and landscape painter — a true polymath in the Romantic mold — also refers only to *Heinrich von Ofterdingen* from among Novalis's works.[56] What Carus — who claimed to have cured himself of melancholia by reading Schelling's *Von der Weltseele* — appears above all to have taken from Novalis's novel is the characteristic enabling fiction of the self as wanderer striving toward the knowledge of nature. Carus is typical of Romantic scientists in that his aesthetic activity was an indispensable adjunct to his research: his geological paintings, which he memorably characterized as "Erdlebenbildkunst," attest to an organic and processual understanding of nature — in them basalt columns appear to grow like tree trunks directly from the earth.[57]

*Fig. 1. Carl Gustav Carus,* Pilger im Felsental *(ca. 1820). Nationalgalerie Berlin. Reproduced with the kind permission of the Bildarchiv Preußischer Kulturbesitz.*

There exists a painting by Carus, dating from about 1820, entitled *Pilger im Felsental*, which I believe is typical of the Romantic tendency to enlist the motif of the wanderer in representations of the self (see fig. 1). This small canvas depicts a solitary wanderer, identifiable as a pilgrim from his staff, facing away from the viewer. The figure is following the course of a stream through a rocky defile, bounded on either side by precipitous cliffs, which convey the idea of an arduous journey. In the background, the sky is apparently suffused with the light of the rising sun, and a single star is visible high above the crags: it is evidently by this star that the wanderer is navigating. It is hard to see the painting as anything other than a visual metaphor for the characteristic Romantic self-conception as wanderer, in which the star represents the transcendental goal upon which the pilgrim's eyes are fixed, and the dawn light, a favored motif in Romantic painting, symbolizes a hopeful future. It seems reasonable to make two assumptions concerning this painting: first, we may take it as an exercise in self-representation, an image that aims to affirm the scientist's ongoing labors by framing them as a pilgrim's journey to salvation. The author of the work, is, after all, primarily a natural scientist, whose skill as artist is subordinated to his investigations in the fields of comparative anatomy and geology. Second, we may suppose that Carus was influenced in this self-representation by Novalis's novel — both the painting and the novel can be read as teleological narratives in which marked sacral overtones are detectable.

I have argued that *Franz Sternbalds Wanderungen* appropriates elements of the ritualized journeying of tradesmen to the end of legitimizing the nomadic and frequently precarious existences of Romantic artists. Read in this way, Tieck's novel is the literary embodiment of a rite of institution, in which the artistic vocation is consecrated by playing up its adventurous distinctiveness. *Heinrich von Ofterdingen*, in effect, does the same for the scientific vocation — although the hero is a poet, he is that in the full sense that the term *poeisis* carried for Novalis, Humboldt, Carus, and Goethe, that is, the sense of creation, the act of making in which the aesthetic and rational faculties are blended.

On 7 January 1826 Goethe wrote to Carus to thank him for sending a copy of his *Vergleichende Anatomie*.

> Wenn ich das neuste Vorschreiten der Naturwissenschaften betrachte, so komm ich mir vor wie ein Wandrer, der in der Morgendämmerung gegen Osten ging, das heranwachsende Licht mit Freuden anschaute und die Erscheinung des großen Feuerballens mit Sehnsucht erwartete, aber doch bei dem Hervortreten desselben die Augen wegwenden mußte, welche den gewünschten erhofften Glanz nicht ertragen konnten.
>
> Es ist nicht zuviel gesagt, aber in einem solchen Zustande befinde ich mich, wenn ich Herrn Carus Werk vornehme, das die Andeutungen alles Werdens von dem einfachsten bis zu dem mannigfachsten Leben durchführt und das große Geheimnis mit Wort und Bild vor Augen legt: daß

> nichts entspringt, als was schon angekündigt ist und daß die Ankündigung erst durch das Angekündigte klar wird, wie die Weissagung durch die Erfüllung.[58]

Goethe's letter is striking, not only for its use of the metaphor of a wanderer moving toward the radiant dawn of knowledge, but also for its juxtaposition of this metaphor with the dialectic of anticipation and fulfillment familiar to us from *Heinrich von Ofterdingen* and other Romantic fictions (such as Eichendorff's *Ahnung und Gegenwart*). The first sentence reads like a piece of ecphrasis (the verbal description of a picture), and it is not inconceivable that Goethe is alluding directly to Carus's *Pilger im Felsental.* What is most significant about Goethe's letter, however, is the support it provides for the thesis that Romantic scientists inclined to view themselves as wanderers, thereby constructing an identity that motivated them to press on with their investigations. We are perhaps not accustomed to classifying Goethe with the Romantics, yet he shared many of their convictions, at least as far as scientific work was concerned — including a belief in the complementarity of aesthetic and empirical practice.[59]

It appears that by the time of Goethe's letter the wanderer motif had become established as the concrete and easily visualized semantic element by means of which scientific pioneers were able to represent the ideas of development and progress to themselves. This is not an insignificant finding, for those very ideas — of development and progress — were to become the lead concepts in the scientific thinking of the nineteenth century: the idea of development according to an inward essence would ultimately inspire the theory of evolution. Of course, such ideas gained currency far beyond the realm of natural science — becoming transferred into the philosophy of history (the progress of the *Weltgeist*, Hegel), and political economy (Marx).

## Unending Journey: The Wanderer and the Fear of the Infinite

The wanderer motif does not only provide the basis of a mobilizing myth for pioneers in the fields of early Romantic art and science; in their literature we find it already being deployed in a contrary sense: to illuminate the problematical aspects of modern subjectivity in general and of their own vocation in particular. Certain texts possess both of these valencies, notably *Franz Sternbalds Wanderungen* — although that work has been interpreted here as an affirmation of the artist's vocation, some critics (Meuthen, Schmidt) see it as a document of the destruction and dissociation of identity. In Tieck's *Märchen*-novella *Der Runenberg*, which first appeared in 1802[60] — significantly, the very year in which Tieck brought out *Heinrich von Ofterdingen* — the wanderer motif is used in an exposition of the perils of untrammeled curiosity. The young hero, Christian, is drawn "wie mit fremder Gewalt" out of his settled life in the fertile plains into the threatening world of the mountains by an unaccountable thirst for knowledge. Leaving his former existence as "Gärtner" behind, he becomes a "Jäger" — not a scientist as such, but we recall that a literary tradition of likening the exploratory drive to the thrill of the hunt has existed at least since David Hume's *Treatise on Human Nature*. However, *Der Runenberg* is the account, not of an initiation into science, but of catastrophic failure on the path from adolescence to manhood. The youth is impelled by a desire for knowledge in the fullest sense (self-knowledge, sexual experience) as well as by a diffuse longing for the sublime. It is in this respect that Christian most resembles those Romantic scientists for whom the exploration of nature was inextricably bound up with the discovery of the imagination and the unconscious, a connection indicated by the metaphor of the mine.

On the threshold of maturity Christian is pulled hither and thither between the competing claims of the old, patriarchal and agrarian, world and the mysterious and alluring world of the mountains, with its prospect of arcane knowledge. A series of dichotomies runs through the text — "Gärtner" / "Jäger," lowlands / mountains, organic / inorganic — throwing the conflict between these two spheres into sharp relief. Doubtless, Christian's movement out of the plains and into the mountains can be read as regression, a quest for "Ganzheitserfahrung" not available in a sphere of cultivation dominated by the principle of specialization.[61] Support for this reading comes from the association in the Romantic mind of the mineral domain with the original, prehistoric state of the world. But since it involves a transition out of the agrarian and into the mineral sphere, Christian's journey can also be read as an allegory of a movement toward a more advanced stage of material culture. The mineral world that so obsesses Tieck's wanderer was, after all, the source of the new materials and technologies then transforming the world. Christian's receipt of a "magische steinerne Tafel" (68) from the queen of the mountains is an initiation into secret knowledge; its runes summon up the idea of the hidden code of nature. From this moment on, the hero's fate is sealed; an attempt to reestablish himself in human society, though initially successful, inevitably fails. The stone tablet exerts an invincible fascination over the revenant, who becomes so withdrawn that his father implores him: "Wirf diese Schrift weg, die dich kalt und grausam macht, die dein Herz versteinern muß" (78). The fascination of the inorganic world atrophies the natural affections: in Christian's perverse vision the organic sphere becomes "der Leichnam vormaliger herrlicher Steinwelten" (77), a realm of death and decay — an inversion of Novalis's optimistic view that nature was developing toward perfection.

It is indisputable that *Der Runenberg* dramatizes the difficulties of negotiating the transition from adolescence to sexual maturity and professional responsibility, but it does so at a time when assimilating to patriarchy and tradition was not the only option, at least for the intellectuals making up the Romantic movement, who felt called upon to explore the natural world and the psyche. Although Romantic science is not in the foreground of the story, the crisis of maturation that it thematizes was experienced most acutely by Romantic artists and scientists. Such individuals were driven by a pressure to innovate, to devise their own *modus vivendi*, and to generate new knowledge. As a result, they found themselves uniquely at odds with their philosophical and religious traditions.

Ultimately Christian succumbs to the attraction of the mineral world, abandoning wife and children to return to it. What makes him return? The story is perhaps overdetermined with regard to motivation: the illicit allure of the "Bergkönigin," the fascination emanating from the stone tablet, and the corrupting influence of the stranger's gold are all implicated. Bearing these in mind, we might say that the movement out of the cultivated plains and into the mine corresponds with a rejection of dependency in favor of fantasized omnipotence.[62] Before his final disappearance Christian reappears briefly, ragged and barefoot, carrying a sack of pebbles, which he maintains are uncut gems — an adept of nature's mysteries. This brief and apparently hastily written story — Tieck claimed to have composed it in one night — is perhaps the most concise and unsettling account of the dangers of an impious *curiositas* driving the exploration of nature. The model for Christian appears to have been the mineralogist Henrik Steffens (1773–1845), whom Tieck met at the Jena literary circle in 1799. At any rate Steffens was convinced of this, pointing with a fine sense of self-irony to his presence in a story

> in welcher ein Mensch vorkömmt, der, durch eine geheime Sehnsucht nach den verschlossenen Geheimnissen der wilden Gebirge getrieben, die fruchtbare Ebene verläßt und, dämonisch verlockt, wahnsinnig wähnt, große Schätze entdeckt zu haben, indem er mühsam einen Sack mit wertlosen Steinen schleppt. Tieck hat gestanden, bei dieser Novelle an mich gedacht zu haben.[63]

Steffens understands the vastness of the natural world as profundity; for him the sphere of human habitation is no more than "eine zwar anmutige, aber leichte Decke" (255), a thin layer draped over the earth's mineral frame. This knowledge of hidden depths confronts the scientist with an epistemological anxiety, and in its extreme form it threatens him with despair.

In a motif study of exemplary breadth Manfred Frank has argued that the rise to prominence of the figures of Ahasver and the Flying Dutchman — the most fertile embodiments of the motif of the journey without end — in the nineteenth century is the result of a growing tendency in literature to reflect critically upon the whole notion of progress.[64] In essence, Frank argues that the motif of the unending journey is a specifically modern derivative of the Christian *navigatio vitae*. The motif acquires its virulence from its expression of the idea that with the demise of belief in a redemptive order man is cast adrift in the universe, eternally sailing, without prospect of gaining the safe haven of salvation. I have taken Tieck's *Runenberg* as an example of a fiction in which the wanderer motif is employed in a contrary sense to that prevailing among the early Romantics, for whom it was a more or less unproblematic emblem of dynamism. In these alternative treatments the unending nature of the journey is used to question the Romantic actionism mentioned earlier — an actionism that persisted in the collective consciousness well into the nineteenth century. The *Runenberg* foreshadows those fictions of late Romanticism in which "die Perspektive der Selbsterlösung des Menschen durch die eigene Tat"[65] is subjected to thorough and unsparing scrutiny. Frank exemplifies this tendency by reference to Adelbert von Chamisso's story *Peter Schlemihls wundersame Geschichte* (1814) and Wilhelm Müller's *Wanderlieder* sequence, *Die Winterreise* (1823/4). Chamisso's hero enters into a Faustian pact, trading his shadow for the inexhaustible money-bag of Fortunatus. By thus selling an insubstantial but essential attribute of his humanity, Schlemihl turns himself into a pariah — the lack of a shadow, a stigma worse than any mark of Cain, forces him to shun broad daylight, condemning him literally to a twilight existence. After futile attempts to regain his shadow, the hero opts for the life of a solitary explorer, seeking to compensate his outcast status in restless scientific investigation: "Durch frühe Schuld von der menschlichen Gesellschaft ausgeschlossen, ward ich zum Ersatz an die Natur, die ich stets geliebt, gewiesen."[66] The unexpected acquisition of seven-league boots assists him in this aim, enabling the wanderer to traverse the world at lightning speed in the pursuit of scientific knowledge: "Ich habe, so weit meine Stiefel gereicht, die Erde, ihre Gestaltung, ihre Höhen, ihre Temperatur, ihre Atmosphäre in ihrem Wechsel, die Erscheinungen ihrer magnetischen Kraft, das Leben auf ihr, besonders im Pflanzenreiche, gründlicher kennen gelernt, als vor mir irgend ein Mensch" (95). Considered as a scientist, Peter Schlemihl is not a Romantic but one of the new breed of positivists, scornful of *Naturphilosophie*, who by mid-century would dominate scientific discourse. His shadow, that aspect of himself that he casts off prior to becoming a successful researcher and explorer, is a "Schatten" in the Jungian sense of the unconscious, the "Nachtseite" of Gotthilf Heinrich Schubert's epochal book,[67] it is, in short, the very basis of his subjectivity. The feverish investigation, the unceasing movement, are therefore preceded by something like a violent act of repression, a quashing of the natural faculties and affections. Chamisso's story exposes actionism of an apparently Romantic kind, but one that is divorced from the Romantic conviction that the natural world could not be studied without attending also to inner, psychic nature.

If the foregoing has made anything clear, it is perhaps that already within Romanticism itself the full semantic gamut of the wanderer motif has been run. The recognition that there was no *rerum natura*, no settled order of the world, brought with it unique dangers for the Romantic imagination. To conceive of nature as unending flux, constantly bringing forth new forms, was in one respect a liberating idea, but it also gave rise to an uneasy awareness of the inexhaustibility of the universe. For as long as the idea of a great chain or scale of being had persisted, it was possible to imagine that man might one day attain fairly comprehensive knowledge of the vast, but finite, array of forms. But the temporalization or dynamization of the worldview had repercussions far beyond the scientific field. The whole notion of a stable and social order in which the individual could find a lasting abode was called into question. The wanderer motif is thus used not only as a vehicle for the theme of scientific curiosity, or its potentially dire consequences, but also to cast doubt on the individual's capacity to take charge of his own existence.

## Notes

[1] Ludwig Tieck, *Franz Sternbalds Wanderungen: Studienausgabe*, ed. Alfred Anger, 2nd ed. (Stuttgart: Reclam, 1994). Further references to the *Studienausgabe* (which is based on the 1798 first edition) will be given in the text using page numbers alone.

[2] When Jakob and Wilhelm Grimm were compiling their *Deutsches Wörterbuch*, the definition of *wandern* as artisan's journey still took precedence over the newer sense of recreational walking: "erst die neuere zeit kennt *wandern* als das frohe durchstreifen der natur, um körper und geist zu erfrischen, nachdem durch die romantik und die turnerei die wanderfreude erweckt war, ist das wort in diesem sinne beliebt (*Seume* gebraucht im spaziergang nach Syrakus noch meist *wandeln*); die dichtung knüpft dabei gern an die wanderlust der handwerksgesellen . . . an." Jakob Grimm and Wilhelm Grimm, *Deutsches Wörterbuch*, 33 vols. (Leipzig: Hirzel, 1854–1971), vol. 13, col. 1667.

[3] Frank Möbus and Anne Bohnenkamp, *Mit Gunst und Verlaub! Wandernde Handwerker: Tradition und Alternative*, 5th ed. (Göttingen: Wallstein, 2001), 27.

[4] See Wolfgang Kehn, "Die Schönheiten der Natur gemeinschaftlich betrachten: Zum Zusammenhang von Freundschaft, ästhetischer Naturerfahrung und 'Gartenrevolution' in der Spätaufklärung," in *Frauenfreundschaft-Männerfreundschaft: Literarische Diskurse im 18. Jahrhundert*, ed. Wolfram Mauser and Barbara Becker-Cantarino (Tübingen: Niemeyer, 1991), 173–74, on friendship as natural social form. See also Roger Paulin, *Ludwig Tieck* (Stuttgart: Metzler, 1987), 21–22, on the Romantic cult of friendship.

[5] "Die Organisation der Handwerksgesellen in ihren Bruderschaften bis etwa 1850 war hochritualisiert. Sie regelte detailliert die Sozialbeziehungen, schirmte die Bruderschaften gegen gesellschaftliche Einflüsse ab und sicherte den sozialen Status der Gesellen." Wolfgang Braungart, *Ritual und Literatur* (Tübingen: Niemeyer, 1996), 103.

[6] Doris Bachmann-Medick characterizes the threshold status of initiates as follows: "Sie schweben in einer labilen Zwischenexistenz, sind weder das eine noch das andere, sondern befinden sich zwischen den vom Gesetz, der Tradition, der Konvention und dem Zeremonial fixierten Positionen." Bachmann-Medick, "Kulturelle Spielräume: Drama und Theater im Licht ethnologischer Ritualforschung," in *Kultur als Text: Die anthropologische Wende in der Kulturwissenschaft*, ed. Doris Bachmann-Medick (Frankfurt am Main: Fischer, 1996), 98–121; here, 103. The concept of liminality originated with Arnold van Gennep and was adopted by the cultural anthropologist Victor Turner for his analysis of theatrical performance as social drama.

[7] Detlef Kremer, *Prosa der Romantik* (Stuttgart: Metzler, 1996), 129.

[8] Korff holds that what is innovative in Tieck's figures is not so much their wandering *per se* — the adventurer being the archetypal hero of the novel — as the "*unbestimmte romantische Sehnsucht*, die etwas Geistigeres und Sublimeres als die bloße Lust am Abenteuer ist. . . . Die Sehnsucht nach dem Ewigen verwandelt sich in ewige Sehnsucht, und sie schweift nunmehr im irdischen Raum umher, ohne doch in irgendeinem Irdischen je ihr Ziel zu finden." Hermann August Korff, *Geist der Goethezeit: Versuch einer ideelen Entwicklung der klassisch-romantischen Literaturgeschichte*, 3rd ed., 5 vols. (Leipzig: Koehler & Amelang, 1957), 3:75.

[9] Kremer, *Prosa der Romantik*, 129.

[10] Jakob Grimm and Wilhelm Grimm, *Deutsches Wörterbuch*, 33 vols. (Leipzig: Hirzel, 1854–1971), vol. 10, col. 157, "Sehnsucht."

[11] The removal of the reference to a "Wollustozean" from the 1843 edition was likely prompted by objections raised by August Wilhelm Schlegel in his letter of 7 Dec. 1798. Thomas E. Schmidt, *Die Geschichtlichkeit des frühromantischen Romans: Literarische Reaktionen auf Erfahrungen eines kulturellen Wandels* (Tübingen: Niemeyer, 1989), 77.

[12] "Diese Verehrung der Kunst, diese Begier, Italien mit seinen Werken zu sehn, hatte er immer für sein einziges Verdienst gehalten, und nun vernichtete ein verehrungswürdiger Meister ihm auch dieses gänzlich" (101–2).

[13] Erich Meuthen, "'... denn er selbst war hier anders': Zum Problem des Identitätsverlusts in Ludwig Tiecks 'Sternbald'-Roman," *Jahrbuch der deutschen Schiller-Gesellschaft* 30 (1986): 383–403; here, 400. Korff has remarked of Tieck's creation of the figure of Florestan: "Er hat mit ihm einen Typus aufgestellt, der für die ganze romantische Erzählungsliteratur von außerordentlicher Bedeutung gewesen ist, den *vagabundierenden Romantiker*, der Romantiker als Vagabund" (*Geist der Goethezeit* 3:75).

[14] See Irmgard Osols-Wehden, *Pilgerfahrt und Narrenreise: Der Einfluß der Dichtungen Dantes und Ariosts auf den frühromantischen Roman in Deutschland* (Hildesheim: Weidmann, 1998). Osols-Wehden does not, despite the suggestive title, discuss the significance of these influences for the theme of wandering in the early Romantic novel.

[15] See Doris Bachmann-Medick, "Kulturelle Spielräume," 104, for a discussion of Turner's concept of *communitas*. Victor Turner, "Liminal to Liminoid in Play,

Flow, Ritual: An Essay in Comparative Symbolology," in *From Ritual to Theatre: The Human Seriousness of Play* (New York: PAJ, 1982), 20–60.

[16] Rudolf Köpke, *Ludwig Tieck: Erinnerungen aus dem Leben des Dichters nach dessen mündlichen und schriftlichen Mitteilungen* (Leipzig: Brockhaus (1855; repr., Darmstadt: Wissenschaftliche Buchgesellschaft. 1970), 144.

[17] Heinrich Bosse, "Zur Sozialgeschichte des Wanderliedes," in *Wanderzwang — Wanderlust: Formen der Raum und Sozialerfahrung zwischen Aufklärung und Frühindustrialisierung* (Tübingen: Niemeyer, 1999), 135–58.

[18] The institution of the *Bildungsreise* is one of the numerous targets of Ludoviko's cynicism: "Nichts ist lächerlicher als die Menschen, die mit ernsthaftern Gesichtern zurückkommen, weil sie etwa entfernte Gegenden gesehn haben, alte Gebäude und wunderliche Sitten" (309).

[19] See Hans-Jürgen Schings, *Melancholie und Aufklärung: Melancholiker und ihre Kritiker in Erfahrungsseelenkunde und Literatur des 18. Jahrhunderts* (Stuttgart: Metzler, 1977), 253. Schings identifies dilettantism as a symptom of Anton Reiser's melancholy.

[20] The phrase is Goethe's, from his marginal notes to *Franz Sternbalds Wanderungen* (*Franz Sternbalds Wanderungen.* [Studienausgabe], 505).

[21] *Franz Sternbalds Wanderungen* (Studienausgabe), 573.

[22] Meuthen, "'... denn er selbst war hier anders,'" 385.

[23] Friedrich Schlegel, *Athenäum*, 1.2 (Berlin: n.p., 1798; repr. Stuttgart: Cotta, 1960), 205–6, fragment no. 116.

[24] Pierre Bourdieu, *Language and Symbolic Power* (Cambridge: Polity, 1991). See 117–26 on "rites of institution."

[25] "Die romantische Schule [entwickelte] ihre hohen Vorstellungen aus einem gesellschaftlichen und politischen Außenseiterdasein heraus, in dem der Freundeskreis, der Kreis der wenigen Gleichgesinnten den eigentlichen Adressatenbezug darstellt." Gert Ueding, "Klassik und Romantik im Zeitalter der französischen Revolution," in *Hanser Sozialgeschichte der deutschen Literatur vom 16. Jh. bis zur Gegenwart*, ed. by Rolf Grimminger (Munich and Vienna: Hanser, 1980–), 4:461–80; here, 462.

[26] Schlegel, *Athenäum*, 1.2 (1798): 209–10, fragment no. 125.

[27] See Kehn, "Die Schönheiten der Natur gemeinschaftlich betrachten."

[28] Novalis, *Schriften: Die Werke Friedrich von Hardenbergs (Historisch-kritische Ausgabe)*, ed. Paul Kluckhohn and Richard Samuel (Stuttgart: Kohlhammer, 1977–), 3:638–39. References to the text of *Heinrich von Ofterdingen* (which appears in vol. 1) will be given by page number alone in the main body of the text. References to other volumes of this edition will be indicated by volume and page number.

[29] Herbert Uerlings refers to the persistence of this interpretive model: "'Übernahme der Form bei Ablehnung des Gehaltes' und eine Deutung des 'Ofterdingen' als 'Anti Meister' lauten im Grunde bis heute die Paradigmen der Forschung." *Friedrich von Hardenberg genannt Novalis: Werk und Forschung* (Stuttgart: Metzler, 1991), 449. Uerlings also notes the distorting effect that the

comparison of the two works has had on the interpretation of *Heinrich von Ofterdingen:* "Fraglich ist, wie weit der immer wieder angestellte Vergleich mit Goethes Roman trägt und ob er nicht zugleich den Blick verstellt für die Besonderheiten des 'Ofterdingen'" (453). Dennis F. Mahoney, *Friedrich von Hardenberg (Novalis)* (Stuttgart and Weimar: Metzler, 2001), 131–34, provides a useful discussion of Novalis's reception of the *Lehrjahre.*

30 "Die Teleologie ist Wirklichkeit — nicht nur, wie Kant gelehrt hatte, eine notwendige Fiktion." Korff, *Geist der Goethezeit,* 3:594.

31 Kremer, *Prosa der Romantik,* 124.

32 Theodore Ziolkowski, *German Romanticism and Its Institutions* (Princeton: Princeton UP, 1990), 21.

33 A fuller discussion of the sublime (and its aporias) is provided in my analysis of Büchner's *Lenz,* where Schiller's essay *Über das Erhabene* is taken as exemplifying the contemporary understanding of an "aesthetics of the infinite" (Nicolson). Marjorie Hope Nicolson's seminal *Mountain Gloom and Mountain Glory: The Development of the Aesthetics of the Infinite* (1959; repr., Seattle: U of Washington P, 1997) provides an unequalled account of the significance of mountaineering for the rise of an aesthetics of the sublime in this period. Theodore Ziolkowski sees the interest in the subterranean as a complement to the growth from the mid-eighteenth century onward in mountaineering: "Inevitably the fascination with the outsides of mountains was transferred to their inner recesses." (Ziolkowski, *German Romanticism and Its Institutions,* 22).

34 The full titles of these treatises are as follows: *Ideen zu einer Philosophie der Natur als Einleitung in das Studium dieser Wissenschaft* and *Von der Weltseele, eine Hypothese der höheren Physik zur Erklärung des allgemeinen Organismus.*

35 See Wolf Lepenies, *Das Ende der Naturgeschichte: Wandel kultureller Selbstverständlichkeiten in den Wissenschaften des 18. und 19. Jahrhunderts* (Munich and Vienna: Hanser, 1976); and Peter Matussek, ed., *Goethe und die Verzeitlichung der Natur* (Munich: Beck, 1998).

36 See Robert J. Richards, *The Romantic Conception of Life* (Chicago, IL and London: U of Chicago P, 2002), esp. chapter 3, 114–92, for a useful account of Schelling's *Naturphilosophie.*

37 This idea has persisted in modern theories of the "self-organization" of matter. See Erich Jantsch, *Die Selbstorganisation des Universum: Vom Urknall zum menschlichen Geist.* (Munich: Deutscher Taschenbuch Verlag, 1979).

38 Einem gelang es — er hob den Schleyer der Göttin zu Saïs —
Aber was sah er? Er sah — Wunder des Wunders — Sich Selbst. (1:110)

39 Several commentators have pointed to the symbolic connection between the descent into the mine and the exploration of the unconscious. Thus Josef Haslinger: "Er [der Bergmann] ist mit der Natur liebevoll verbündet, mehr noch, er steigt in ihre verschlungenen Gänge hinab, in ihr Inneres, was durchaus einen Abstieg ins Unbewußte meint, in die verdrängte Natur." Haslinger, *Die Ästhetik des Novalis* (Königstein im Taunus: Hain, 1981), 159. Theodore Ziolkowski similarly emphasizes the psychological or proto-psychoanalytical dimensions of the mine in Romantic literature, but attributes to the Romantics a non-technical,

pre-industrial view: "The mine in German Romanticism is a mine of the soul, not a technological site" (*German Romanticism and Its Institutions*, 28) However, *Heinrich von Ofterdingen* is conditioned, not by a denial of the technical sphere, but by the terms of Novalis's aesthetics: "Die Kunst auf eine *angenehme* Art zu befremden, einen Gegenstand fremd zu machen und doch bekannt und anziehend, das ist die romantische Poetik" (3:685). Herbert Uerlings sees it differently than does Ziolkowski; see Uerlings, "Novalis in Freiberg: Die Romantisierung des Bergbaus — Mit einem Blick auf Tiecks *Runenberg* und E. T. A. Hoffmanns *Bergwerke zu Falun*," *Aurora* 56 (1996): 57–77.

[40] Kremer, *Prosa der Romantik*, 126.

[41] "Aus der Enzyklopädistik romantisch interpretierter Wissenschaften [wird] das enzyklopädisch angelegte Kunstwerk, das ein utopisches Bild einer neuen Zeit gibt" (Uerlings, *Friedrich von Hardenberg*, 400).

[42] Hans-Joachim Mähl provides the fullest account of the influence of the idea of a Golden Age on Novalis's literary production, characterizing Novalis's conception of the Golden Age in terms of process, as "den Erlösungsweg, den Prozeß der Verbindung alles Getrennten, der Versöhnung der äußeren Welt mit der inneren." Mähl, *Die Idee des goldenen Zeitalters im Werk des Novalis: Studien zur Wesensbestimmung der frühromantischen Utopie und zu ihren ideengeschichtlichen Voraussetzungen* (Heidelberg: Winter, 1965), 397.

[43] Kremer, *Prosa der Romantik*, 124.

[44] "Der zweite Teil des Romans aber sollte nun den Weg nach außen, die Verwandlung der Natur- und Menschenwelt . . . schildern" (Mähl, *Die Idee des goldenen Zeitalters*, 412).

[45] See Mähl, *Die Idee des goldenen Zeitalters*, esp. part 2, chapter 3: "Das goldene Zeitalter als poetisches 'Postulat' und als 'Approximationsprinzip,'" and chapter 6: "Die poetische Vorstellungsform des goldenen Zeitalters."

[46] "Mathematische Studien. Bekanntmachung mit der Landesverfassung und den andern Zweigen des Finanzfachs. . . . *Chémische*, Physicalische und technische Studien. (Bes[onders] das Maschinenwesen)" (5:95–96).

[47] The idea of organic life developing in accordance with an internal principle is to be found, for instance, in Goethe's studies of morphology, beginning with his *Versuch die Metamorphose der Pflanzen zu erklären* (1790).

[48] Ernst Bloch, *Gesamtausgabe* (Frankfurt am Main: Suhrkamp, 1959–), 5:254.

[49] Alexander von Humboldt: "Was mir den Hauptantrieb gewährte, war das Bestreben, die Erscheinungen der körperlichen Dinge in diesem allgemeinen Zusammenhang, die Natur als ein durch innere Kräfte bewegtes und belebtes Ganzes aufzufassen." Humboldt, *Kosmos für die Gegenwart*, ed. Hanno Beck (Stuttgart: Brockhaus, 1978), xxv.

[50] "Schelling's theory suggested that nature might furnish a path back to the self: one might go into nature, enter the lush forests of central Europe or travel to the tropics of foreign lands, and there in the wild, tangled growth of primitive nature discover the self. But not only might one discover oneself in nature; the exploration of nature might even be regarded as a necessary propaedeutic to the development of the self, of one's character and personality. This implication of Schelling's

philosophy greatly appealed to Alexander von Humboldt, whose retrospective creation of his experiences in the jungles around the Orinoco — where he grew into that true self he became — ... bear the mark of his engagement with Schelling" (Richards, *The Romantic Conception of Life*, 134).

[51] Schlegel, *Athenäum*, 1.2 (1798): 205, fragment no.116.

[52] Humboldt, *Kosmos*, xxx.

[53] See Petra Werner, *Himmel und Erde: Alexander von Humboldt und sein Kosmos* (Berlin: Akademie, 2004), 115.

[54] Isaiah Berlin, *The Roots of Romanticism*, ed. Henry Hardy (London: Pimlico, 2000), 106. This edition contains the published text of the Mellon Lectures held in Washington, DC, in 1965. Berlin's writings continue to serve as an invaluable source on the philosophical background of the Romantic movement.

[55] Novalis, *Schriften*, 1:190.

[56] Uerlings, *Friedrich von Hardenberg*, 167.

[57] For a valuable treatment of the links between Carus's painting and geological investigations see Richard Hoppe-Sailer, "Genesis und Prozeß: Elemente der Goethe Rezeption bei Carl Gustav Carus, Paul Klee und Joseph Beuys," in Matussek, *Goethe und die Verzeitlichung der Natur*, 276–300.

[58] Quoted from Stefan Grosche, *"Zarten Seelen ist gar viel gegönnt": Naturwissenschaft und Kunst im Briefwechsel zwischen C. G. Carus und Goethe* (Göttingen: Wallstein, 2001), 46.

[59] "Wenn wir von ihr irgend eine Art von Ganzheit erwarten, so müssen wir uns die Wissenschaft notwendig als Kunst denken." Johann Wolfgang Goethe, *Die Schriften zur Naturwissenschaft, im Auftrage der Deutschen Akademie der Naturforscher (Leopoldina) zu Halle*, ed. Wolf von Engelhardt and Dorothea Kuhn, 11 vols. (Weimar: n.p., 1947–), vol. 1, part 6, 77. (= Leopoldina Ausgabe).

[60] Ludwig Tieck, *Werke in vier Bänden*. ed. Marianne Thalmann (Darmstadt: Wissenschaftliche Buchgesellschaft, 1978), 2:59–83. Subsequent references to this work are given in the text using page numbers alone.

[61] Thus Klaus F. Gille, "Der Berg und die Seele: Überlegungen zu Tieck: 'Der Runenberg.'" *Neophilologus* 77 (1993): 611–23.

[62] In his vacillation between the two spheres Christian resembles Elis in E. T. A. Hoffmann's *Die Bergwerke zu Falun*, who is beset by "ein ständiges Pendeln zwischen antinomischen Gefühlszuständen." Hartmut Böhme, *Natur und Subjekt* (Frankfurt am Main: Suhrkamp, 1988), "Geheime Macht im Schoß der Erde: Das Symbolfeld des Bergbaus," 67–144; here, 129. (Böhme's further remarks concerning Elis are equally applicable to Christian: "In diesem Pendeln verläuft der Kampf um das Selbst, um die Formen bürgerlicher Subjektverfassung, die in der Romantik in Krise geraten sind. Denn das verlockende Glück des Berges ist zugleich der Abgrund, der sich mitten in der absoluten Selbst-Setzung der romantischen Kunst öffnet.")

[63] Henrik Steffens, *Was ich erlebte: Aus der Erinnerung niedergeschrieben*, 4 vols. (Breslau: Josef Max, 1841), 3:22–23 (quoted from Uwe Schweikert, *Dichter über ihre Dichtungen: Ludwig Tieck*, 3 vols. [Munich: Heimeran, 1971], 1:255–56).

[64] Manfred Frank, *Die unendliche Fahrt: Die Geschichte des fliegenden Holländers und verwandter Motive* (Leipzig: Reclam, 1995). The myth of Ahasver, the "cobbler of Jerusalem," condemned to wander the earth eternally for mocking Christ on the way to Calvary, probably based on the medieval legend of Cartophilus, makes its first appearance in writing in a seventeenth-century *Volksbuch.* Frank sets the first appearance in print of the saga of the Flying Dutchman and the proliferation of versions of the Ahasver story in the early nineteenth century in the context of growing concern about the project of modernity (69–91). Among the many Romantics to rework the Ahasver myth were Wordsworth, in his *Song for the Wandering Jew* (1800), Byron, whose *Childe Harold's Pilgrimage* (1812) has a "gloomy wanderer" as its protagonist, and Lenau, in the verse epic *Ahasver, der ewige Jude* (1831). For a recent survey of nineteenth-century versions of the myth of the Wandering Jew see Judith Chernaik, "No resting could he find: The Mariner, the Dutchman and the Wandering Jew," *Times Literary Supplement*, 24 Jan. 2003.

[65] Frank, *Die unendliche Fahrt*, 169.

[66] Adelbert von Chamisso, *Peter Schlemihls wundersame Geschichte* (Nuremberg: Schrag, 1814; repr., Munich: dtv, 2003), 86.

[67] Gotthilf Heinrich Schubert, *Ansichten von der Nachtseite der Naturwissenschaft* Dresden: Arnold, 1808).

# 3: The Wanderer in Political Discourse

## The Wanderer as *Weltbürger*: Heine's *Harzreise* (1826)

### The *Harzreise* and the Legacy of the Enlightenment Travelogue

When the *Reisebilder: Erster Theil* first appeared in the imprint of Hoffmann and Campe in May 1826, Heine's literary contemporaries were not slow to recognize that the publication — comprising two novella-length prose texts: the *Harzreise* and the first part of the *Nordsee*, together with several poems, including the *Heimkehr* cycle — marked a decisive break with traditional literary models. Many reacted with confusion and distaste, and even those who greeted the new work with favorable notices confessed to some puzzlement. Karl Immermann was one of these. In his review in the May 1827 issue of the *Jahrbücher für wissenschaftliche Kritik*, an enthusiastic treatment of the poems stands alongside a more sober assessment of the prose: "Ueberhaupt findet sich in der Harzreise zu viel nüchterne Reflexion, die Darstellung wird zwar an einzelnen Punkten zur runden, poetischen Gestalt, jene Punkte stehen aber zu isolirt da."[1] Other reviewers made reference to Heine's originality, as in the following anonymous contribution to the *Literatur-Blatt* of the *Allgemeine Unterhaltungs-Blätter* (January 1828): "Man täuscht sich sehr, wenn man diese Reisebilder als eine gewöhnliche Reisebeschreibung hält, wie sie jede Messe zu Dutzenden zu Tage fördert . . . Vielmehr ist dieses Buch ein ganz neues Genre in unserer Literatur, das sich eine eigene Bahn vorgeschrieben und darauf selbständig und nachahmungslos vorwärts wandelt."[2]

The confused contemporary reactions have set the tone for the subsequent reception: while some Germanists have seen the advent of the *Reisebild* (the term first appears in Heine's letter of 14 December 1825 to Moses Moser) as the birth of a new literary genre,[3] others have insisted on classifying Heine's prose as journalism rather than literature.[4] While there is broad agreement that the *Harzreise*, the cornerstone text of the *Reisebilder: Erster Theil*, inherits some traits from the late Enlightenment travelogue,[5] the traits themselves are seldom specified. Yet any attempt to characterize the *Reisebild* as a new genre must attend to the question of influences from Enlightenment travel literature, and from the *Wanderbericht* in particular.[6] In the following I will attempt to do just that, concentrating on the *Harzreise* to the exclusion of the remainder of the *Reisebilder* for the reason that the wanderer motif occurs here in a sharply contoured form, while in the later *Reisebilder* it is eclipsed by the political commentary. The *Harzreise* is constructed around a wandering protagonist, and in this respect it harks back not only to the Enlightenment travelogue but also to the fictions of the Romantic era. Despite the text's high degree of biographical referentiality, its wanderer ought not to be equated with Heine but is better regarded as a construct, a persona. Since it is precisely in the motif of the wanderer that the Enlightenment and Romantic traditions appear to coalesce in the *Harzreise*, we need to ask what of each of these traditions is present in Heine's interpretation of the motif.

A number of factors combined to make the *Wanderbericht* the favored documentary form of the late Enlightenment period. The first was the symbolism of walking itself, which, in its negative aspect — the refusal of coach travel — implied a critical stance toward civilization. In its positive aspect, walking symbolized a commitment to egalitarian principles, a will to overcome social barriers. And, as we have seen, the upright gait of the pedestrian had come to stand for the project of self-emancipation and independent thought itself.

Apart from its symbolic affinity for ideas of liberty and equality, pedestrian travel also commended itself to the Enlightenment mind on account of its empirical value. Whether in botany or geology, it was only by walking that one could get up close to the object of interest. The arguments in favor of walking were still more compelling when the object was the land itself and its people. Walking allowed both detailed scrutiny of the land and direct access to its inhabitants: the rural poor were rarely encountered in the post coach. For the ethnographer, or the political writer, both of whom sought contact with the members of these classes, tramping the roads offered one way of reducing the visible social distance that separated him from his interlocutors.

Freed from the constraints of post-coach timetables and itineraries, the pedestrian observer was able to traverse the land at will, accessing little-frequented areas and adapting the schedule to the requirements of his researches — "kreuz und quer" is the oft-repeated formula for such unsystematic wandering. Georg Friedrich Rebmann (1768–1824), an ardent partisan of the French Revolution, emphasizes flexibility as a key advantage of walking in the first letter of his travelogue *Kosmopolitische Wanderungen durch einen Theil Deutschlands* (1793):

> Es ist ein anderes Ding um den Reisenden, der in einer stolzen Extrapost ankommt, im besten Gasthof seines Leibes pflegt und sich auf Assembleen, Picknicks und Bällen herumwirbelt und jedem Gegenstand, der seine Betäubung zerstreuen könnte, sorgfältig ausweicht, und um denjenigen, der, wie ich, im Zickzack durch ein Land, bald zu Fuß, bald in der Diligence, bald mit Extrapost, umherschweift und jede

> Menschenklasse seiner Aufmerksamkeit wert hält. Gerade die mittleren und niedrigsten Klassen liefern dem Beobachter am meisten Stoff, bei ihnen ist das eigentümliche Gepräge noch unverwischt, während die höhern Stände "unerzogen und nur gebildet," sich im ganzen überall gleichen.[7]

For Rebmann, whose *Kosmopolitische Wanderungen* will serve as a reference point for the discussion of Enlightenment influence on Heine's *Harzreise*, it is precisely the non-systematic nature of the journey that provides a guarantee of its information value. It is worth emphasizing this point, if only to modify the widely held view that Enlightenment travel was invariably planned and systematic. While this is broadly true, the openness to contingency, which is sometimes cited as if it were an entirely new feature of the *Harzreise*,[8] is already cited as desirable in travelogues like Rebmann's.

For Rebmann, the meandering mode of travel, and walking in particular, enables the study of the social ensemble, but especially the common people, who in the extract quoted above are idealized in a Rousseauesque vein as natural and uncorrupted. Heine's wanderer in the *Harzreise* exhibits a similar ethnographic interest, using the journey to converse with interlocutors from social groups to which he would have had no access in the urban and academic milieus. Moreover, Heine — like Rebmann — invokes the qualities of naturalness and originality in portraying the common people, though his idealization is at times ironically broken, as in the depiction of the Clausthal miners, whose sympathetic portrayal is qualified by an unsparing exposition of their servility and conservatism.

As is the case in Rebmann's *Kosmopolitische Wanderungen*, the (qualified) idealization of ordinary people in the *Harzreise* is coupled with a socially critical stance of a distinctly anti-urban cast. Both texts articulate this stance with recourse to the "Hütte und Palast" topos; this makes its first appearance in the *Harzreise* in the opening poem "Schwarze Röcke, seid'ne Strümpfe." Here the narrator announces his intention to exchange the "glatten Säle" for "die frommen Hütten," thereby specifying the destination of the journey at the outset; the *Bergidylle* poem marks the point at which this destination has been reached.[9] The *Bergidylle* reinterprets the familiar topos, linking the two locations, cabin and palace, in a novel way. Beginning with the seclusion of the miner's hut, the poem concludes with the wanderer united with his beloved in the surroundings of a castle, which is conjured out of its ruinous state when "das rechte Wort"[10] is uttered. Instead of merely describing both locations, the poem enacts a movement from one to the other — out of the cabin and into the palace. This dynamic reinterpretation of the cabin-palace topos provides a vivid illustration of Heine's understanding of history in the Hegelian sense of "Fortschritt im Bewußtsein der Freiheit."[11]

We have identified certain features that the *Harzreise* shares with the political *Wanderbericht*. First, both Heine's text and its forebears are marked by an emphatic turn to the common people, who are associated with some unalienated state of "Unmittelbarkeit." Second, the *Harzreise* follows the *Wanderbericht* genre in its reliance on the pedestrian perspective in the close observation of political and social circumstances. But what is the source of the cutting satire, which is the most prominent stylistic feature of the *Harzreise*? Humor is certainly not apparent in Gottschalk's *Taschenbuch für Reisende in den Harz* (first published 1806, third edition 1823), the guidebook that Heine parodies throughout the *Harzreise*. Nor is it a significant moment of *Wanderberichte* like Rebmann's, where philanthropic pathos rather than levity is the dominant tone. We must look elsewhere to find anything resembling Heine's acidulous humor, namely to the travel satire, a prolific genre in the eighteenth century.[12] Unlike the *Wanderbericht*, with its claim to authenticity, the travel satire exploited exotic or imaginary locations to mask an indictment of the domestic political scene. It is here that we find parody, drastic comparisons, and grotesque caricature of the kind that characterizes the satiric moment of the *Harzreise*. Beginning with the notorious description of Göttingen, the *Harzreise* is built on a sustained parody of Gottschalk's popular travel guide; comic effect is produced by ridiculing the guide's encyclopedic tendency and its pedantic use of statistics. In the opening sketch of Göttingen such pretensions to systematicity are mocked with the *reductio ad absurdum* of topographical description to a jumble of abstract and concrete nouns: "Schnurren, Pudeln, Dissertazionen, Theedansants, Wäscherinnen, Kompendien, Taubenbraten, Guelfenorden, Promozionskutschen, Pfeifenköpfen, Hofräthen, Justizräthen, Relegationsräthen, Profaxen und anderen Faxen" (6:83).[13]

The travel satire is a distinct genre from the *Wanderbericht:* while the latter presents itself as a critical but essentially sober eyewitness account of the state of affairs in a particular place and time, the former frequently uses techniques of masking, shifting the plot to a remote or fictional location. Satiric humor is kept out of the *Wanderbericht*, perhaps because the technique was seen as incompatible with the status of that genre as reportage. Rebmann, who tries his hand at both forms (*Wanderungen*, *Empfindsame Reise nach Schilda*), observes the distinction between them assiduously. With the *Harzreise*, however, elements of both forms are brought together in a new synthesis: the claim to an authenticity grounded in personal observation is fused with the technique of the travel satire in a new blurred genre.

One further residue of the Enlightenment *Wanderbericht* appears in the *Harzreise:* the theory of national character, a common feature of the ethnographic travelogues in this period. Motivated by the philanthropic desire to identify the universal characteristics of a postulated human nature, the ethnographers of the eighteenth century set out to inventory the visible features (physiognomomy, dress, and custom) of the world's peoples. Their observations were then used to form hypotheses concerning the distinct national character each people was thought to embody. Such observations were linked to an ongoing debate concerning the optimal form of government. This debate centered on the question of whether national character, formed by climate and other environmental conditions, determined the constitutional form appropriate to a particular land.[14] Heine plays on this theory when he ascribes "einen deutsch langsamen Charakter" (6:86) to the maltreated horses of the students at Rauschenwasser, and when he introduces a tongue-in-cheek disquisition on the character of the Brocken:

> Der Brocken ist ein Deutscher. Mit deutscher Gründlichkeit zeigt er uns, klar und deutlich, wie ein Riesenpanorama, die vielen hundert Städte, Städtchen und Dörfer, die meistens nördlich liegen, und ringsum alle Berge, Wälder, Flüsse, Flächen, unendlich weit. . . . Der Berg hat auch so etwas Deutschruhiges, Verständiges, Tolerantes; eben weil er die Dinge so weit und klar überschauen kann. . . . Durch seinen Kahlkopf, den er zuweilen mit einer weißen Nebelkappe bedeckt, giebt er sich zwar den Anstrich von Philiströsität; aber wie bey manchen andern großen Deutschen, geschieht es aus purer Ironie. Es ist sogar notorisch, daß der Brocken seine burschikosen, phantastischen Zeiten hat, z.B. die erste Maynacht. Dann wirft er seine Nebelkappe in die Luft und wird, eben so gut wie wir Uebrigen, recht echtdeutsch romantisch verrückt. (117–18)

While he ironizes the theory of national character, one of the key theoretical assumptions of the ethnographers, Heine appropriates the physiognomic mode of description prominent in the ethnographic writing of the time. This is used to produce drastic effects, as in the description of a traveling party of philistines met at the inn in Northeim. Here the authorial narrator adopts a position analogous to that of an ethnographer among a foreign people: the aim is not, however, to introduce generalizations about national character but to make visible a particular social type whose characteristics are narrow-mindedness and stubborn complacency, and who, for Heine, embodies the forces of inertia and reaction. The antithesis of this group is the personified Brocken, whose farsightedness and tolerance are presented as the *true* German traits. The participatory effect of humor is exploited above and in the physiognomic sketches to make the reader complicit in this superior gaze announced in the prefatory poem: "Auf die Berge will ich steigen, / Lachend auf euch niederschauen" (83).

### The *Harzreise* as Critique of Patriotic Tourism

In his study Hildebrand has chosen to characterize the *Harzreise* as a primarily literary journey, an odyssey in textual rather than topographical space. Given the wealth of references, overt and tacit, to other literary and non-literary texts, this is an entirely plausible assertion to make. It should not be forgotten, however, that Heine's story is not confined to an exclusively literary dimension; instead, like the *Wanderbericht*, with which it shares certain features, it describes — albeit in highly modified form — wanderings in a real geographical area. Moreover, the space which Heine's wanderer traverses, the Harz mountains, is burdened with an abundance of mythical and literary associations; it is *terra cognita*, a terrain thoroughly explored and mapped, and made accessible in numerous guides and handbooks. As Klaus Pabel has put it, what Heine undertook in the autumn of 1824 was "[eine] Wanderung in die Gegend fast vor der Tür."[15] The historical journey and the literary product that was forged out of it therefore inevitably involve a confrontation with the phenomenon of mass tourism. Hence, the *Harzreise* does not merely engage with a literary canon; it also addresses itself to a new and flourishing cultural practice. That the practice of traveling to sites deemed to possess outstanding natural beauty or especial national significance was widespread and transcended class barriers is evident from the social mix — students, commercial travelers, journeymen, and the members of the leisured classes — encountered in the hostel on the summit of the Brocken. In the following I will argue that Heine engages critically with the practice of tourism on two fronts: by unmasking the bankrupt aesthetic of nature underlying it, and by satirizing the virulent nationalism it sought to promote.

What were the reasons for the remarkable popularity of what we might now call domestic tourism in the Restoration period? The first factor was the rise in national sentiment following Napoleon's defeat and the establishment of the German Confederation at the Congress of Vienna. As early as 1815, the year of the Congress, the first of the patriotic student fraternities or *Burschenschaften* was founded at the University of Jena. These organizations traced their roots to volunteer bodies like the *Lützower Freicorps* that fought in partisan actions against French hegemony in 1813–14, and, accordingly, espoused a nationalism of a militant stamp. Although this youth movement was driven underground by the Karlsbad decrees of 1819, it had by then already played an important role in popularizing the idea of national unity. Moreover, the leaders of the movement, especially Friedrich Ludwig Jahn, advocated pedestrian tours as a means of furthering this political aim, taking the view that these would foster a sense of the essential unity of the German people. These ideas, far from remaining confined to a coterie of nationally minded students and the members of Jahn's athletics movement, the *Turnbewegung*,[16] were effectively communicated to the wider populace, with the result that patriotism became an important motive for domestic tourism. The second reason for the popularity of pedestrian tours in this period — as opposed to foreign travel — was economic. Hiking and wandering through regions that were close at hand proved an affordable recreation in the economic recession of the early post-Napoleonic period.

The *Harzreise* engages with the new phenomenon of popular tourism and its associated nature-aesthetic in a complex manner. It is characterized by a stance that is primarily, but not exclusively, critical. While Heine's wanderer, in common with contemporary tourists, undertakes a journey in an approved part of his own fatherland, guidebook in hand, there are certain respects in which he fails to conform with the conventions of the practice. For one thing, the wanderer travels for the greater part of his journey in solitude; by contrast, the national-patriotic wandering of the *Burschenschaften* was primarily a companionable activity, intended to promote a sense of *esprit de corps* among its participants. And the decision to dispense with the clichéd opening of the first version of the story, published in *Der Gesellschafter* (which has the wanderer setting out at daybreak from the inn at Osterode) effectively distances the story from the canonic Romantic narratives that inspired such wandering, thereby making the critical intention plain. It is precisely the possession of this critical faculty, the ethnographer's sharpened view for the characteristics of the society with which he comes into contact, that sets the wanderer apart from his fellow tourists.

In the *Harzreise* this acute gaze is focused on the particular understanding of nature on which the practice of tourism is founded, and on the objective conditions determining that understanding. It is no coincidence that Heine's observation concerning the loss of "Unmittelbarkeit" (96) from man's relationship to nature occurs in the Clausthal episode. In a Germany still scarcely touched by the phenomenon of large-scale industrial manufacturing, the Clausthal miners form the unwitting vanguard of a movement toward the division of labor and technical exploitation that set the seal on man's estrangement from nature.

> Da unten ist ein verworrenes Rauschen und Summen, man stößt beständig an Balken und Seile, die in Bewegung sind, um die Tonnen mit geklopften Erzen, oder das hervorgesinterte Wasser herauf zu winden. Zuweilen gelangt man auch in durchgehauene Gänge, Stollen genannt, wo man das Erz wachsen sieht, und wo der einsame Bergmann den ganzen Tag sitzt und mühsam mit dem Hammer die Erzstücke aus der Wand heraus klopft. Bis in die unterste Tiefe, wo man, wie einige behaupten, schon hören kann, wie die Leute in Amerika "*Hourrah Lafayette!*" schreien, bin ich nicht gekommen; unter uns gesagt, dort, bis wohin ich kam, schien es mir bereits tief genug: — immerwährendes Brausen und Sausen, unheimliche Maschinenbewegung, unterirdisches Quellengeriesel, von allen Seiten herabtriefendes Wasser, qualmig aufsteigende Erddünste, und das Grubenlicht immer bleicher hineinflimmernd in die einsame Nacht. (94)

In his description of the Clausthal miners Heine reveals the rift between a domestic life still dominated by the communal activity of storytelling, and a working existence that finds the miner isolated from his fellows for the duration of his shift. Unlike Novalis, who, in *Heinrich von Ofterdingen*, imagines the descent into the earth as a reconciliation between man and nature, drawing a veil over the brute facts of industrial mining in the process, Heine refuses any harmonizing transfiguration; in his version it is not so much the labor of men that is foregrounded, but the impersonal, incomprehensible movement of machinery, which at all times threatens to sweep the observer away to his doom.[17]

Heine's exposition of what goes on underneath one mountain — the restless technical exploitation of nature — furnishes the reader with an understanding of the nature-worship taking place on the summit of the Brocken. As Pabel has shown, the former is the condition of the latter: tourists in the Restoration period seek to compensate their estrangement from nature by staging rituals of nature-worship, which, although thoroughly secular in character, stimulate something like religious feeling in their participants:[18]

> Es ist ein erhabener Anblick, der die Seele zum Gebet stimmt. Wohl eine Viertelstunde standen Alle ernsthaft schweigend, und sahen, wie der schöne Feuerball im Westen allmählig versank; die Gesichter wurden vom Abendroth angestralt, die Hände falteten sich unwillkürlich; es war, als ständen wir, eine stille Gemeinde, im Schiffe eines Riesendoms, und der Priester erhöbe jetzt den Leib des Herrn, und von der Orgel ergösse sich Palestrinas ewiger Choral. (119)

By unmasking such rituals as one side of the debased coin of an alienated relationship to nature — the other being economic exploitation — Heine's narrator adopts a critical stance toward tourism. But if the wanderer is elsewhere separated from the other figures by virtue of his skepticism, he appears here as a participant, for, as Altenhofer has pointed out, the spectacle of the sunset is not itself subject to ironic rupture, the illusion is not shattered until the commercial traveler's banal exclamation: "Wie ist die Natur doch im Allgemeinen so schön!" For the duration of the spectacle the narrator is content for his own individuality to be subsumed under the collective experience.[19] The desire for differentiation from the philistines expressed in the superior gaze is tempered here by the will to integration: alongside the critical "ich" there appears a companionable "wir." On the Brocken the wanderer feels himself embraced and kissed by his fellow countrymen, and he plays an exuberant part in the chaotic evening revelries. That is not to say that the critical view is abandoned: the satiric gaze is never keener than in the description of the bacchanal, which becomes a nightmarish sketch of Restoration society. Rather, the adoption of an insider view allows Heine to pursue a subtle critique of tourism that nevertheless pulls up short of condemning the practice *per se*. It is not Heine's intention to deprive the reader of his or her enjoyment of such recreation; instead he must have hoped that the popularity of Harz tourism would help his book to commercial success. Apart from contributing to the popularity of wandering as a low-cost recreation, the post-Napoleonic economic depression had also stimulated an appetite for a literature that allowed the reading public to indulge its taste for vicarious travel.[20]

The relentless commercial exploitation of nature is one reason offered in the *Harzreise* for the loss of unmediatedness from man's relations to nature. Another reason lies in the omnipresence of artistic representations which interpose themselves between the beholder and nature, prestructuring both perception itself and the responses to it. The following passage addresses the mediating role of art in the experience of nature:

> Die Wolken, so bizarr gestaltet sie auch zuweilen erscheinen, tragen ein weißes oder doch ein mildes, mit dem blauen Himmel und der grünen Erde harmonisch correspondirendes Colorit, so daß alle Farben einer Gegend wie leise Musik in einander schmelzen, und jeder Naturanblick krampfstillend und gemüthberuhigend wirkt. — Der selige Hoffmann würde die Wolken buntscheckig bemalt haben. — Eben wie ein großer Dichter, weiß die Natur auch mit den wenigsten Mitteln die größten Effekte hervor zu bringen. (91)

As Pabel has remarked, it is not nature itself, but rather its "harmonisch correspondirendes Colorit" — that is, its apperception in the medium of art — that is presented as having an antispasmodic and calmative effect. The reference to Hoffmann and the comparison of nature to "ein großer Dichter" work to make visible the presence of the author who scrutinizes his tableaux even as he makes them. By thus putting the aesthetic machinery on view, the narrator demonstrates the necessary derivativeness of the literary representation of nature which must endlessly recycle the phrasal stock of its predecessors and of art criticism. This derivativeness is recapitulated in a touristic appreciation of nature that has sunk to the level of cliché; so much is clear from the tradesman's bathetic exclamation ("im Allgemeinen"), and from the fact that the Brocken visitors foregather to take in the view at specific times — sunset and sunrise, as if viewing a diorama.[21]

By foregrounding the author's role, Heine shows that nature, far from being a moral source in the sense understood by the Romantics, amounts to a storehouse of freely available symbols whose human value is dependent on the specific construction put on them. Such a disillusioning approach might be considered inimical to pathos, but Heine convincingly evokes an ecstatic response to nature that is no less authentic for its being accompanied by reflections on the mediatedness and constructedness of that experience. Indeed, the emotional content of the response may seem all the more intense for such reflections.

The second significant dimension of Heine's critical engagement with tourism gets to grips with the use of the practice in shoring up nationalist ideology. I will want to argue that the text subverts the patriotic tourism practiced by the *Burschenschaften*, thereby paving the way for Heine's later adoption of cosmopolitanism. In his *Deutsches Volkstum*, which appeared in 1810, Friedrich Ludwig Jahn, then a teacher at the Plamann Institute in Berlin, specifically advocates what he calls "Vaterländische Wanderungen" as a means of building up a specifically German national consciousness. Central to Jahn's political convictions was the idea of the people (*Volk*), whose essential unity Jahn conveyed in the metaphor of a living organism. The people must be brought to awareness of its common identity if political unity — the ultimate goal for Jahn and the nationalists — is to be attained: "Kennenlernen muß sich das Volk als Volk, sonst stirbt es ab."[22] In asserting a distinct German identity, Jahn takes up the theory of national character, but, unlike the eighteenth-century philanthropists, he employs it in an effort to demonstrate the cultural superiority of the German nation. Among those traits cited as specifically German is the desire to wander itself ("Uralt ist des Deutschen Reisetrieb") — an attribute which Jahn approvingly links to the warlike nature of the Germanic tribes.[23]

Despite the avowedly xenophobic and militant nature of the patriotic student movement — expressed in the writings of Arndt and Jahn — Heine found it possible, at least for a time, to move in such circles. This requires some explanation, since the inflated rhetoric of its canonical texts can all too easily obscure our view of the early nationalist movement. Their bombast was a product of its time, of the crushing sense of national inferiority that weighed heavily on the members of a disenfranchised bourgeoisie. This party saw the fragmentation of the German-speaking lands as the chief obstacle to political progress; it saw national unity as the means to a citizens' parliament. It was a paradox of early German nationalism to be at once narrowly chauvinistic and fervently committed to the ideals of constitutionalism. Jahn had even played an active part in the Stein-Hardenberg reforms in Prussia, serving briefly on a committee overseeing army reform. It was ultimately because of its constitutional and national enthusiasms that the student movement would fall foul of the forces of reaction in the German Confederation.

Heine's repudiation of national-liberal ideology and his movement toward cosmopolitanism has to be viewed against the background of the worsening social position of German Jews in the early Restoration. Anti-Jewish sentiment, intensified by the pressures of economic recession, had flared up in the so-called "Hep Hep" riots of 1819. Moreover, German Jews were the principal losers when the reform process was sent into reverse in Prussia. When the equality laws, introduced during the French occupation, were finally repealed in 1822, Jews found themselves barred from public office.[24] This development put an end to Heine's prospects of a legal career in Prussia and set his hopes of securing a respectable place in German society back considerably. For as long as those hopes remained viable, Heine had been able to entertain the idea of reform on national-liberal lines; with their demise, the xenophobic and anti-Semitic rhetoric of the nationalists — and especially of the *Burschenschaftler* — must have seemed intolerable.

In the *Harzreise* nationalist complacencies are attacked on two levels: physiognomic description is employed to produce a caricature of a typical corps student, and stereotypical assumptions about the German national character are subverted. In the course of the unruly evening meal in the *Brockenhaus*, a confrontation takes place between a Swiss citizen and a student from Greifswald, a new university then notorious for the jingoistic fervor of its students. Taking offense at the assertion that the Germans "wie mit der wahren Freyheit, so auch mit der wahren Genügsamkeit unbekannt seyen" (122–23), the Greifswald student responds with a show of aggression: "er beteuerte, dass deutsche Thatkraft und Einfältigkeit noch nicht erloschen sey, schlug sich dröhnend auf die Brust, und leerte eine ungeheure Stange Weißbier." There follows a caricature of the man from Greifswald, which focuses on the medieval dress then affected by nationally minded students:

> Dieser war ein Mann aus jenen Zeiten, als die Läuse gute Tage hatten und die Friseure zu verhungern fürchteten. Er trug herabhängend langes Haar, ein ritterliches Barett, einen schwarzen altdeutschen Rock, ein schmutziges Hemd, das zugleich das Amt einer Weste versah, und darunter ein Medaillon mit einem Haarbüschel von Blüchers Schimmel. Er sah aus wie ein Narr in Lebensgröße. (123)

Wherever assertions are made about the character of the Germans, these are in conflict with the reigning assumptions of ideologues like Jahn. The description of the "character" of the Brocken itself begins with an apparent affirmation of German thoroughness; this is followed by a reference to a philistinism alleviated only by episodes in which the personified Brocken "wie wir Übrigen" becomes "recht echt-deutsch romantisch verrückt." Inverting an anecdote concerning two Chinese scholars who had appeared before a paying public in Berlin, Heine imagines a German being put on show in China, with a sign stating his qualities as consisting in "Philosophiren, Tabakrauchen und Geduld" (121). Here Heine departs from the stereotype, fostered by Jahn and Arndt and invoked by the Greifswald student, of German energy, forcefulness, and militance. (We recall the reference to the "deutsch langsamen Charakter" of the horses seen at Rauschenwasser.) Far from recognizing the oft-affirmed combativeness of the Germans, the *Harzreise* diagnoses a people in the grip of a profound lethargy. Having set a naïve corps student to rights on the esoteric sense of the Berlin ballet, the narrator suggests that Spontini's operas with their bombastic, martial music might be "ein heroisches Mittel . . . um unser erschlafftes Volk kriegerisch zu stärken" (122). The quip is only half in irony, for the task that Heine sets himself in the *Harzreise* is to shake his readership out of the leaden despondency and resignation that had paralyzed all political debate. This is the esoteric sense of the second night's dream, in which the narrator finds himself in the role of a knight who descends into the depths of the earth in an attempt to waken the sleeping princess with a kiss — an allegory of the author's mission to bring his readership to political awareness.

Heine's rejection of the narrow and zealous variant of nationalism that he found among the student fraternities cleared the way for his embrace of cosmopolitanism, a political ideal that had enjoyed widespread currency in the late Enlightenment.[25] Although Heine did not set out his views on the ideal of a universal brotherhood of man until after the July 1830 revolution (in *Die romantische Schule*), we know he was already styling himself as a cosmopolitan at the time of his Harz journey. In a supplement to *Der Gesellschafter*, published on 30 August 1826, Karl Dörne, a commercial traveler, reacting to his representation in the *Harzreise* as a sentimental journeyman tailor, provided the following account of his meeting with Heine:

> Im Herbst 1824 kehrte ich von einer Geschäfts-Reise von Osterode nach Clausthal zurück. . . . Etwa auf der Hälfte des Weges traf ich mit einem jungen Manne zusammen, den ich genau beschreibe, damit er sich überzeugt, daß ich ihn wirklich damals gesehen. Er war etwa 5 Fuß 6 Zoll groß, konnte 25–27 Jahr alt seyn, hatte blonde Haare, blaue Augen, eine einnehmende Gesichtsbildung, war schlank von Gestalt, trug einen braunen Ueberrock, gelbe Pantalons, gestreifte Weste, schwarzes Halstuch und hatte eine grüne Kappe auf dem Kopfe und einen Tornister von grüner Wachsleinwand auf dem Rücken. . . . Der Fremde sah mich mit einem sardonischen Lächeln von der Seite an, nannte sich Peregrinus und sagte, er sey ein Cosmopolit, der auf Kosten des türkischen Kaisers reise, um Rekruten an zu werben.[26]

The accuracy of this reported exchange can be taken for granted since Heine, who read Dörne's account, did not dispute any of its details. Robertson, pointing to the enlightened treatment of the Jews in the Ottoman Empire, sees Heine's play-acting in terms of compensatory fantasy.[27] While it is true that Heine occasionally imagined himself into a foreign, non-German identity — his declaration "Ich bin stolz darauf ein Perser zu seyn,"[28] made in 1824, is characteristic — this tendency was countered by his awareness of his almost visceral attachment to the language and culture of Germany, a point that Robertson acknowledges.

Dörne's account provides support for the view that Heine conceived of his Harz journey as a cosmopolitan journey in the sense understood by Rebmann and other Enlightenment authors. Given that Heine undertakes "eine Reise vor der eigenen Tür" it is not immediately obvious that this is the case. But what marks Heine's and Rebmann's wanderings as cosmopolitan is not so much the area traversed as the sensibility brought to bear on all that is observed. What both men possess is a critical awareness that constantly refers the phenomena observed on a local level to a global political horizon. I have already remarked that the narrator's adoption of the gaze of the ethnographer produces a defamiliarizing effect, as if the wanderer were reporting on a foreign culture. Indeed the foreign and the exotic are constantly present in the *Harzreise*, serving as a standard against which the narrator constantly assays the state of his own nation's culture. The Orient (represented by Turkey and China) serves as the antipode of a European world gripped by an ideology of asceticism and renunciation. In the Goslar episode, which tackles the Christian *memento mori* ethos, the burial customs of the Orient are invoked as examples of an approach to death that does not negate the claims of the living:

> Die Türken begraben ihre Todten weit schöner als wir, ihre Kirchhöfe sind ordentlich [*sic*] Gärten, und da sitzen sie auf ihren weißen, beturbanten Grabsteinen, unter dem Schatten einer Zypresse, und streichen ihre ernsthaften Bärte, und rauchen ruhig ihren türkischen Tabak aus ihren langen türkischen Pfeifen; — und bey den Chinesen gar ist es eine ordentliche Lust zuzusehen, wie sie auf den Ruhestätten ihrer Todten manierlich herumtänzeln, und beten, und Thee trinken, und die Geige spielen, und die geliebten Gräber gar hübsch zu verzieren wissen mit allerley vergoldetem Lattenwerk, Porzellanfigürchen, Fetzen von buntem Seidenzeug, künstlichen Blumen, und farbigen Laternchen. (100–101)

This affirmative discourse on oriental funerary culture provides the bridge between the leaden gloom of the Goslar cathedral and the enlivening love escapade that follows. For the wanderer, the cathedral's medieval wooden crucifix depicts "das Hinsterben eines Menschen, aber nicht eines gottgebornen Heilands" (100), thus epitomizing a life-denying Christian ethos of renunciation, subsequently banished by "das schöne Antlitz" (101) of a young woman of Goslar. Having witnessed the sunrise that follows the night of dissipation, the narrator again invokes the Orient as the realm of a joyous sensuality, formerly present in Hellenic culture but effaced in the modern Europe:

> In meinem Magen sah es so nüchtern aus, wie in der Goslarschen Stephanskirche. Aber mit dem arabischen Trank rieselte mir auch der warme Orient durch die Glieder, östliche Rosen umdufteten mich, süße Bulbullieder erklangen, die Studenten verwandelten sich in Kameele, die Brockenhausmädchen, mit ihren Congrevischen Blicken, wurden zu Houris, die Philisternasen wurden Minarets u.s.w. (128)

Though this is a jocular rehearsal of the stereotypical trappings of a modish literary Orientalism, the picture of a mythic Orient again invites comparison with the realities of contemporary Germany. The rhapsody of the Orient flows naturally from the description of the rising sun: here, the idea of a sensuality of a kind different from the gross self-indulgence of the previous night's revels is introduced. As elsewhere in the *Harzreise*, light is seen banishing night — and the fog that Heine employs as a metaphor for obscurantism and delusion, but also for alcoholic intoxication.[29] The fog of alcoholic excess that had veiled the Brocken, dulling the senses and the will of the revelers, is implicitly contrasted with the wakefulness imparted by the Arabian stimulant, coffee. Thus the Orient appears as the preserve of a sensual enjoyment linked with undimmed awareness of the world, by contrast with an Occident which takes its solace in narcosis.

Although the Harz mountains form the backdrop for the narrated journey, the city of Berlin looms on the horizon, casting its shadow over the work. As Karl Varnhagen von Ense rightly noted in his review of the *Reisebilder: Erster Theil:* "Der Verfasser geht von Göttingen aus und besucht den Harz, hat aber dabei beständig Berlin vor der Seele."[30] This is true in the important respect that the *Reisebilder* — though composed with an eye to the wider market — are addressed in the first instance to a readership in the Prussian capital. This readership comprised, as Norbert Altenhofer has observed, habitués of Rahel Varnhagen von Ense's literary salon, students in Berlin and Göttingen, and the members of the *Verein für Cultur und Wissenschaft der Juden*. Both the humorous discourse on the esoteric meaning of the Berlin ballet and the ironic juxtaposition of the mores of an "ästhetische Theegesellschaft" with the wild revelry of Walpurgisnacht are knowing in-jokes, calculated to appeal to this metropolitan set. But the salon provides more than a target readership; it is the source both of the characteristic discursive style — "das assoziative Verfahren, der Konversationston, die Anspielungstechnik"[31] — and of the urbane skepticism in which current events are weighed. These are key components of the distinctly cosmopolitan consciousness with which the wanderer views the mores of Restoration Germany.

This critical consciousness is at work everywhere, destroying the illusions cherished by nationalist ideologues and fostered by Romantic literature. Hildebrand has remarked of Heine's disillusioning treatment of the mines episode: "Er entwirft eine parodistische Kontrafaktur der mystischen Bergwerksromantik mit ihrem Hang zur geheimnisvollen Verdunklung, phantastischen Selbstversenkung ins Innere und ihrem — dem Lichtsymbol der Aufklärung entgegensetzten — politischen Obskurantismus."[32] But Heine also uses this episode to combat the political quietism that he deprecates in Romanticism by imagining the mine as a place which, for all its remoteness, is inextricably bound up with the outside world. Thus the innermost recesses of the mine correspond not to the profundities of the soul but to a place "wo man, wie Einige behaupten, schon hören kann, wie die Leute in Amerika 'Hourrah Lafayette!' schreien" (94). With this topical reference to the enthusiastic reception in America of General Lafayette, hero of that nation's War of Independence, the text establishes a connection between the privations of the miners in a remote corner of the Harz and the struggle for emancipation on the global political stage.

The struggle being conducted on the miners' behalf is not their only link with the global dimension, for the terms of their servitude are also dictated from afar. The wanderer's guide, a miner, regales him with an account of the visit of the Duke of Cambridge to the Dorothea pit some years previously. One of the mine galleries had been decorated for the occasion with lanterns, flowers, and greenery. The guide ("eine kreuzehrliche, pudeldeutsche Natur"; 95) concludes with a heartfelt expression of loyalty to the Duke and the House of Hanover, which controlled both Göttingen and part of the Harz. Here, as elsewhere, the text takes up the theme of national character, reflecting on the nature of German loyalty as embodied by the guileless miner. This loyalty, fervent and unquestioning, is shown to be misplaced, invested as it is in the person of a foreign sovereign. The sense of deception is intensified by the description of the mock-idyll staged for the benefit of the Duke; testifying to a degenerate nature-aesthetic, this subterranean banquet is a travesty of the simple, unalienated existence lost to the miners. Overall, the mines episode ministers to a cosmopolitan or anti-national political analysis by showing a world governed by interested parties rather than by nation states.

Nor does the critical gaze spare places of iconic significance to nationalists: thus the dilapidated condition of the former imperial free city of Goslar is made to stand, *pars pro toto*, for the moribund Holy Roman Empire: "tausendjährige Döme werden abgebrochen, und Kaiserstühle in die Rumpelkammer geworfen" (6:100). Although the fate of the Empire had been sealed by the advance of Napoleon in 1806, it continued to provide a focus for national sentiment. In Heine's treatment the sooty figures of the emperors that adorn the town hall are reduced to "gebratene Universitätspedelle" (99), scorched, as it were, by the recent European conflagration. The text tackles the ruin cult, a characteristic feature of patriotic tourism, with similar irreverence.[33] This craze, which grew out of the Romantic exaltation of the Middle Ages, lent itself to a nationalist ideology that propagated the myth of the essentially Germanic character of that era. Gottschalk's *Taschenbuch* is typical of contemporary guidebooks in linking the appreciation of medieval ruins to the idea of a specifically national heritage: "Ergriffen wird sich der Freund altdeutscher Geschichte fühlen bei'm Anschauen der vielen Trümmern und ehrwürdigen Reste aus der Vorzeit unserer Nation."[34] Such banalities must have been an irresistible provocation to Heine's satiric ire. His text mischievously alludes to Gottschalk before remarking dismissively of the ruins at Osterode: "Sie bestehen nur noch aus der Hälfte eines großen, dickmaurigen, wie von Krebsschäden angefressenen Turms" (89). The Brocken, itself a preeminent national shrine, is demythologized, as we have seen, by association with a crapulous student body. Even the wanderer's description of a roast of veal "groß wie die Chimborasso in miniatur" (6:92) may be read as a comically belittling reference to the Brocken. Chimborazo, a peak in the Ecuadorian Andes, was at the time regarded as the highest mountain in the world: the first European to ascend it, Alexander von Humboldt, had described the mountain in his *Ansichten der Natur* (1807) as "sechsmal höher als der Brocken." In any event, the mention of Mount Chimborazo demonstrates that the wanderer in the German heartland remains mindful of grander peaks elsewhere in the world.

Much of what has been described previously (the trenchant criticism of national chauvinism, the questioning of assumptions about national character, the surreptitious introduction of a global dimension to the narrative of a provincial journey) can be regarded as elements of an incipient cosmopolitan analysis. This becomes apparent when we compare these elements with the apparently full fledged cosmopolitanism articulated by Heine in *Die romantische Schule*. A lengthy citation from that work is required to clarify this:

> Man befahl uns den Patriotismus und wir wurden Patrioten; denn wir tun alles, was uns unsere Fürsten befehlen.
>
> Man muß sich aber unter diesem Patriotismus nicht dasselbe Gefühl denken, das hier in Frankreich diesen Namen führt. Der Patriotismus des Franzosen besteht darin, daß sein Herz erwärmt wird, durch diese Wärme sich ausdehnt, sich erweitert, daß es nicht mehr bloß die nächsten Angehörigen, sondern ganz Frankreich, das ganze Land der Civilisazion, mit seiner Liebe umfaßt; der Patriotismus des Deutschen hingegen besteht darin, daß sein Herz enger wird, daß es sich zusammenzieht, wie Leder in der Kälte, daß er das Fremdländische haßt; daß er nicht mehr Weltbürger, nicht mehr Europäer, sondern nur ein enger Teutscher seyn will. Da sahen wir nun das idealische Flegelthum, das Herr Jahn in System gebracht; es begann die schäbige, plumpe, ungewaschene Opposizion gegen eine Gesinnung, die eben das Herrlichste und Heiligste ist, was Deutschland hervorgebracht hat, nemlich gegen jene Humanität, gegen jene allgemeine Menschen-Verbrüderung, gegen jenen Cosmopolitismus, dem unsere großen Geister, Lessing, Herder, Schiller, Goethe, Jean Paul, dem alle Gebildeten in Deutschland immer gehuldigt haben. (8/1:141)

What is interesting about this passage is its appropriation of the rhetoric of patriotism to make the case for cosmopolitanism, equated with "Humanität." This tactic is dictated by the expectations of the French readers to whom *Die romantische Schule* was addressed in the first instance. Given this fact, it is important not to make too much of the distinction between "French" and "German" varieties of patriotism, although the scorn poured on the latter smacks of the bitterness of recent exile — following his move to Paris in 1831, Heine would never again reside in Germany. The implicit and crucial distinction is that between a broader and more generous patriotism akin to that current in the late Enlightenment, and a narrow variety predicated on the nation state in all its linguistic and ethnic uniqueness. In the above passage Heine recurs to the Enlightenment position, encapsulated in the definition of "Der Patriot" offered by Adelung's *Grammatisch-kritisches Wörterbuch:* "eine Person, welche das allgemeine Beste auch zum Nachtheile ihres eigenen Besten befördert, welche die allgemeine Wohlfahrt ihrer eigenen vorziehet." Characteristically, the same dictionary contextualizes the term "Vaterland" in the sentence: "Die Erde ist unser aller Vaterland."[35] In this perspective the true patriot is the world citizen, whose concern for the common good embraces the whole of humanity. The above extract from *Die romantische Schule* makes a similar appeal to a patriotism grounded in altruism, in which allegiance to France as "das ganze Land der Civilisazion" in reality entails loyalty to the ideal of the Universal Nation born with the advent of the French Republic.

In *Die romantische Schule*, patriotism of the narrow kind is linked with servility, just as it had been in the *Harzreise:* the glorification of the people considered as the fundament of the nation state is represented as a falsehood perpetuated by the true beneficiaries of nationalist ideology, the aristocracy. Once again, the attack is intensified by focusing on the person of Jahn — not named in the *Harzreise*, but recognizable from the caricature of the Greifswald student and the use of the sarcastic neologism "Turngemeinplätzen" (128) to dismiss the platitudes of the Brocken visitors' book. Jahn becomes the embodiment of the "schäbige, plumpe, ungewaschene Opposition" to a generous cosmopolitanism, which, Heine tells his readers, had been cherished by Germany's foremost writers. Skepticism about the war of liberation, presented as the project of the aristocracy in *Die romantische Schule*, is also foreshadowed in the earlier work: we recall the walls of the inn decorated with "Bilder aus dem Befreyungskriege, worauf treu dargestellt stand, wie wir alle Helden waren" (89). In several respects, then, the *Harzreise* can be seen as heralding the cosmopolitanism in whose cause Heine would labor for the rest of his life, and which he believed would eventually become "die allgemeine Gesinnung in Europa."[36]

## Wandering as Sensual and Political Emancipation

Before characterizing the *Harzreise* as a stage on Heine's path to the programmatic "Versöhnung von Geist und Materie," Hildebrand sums up his findings as follows: "Die *Harzreise* — so hat die Analyse gezeigt — ist insgesamt von dem Bemühen getragen, den für Heine problematischen Dualismus zwischen Seele und Verstand, Gemüts- und Erscheinungswelt im Horizont eines sensualistischen Ganzheitsideals zu überwinden."[37] While this argument is compelling, what it leaves unstated is that the text strives toward a reconciliation of body and spirit by presenting its protagonist as a wanderer. As will be seen in the discussion of Büchner's *Lenz*, the wanderer motif lends itself to narratives that seek to comprehend man as a mind-body duality, that is, in anthropological terms. (Hildebrand makes no reference to the tradition of empirical anthropology in his discussion of Heine's sensualism.) Moving through the terrain of the Harz, Heine's wanderer feels the exigencies of physical desire (hunger, thirst, fatigue), and the pleasure of its satisfaction. At the same time, his senses and his critical faculty are stimulated by the unaccustomed circumstances of the journey.

In a similar way to Büchner, Heine grounds the claims of the individual to emancipation in the *a priori* experience of corporeality in wandering. For Heine, however, this experience leads not only to an awareness of man's unfree state in a society that places undue value on renunciation and individualism but also to a revelation of his immense capacity for taking pleasure in the physical world. Hence, the imperative of emancipation is based on the awareness of a discrepancy between the human capacity for enjoyment and its suppression in a society where renunciation — "das dunkle Hirngespinst / Das uns Lust und Lieb' verleidet" (109) —; of both the material and the political kind has become the norm.

Although the research, perhaps taking its cue from Sammons's thesis concerning Heine's "fundamental instability,"[38] has persisted in claiming that Heine's narrators are protean shape-shifters lacking a stable identity, it can be countered that Heine is "one of the most corporeally present personas in the whole of German writing."[39] The corporeal dimension gives substance to the agile, combative narrator who is constantly getting the better of dull-witted philistines and boorish chauvinists. It is in this combative persona, lashing his enemies with the Harlequin's whip, that the "carnivalising tendency," which Grubacic perceptively identified as the hallmark of the narrative style of the *Reisebilder*, is most evident.[40] And it is the very physicality of the narrator's persona — made manifest in his wanderings — that itself plays an important part in the carnivalization of the narrative. From the encomium of Göttingen's beer and sausages to the breakfast in the Brocken guest house, appetite is the wanderer's constant companion and signature trait. It is worth noting that, on one of the only two occasions on which the term "Sehnsucht" — the defining attribute of Romantic wandering — is mentioned, the narrator is referring to his "Sehnsucht nach einem Frühstück" (128).[41]

There is an ironical boastfulness in the narrator's references to his capacity for food and drink, which attests to a vitality strengthened by wandering through the Harz: in Clausthal he tackles a roast of veal "groß wie der Chimborasso in miniatur"; of his consumption of drink on the Brocken he remarks laconically: "Ich kann viel vertragen" (126). The impression is created of a Rabelaisian rebel whose strength and insubordination announce themselves in a prodigious appetite. It would be wrong, however, to see such braggadocio as an exercise in self-aggrandizing on Heine's part:[42] it is no more to be identified with author's historical person than assertions like the following: "Was mich betrifft, so habe ich in der Naturwissenschaft mein eigenes System, und demnach theile ich Alles ein: in dasjenige, was man essen kann, und in dasjenige, was man nicht essen kann" (129–30). Here the narrator briefly dons the mask of a philistine in order to lampoon an arid rationalism capable of comprehending nature only in terms of taxonomic categories.

The wanderer's increased vitality is not only a matter of physical stamina and mental agility: the journey also enables the demonstration of amatory prowess. In Goslar the sight of a beautiful woman — who bestows a smile on the stranger passing in the street below — gives rise to an adventure in which the erotic and subversive moments are blended. Returning to the scene, the wanderer climbs to the window to steal a spray of flowers, defying "die aufgesperrten Mäuler, versteinerten Nasen und Glotzaugen" (101) of the passers-by. In its stereotypical components — the woman at the window, the knapsack-bearing wanderer outside; the use of the formula "Ich reis' morgen fort und komme wohl nie wieder!" — this scene reprises elements of the erotic vagrancy of such Romantic narratives as *Franz Sternbalds Wanderungen*.

Heine's sensualistic ideal, which seeks to reconcile the spiritual and corporeal dimensions of the individual, would eventually set him at odds with Hegel's philosophy of history, which asserts the primacy of the "objective spirit." Proceeding from the well-founded assumption that the tripartite structure of the *Bergidylle* is modeled on Hegel's triadic model of history, Hildebrand argues that Heine interprets Hegel in a sensualistic direction.[43] As we have seen, Heine's use of the wanderer motif specifically foregrounds the appetitive and corporeal dimensions. By fleshing out his narrator in this way, Heine lends especial weight to the individual human subject. This position was bound to lead to a conflict with a Hegelian objectivism. In the essay *Verschiedenartige Geschichtsauffassung* (1833), Heine voices objections to the Hegelian understanding of history as an ineluctable and impersonal process. There the claim to happiness in the here-and-now is emphatically asserted against a teleological philosophy that sees liberation as the end point of a historical process of indeterminate length:

> Das Leben ist weder Zweck noch Mittel; das Leben ist ein Recht. Das Leben will dieses Recht geltend machen gegen den erstarrenden Tod, gegen die Vergangenheit, und dieses Geltendmachen ist die Revoluzion. Der elegische Indifferentismus der Historiker und Poeten soll unsere Energie nicht lähmen bey diesem Geschäfte; und die Schwärmerey der Zukunftbeglücker soll uns nicht verleiten, die Interessen der Gegenwart und das zunächst zu verfechtende Menschenrecht, das Recht zu leben, aufs Spiel zu setzen. (10:302)

This affirmation of the right of the individual to the enjoyment of the present moment and the rejection of the millenarianism of the "Zukunftbeglücker" partakes of the spirit of the humanistic *carpe diem* maxim. It is this refusal to subordinate the real interests of living persons to an eschatology, whether of Christian or idealistic origin, that forms the basis of Heine's political convictions. Heine's wanderer presses the claims of the individual to the enjoyment of life, and, in so doing, asserts the rights of the individual to be considered as the creative subject of history.

## Demolishing the Sublime: Büchner's *Lenz* (1839)

### Lenz and the Wanderliteratur of the Biedermeierzeit

The opening sentences of Georg Büchner's *Lenz* (1839) appear to set the scene for a conventional account of an excursion in the mountains, a favored setting for the practice of recreational wandering in the *Biedermeier* era:[44] "Den 20. [Januar] ging Lenz durch's Gebirg. Die Gipfel und hohe Bergflächen im Schnee, die Täler hinunter graues Gestein, grüne Flächen, Felsen und Tannen."[45] As the narrative unfolds, it becomes clear that the uncanny stillness conveyed by the absence of the verb in the elliptical second sentence relates to the protagonist's malaise, but at this point the impression created by the enumeration of static objects is of a pared-down description of a landscape painting. The mention of a date and the suggestion of landscape would likely have put a contemporary reader in mind of a *Wanderbericht*, an account of an actual journey undertaken on foot, a genre best exemplified by the series *Das malerische und romantische Deutschland*. But such expectations are already unsettled by the mention of the branches of the firs hanging heavily in the damp air, by the attributes "schwer" and "feucht," and by the description of the sluggish movement of the fog through the undergrowth: "so träg, so plump" (the adverb "so" serving to meld our perspective with that of Lenz).

The apparent similarity to a *Wanderbericht* is finally dispelled in the next pair of sentences: "Er ging gleichgültig weiter, es lag ihm nichts am Weg, bald auf- bald abwärts." For a bourgeois wanderer embarked on a pedestrian tour, the path is naturally of great importance, as are the surroundings. Lenz's indifference to these indicates the degree to which he is sunk in melancholy solipsism. It is the next sentence, however, that reveals that the situation described cannot be reduced to a conventional narrative of wandering: "Müdigkeit spürte er keine, nur war es ihm manchmal unangenehm, daß er nicht auf dem Kopf gehn konnte." This formulation has provoked more interpretive hand-wringing than perhaps any other in the entire story. Niccolini, who reads *Lenz* as an allegory of the act of writing, sees the image of inversion as an expression of Lenz's will to remake the world perceived by him into a literary construct. Knapp asserts that the image gives the reader immediate insight into the disturbed mental state of the protagonist, while at the same time appealing for understanding. Kubitschek has pointed to the ambivalence of the sentence, which makes it unclear as to whether Lenz or the world itself is to be understood as disordered.[46]

I will not list the other obvious differences between *Lenz* and contemporary *Wanderberichte*. The object of the exercise is to introduce a general thesis about the way in which Büchner's narrative relates to the cultural practice of recreational wandering, namely that the text, apart from breaking with the boundaries of contemporary genre, denies the commonly held view that the contemplation of landscape is a remedy for melancholia, or what today we would label depression.[47] Verifying this thesis and establishing its implications will require detailed attention to the representation of landscape in *Lenz*.

## Wanderliteratur and the Biedermeier Landscape Aesthetic

Recreational wandering in the *Biedermeierzeit* was not primarily a matter of therapy: the emphasis was on enjoyment and recreation, on the pleasures to be had from landscape and from moderate physical exertion. Nevertheless, therapeutic and prophylactic considerations formed an implicit part of the program. In his discussion of the pre-1848 *Wanderliteratur*,[48] Wolfgang Albrecht argues that the characteristic conception of nature in this genre is that of "einem . . . jedem Bürger offenstehenden *schönen* Erholungs-, Flucht-, oder Kompensationsraum."[49] In other words, the assumption that the practice of wandering is essential to the maintenance of psychic health is always present in the *Wanderliteratur*, even where it is not explicitly presented in terms of preventing or alleviating melancholia. Albrecht discerns a pattern of behavior common to the *Wanderberichte* he assessed:

> Gewandert und auf Gipfel gestiegen wurde zwecks intensivierter und vor allem genußvoller, mannigfaltiger Naturwahrnehmung; um gründlichere Ein- und Rundblicke zu gewinnen, um sich Panoramen zu vergegenwärtigen, wie es von den frühen Alpenwanderern bis zum "Spaziergänger" Seume feste Tradition unter Fußreisenden geworden war.[50]

At some point in the excursion the wanderer typically ascends to some elevated position in order to survey the terrain through which he is passing. The ascent to a high point has two effects: it produces a pleasurable physical sensation associated with deeper breathing and the swelling breast; and it allows the surroundings to be viewed as landscape, thus fulfilling the aesthetic requirement. These two elements, the expansive physical sensation and the aesthetic view, combine to create the impression of freedom. The elevated perspective is particularly important since this conveys the sense of being borne aloft, far above the mundane world with its cares and pressures, in short, a feeling of sublimity. Since the *Sturm und Drang* period, to which Lenz belonged, the Alpine landscape had been hymned as a realm of liberty, an idea that found its most frequently quoted expression in Schiller's "Auf den Bergen ist die Freiheit!" from the drama *Die Braut von Messina* (1803) — the phrase appears in modified form as the motto to Blumenhagen's *Wanderbuch.*[51] It is worth quoting Blumenhagen's prefatory poem, as Albrecht does, to clarify the nature of the sense of freedom sought out and experienced by wanderers in the mountains:

> Auf den Bergen wohnt die Freiheit;
> Auf den Bergen wohnt das Licht!
> Menschenbrust wird leichter droben,
> Was sie drückte, fühlt sie nicht.
> Hin drum zu den blauen Höhen,
> Wo die frischen Lüfte wehen;
> Fern der Erdmisere da,
> Und der Sternenhimmel nah! —

In these lines freedom is associated both with the expansive and uplifting physical sensation of the swelling breast and with the aesthetic elements of spaciousness and light — the reference to "Erdmisere" shows that compensation of a specifically emotional kind is expected of the excursion into the mountains. The idea of landscape as therapy for melancholia as promulgated by C. C. L. Hirschfeld is thus implicitly but recognizably present.

This brings us to the primary purpose of the wanderer's ascent to the hilltop or mountain summit: the possibility this offers for viewing nature as landscape. At this point we need to consider what is meant by the term landscape. Ritter provides an explanation:

> Landschaft ist Natur, die im Anblick für einen fühlenden und empfindenden Betrachter ästhetisch gegenwärtig ist: Nicht die Felder vor der Stadt, . . . nicht die Gebirge und die Steppen der Hirten und Karawanen . . . sind als solche schon "Landschaft." Sie werden dies erst, wenn sich der Mensch ihnen ohne praktischen Zweck in "freier" genießender Anschauung zuwendet, um als er selbst in der Natur zu sein. Mit seinem Hinausgehen verändert die Natur ihr Gesicht.[52]

This definition is useful in that it makes clear that landscape as such is constituted in the act of seeing. Ritter's assertion that viewing nature as landscape is a "free" and disinterested activity (in the sense of the "reines uninteressiertes Wohlgefallen" that for Kant is essential to the appreciation of nature and of art)[53] does, however, require some qualification. Insofar as bourgeois wanderers were seeking a form of compensation, they inevitably had a purpose in mind.[54] To this extent viewing nature as landscape is arguably a far from disinterested activity. Further, classical landscape painting constructs nature as space organized around a unique central perspective. Such a treatment has the effect of privileging the viewer over what is viewed, presupposing the existence of a sovereign subject for whom the landscape exists. We might say, therefore, that the classical landscape carries a certain ideological charge, since it places the subject in a commanding position with respect to nature.

To judge from the *Wanderliteratur* produced in the *Biedermeierzeit*, bourgeois wandering was demonstrably in thrall to a painterly aesthetic: this is evident from the title of the series *Das malerische und romantische Deutschland*, and it is borne out by an examination of the engravings that accompany the verbal descriptions of wandering in that series. And although the central perspective of classical landscape painting is no longer characteristic of the engravings and vedute[55] of the time, the same tendency to represent human sovereignty over nature is discernible in these mass-produced equivalents of landscape paintings.

Because of their status as mass art, vedute and engravings have long been regarded as unworthy of study by art historians. In recent times, however, such mass-produced images have undergone a reevaluation and are increasingly viewed as valuable documentary sources in the study of the material culture of the nineteenth century. Gudrun König's cultural history of recreational pedestrianism has benefited greatly from the extensive use of vedute, from which she has gained insights into recreational walking as a social activity and the prevailing view of nature in the first half of the nineteenth century.[56] The importance of engravings and vedute as mass-produced images — collected in book form or sold singly as ornamental prints — in forming a specifically bourgeois view of nature should not be underestimated. The study of such images is especially revealing of the expectations and conditions that attend the encounter with nature.

So it is with the illustrations in the series *Das malerische und romantische Deutschland*, whose conventionality is reflected by the recurring clichés "pittoresk," "romantisch," "anmutig," and "erhaben" in the accompanying landscape descriptions.[57] The foreground is dominated for the most part by staffage figures depicted at work or at leisure. Commercial travelers and tourists appear frequently, and the solitary male wanderer — often accompanied by a dog — is a frequent motif. The overall impression is of a populous harmony and of nature domesticated (see the engraving from Blumenhagen's *Wanderung durch den Harz*, fig. 2).

The popularity of vedute and their very status as collectible items is itself revealing of the *Biedermeier* attitude toward nature, and it also throws light on the acquisitive tendency inherent in the practice of recreational wandering, a practice aimed at the collection and appropriation of landscapes. This tendency is evident in Friedrich Rückert's poem *Der*

*Fig 2. Clausthal, engraving by Ludwig Richter. Reproduced from Wilhelm Blumenhagen,* Wanderung durch den Harz: Mit 30 Stahlstichen (1838). *Reproduced with the kind permission of the Georg Olms Verlag, Hildesheim.*

*Wanderer*, which Gustav Adolf Riecke uses as the motto to his book *Süddeutschland*, published in 1844:

> Dem Wandersmann gehört die Welt
> In allen ihren Weiten,
> Weil er kann über Thal und Feld
> So wohlgemuth hinschreiten.
>
> . . . . . . . . . . . . . . . . . . . . . . . . . .
>
> Die Lüfte sind mir dienstbar auch,
> Die mir im Rücken wehen,
> Sie wollen doch mit ihrem Hauch,
> Mich fördern nur im Gehen.[58]

These lines are symptomatic of the pervasive influence of a utilitarian mode of thought on the bourgeois view of nature: even the winds are seen as "dienstbar," helping the wanderer on his way. Nor are considerations of profit and loss ever far from the surface for bourgeois wanderers, for whom the investment of effort must always yield a dividend in terms of a conventionally beautiful prospect: excursions to such spots are repeatedly characterized in contemporary guides and handbooks as "lohnend," a far cry from the "reines uninteressiertes Wohlgefallen' considered by Kant as indispensable to aesthetic experience.

The utilitarian tendency in the *Wanderliteratur* of the *Biedermeierzeit* is accompanied by a toning-down of the emancipatory symbolism of wandering. The shift of the culture of bourgeois wandering, away from the political program of the Enlightenment, is evident in the altered sense of freedom enjoyed by wanderers in the encounter with nature. As we have seen, freedom continues to be invoked in the *Biedermeier*, and with considerable pathos, as the specific gain to be had from wandering. However, although the *Wanderliteratur* frequently makes reference to Schiller, his idea of nature as a space outside the stultifying social and political order of absolutism is considerably weakened. True, mountainous nature is still prized as a space in which the wanderer feels elevated above mundane concerns and pressures, but, although the sense of exaltation persists, in the *Biedermeier* aesthetic it is attenuated, as I shall show presently.

Wanderers still climb to high places in order to gaze upon the land below in the *Biedermeierzeit* — indeed walking tours of the Harz and other mountainous regions had attained an unprecedented level of popularity by the 1820s, as the Brocken visitors' books show — but the nature of that gaze, and of the emotion of freedom produced by it, is altered. That emotion now depends on pleasurable physical sensation of mild exertion and on a view that imparts a sense of ownership, of sovereignty over what is surveyed. Those moments of terror and awe upon which the classic sublime experience depends are not banished from the *Wanderliteratur*, but they are domesticated. From his (such excursions remain a predominantly male pastime) elevated vantage the wanderer takes untroubled pleasure in the conquest of space and in the appropriation of landscape, the contemplation of which fosters a sense of individuality and strengthens him for his return to a society governed by an ethos of competitive striving.

The *Wanderliteratur* of the *Biedermeierzeit* was appropriative in its responses to landscape, but — more fundamentally — it was empirical. Indeed empiricism, the key epistemological trait of the *Biedermeier*, was the precondition of the utilitarian view of nature just described. On the textual level this trait is reflected in the close interrelationship of text and image, a hallmark not only of *Wanderliteratur* but also of other contemporary genres such as the urban sketch.[59] As a natural scientist, Büchner was steeped in this current of empiricism, and it was this habit of mind above all that led him to repudiate the aesthetics of idealism and the bourgeois ideology that he saw as depending upon it.

## "sie war so eng, daß er an alles zu stoßen fürchtete": The Blocked Sublime

We noted above that the term "erhaben" (sublime) is one of the most frequently used attributes of landscapes in the *Wanderliteratur.* For the Romantics, as for Goethe and Schiller, the word "sublime" denotes a distinct experience, which begins with awe and a sense of personal insignificance in the face of an overwhelming natural phenomenon, followed by a heightened awareness of the consciousness that separates the observer from, and elevates him above, the rest of nature. Hartmut Böhme provides a compelling explanation for the appearance of the category of the sublime in eighteenth-century aesthetics by putting it in the context of the bourgeois project of the domination of nature.[60] Böhme notes that the category of the sublime pertained precisely to those parts of the natural world — especially mountainous regions — then being opened up for exploitation, arguing that the conception of the sublime mobilized the imagination in managing and overcoming the fears associated with such regions.

Schiller's account in his essay *Über das Erhabene* (1801) of the emotional impact of the contemplation of a sublime object on an observer, and of the edifying effects of such an encounter, is exemplary of the classicistic-idealistic concept of the sublime:

> Zwey Genien sind es, die uns die Natur zu Begleitern durchs Leben gab. . . . In dem ersten dieser Genien erkennt man das Gefühl des Schönen, in dem zweyten das Gefühl des Erhabenen. . . . Das Gefühl des Erhabenen ist ein gemischtes Gefühl. Es ist eine Zusammensetzung von *Wehseyn*, das sich in seinem höchsten Grad als ein Schauer äußert, und von *Frohseyn*, das bis zum Entzücken steigen kann. . . . Diese Verbindung zweyer widersprechender Empfindungen in einem einzigen Gefühl beweist unsere moralische Selbständigkeit auf eine unwiderlegliche Weise. Denn da es absolut unmöglich ist, daß der nehmliche Gegenstand in zwey entgegengesetzten Verhältnissen zu uns stehe, so folgt daraus, daß *wir selbst* in zwey verschiedenen Verhältnissen zu dem Gegenstand stehen, daß folglich zwey entgegengesetzte Naturen in uns vereiniget seyn müssen, welche bey Vorstellung desselben, auf ganz entgegengesetzte Art interessiret [*sic*] sind. Wir erfahren also durch das Gefühl des Erhabenen, daß sich der Zustand unsers Geistes nicht nothwendig nach dem Zustand des Sinnes richtet, daß die Gesetze der Natur nicht nothwendig auch die unsrigen sind, und das wir ein selbständiges Prinzipium in uns haben, welches von allen sinnlichen Rührungen unabhängig ist. . . . Das Erhabene verschafft uns also einen Ausgang aus der sinnlichen Welt, worinn uns das Schöne gern immer gefangen halten möchte.[61]

Schiller's essay differentiates clearly between the categories of the beautiful (that which is congenial to our sensual nature) and the sublime (which is antagonistic to our sensuality). The feeling of sublimity depends for its effect on making the observer aware of his own fragility in the face of an implacable natural world: "eine Macht, gegen welche die unsrige in Nichts verschwindet"(*NA* 12:42). This sense of fragility gives way to a heightened awareness on the part of the subject of his or her status as rational being, based on the awareness of two contending feelings, terror and joy. It is the knowledge of the ability to accommodate these feelings simultaneously that grants the subject a feeling of superiority to insensate nature. Schiller's idealism is the philosophical context for his theory of the sublime: his intention is to demonstrate the existence of a "selbständiges Prinzipium" in man not susceptible to sensual or material determination.

It is not surprising that the aesthetic of the sublime did not sit easily with a *Biedermeier* ideal of a quiet, circumscribed existence, an ideal reflected in the predilection for framed prospects and views of delimited spaces: the adjective that best describes the taste in landscape then prevailing is "überschaubar."[62] On the other hand, there was a place in *Biedermeier* art for an aesthetic that offered "einen Ausgang aus der sinnlichen Welt," since this underpinned the dominant ideology of renunciation and asceticism. Nevertheless the blurring of the distinction between *erhaben* and *schön* in the contemporary *Wanderliteratur* seems to indicate a weakening of the category of the sublime. This weakening may have been connected to the fact that by the end of the first half of the nineteenth century there was little wilderness left to conquer in Europe. But what was probably most decisive in loosening the grip of the sublime on the imagination was the rise of an empirical mode of thought.

Elements of the sublime, elided or toned down in the *Biedermeier* aesthetic, are amplified in Büchner's treatment of landscape in *Lenz*. Harald Schmidt has shown that the scenery in *Lenz* corresponds in its bareness and in its bold and simple contours — the mountain spurs stretch out like "gewaltige Glieder" (137) — to the classicistic ideal of "das Einfach-Erhabene" expressed in Winckelmann's formula "edle Einfalt und stille Größe" and theoretically elaborated in such works as the aforementioned essay by Schiller[63] and in Kant's writings on the sublime in the *Kritik der Urteilskraft*. To this extent the representation of nature in Lenz is at odds with the conventions of the *Biedermeier*, which inherits, albeit in attenuated form, its idealizing tendencies from Weimar classicism.

Büchner's mountain landscape owes more to a Romantic conception of the sublime than it does to the classicistic model, in which the experience of the sublime serves to affirm "unsere moralische Selbständigkeit." While the Romantics recognized the classicistic model, they inclined to play up the threatening aspects of the sublime. In the topology of Romantic literature, mountains were the place of madness: in Tieck's fictions *Der Runenberg* (1802) and *Der Aufruhr in den Cevennen* (1826) the sublime does not bring the individual to the awareness of his essence as a rational being but rather sets him in a state of giddiness ("Taumel") or anxiety.[64]

For the most part, Lenz perceives the sublimity of the mountain landscape as crushing and oppressive. There are also euphoric moments, about which I will say more presently. At this point, however, I will concentrate on the dysphoric moments. Let us return to the opening description of Lenz's anguished progress:

> Es war ihm alles so klein, so nahe, so naß, er hätte die Erde hinter den Ofen setzen mögen, er begriff nicht, daß er so viel Zeit brauchte, um einen Abhang hinunter zu klimmen, einen fernen Punkt zu erreichen; er meinte, er müsse Alles mit ein Paar Schritten ausmessen können. (137)

This passage is striking, because a mountainscape, the very setting, which, since the Enlightenment, is repeatedly apostrophized by wanderers as "die freie, offene Natur" is experienced as an hermetically sealed and oppressive space.

Before descending into the valley of Waldbach, Lenz pauses at a high point in the mountains. His dominant impression is of emptiness and monotony: "nichts als Gipfel" (138). The view from the summit, which in the *Wanderliteratur* invariably gives rise to the emotion of freedom, stimulates in him an awareness of personal isolation and insignificance, feeding a growing anxiety, which culminates in panic-stricken flight:

> Gegen Abend kam er auf die Höhe des Gebirgs, auf das Schneefeld, von wo man wieder hinabstieg in die Ebene nach Westen, er setzte sich oben nieder. Es war gegen Abend ruhiger geworden; das Gewölk lag fest und unbeweglich am Himmel, so weit der Blick reichte, nichts als Gipfel, von denen sich breite Flächen hinabzogen, und alles so still, grau, dämmernd; es wurde ihm entsetzlich einsam, er war allein, ganz allein . . .; es faßte ihn eine namenlose Angst in diesem Nichts, er war im Leeren, er riß sich auf und flog den Abhang hinunter. (138)

Here the basic trajectory of Lenz's psychosis appears for the first time: an initial feeling of confinement and oppression triggers growing anxiety, which finds release in violent action or headlong flight. A significant factor is the failing light. The light-darkness antinomy is just one of a series of oppositions upon which the text is constructed. For Peter Hasubek, the most significant of these is that between stillness and movement.[65] On a prosaic level the unceasing up-and-down motion recalls the strenuous business of traversing mountainous terrain. But it also relates directly to the fluctuations of Lenz's psychic condition; it is "Sinnbild für die Beschaffenheit der Psyche des Lenz."[66] If we accept that this vertical movement corresponds to the dynamic of Lenz's sufferings, then the amplitude of the waves is clearly much greater in the second half of the narrative, that is, after the *Kunstgespräch* and Oberlin's departure. As Lenz's condition deteriorates, the poles of inertia and of movement move farther apart: the melancholy paralysis becomes more total, and the moment of release more violent: "Ein gewaltsames Drängen, und dann erschöpft zurückgeschlagen; er lag in den heißesten Tränen, und dann bekam er plötzlich eine Stärke und erhob sich kalt und gleichgültig, seine Tränen waren ihm dann wie Eis, er mußte lachen. *Je höher er sich aufriß, desto tiefer stürzte er hinunter*" (149; emphasis added).

In the early stages the release of tension takes the form of relatively inconsequential acts of self-injury: Lenz tears at himself with his fingernails and douses himself in the icy water of the spring. As the paralysis takes a firmer grip, so do the despairing attempts to counter it. One morning Lenz appears before Oberlin with a dislocated arm, having thrown himself from his window. A shocked Oberlin tends the injury and summons the schoolmaster to watch over Lenz and hinder any further attempts at self-harm. When the schoolmaster arrives, Lenz proposes a walk to Fouday, where he intends to visit the grave of the girl whom he had tried to revive. During this walk Lenz's anxiety is expressed in frenzied motor activity: "Bald ging er langsam und klagte über große Schwäche in den Gliedern, dann ging er mit verzweifelnder Schnelligkeit" (154). By this point the claustrophobic experience of the landscape has reached its apogee: "Die Landschaft beängstigte ihn, sie war so eng, daß er an alles zu stoßen fürchtete" (154). In an effort to shake off his two chaperones — the schoolmaster and his brother — Lenz makes for Waldbach, before turning about "wie ein Blitz" to sprint "wie ein Hirsch" back in the direction of Fouday. These violent and abrupt actions correlate with Lenz's increasingly frequent attempts at suicide.

The image of the wave suggests a wider congruence between the mountain landscape and a seascape, itself a much-used topos of the sublime. The resemblance has not escaped Schmidt's attention. In an attempt to convey the effect of the mountain landscape constructed by Büchner, Schmidt compares it with Caspar David Friedrich's painting *Mönch am Meer* (first exhibited 1810), citing "deutliche Parallelen zwischen Friedrichs innovativer, die Grenzen der Landschaftvorstellung schon überschreitender romantischer Malerei und Büchners literarischer Evokation eines monotonen, entleerten und schier unendlichen Naturraums in der zweiten Vogesenschilderung."[67] Friedrich's representation of a solitary figure on a pale strip of strand staring outwards at a tenebrous waste of sea overarched by a lowering sky succeeds paradoxically in making a vast space appear oppressive. Schmidt recalls Heinrich von Kleist's remarks in the *Berliner Abendblätter* of 13 October 1810 — "Nichts kann trauriger und unbehaglicher sein, als diese Stellung in der Welt: der einzige Lebensfunke im weiten Reiche des Todes, der einsame Mittelpunkt im einsamen Kreis . . . so ist es, wenn man es betrachtet, als ob einem die Augenlider weggeschnitten wären."[68] Schmidt rightly concludes: "Statt der romantischen Sehnsucht und der Steigerung der Gemütskräfte im Erhabenen provoziert Friedrichs Bild unangenehme Traueraffekte und kündet von schwarzer Melancholie."[69]

In *his* representation of landscape Büchner deploys all the requisites of the sublime, but the sublime experience itself is blocked: only one of the two components of that experience, as described by Schiller, is present, that of "Wehsein." At no time does Lenz become aware of the presence within himself of "ein selbständiges Prinzipium." By amplifying the requisites of the sublime while simultaneously denying their effects, Büchner delivers a resounding blow to an aesthetic category that formed the cornerstone of the aesthetics of idealism. This category was already under pressure in the *Biedermeierzeit*, both from the prevailing intellectual current of empiricism and from the growing appetite for an art that conveyed ideas of stability and permanence, preferences that were part of a reaction to the growing pace of social and economic change.

## The Body as Locus of Suffering and Euphoria in Lenz

What is remarkable about Büchner's treatment of psychic suffering is the degree to which this is presented as being experienced on the body. I have already mentioned the very physical nature of the symptoms of Lenz's melancholia: the recurring impressions of confinement and oppression are felt as a pressure weighing upon his body, and the very atmosphere bears down on the sufferer as an intolerable weight. He is immobilized by the "ungeheure Schwere der Luft" (157). To Madame Oberlin he complains: "Jetzt ist es mir so eng, so eng, sehn Sie, es ist mir manchmal, als stieß ich mit den Händen an den Himmel; o ich ersticke!" and continuing, he describes the pain of separation from "das Frauenzimmer . . . dessen Schicksal mir so zentnerschwer auf dem Herzen liegt" (149) expressly as a "physischen Schmerz, da in der linken Seite, im Arm, womit ich sie sonst faßte" (150).

The physical dimension is also manifest in the episodes of euphoria, the first of which occurs in the opening scene. Here the predominant sense of a pervasive and threatening stillness is broken for a moment that is described in the long sentence introduced by the hypotactic construction "Nur manchmal, wenn . . ." and concluding with the image of a rushing stream. This extraordinary structure is made up of two extended series of clauses, the first of which concludes with the closure of the main clause: " . . . riß es ihm in der Brust."[70] The syntactic tension created by the distance between the opening and conclusion of the main clause reproduces the fervid style of the *Sturm und Drang*, and evokes uncanny psychic strain. For as long as the moment and the sentence persist, the wanderer finds himself in a rhapsodic state, the brevity of which is indicated by the phrase: "Aber es waren nur Augenblicke."

> Nur manchmal . . . riß es ihm in der Brust, er stand, keuchend, den Leib vorwärts gebogen, Augen und Mund weit offen, er meinte, er müsse den Sturm in sich ziehen, Alles in sich fassen, er dehnte sich aus und lag über

> der Erde, er wühlte sich in das All hinein, es war eine Lust, die ihm Wehe tat; oder er stand still und legte das Haupt in's Moos und schloß die Augen halb, und dann zog es weit von ihm, die Erde wich unter ihm, sie wurde klein wie ein wandelnder Stern und tauchte sich in einen brausenden Strom, der seine klare Flut unter ihm zog. (137)

In the space of that moment Lenz's contemplation of the landscape produces in him a euphoric state in which he apparently transcends the boundaries of his own existence. The self feels greatly extended, to the point where Lenz feels capable of drawing the storm into himself, and, at the same time, raised up above the earth, which appears "klein, wie ein wandelnder Stern." The prevailing sense is of the self merging with the universe. More will be said presently about these moments. At this point, though, what is of interest is the participation of the whole body in the fleeting access of ecstasy: "Brust," "Leib," "Augen," and "Mund" all have their parts to play in the reaction to the synaesthetic vision of a landscape suddenly set in motion by the storm.

In emphasizing the physical dimensions of Lenz's suffering, Büchner demonstrates the reality of those sufferings for his protagonist. He thereby follows a strategy similar to that of Moritz, who, in representing Anton Reiser's melancholia, draws attention to the body as the point at which therapy can be applied. But while Moritz asserts the reality of his subject's sufferings,[71] moral judgment is never entirely absent from the psychological novel. *Anton Reiser* thus never quite escapes the characteristically ambivalent Enlightenment view of mental illness entailed by the double sense of the word "moral," which could then serve as a non-evaluative antonym for "physical," but which was also used to refer to the field of "Sittlichkeit" (moral standards).[72] By opting to narrate the story entirely from the sufferer's perspective, Büchner succeeds to a greater degree than Moritz in avoiding any suggestion that Lenz bears any moral responsibility for his illness.

The single most important difference between Oberlin's report on the sufferings of the historical Lenz, Büchner's main source, and the narrative fiction he made out of it lies in the presentation of Lenz as a solitary wanderer in a mountain landscape. It is this presentation, above all, that allows emphasis to be placed on the physical aspects of Lenz's suffering. As is the case in the *Harzreise*, the motif of the wanderer is enlisted in an assault upon an ideology of renunciation. However Büchner attacks the problem from the opposite pole from Heine: rather than summoning up corporeal man's capacity for pleasure, the motif becomes in Büchner's hands an organon for registering the physicality of suffering wrought by ideological and social mechanisms of repression. Büchner's understanding of the whole body as the place in which the symptoms of melancholia, depression, and anxiety manifest themselves is at odds with one of the founding assumptions of psychology, namely that the mind exists apart from the body as a separate repository of experience.

The presentation of the protagonist as a wanderer highlights both the phenomenal reality of his sufferings and the immediacy with which they are felt; but it also locates their causes decisively in the *external* world. Far from being the projections of Lenz's consciousness, as Reuchlein[73] avers, the landscapes of Büchner's story represent the objective external conditions upon which psychic equanimity is utterly dependent. Lenz is, of course, not only exposed to atmospheres in the high mountains: the particular emotional atmosphere that obtains in Waldbach, that emanating from Oberlin's household, has a direct influence on the course of his illness. This emotional atmosphere is constituted, in part, by the glances of others. The sense of ease experienced by Lenz on his first day accompanying Oberlin on his rounds is produced by the "zutrauensvolle Blicke" of the valley's inhabitants and "die mächtige Ruhe" in Oberlin's own gaze (140). For as long as Oberlin treats him with consideration and refrains from judgment, the symptoms of Lenz's melancholia are held in check and his integration appears a real possibility.[74]

With the appearance of Kaufmann, however, the harmonious atmosphere is disturbed. The visitor is a source of information on Lenz's personal history and illness; Oberlin, who hitherto had known nothing of Lenz's past, now has a material basis on which to judge him. From now on, the pastor's attitude toward Lenz, though still compassionate, includes a nuance of disapproval and censure: "Oberlin blickte ihn unwillig an" (153). Lenz's labile equanimity is shattered when Kaufmann admonishes him to seek reconciliation with his father, reproving him for wasting his time in Waldbach instead of engaging in purposeful activity. Lenz's response is anguished: "Hier weg, weg! nach Haus? Toll werden dort? . . . Ich würde toll! toll! Laßt mich doch in Ruhe! Nur ein bißchen Ruhe, jetzt wo es mir ein wenig wohl wird!" (146). Although the atmosphere in the vicarage at Waldbach has shifted only by a nuance, Lenz is sensible of the change. Kaufmann's accusations are followed in short order by the departure of Oberlin and Kaufmann, a development that Lenz interprets as abandonment and as implicit reproach and that brings his submerged guilt complex to the surface. For Lenz, Oberlin's departure is equivalent to being abandoned by God: it is this that leads him to attempt the awakening of the dead child — an experiment in theodicy.

In his impassioned plea, cited above, the reactive nature of Lenz's melancholia and the external factors that drove him to seek a refuge in Waldbach become apparent: the conflict with his father and the objective conditions of a bourgeois existence whose relentless ethic of individual striving is sketched by Lenz thus: "Immer steigen, ringen und so in Ewigkeit Alles was der Augenblick gibt, wegwerfen und immer darben, um einmal zu genießen; dürsten, während einem helle Quellen über den Weg springen" (146).

The arrival of Kaufmann, who represents the individualistic ethic that has made Lenz ill, makes it clear that there are no refuges into which the sufferer can withdraw from the ramifications of bourgeois civilization, which have penetrated even the backwoods idyll of Waldbach with its apparently intact Christian social model.[75]

In its emphasis on the corporeality of Lenz's sufferings, the text succeeds in showing the interpenetration of subject and environment, the inescapable embeddedness of the subject in physical circumstances. It is this awareness that subjectivity is inseparable from corporeality, and hence from material conditions, that informs Büchner's political philosophy.

### "Es waren nur Augenblicke": Euphoric Moments in the Landscape

Having noted that it is the conditions of bourgeois existence, in particular the individualistic ethic of performance, that underlie the sufferings of Lenz, we are in a better position to understand his brief moments of euphoria in the sublime landscape. I have already cited the first such moment above, in which the oppressive monotony is very briefly dispelled and Lenz in his ecstasy feels merged with the universe.

Such moments need to be explained in view of the fact that Lenz predominantly experiences the vast and lifeless monotony of the mountainscape as crushingly oppressive. We have seen that that monotony calls to the wanderer's mind his vulnerability in the face of nature — which, we may suppose, stands for all the impassive and unknowable forces confronting the individual — and, in its very lifelessness, it recalls to him his utter isolation. Alone in the mountains, he becomes acutely aware of his own individuality, of the gulf that separates him from a sustaining collective existence. The mountain, in the scriptural tradition the place of revelation of God's law, becomes the place of revelation of universal anomie and the backdrop for Lenz's apostate rage. Highly significant is his self-identification with the mythical figure of Ahasver[76] — which we should see not just in the context of Lenz's delusions of guilt but also as an indication of his profound sense of isolation, of being engaged in a journey without end. It is, as Manfred Frank has pointed out, no accident that the medieval legend of the Wandering Jew was energetically appropriated and reworked by the Romantics.[77] In that figure they found an icon of the predicament of the individual, then in danger of coming to grief as the bundle of processes we summarize by the term modernity gathered pace. The mythical figure of Ahasver embodied for that generation the sense of what Lukács has called "transcendental homelessness,"[78] the existential uncertainty that arose from the collapse of the Christian *ordo universalis* and the accompanying rise of an instrumental rationality of a decidedly economic character. In Ahasver's restlessness, his eternal voyaging, the Romantics saw a metaphor for the ceaseless striving and the unending torment of an never-satisfied will that formed the lot of the individual. It is the predicament for which Schopenhauer found the following expression in book 4 of *Die Welt als Wille und Vorstellung:*

> Denn, wie auf dem tobenden Meere, das, nach allen Seiten unbegränzt, heulend Wasserberge erhebt und senkt, auf einem Kahn ein Schiffer sitzt, dem schwachen Fahrzeug vertrauend; so sitzt, mitten in einer Welt voll Quaalen, ruhig der einzelne Mensch, gestützt und vertrauend auf das *principium individuationis*, oder die Weise wie das Individuum die Dinge erkennt, als Erscheinung.[79]

Büchner's protagonist is no less encaged in his individuality than the boatman in Schopenhauer's metaphor, even if the *principium individuationis* is, for him, no bastion of serenity. The euphoric moments in *Lenz* all involve in some measure the suspension of this individuality, whether in the experience of landscape or in conversation and other forms of social interaction. They are ecstatic in the sense that they involve a displacement (*ekstasis*), a movement out of the self — "er war weg, weit weg" (139), it is said of Lenz in conversation. One such moment occurs when Lenz, having accompanied Oberlin and Kaufmann to the edge of the valley, turns back and wanders aimlessly for a time:

> Er ging allein zurück. Er durchstrich das Gebirg in verschiedenen Richtungen, breite Flächen zogen sich in die Täler herab, wenig Wald, nichts als gewaltige Linien und weiter hinaus die weiter rauchende Ebene, in der Luft ein gewaltiges Wehen, nirgends eine Spur von Menschen als hie und da eine verlassene Hütte, wo die Hirten den Sommer zubrachten, an den Abhängen gelehnt. Er wurde still, vielleicht fast träumend, es verschmolz ihm Alles in eine Linie, wie eine steigende und sinkende Welle, zwischen Himmel und Erde, es war ihm als läge er an einem unendlichen Meer, das leise auf- und abwogte. (147)

What happens on this and on the other ecstatic occasions is similar to the effects described by Schopenhauer of the contemplation of a sublime landscape:

> Versetzen wir uns in eine sehr einsame Gegend, mit unbeschränktem Horizont, unter völlig wolkenlosem Himmel, Bäume und Pflanzen in ganz unbewegter Luft, keine Thiere, keine Menschen, keine bewegte Gewässer, die tiefste Stille; — so ist solche Umgebung wie ein Aufruf zum Ernst, zur Kontemplation, mit Losreißung von allem Wollen und dessen Dürftigkeit: eben dieses aber giebt schon einer solchen, bloß einsamen und tiefruhenden Umgebung einen Anstrich des Erhabenen. Denn weil sie für den des steten Strebens und Erreichens bedürftigen Willen keine Objekte darbietet, weder günstige noch ungünstige, so bleibt nur der Zustand der reinen Kontemplation übrig, und wer dieser nicht fähig ist, wird der Leere des nichtbeschäftigten Willens, der Quaal der Langenweile, mit beschämender Herabsetzung Preis gegeben.[80]

In the reference to the "Quaal der Langenweile" we recognize Lenz's habitual state in the face of the empty landscape: unable to transcend the feeling of emptiness in contemplation, he is thrown back on the pain of his unoccupied will. (For Schopenhauer willing and suffering are interchangeable terms since "Alles Wollen entspringt aus Bedürfnis, also aus Mangel, also aus Leiden."[81]) Instead of having his individuality and his will affirmed, Lenz finds it denied, negated by the implacable, uninhabitable monotony. But for an instant Lenz, absorbed in perception, is detached from all willing, arriving at a state in which he forgets his individuality. He loses himself in the object and attains a state of quietude akin to that claimed by Schopenhauer for the aesthetic mode of contemplation.[82] Significant here is the image of the endless sea, in the language of psychoanalysis the symbolic place of narcissistic regression, the place where all individuality ceases. Lenz is no longer Schopenhauer's solitary boatman; he has abandoned himself to the waves, yielding to the unconscious desire to relinquish the individuality that agonizes him.

Another scene in which images of water and waves play a significant part is the one in which Lenz appears before Oberlin's parishioners to give a sermon. On the way to the church, the valley is bathed in warmth and light: "Es war als löste sich alles in eine harmonische Welle auf" (142). Voices raised in choral harmony put him in a trance "als schaue man in reines durchsichtiges Bergwasser" (later, Oberlin tells how, on looking into a mountain stream, he had fallen into "eine Art von Somnambulismus"). Under the influence of the music Lenz's melancholic paralysis ("Starrkrampf") is dispelled. At this moment Lenz's pain reawakens, but he is overcome at the same time by a "süßes Gefühl unendlichen Wohls." The singing resumes, the words of the chorale with their reference to deep springs bursting forth reflect the transition from a state of psychic and emotional inertia to one of flux. Once again, the meteorological and psychic conditions accord: "es war Tauwetter eingefallen" (141).

The process of dissolution signaled by the water metaphors is one in which the boundaries of the self become fluid. Again, as in the ecstasies of landscape, Lenz feels himself melding with the universe. This time, however, the ecstatic merger has a new quality: it is accompanied by a revelation of the universal nature of suffering — "das All lag für ihn in Wunden" — and an implicit desire to become absorbed into "das von materiellen Bedürfnissen gequälte Sein." In Schopenhauer's terms, Lenz has for an instant seen through the *principium individuationis* to the universal suffering that is the ground of all being. But the release is a temporary one. Alone, the feeling of the dissolution of the bounds of self ebbs away in diffuse "Wollust," and the capsule of individuality recloses.

In his recognition that suffering is universal and demands an appropriate ethical response, Büchner is strikingly close to Schopenhauer. What is more, the two writers are at one in emphasizing the body (which for

Schopenhauer has the status of "objectified will") as the prime locus of human suffering. For Schopenhauer, the individual, having seen through the *principium individuationis*, which blinds him to the "boundless world of suffering," is called upon to enter into a relation of sympathy with all being, thereby escaping the bonds of his own particular torment. The knowledge that creation is filled with suffering is, in the words of Thomas Payne in *Dantons Tod*, "Der Fels des Atheismus."[83] This rock, on which Lenz comes to grief, is the rock upon which Büchner grounds his political commitment.

I have argued above that the practice of recreational wandering in the *Biedermeierzeit*, as well as the aesthetic to which it is allied, is aimed at bolstering individualistic feeling. In the case of Lenz, by contrast, the perception of landscape intensifies the awareness of an agonized individuality and, on occasion, gives rise to ecstatic moments in which the unconscious desire to relinquish it gains the upper hand. What distinguishes Büchner from his *Schmerzensmann* is the response to a landscape perceived, not as a mirror of divine order, but as a space whose anomie is revealed in its absurdity: "Der Himmel war ein dummes blaues Aug, und der Mond stand ganz lächerlich drin, einfältig" (151). While the sight of the "vast and infinite deformity"[84] of a godless landscape appalls Lenz, to Büchner it is a summons to work for the construction of a human order dedicated to the alleviation of suffering.

In its presentation of landscape the text thus repudiates an idealist aesthetic that regards nature as the place where harmony is revealed, or — more specifically — as a place whose sublimity brings the observer to the knowledge of the primacy of his own will. Because it fails to acknowledge the existence of imperfection, specifically of pain, such an aesthetic is, in the words that Büchner gives Lenz to utter: "die schmählichste Verachtung der menschlichen Natur" (144). It is as abhorrent to him as the utopianism of the "Zukunftbeglücker" is to Heine. By reprising the (early) Romantic topos of the mountains as the place of madness, Büchner refuses a conception of nature that glosses over imperfection and deformity. In doing so he does not, however, deny the orderedness of the world: rather he takes the view that imperfection and deformity must be considered as parts of a higher order that eludes understanding.[85]

The *Kunstgespräch*, a monologue disguised as a dialogue, is the place in the story where Büchner articulates his own aesthetic position as an alternative to the idealistic model of Weimar classicism.[86] Niccolini sees this passage as having a poetological function; it is the articulation of Büchner's theory of the ends of art.[87] She argues that Büchner distinguishes two aims of aesthetic practice — first, that art should strive for fidelity to life[88] and, second, that it should be informed by the love of humanity[89] — and that both of these postulates are substantially fulfilled by the narrative itself. By refusing an idealistic aesthetic, Büchner also implicitly rejects the notion that the encounter with nature is capable of restoring the individual to a notional prestabilized harmony in an disenchanted modern society. Lenz, in common with the pedestrian tourists of the *Biedermeierzeit*, seeks a refuge in nature and, like them, returns to the horizons of that society. His melancholia, caused by the demands made of the individual in that era, remains uncured. By thus exposing the inadequacies of aesthetic practice — including the consumption of landscape in recreational wandering — in reconciling the individual to the social order that is the source of his suffering, the text challenges the reader to engage more thoroughly with the question of suffering and its causes.

The focus on the body as the locus of suffering is highly consistent with the Biedermeier current of empiricism, but Büchner radicalizes this current in the direction of uncompromising materialism. We have already encountered this empirical strain in the *Harzreise*, where I treated it as a legacy of the Late Enlightenment travelogues, and indeed *Lenz* in many respects seems like a *Doppelgänger* of Heine's text, sharing philosophical and political preoccupations with it, but approaching its problem from the opposite anthropological perspective. Staging corporeality via the wanderer motif is central to Büchner's strategy of demolishing the sublime, and with it the aesthetics of idealism, which, for Büchner, is the inhuman foundation of the bourgeois ideology of renunciation.

## Fontane's *Wanderungen durch die Mark Brandenburg* (1861–81)

### "Wanderungen" as Principle of Composition and Mode of Reception

In 1859 Theodor Fontane returned to Berlin, after spending three years in London as a journalist in the pay of the Prussian government. From that time onward, and until the end of his life, the project that would preoccupy him above all was the literary representation of the Mark Brandenburg. Nor did that preoccupation cease with the beginning of his career as a novelist. The fruits of that labor were published in four volumes by Wilhelm Hertz. The first volume, entitled *Wanderungen durch die Mark Brandenburg* (retitled *Die Grafschaft Ruppin* in subsequent editions) appeared in 1861, predated 1862; this was followed by *Das Oderland* (1863), *Osthavelland* (later retitled *Havelland*), and *Spreeland*, which bore the impression dates 1873 and 1882 respectively. Although the volume *Fünf Schlösser* (1889) is thematically linked with the *Wanderungen*, its omission from the *Wohlfeile Ausgabe* of 1892 is sufficient reason to consider it a separate work.

The *Wanderungen* are usually regarded as an interim stage, a bridge between the early journalism and the later novelistic work. For this reason, and because of an enduring prejudice against the supposedly provincial character of the work, the volumes have long occupied something of a blind spot in Fontane research. The complex history of the various editions of the *Wanderungen* may also have been a factor inhibiting study. Nevertheless, the neglect of the *Wanderungen* by Germanists is puzzling, when we recall that it was for this work and *not* for his novels that Fontane was acclaimed in his lifetime.[90] The post-1989 period has, however, seen something of an upturn in research interest — prompted in part by the appropriation of Fontane as an icon of the *Bundesland* Brandenburg. Among the more important recent studies are those of Peter J. Brenner, Walter Erhart, and Hubertus Fischer.[91] Further valuable contributions made at a conference in 2002, jointly organized by the Theodor-Fontane-Archiv and the Theodor Fontane Gesellschaft, collected in a volume edited by Hanna Delf von Wolzogen, have gone some way to redressing earlier neglect.[92] My study here will concentrate on two aspects: first, I will seek to show what use Fontane makes of the motif of the wanderer to produce a politically motivated literary work, and, second, I will attempt to show how the use of motif sets Fontane apart from a group of contemporaries, the historicists. Given the scale of the *Wanderungen*, a work that merits a monograph in its own right, the discussion will focus especially on the first two volumes, which can be said to embody the aesthetic and political concerns underpinning the whole work.

Like Heine, Fontane opts for a narrative of wandering, partly with an eye to a booming market for travel literature. In his review of Anton von Etzel's *Die Ostsee und ihre Küstenländer*[93] in the *Preußische Zeitung*, Fontane deplores the lack of a "historisch-romantischen Reiseliteratur" in Germany, remarking: "Es fehlt östlich von der Elbe durchaus noch die Wünschelrute, die den Boden berührt und die Gestalten erstehen macht. Wer Gelegenheit genommen hat, zu beobachten, wie dieser eigentümliche, wichtige Literaturzweig in England blüht, der wird uns zustimmen."[94] With Etzel's "discovery" of the Baltic, it could only be a matter of time before such a literature emerged for the similarly neglected Mark Brandenburg. Fontane knew that the prize for the first author to venture into such territory would be very great, given the size and rapid growth of Berlin as a literary market. While Fontane follows Heine in reprising the Romantic motif of the wanderer in order to create commercially successful (and politically motivated) texts, Fontane's wandering narrator has none of the corporeal substantiality of Heine's; rather, his is a shadowy and more unobtrusive presence. The two narrators are further differentiated by the claims made for the perspectives they embody. As I have argued, the physical presence of Heine's narrator corresponds to a radical subjectivism; Fontane, by contrast, at least professes his concern for objectivity and Realism.[95] The *Wanderungen* are primarily presented to the reader as the document of a culture rather than as the expression of an individual sensibility.

It is also apparent that Fontane has a broad understanding of what is meant by "wandering." As Hubertus Fischer has observed: "Er war nicht gut zu Fuß und alles andere als ein Wandervogel, vielmehr ein Spaziergänger, für den sich die Sache im besten Fall nach einem *'halbstündigen Gang'* erledigt hatte."[96] Wandering, in the sense of a strenuous pedestrianism, is nowhere especially prominent. Instead, Fontane makes extensive use of trains, post-chaises, and boats in his explorations of the Mark Brandenburg, walking only in order to inspect the object of interest. Indeed, Fontane's *Wanderungen* can also be understood in a more abstract sense: as a procedure of textual construction, and as a mode of reception that the author seeks to control. A procedure of textual construction? Fontane repeatedly represents himself as a searcher and collector: "sorglos hab' ich es gesammelt," he says of his material in the foreword to the first edition, "nicht wie einer, der mit der Sichel zur Ernte ging, sondern wie ein Spaziergänger, der einzelne Ähren aus dem reichen Felde zieht" (2/1:11) His numerous excursions into the Mark Brandenburg were undertaken with the object of amassing the material — topographical, historical, mythological, archaeological — out of which the *Wanderungen* were gradually assembled. Vital though these excursions were, he also garnered much material from textual sources: histories of Prussia, memoirs, and private correspondence, constantly augmented by oral and written communications from knowledgeable informants — especially his sister, Lise. Thus, "wandering" can also be said to connote an odyssey through a maze of written matter on the history of the Mark, with the important proviso that the most highly valued material is not that of official historiography but the anecdotal and the personal.

In the foreword to the first volume Fontane sets out a visual program, a set of specifications intended to enable the tourist to see the Mark "correctly." These specifications are threefold: first, the prospective tourist must eschew prejudice, traveling with "Liebe zu 'Land und Leuten'" (2/1:12) — an injunction that aims to overcome the still current view of Brandenburg as a sandy waste devoid of aesthetic appeal. Second, the tourist is called to cultivate "Natur und Landschaftssinn," that is, to become accustomed to viewing the country as landscape.[97] And, third, he or she is enjoined to acquire a thorough knowledge of the region's history. Apart from specifying a particular mode of seeing to the *tourist*, these strictures also attest to a will to steer the *reader's* reception of the literary work. Although the *Wanderungen* sets out to build up a canon of views and scenic locations in an undervisited Brandenburg, the work cannot in any conventional sense be regarded as a guidebook, for it lacks the pragmatic focus of the Baedeker guides.[98] Instead the "wanderings" on which the reader is invited to embark are, in the first instance, of a textual nature: what is envisaged is a foray into a Brandenburg that exists as primarily a literary construct, a weave of landscapes, historiography, biographical sketches, and local lore. At every turn the reader is accompanied by the narrator, a cicerone whose gently insistent tone advises as to the authorized interpretation of the whole.[99]

In a discussion of the visual program of the *Wanderungen*, Erdmut Jost argues that the landscapes are evoked in such a way as to meet the expectations of a readership accustomed to the visual conventions of the panorama and the diorama. As we have seen in the discussion of the *Harzreise*, these popular media, together with mass-produced vedute, played a significant part in pre-structuring the experience of nature in wandering. Fontane imitates these media by carefully setting the scene, striving at all times for what Jost terms "den *perfekten* Blick, das *perfekte* Bild," a strategy that may be characterized as "die im Text allanwesende Wahrnehmungslenkung."[100] I will say more about the significance of these media for the aesthetic of the text presently. For now it is enough to note that the process of wandering is itself narrated so as to draw the reader into the narrator's perspective. The following sample should serve to illustrate this: "Wir verlassen nun den Saal und das Haus, passieren die mehr dem Dorfe zu gelegene Hälfte des Parkes, überschreiten gleich danach die Dorfstraße und stehen jetzt auf einem geräumigen Rasenfleck, in dessen Mitte sich die Dorfkirche erhebt" (2/1:24). In such passages the use of the present tense gives the illusion of immediacy, while the embracing "wir" tends to forestall any dissent from the historical interpretation that follows.

The postscript to the final volume of the *Wanderungen* expresses regret that the "ursprüngliche Plauderton eines Touristen" (2/2:870) had given way to a "historische Vortragsweise" in the second volume (*Das Oderland*), remarking that the author had sought to find his way back to "die frühere Weise" in the final two volumes. In fact, the two narrative modes alternate throughout the *Wanderungen*, the casual tone of the tourist securing sympathy for the convictions articulated in the historiography. Styling the work as *Wanderungen* is intended to create the impression of casualness, of inconsequentiality; it is as if the work were the product of whim rather than elaborate artifice.[101] This is both a dissimulation — a distraction from the ideological program subtending the work — and a gesture of humility, a *captatio benevolentiae* similar to the one we find in the postscript to the final volume: "Wer sein Buch einfach 'Wanderungen' nennt und es zu größerer Hälfte mit landschaftlichen Beschreibungen und Genreszenen füllt . . ., der hat wohl genugsam angedeutet, daß er freiwillig darauf verzichtet, unter die Würdenträger und Großcordons historischer Wissenschaft eingereiht zu werden" (2/2:871).

## The Dialectic of Domestic and Foreign in the "Wanderungen"

"'Erst die Fremde lehrt uns, was wir an der Heimat besitzen'" (2/1:9). This remark — identified as a commonplace by its enclosure in quotation marks — opens the foreword to the first (1862) edition of the *Wanderungen*, introducing the oft-cited reminiscence of Loch Leven and the aesthetic program outlined above. The foreign manifests itself in many forms on Fontane's excursions: in the Italian artworks hidden away in the country house at Radensleben, in the Wendish inhabitants of the Mark, in the Dutch and French settlers of Friedrich II's great colonization. It is present in Gustav Kühn's colorful news-sheets — "der dünne Faden, durch den weite Strecken unseres eigenen Landes . . ., mit der Welt draußen zusammenhängen" (2/1:136) — but especially in an aesthetic that Fontane, like his paragon Schinkel, applies to the landscape of Brandenburg. As is the case in Heine's *Harzreise*, what first appears as "eine Reise vor der eigenen Tür" turns up manifold connections between the local and global dimensions. Fontane perhaps differs from Heine, however, in that the foreign serves less as the basis of a thoroughgoing critical evaluation of the homeland than as the source of the palette of painterly effects used to aestheticize it. Naturally this is a simplification: in my discussion of the *Harzreise* it was argued that Heine's critical gaze was formed in part by his experience of Berlin. Similarly, Fontane's time in London provided him with a critical awareness that secured his writing against all patriotic excess. But the knowledge that "hinterm Berg auch noch Leute wohnen"[102] never becomes for Fontane the basis of a cosmopolitanism in the way that it does for Heine. If Fontane's Prussianism is controlled by "die Dialektik zwischen Heimat und Welt,"[103] then the balance in that dialectic at all times favors "die Belebung des Lokalen."[104] London and Scotland were, above all, the key stations of an aesthetic education: it was there that the foundations of Fontane's literary realism were laid. Apart from fostering his powers of observation, the British episode also stimulated in Fontane the desire to employ those powers in the literary representation of his own land. Like the architect Karl Friedrich Schinkel (1781–1841) and the painter Carl Blechen (1798–1840), both of whom he admired, Fontane adds Italianate touches — "südlich Land und blauen Himmel" (2/1:981) — to his Brandenburg landscapes. In this he follows the long-established practice of those northern European artists who appropriated the techniques of Italian landscape painting, applying them in the representation of their own lands.[105] Similarly, by revealing hidden art treasures such as the Italian paintings and sculptures housed at Radensleben, Fontane exploits the foreign to endow the Mark with cultural prestige.

The stipulation that the wanderer should travel with "Liebe zu 'Land und Leuten'" points to the ethnographic interest underlying the work.[106] Fontane is wedded to the notion of a distinctive national — and regional — character determined by the conditions obtaining in a particular locality. "Der modelnde Einfluß, den die Wohnstätte des Menschen auf den Menschen selber übt" (2/1:598) plays an important role in Fontane's conception of national character, just as it had for Enlightenment theorists. Fontane's conviction that the Markish character is the product of the struggle with the soil is demonstrated *ex negativo* by reference to the colonists of the drained Oder marshes. Whereas elsewhere in the Mark the harsh, unyielding nature of the land had given rise to hardiness, diligence, and thrift, the ease of cultivation of the rich alluvial soil of the Oder marsh encouraged moral laxity and indolence in the first generation of colonists.

By and large, the text avoids generalizations about particular groups in its reflections on questions of regional or national character — the excursus on the subject of the Wends in *Havelland* is an exception in this regard. Instead the main focus is on individual (historical) persons, each of whom is linked with the localities visited by the wanderer. What does the text represent as the salient features of the Markish character? Certain traits recur throughout the character sketches: loyalty, discipline, self-abnegation, hardiness; but reticence, suspiciousness, and a certain philistinism appear as the other side of the coin. These traits, although associated in the first instance with the landed gentry — seen as the class most bonded to their native soil — are also exhibited by bourgeois subjects. Thus, General von Günther, born of bourgeois stock, is likened to the aristocratic "Husarenvater," Zieten. Indeed, two things are notable about the character portraits in the *Wanderungen:* first, those virtues asserted as Prussian are by no means exclusively associated with the nobility and second, despite the looming presence of the military, it is not the martial qualities that are given especial prominence. Thus, Fontane is remarkably sparing in his praise of the elder Zieten and of Field Marshal von dem Knesebeck. As for Zieten, it is his earnestness, sobriety, and straightforwardness that are extolled. Not uniquely martial attributes, one might argue; indeed, on examination neither Zieten nor Knesebeck proves particularly combative. The "Husarenvater" has drawn his sword only once in combat; Knesebeck is less a warrior than a rather sedentary military strategist, "der zeitlebens wie ein Poet gedacht und gefühlt hatte" (2/1:37). His bellicose *Lob des Krieges* is passed over without comment, and the poem "Mit dem Schwerte sei dem Feind gewehrt, / Mit dem Pflug der Erde Frucht gemehrt," is reservedly characterized as "vielleicht ein treffendes Motto märkischen Adels" (2/1:38). Moreover, the counts of Ruppin appear not as "comites bellicosissimi" but as "viri nobiles et generosi'" (2/1:59), and — strikingly — as masters of "die schwere Kunst der Nachgiebigkeit" (2/1:60).

The portraits of General von Günther and Schinkel (both of bourgeois birth) are the most important of the first volume. This is especially clear when we consider the extent to which these two portraits dominated the unaugmented first edition (1862) of the *Wanderungen*. It is here that we find those qualities Fontane regards as characteristically Prussian. Of Günther — who is likened to Zieten — it is asserted: "Bis zuletzt war ihm das 'ich dien' ein Stolz und ein Bedürfnis gewesen. . . . An Gehorsam, an Diensttreue, war ihm keiner gleich. . . . Das Opfer war Gebot, war *Leidenschaft.* Preußen über alles" (2/1:104, 106). As for Schinkel, the "Schöpfer unsrer Baukunst" is exalted over the "Husarenvater," Zieten. As is often the case with Fontane, the traits attributed to Schinkel — "eiserne Ausdauer," "Selbstverleugnung" (2/1:125) — are, in part, those to which he himself aspires, though the fact that Schinkel's early death was reputedly brought on by overwork casts an ambivalent light on this encomium. Character, as Fontane understands it, is not identical with the virtues exhibited by Schinkel, Günther, and other paragons. After all, the boorish Michel Protzen, though a man of character, displays none of these attributes. Instead the term betokens an individual's groundedness in place and tradition; it is "das Prinzip jener beziehungsreichen Verbundenheit von Leben, Person und Lebenswelt,"[107] and as such it is the precondition for the moral standards that Fontane seeks to preserve and encourage.

The ethnographic interest underlying the *Wanderungen* is oriented primarily toward *historical* personages of aristocratic and bourgeois origin. It is in this respect that the *Wanderungen* are most unlike the liberal travel literature of the late Enlightenment and *Biedermeier* periods with its (usually idealizing) emphasis on the rural and urban working classes.[108] As Wolfgang Albrecht has remarked — giving Riehl's *Wanderbuch* as an example — depoliticized ethnography was a feature of contemporary travel writing.[109] While the working classes occupy an undeniably peripheral position in Fontane's Mark, they do play more than a mere staffage role. Thus, the chapters "Das Wustrauer Luch" and especially "Glindow" with its "Bilder eines allermodernsten frondiensthaften Industrialismus" (2/2:449) do not gloss over the privations faced by working men and women. However, such passages of socially critical reportage are the exception, for Fontane is primarily interested in the common people as the bearers of a collective culture that finds its apotheosis in such events as the Möskefest celebrated at Rheinsberg. The transformation of this originally religious festival into a celebration of the victory at the Battle of Prague in 1757 is registered with a note of concern: "*Das Soldatische hat sich zum poetischen Inhalt unseres Volkslebens ausgebildet*" (2/3:411, emphasis in original), a remark suggesting reservations regarding the militarization of Prussian culture.

The dimension of the foreign is, as we have seen, present in many forms; but (as in the *Harzreise*) it is arguably most powerfully embodied in the city of Berlin itself. Fontane's wanderings originate in Berlin, and they circle around it; yet it is the rural periphery and not the urban center that is progressively discovered. Berlin is always viewed from a distance, its towers veiled in a transforming mist. It is more present in the public buildings and monuments constructed by Karl Friedrich Schinkel than in the burgeoning suburbs and industrial quarters. To a considerable extent, however, Berlin is represented in terms of its impact on the Mark: it is the vast fire that devours the turf harvested at Wustrau and the Menzer forest: "Ehe dreißig Jahre um waren, war die ganze Menzer Forst durch die Berliner Schornsteine geflogen. Was Teeröfen und Glashütten in alle Ewigkeit nicht vermocht hätten, das hatte die Konsumationskraft einer großen Stadt in weniger als einem Menschenalter geleistet" (2/1:339). Berlin stands in a relation of consumption to its hinterland, an idea taken up again in the chapter "Glindow": "Was Werder für den *Obst*konsum der Hauptstadt ist, das ist Glindow für den *Ziegel*konsum" (2/2:441). As such the relationship of city to hinterland is a troubled one: "das riesige Wachstum der Stadt" (2/2:442) corresponds to signs of destruction in the countryside. To be sure, Fontane's own relationship to the city that became his permanent residence after 1859 was just as complex: the apparent anti-urbanism of certain passages of the *Wanderungen* has to be set against more positive utterances in private correspondence. Thus, while the prospect from the Ruinenberg in Freienwalde appears as a tonic for the jaded city dweller, "wessen Auge krank geworden in Licht und Staub und all dem Blendwerk großer Städte" (2/1:593), there can be no doubt that, for Fontane, the metropolis was "das helle Licht . . ., das ich nicht aufgeben möchte."[110] Like Fontane's political opinions, his views on the relative merits of the urban and rural cannot be reduced to a simple formula. The two sets of opinions develop in tandem: as Fontane moved from the conservatism of his years at the *Kreuz-Zeitung* (back) toward a more liberal political position, so too did his enthusiasm for urban life increase. The turning point came in the 1870s with his move to the *Vossische Zeitung*;[111] and, after the "Unglücksjahr" of 1876 and his resignation from the Prussian Academy of Arts and Sciences, Fontane's political conformism was at an end. Those portions of the work that appeared during the decade at the *Kreuz-Zeitung*, however, attest to a distanced perspective toward Berlin. The opening sentence of "Rheinsberg," the first of the *Märkische Bilder* series (published October-November 1859) is typical in emphasizing and prizing the relative difficulty of access: "*Rheinsberg* von *Berlin* aus zu erreichen ist nicht leicht" (2/1:262). Here, as elsewhere, the *Wanderungen* present themselves as a search for the hidden, the neglected, and the obscure. Thus the work — especially in its early phase — is marked by a demonstrative turning away from the urban milieu. It would, however, be simplistic to represent this turning away as a Rousseauesque revolt against civilization, even if the text occasionally gestures in this direction: "*Wir* aber, in jenem stolzen Wandergefühl, das sich nach Strapazen sehnt, haben den Omnibus verschmäht" (2/2:606). Elsewhere, technical progress is exalted — not deprecated, as we might be inclined to expect. In "Das Schildhorn bei Spandau" (which appears only in the first edition of the *Wanderungen*) "Der helle Pfiff der Lokomotive," becomes the herald of welcome renewal, banishing "die Stille, die Stagnation, die so leicht zum Brütwinkel alles Finstern und Unheimlichen werden" (2/3:401–2). Here a rhetorical note is struck that would not have been out of place in the liberal travel writing of the Young Germans.

It is significant that the plan to write about "*die Marken*, ihre Männer u[nd] ihre Geschichte" was conceived in London.[112] There Fontane had endured real isolation, exacerbated by a tense relationship with his employers in Berlin, an unhappiness only partly mitigated by an abiding interest in London's theatrical and political life. In *Ein Sommer in London*, a memoir of the summer of 1852, daily existence in the metropolis is characterized in terms of its "*Massenhaftigkeit*" (3/3:9), a term that indicates both the deindividualizing effects of urban life and the absence of a sustaining collectivity. It was the experience of these effects that reinforced the exile's commitment to the notion of *character*, both individual and national. Character, for Fontane the guarantee of a stable individual and collective identity, stems not from the city — which effaces it — but from the unurbanized land, from the soil, a notion deriving ultimately from Herder and other theorists of national character. This understanding of the rural as a source of moral regeneration is influenced by the Romantic idea of nature as moral source, and by the idyllic mode in eighteenth-century German poetry, whose foremost exponent was Johann Heinrich Voss. Fontane clearly articulates this in a letter to Ernst Kossak:

> Ich schreibe diese Bücher aus reiner Liebe zur *Scholle*, aus dem Gefühl und dem Bewußtsein (die mir beide in der Fremde gekommen sind) daß in dieser Liebe unsre allerbesten Kräfte wurzeln, Keime eines ächten Conservatismus. Daß uns der Conservatismus, den ich im Sinne habe, noth thut, ist meine feste Ueberzeugung. Speziell unser guten Stadt Berlin ist die Vorstellung abhanden gekommen, daß Beschränkung, Disciplin, das freimüthige Bekenntniß des Nicht-Wissens und viele andern kleinen Tugenden derart auch Tugenden sind, doppelt vielleicht weil sie bei der Oberflächlichkeit und Zer[s]plitterung unsres Lebens, immer rarer werden.[113]

The letter is remarkable for its use of the interlinked metaphors of soil and growth, which recur not only in the *Wanderungen* but throughout Fontane's writings. Such metaphors express his previously mentioned conviction that individual character is bound up with the character of a particular locality. Taken out of the locality to which he is inextricably linked, the individual finds it difficult to flourish. This sense emerges from a letter written by Fontane to his mother from London on 27 June 1858:

> Was ich hier auf die Dauer nicht ertragen kann, das ist das Alleinstehn, die geistige Vereinsamung . . . die Heimath ist zu fern. Die Verbindung mit ihr ist zu lose und zu locker. Was man sagt, verhallt wie in der Wüste. . . . Wir sind eine Pflanze im fremden Boden, es nutzt nichts, daß man alle Sorten von Mist um sie herpackt, sie geht doch aus, weil sie nun mal an

> andres Erdreich gewöhnt ist und wenn es auch nur der vielverschrieene märkische Sand wäre. (4/1:621–22)

What is voiced here is, of course, not merely the particular anguish of a Prussian émigré in London, but also the writer's convictions concerning the moral uprootedness of all city-dwellers. As we have seen, the notion of a Prussian or Brandenburgish character entails for Fontane a canon of specific moral values; the cited letter to Kossak exudes anxiety over the perceived absence of such values from the metropolis. The *Wanderungen* circle around Berlin, holding it at arm's length, for it is not there that those aspects of the Prussian character that the work seeks to revive are to be found. Had the wanderer chosen to traverse the streets of Berlin he might have been confronted with unconscionable evidence that that character was being effaced, and with it the basis of a nationally distinctive collectivity. Instead he opts for the Mark, and for that most rooted class, the Markish nobility. The peregrinations in the Mark might thus be said to involve an act of double evasion: first, in the turn to the past and second, in the avoidance of Berlin. In this respect, at least, it would seem possible to speak of the work as a counterpart to Fontane's journalism, and the question of the relationship between these two aspects of the writer's career is a pertinent one, though one that cannot be explored here.

### "Vaterländische Wanderungen" in Virtual Space: Affinities with the Panorama

Walter Erhart's 1992 essay represents a landmark in the research on the *Wanderungen*, both because it argues effectively that the work is motivated by "Wille zur Ganzheit, zur Totalität,"[114] the desire to counter the decline of collective social forms in modernity, and because it links that will to totality with the panoramic mode of seeing prevailing in the work. That Fontane brings a panoramic view, schooled by the paintings of Lorrain, Poussin, Schinkel, and Blechen to his representations of landscape has been repeatedly noted in the research.[115] Fontane's perception of the Mark is pre-structured by landscape painting in the same way that his reader's view is by vedute, panoramas, and other mass art forms.

Although Fontane's use of the panoramic view has been repeatedly cited, it may be argued that insufficient attention has been paid to the significance of the mass artform as a model for the *Wanderungen* as a whole. Erhart is alone in applying the far-reaching insights of Hess to Fontane's work. Following a survey of the emergence of the panorama and the (closely related) diorama as mass entertainments in urban centers, Hess argues that the panorama concept became increasingly historicized in the course of the nineteenth century.[116] Following an initial vogue for landscapes, especially representations of the Mediterranean, historical subjects began to become increasingly popular. As early as 1830 Carl Wilhelm

Gropius was exhibiting a diorama with a pronounced historical theme: *Gothischer Dom in Morgenbeleuchtung* (*nach Schinkels Gemälde*). In time, the panorama concept itself underwent change, being used in a metaphorical sense in a range of semantic fields outside the purely aesthetic sphere. Reviewing book titles from the 1840s, Hess notes that the term was then being applied to almost any work claiming an all-encompassing view of its subject. The term was especially favored for historical works that sought to provide an inventory of the antiquities, monuments, and landscapes of a particular region. Thus the term panorama came to denote not merely the apperception of landscape but also a particular historical view — one that emphasized continuity and went hand-in-glove with historicism, in the sense of a conception of history that emphasizes the individuality and uniqueness of each historical period. As a corollary to the view that each historical era could only be understood on its own terms, historicists held that there existed a unique correct interpretation of each era — in other words, they believed that individual historical periods could be represented objectively, as if in a snapshot of frozen time.

We know that Fontane was content to be regarded as a painter of historical landscapes from his approving response to Brachvogel's review of the *Wanderungen*.[117] He may even have seen himself as a successor to Karl Friedrich Schinkel — born like him in Neu-Ruppin — whose encomium occupies such a prominent place in *Die Grafschaft Ruppin*. Fontane shared Schinkel's concern for the restoration and maintenance of Brandenburg's monuments and antiquities and it was probably from Schinkel that he took his propensity for panoramic historic landscapes.[118] The chapter "Karl Friedrich Schinkel" refers to the young Schinkel's career assisting at Gropius's Christmas spectaculars, a reference that proves Fontane knew about Schinkel's collaboration with Gropius in perfecting the diorama (Carl Wilhelm Gropius opened his *Berliner Diorama* in 1827), a form whose realistic reproduction of space made it the forerunner of photography. For Fontane the diorama and the photograph offer a paradigm for the objective fixing of the discrete events of history.

Fontane's panorama of the Mark resembles the mass entertainments of Gropius's *Berliner Diorama*, not only in its attempt to provide an all-encompassing view of its historical subject matter, but also in its definite national-ideological tendency. In the sense that it contains these two conflicting moments — a claim to realistic, objective representation and an idealizing nationalist tendency — the *Wanderungen* reveal themselves to be a thoroughgoing product of historicism.[119] Nationalist ideology made itself felt in even the earliest historical dioramas shown in Berlin. Schinkel's *Gothischer Dom in Morgenbeleuchtung* is typical in this respect. The painting, and the diorama based on it, were imbued with a overtly nationalist symbolism. Interestingly, Schinkel's painting did not depict an actually existing medieval cathedral, but a building commissioned by Friedrich

Wilhelm III in 1814–15 as a memorial to the Wars of Liberation. Although never constructed for lack of funds, that structure was intended to instill awe and patriotic feeling by making manifest the splendor of the Middle Ages, a period considered as marking the origin of a distinct German national history. Such considerations evidently also played a part in the exhibition of the diorama based on Schinkel's painting, which opened on 18 June 1830. Later, these media would be even more overtly utilized for the purposes of state propaganda. Popular enthusiasm for these entertainments, together with their use in the manipulation of public opinion, reached its zenith in the early *Gründerzeit*. Anton von Werner's 1883 panorama of the Battle of Sedan drew large crowds to a specially constructed rotunda on the Alexanderplatz; the opening, attended by Bismarck and the Kaiser, had, as Hess notes, "den Charakter eines Staatsaktes."[120]

The panorama analogy is a particularly fruitful one to apply to the *Wanderungen*, not only because it helps us to grasp the totalizing aesthetic of the work, but also in view of the conflation of landscape and national ideology that characterizes the medium and the literary work itself. There is, however, a further respect in which Fontane's work resembles the mass medium. It does so by replicating what Hess has termed the panorama's "historicistic structure," that is, the capacity of that medium to visualize simultaneously or in succession historical events greatly separated in time — an attribute that it shares with the museum.[121] Thus in the *Wanderungen* early struggles between Germans and Slavs, the settlement of the Mark by the Cistercians, the turmoil of the post-Reformation period, the Battle of Fehrbellin, and the campaigns of the Wars of Liberation are all made simultaneously present in what Erhart, borrowing André Malraux's term, calls a *musée imaginaire*.

Viewing the work as panorama or *musée imaginaire* allows a fuller understanding of the relationship between structure and function within it. In the preface to the fourth edition, dated 14 November 1882, Fontane felt it necessary to correct misconceptions about the nature of the work: the *Wanderungen*, he stresses, "sollen kein Geschichtsbuch sein," adding "auch kein Reisebuch" (2/3:816). From that preface it is evident that the *Wanderungen* were seen by many readers as a handbook in the mold of the Baedeker guides. The author registers this misunderstanding and the reader disappointment resulting from it with chagrin. The *Wanderungen* were not conceived as a sort of vade mecum designed to accompany excursions in the Mark; rather, it might be argued, the work itself creates a space constructed in accordance with a realist aesthetic in which the reader can simulate the effect of moving about. The wanderings that are envisaged are of a virtual or textual nature. Like the panorama and its variants, the specific attraction of the work lies in the fact that it offers a vicarious experience of travel, the completeness of which is enhanced by the wealth of topographical and historical detail.[122] Undoubtedly it was the geographical organization of the *Wanderungen* that caused readers to confuse them with the Baedeker guides: each of the four volumes is devoted to a particular region of the Mark, and these are in turn subdivided into chapters that focus — for the most part — on districts and towns within those regions. This organizational principle lends the work its characteristic openness; it invites the reader to access it at any point, rather than constraining him or her to a linear reading. Erdmut Jost has correctly noted that many individual chapters exhibit a circular structure: the verse epigraph introduces the theme, which is varied throughout the chapter and reprised in the concluding sentences.[123] This finding has implications for the overall structure of the work, insofar as their circularity endows the parts with a high degree of independence with respect to the whole. To return to the idea of the *Wanderungen* as panorama, as a virtual space in which the reader can simulate the experience of wandering, we might say that each chapter represents a self-contained excursion in a particular landscape. Because the individual chapters represent self-contained excursions, the reader can set the itinerary; but this degree of freedom afforded by the structure is offset by the careful steering of perception alluded to earlier, which constantly refers the reader to the ideological framework. The ideological framework, the canon of moral attributes as manifested in the persons associated with a particular locality, is what binds the individual chapters to the whole. The moral canon is normative, since it represents an ideal standard of Prussian character to which the individuals portrayed are held to conform to a greater (Schinkel, Günther) or lesser (Michel Protzen) degree.

Although the *Wanderungen* are characterized by a totalizing view at the service of a specific ideology, it would be a gross oversimplification to liken it to propagandistic spectacles like Anton von Werner's panorama of the Battle of Sedan. To be sure, Fontane, like the constructors of memorials, museums, and panoramas, operates with a patriotic program in mind, but he differs from them in that, rather than validating the contemporary political situation, he is engaged in an attempt to recover and revive the values of the past.[124] Fontane's "ächter Conservatismus" proceeds from the perception that the ethical basis of Prussia's greatness was being undermined even as Prussia achieved supremacy as the leading power in the newly established Empire. The dominant trends of the time were rampant mercantilism and Bismarckian chicanery, and Fontane — for all the esteem in which he held the person of Bismarck — was by no means blind to the latter. Although he would not permit himself to call the Chancellor a "Prinzipienverächter" until much later, and then only in private correspondence, Fontane's misgivings about Bismarck's "blood and iron" policy were already incipient in his accounts of the campaigns of 1864 and 1866.[125] While the sacrifice of the officers and men who perished in those wars is given due honor, these accounts reserve judgment on the question of the foreign policy of which they were an instrument. In the

*Wanderungen*, too, commemorating the fallen can imply a critique of power. The obelisk at Rheinsberg, by memorializing those commanders unjustly neglected by official historiography, is presented as a critical commentary to Friedrich II's version of the Seven Years' War.

In the sense that it intends a recovery of declining values and principles, Fontane's most Prussian book implies not an affirmation but a (tacit) critique of the contemporary situation. This critical tendency is already suggested by the title of the work. We have seen that for Fontane that term can denote a range of travel modes, but in the railway age "Wanderungen" has a specific signal value. It is a declaration of allegiance to pedestrianism; what is tendentiously indicated in the title is thus a commitment to deceleration, to a travel mode that enables the recovery of the fine detail erased in the moving panorama of the rail passenger's window. And the panoramic view of the Wanderungen is indeed one that encompasses the minutiae of "Storchennest" and "Hagebuttenstrauch." In a Mark whose values are threatened by the burgeoning metropolis, this mode of travel is indispensable in recuperating those elements of difference that remain and, with them, the vestiges of a Prussian character.

In certain respects the *Wanderungen* seem to match the specifications made by Hegel for the early epics of the world's peoples: these are "die poetischen Grundbücher," the memorials of cultures, which provide "eine Totalanschauung des ganzen Volksgeistes."[126] Although Fontane's aversion to speculative philosophy certainly also precluded any in-depth study of aesthetics, his chapter "Wilhelm Gentz" (which first appeared in the *Wohlfeile Ausgabe* of 1892) contains a quotation from Gentz's travelogue that articulates a vision of art tantalizingly close to Hegel's: "Wie Egypten selbst als ein eigentümlicher, nur aus sich selbst verständlicher Organismus anzusehen ist, so prägen auch die egyptischen Kunstwerke: ganze Ortschaften mit Tempeln, Obelisken, Grabdenkmälern, Sphinxalleen eine in sich einige Totalität aus, welche der hierarchischen Gliederung und Ordnung des Lebens entspricht" (2/1:159). It might be said that the above quotation captures something of the spirit of Fontane's own intentions for the *Wanderungen:* a work of parts, individual feuilletonistic essays, all of which are bound together in a whole providing a panoramic overview of the history of Brandenburg. In their striving for wholeness, roundedness, and objectivity, and their avoidance of ironic rupture, Fontane's *Reisefeuilletons* are the antithesis of Heine's *Reisebilder*, which sought to break with Hegel's classicism.[127]

## "Keime Pflanzen für künftige Saat": Wandering and Cultivation

Also Hegelian is Fontane's recognition of the state as the objectified reason within which the individual must take his place. Like his hero, the reformer Marwitz, Fontane strives for a moral regeneration of Prussia in which "der Egoismus . . . ausgefegt, die Zugehörigkeit zum Staat und das

Bewußtsein davon neu geboren werden [sollte]" (2/1:772). But the self-submission Fontane advocates is not so much to the state as accomplished fact as to the nation in its process of evolution and growth. The prominence given to metaphors of growth has already been noted; these attest to Fontane's historicism, to his conviction that nations develop in accordance with internal principles. For Fontane, the anthropological principle driving historical change is "character." As we have noticed, he holds that character is the product of environmental factors; in this he is close to the environmental determinism articulated by Herder in *Ideen zur Philosophie der Geschichte der Menschheit* (1784–91). This environmental determinism is not total, for Herder postulates an internal principle — "genetische Kraft" — by means of which the individual organism adapts to its surroundings.[128] Although Herder uses the concept of "Kraft" primarily in a biological context, he also ascribes vital force to historical agencies, regarding history in terms of conflict among contending "Kräfte." This idea of history as the product of contending forces is brought out clearly in the chapter "Die Wenden in der Mark" in *Havelland:*

> Die Wenden waren tapfer und gastfrei und, wie wir uns überzeugt halten, um kein Haar falscher und untreuer als ihre Besieger, die Deutschen; aber in einem waren sie ihnen allerdings unebenbürtig, in jener gestaltenden, große Ziele von Generation zu Generation unerschütterlich im Auge behaltenden Kraft, die zu allen Zeiten der Grundzug der germanischen Race [*sic*] gewesen und noch jetzt die Bürgschaft ihres Lebens ist. *Die Wenden von damals waren wie die Polen von heut.* Ausgerüstet mit liebenswürdigen und blendenden Eigenschaften, an Ritterlichkeit ihren Gegnern mindestens gleich, an Leidenschaft, an Opfermut ihnen vielleicht überlegen, gingen sie dennoch zugrunde, weil sie jener gestaltenden Kraft entbehrten. Immer voll Neigung, ihre Kräfte nach außen hin schweifen zu lassen, statt sie im Zentrum zu einen, fehlte ihnen das Konzentrische, während sie exzentrisch waren in jedem Sinne. Dazu die individuelle Freiheit höher achtend als die staatliche Festigung — wer erkennte in diesem allen nicht polnischnationale Züge? (2/2:26–27)

In the above passage we recognize some of the key features of the historicism prevalent in Fontane's time: the belief that each of the world's peoples and each historical epoch is in some sense individual, unique, and unrepeatable, that peoples and epochs can only be understood on their own terms. Also typical is the effort to be even-handed, to do justice to all the parties described. Furthermore, the passage envisages history as a process directed toward the end point of "staatliche Festigung." But what is interesting about the above passage is its notion of a vital force embodied in a people as the motor of historical change. Fontane's view of history thus contains a strong element of vitalism, and in this respect it may be regarded as distinct from the prevalent form of historicism. The practitioners of that brand of historicism — conservative historians such as

Leopold von Ranke, Friedrich Karl von Savigny, and Heinrich von Treitschke — represented contemporary political and social reality as the culmination of all prior historical development; their primary concern was to narrate history in such a way as to legitimate the present. As Walter Müller-Seidel has remarked:

> Geschichtliches Denken im Verständnis der Historischen Schule ist der Vergangenheit liebevoll zugetan und dem Gewordenen als der staatlichen Gegenwart des eigenen Volkes, erst recht. Aber das Werden selbst, der Ablauf, die Formen der Erneuerung finden nicht gleicherweise Interesse, und am wenigsten dann, wenn sie über die Gegenwart hinaus und in die Zukunft hinein weisen. . . . Dem Geschichtsdenken des 19. Jahrhunderts, wie es sich im Historismus entwickelt hat, fehlen Kategorien wie Zukunft, Erneuerung oder Fortschritt.[129]

It is generally held that the Fontane of the *Wanderungen* operates within the parameters of historicism.[130] Like other members of the "Historische Schule" he claims impartiality while simultaneously employing historiography as the instrument of national ideology. In the above passage, however, we get a glimpse of a view of history whose horizons are not restricted to the present. Here history is viewed not from the vantage of a end point already attained but as a dynamic process, for the "gestaltende Kraft" here attributed to the German people is "noch jetzt die Bürgschaft ihres Lebens." For Fontane, then, German history had not reached its terminus in the establishment of the *Reich*, as it had for Gustav Freytag — who shares his predilection for biologistic metaphors — but was still very much in the making. Culturally mediated evolution — and not revolution — is the mode of social change in which Fontane puts his trust. Cleaving to a gradual view of historical change, he is convinced of the necessity of maintaining continuity with the past. He envisages not rupture but gradual development in which remnants of the past will endure and persist. It is the desire to rescue cultural goods for the future and thereby to exercise a beneficent influence on the future development of Prussia — and thus, of the Reich as a whole — that motivates Fontane's search for cultural artifacts and exemplary persons in the Mark.

The frequency with which metaphors of growth occur is not least due to the status of agriculture within the literary work. Everywhere the wanderer turns he is confronted with a landscape that is shaped by cultivation: "Kein Fußbreit Landes, der nicht die Pflege der Menschenhand verriete" (2/2:557). Much attention is devoted to accounts of the draining of the Oder and Havel marshes and of the subsequent unrelenting efforts to make the reclaimed land fertile. A recurring theme is the capacity of strenuous labor to make even the most unpromising material bear fruit. This theme can be understood in a purely poetological sense as an expression of Fontane's will to fashion a work of art out of the scarce stuff of Markish lore and legend, but cultivation as it appears in the *Wanderungen* is always also associated with the process of civilization itself. Thus those figures who are presented as having contributed the most to the evolution and growth of Prussia are those who had played a leading role in its agricultural development: from the soldier-king Friedrich Wilhelm I and his successor Friedrich II, with their ambitious land-reclamation and settlement programs, to the pioneers of rational agriculture ("Die Besiegung der Natur durch Arbeit"),[131] Daniel Albrecht Thaer and the industrious Frau von Friedland. Indeed, Fontane describes a mode of wandering that is allied with cultivation inasmuch as it aims to shape the future by recovering and transmitting the cultural goods of the past.[132] And the reader, too, is afforded the opportunity of participating in the material labor of recovering the past: both by wandering through the *musée imaginaire* of the work itself and by recapitulating the author's own travels in the Mark. Either way, the work seeks to encourage a form of wandering by means of which Berliners can reconnect with the soil of the Mark and with the moral heritage from which, in Fontane's opinion, they have become detached. The animation of the local, the poeticizing of times past[133] is therefore carried on with an eye to the future social and political development of Prussia. Hope in the future — and in its amenability to reform — is always present in the *Wanderungen*. Of all the *motti* adorning the individual chapters, the one which perhaps best encapsulates Fontane's intentions is the short verse dedication to Thaer:

> Ehre jedem Heldentume,
> Dreimal Ehre deinem Ruhme,
> Aller Taten beste Tat
> Ist: Keime pflanzen für künftige Saat. (2/1:654)

It has been noted that "Wanderungen" implies a commitment to pedestrianism as a decelerated mode of travel. What the work envisages is a gradual progress through the landscape that fosters a sense of continuity. Fontane's trust in continuity, in stable, measured growth as a principle of historical change, comes to the fore in a piece originally written for the Christmas Day edition of the *Kreuz-Zeitung* and subsequently reprinted in *Havelland*, "Der Eibenbaum im Parkgarten des Herrenhauses." The subject is an ancient yew standing in the garden of a baron's house in the Tiergarten. In the text the mighty tree, whose origins Fontane traces to the arrival of the Hohenzollerns in the Mark, provides the symbolic link between monarchy and democracy. The latest scion of that dynasty, the crown prince, Friedrich Wilhelm IV, had, as a boy, played under its branches. Later, Fontane recalls, the tree had come under threat when the Prussian Upper House, as a result of a fire in 1852, was forced to move to the former baronial residence. When it became apparent that an extension to the building would be required to accommodate the legislature, the decision was taken to fell the ancient yew. Only the intervention of the King prevented this decision from being carried out: "Wer überhaupt dankbar ist, ist es gegen alles, Mensch oder Baum" (2/2:125). The anecdote can be read as a parable of the parliament's steady encroachment on royal territory, a process countervailed by royal decree; but it is also the account of a clash between reckless progressivism and a conservatism characterized by gratitude toward the past. The outcome — the new Upper House was finally constructed in such a way as to accommodate the yew tree — gestures toward a hoped-for reconciliation between the parliamentary and monarchic traditions.

Of course, wandering in the Mark does not inevitably foster a sense of continuity but can instead confront the wanderer with the irrefutable evidence of decline and loss. Erhart has particularly stressed "die melancholische Begleitmelodie der Vergänglichkeit," which he likens to the kind of nostalgia supposedly found in Lévi-Strauss's *Tristes tropiques.*[134] At times the terrain seems stubbornly resistant to the wanderer's attempts to make it yield up historical material, to make it speak. The silence of absence and death envelops the ruins of the Cistercian monastery at Chorin, described in *Havelland:* "Da sind keine Traditionen . . ., da ist kein See, kein Haus, kein Baum, die als Zeugen blutiger Vorgänge in irgendeine alte Klosterlegende verflochten wären; . . .; alles ist tot hier, alles schweigt" (2/2:93). Perhaps nowhere is the dissonance between past and present more evident than in those excursions where the urban and rural spheres collide. Thus the opening paragraphs describing an excursion on foot from Berlin to the residence of Wilhelm von Humboldt at Tegel are mired in contradiction (2/2:156–57). The first part of the journey takes the wanderer through the suburb of Oranienburg, "die volkreichste und vielleicht interessanteste der Berliner Vorstädte." Almost incredibly, Fontane, having noted that this suburb is almost entirely dominated by steelworks, railway yards, barracks, and cemeteries, goes on to contrast it favorably with the neighboring village of Wedding. The suburb of Oranienburg is identified as "das Kind einer neuen Zeit und eines neuen Geistes" in contrast with Wedding, which typifies an old-fashioned Markish dourness. While the old village is decried as prosaic and unlovely — "In erschreckender Weise fehlt der Sinn für das *Malerische*" — the industrial suburb is praised for the "feinen Geschmack" of its buildings. The effect here, where the text struggles to accommodate the Mark and Berlin simultaneously, is one of strain. At the threshold between the city and the Mark, the wanderer feels compelled to uphold the values of the new age in the face of the old, a decision that seems at odds with the fundamental tendency of the *Wanderungen.*

Nevertheless, this is only an apparent contradiction, for the *Wanderungen*, despite its conservatism and antiquarianism, is essentially committed to the future, to the moral regeneration of Prussia. In a sense the project of recovering the cultural goods of the past is necessarily accompanied by a certain melancholia, for the wanderer must turn to churches and graveyards, to monuments and inscriptions as his primary sources; and, in the course of his work he is inevitably confronted with lacunae and absences. By placing too much emphasis on the melancholic undertones, undeniably present though they are, interpreters risk overlooking the prospective and reforming intention of the work. Even those passages that apparently lend themselves most naturally to such a reading are not always devoid of optimism. Thus Erhart may well use the description of *Schloß Oranienburg* to argue that the *Wanderungen* is a document of an ailing culture, pointing to the ill-usage to which the former residence of Friedrich I had been put, its conversion into a cotton mill and, later, into a sulphuric acid plant: "Die Schwefeldämpfe ätzten und beizten den letzten Rest alter Herrlichkeit hinweg" (2/2:152). But that is not the end of the matter, for the building has acquired a new purpose, as a teacher-training college. Doubtless, the old splendor has vanished; the building now wears "das moderne Allerweltskleid." There are, however, grounds for hope in the future, and specifically in the new generation of teachers, whom Fontane sees as the bearers of the historical and cultural legacy of which *Schloß Oranienburg* forms a part. The reflections on decline and loss that form a significant part of the *Wanderungen* are by no means incompatible with a belief in historical evolution and progress, for Fontane shares with Herder an organicist view of history in which the decay of a particular culture or historical era is followed by the blossoming of another.

## Notes

[1] Eberhard Galley et al., *Heinrich Heines Werk im Urteil der Zeitgenossen*, 13 vols. (Hamburg: Hoffmann & Campe, 1981–2006), 1:244–52; here, 250.

[2] Galley, *Heinrich Heines Werk*, 1:289–91; here, 291.

[3] Among the modern scholars to assert that the *Reisebild* represents an innovative genre are Wolfgang Preisendanz and Karol Sauerland. See Wolfgang Preisendanz, "Der Funktionsübergang von Dichtung und Publizistik bei Heine," in Hans Robert Jauß, *Die nicht mehr schönen Künste: Grenzphänomene des Ästhetischen* (Munich: Fink, 1968), 343–74; and Karol Sauerland, "Heinrich Heines *Reisebilder* — ein besonderes literarisches Genre?" in *Heinrich Heine: Streitbarer Humanist und volksverbundener Dichter*. Internationale Wissenschaftliche Konferenz aus Anlaß des 175. Geburtstages von Heinrich Heine vom 6. zum 9. Dezember 1972 in Weimar, ed Karl Wolfgang Becker (Weimar: Nationale Forschungs- und Gedenkstätten der klassischen deutschen Literatur, 1973), 145–58 and 472–74. Peter Brenner's survey of the extensive body of research into Heine's *Reisebilder* remains the most comprehensive; see Brenner, *Der*

*Reisebericht in der deutschen Literatur: Ein Forschungsüberblick als Vorstudie zu einer Gattungsgeschichte* (Tübingen: Niemeyer, 1990), 361–442.

[4] "Hier nach 'Dichtung' zu suchen, wäre von vornherein verfehlt. Denn die meisten Vertreter dieser Bewegung betrachteten sich voller Stolz als öffentlich wirksame Publizisten und nicht als weltfremde Literaten." Jost Hermand, *Das junge Deutschland: Texte und Dokumente* (Stuttgart: Reclam, 1966), 373–74.

[5] Carolyn Becker disagrees, arguing that the *Harzreise* marks a decisive break with Enlightenment travel literature. See *From the Jacobins to the Young Germans: The Liberal Travel Literature from 1785 to 1840* (Ph.D. diss., University of Wisconsin, 1974), 71–72.

[6] Albrecht defines "Wanderberichte oder -beschreibungen" as "Schriften, die nach unterschiedlichen narrativen Grundsätzen ganz oder partiell handeln von authentischem Wandern im Sinne einer Reise zu Fuß, bei der ein Orts- oder Raumwechsel zur Begegnung mit Fremden führt." Wolfgang Albrecht, "Kultur und Physiologie des Wanderns: Einleitende Vorüberlegungen eines Germanisten zur interdisziplinären Erforschung der deutschsprachigen Wanderliteratur," in *Wanderzwang — Wanderlust: Formen der Raum und Sozialerfahrung zwischen Aufklärung und Frühindustrialisierung*, ed. Wolfgang Albrecht and Hans-Joachim Kertscher (Tübingen: Niemeyer, 1999), 1–12; here, 2. The main exemplar of the genre in the pre-1848 period is the ten-part series *Das malerische und romantische Deutschland*, published by Wigand of Leipzig, including the following works: Gustav Schwab, *Wanderungen durch Schwaben* (Leipzig: Wigand, 1837/38; part 2 of *Das malerische und romantische Deutschland*); Wilhelm Blumenhagen, *Wanderung durch den Harz* (Leipzig: Wigand, 1838; repr., Hildesheim: Olms, 1984; part 5); Georg Carl Herloßsohn, *Wanderungen durch das Riesengebirge und die Grafschaft Glatz* (Leipzig: Wigand, 1840/41; part 6).

[7] Georg Friedrich Rebmann, *Werke und Briefe*, ed. Wolfgang Ritschel, 3 vols. (Berlin: Rütten & Loening, 1990), 1:67.

[8] Karol Sauerland (*Heinrich Heines Reisebilder*, 150–54) argues that Heine's use of contingency as a principle structuring both the journey and the text distinguishes the *Harzreise* from its forebears. See also Françoise Knopper, "Heine et la tradition des chroniques de voyage," in *Heine voyageur*, ed. Alain Cozic, Françoise Knopper, and Alain Ruiz (Toulouse: Mirail, 1999), 99–111; here, 102: "Les bourgeois érudits avaient surtout l'ambition d'être exhaustifs, encyclopédiques, précis, techniques, utiles. . . . Leur plan était rigide, leur parcours fixé à l'avance et scrupuleusement respecté . . . Heine s'écartera de cette ambition scientifique: à la continuité objective du parcours il opposera ses associations d'idées, discontinues." Heine uses the formula "die Kreuz und die Quer" in the opening sentence of his travelogue *Ueber Polen* (1822).

[9] The *Bergidylle* "bildet sowohl den strukturellen Mittelpunkt wie auch den programmatischen Höhepunkt der 'Harzreise,' da hier nicht nur die wichtigsten Motive des Textes zusammenlaufen, sondern der im Prolog genannte Zielort der Reise erreicht ist." Olaf Hildebrand, *Emanzipation und Versöhnung: Aspekte des Sensualismus im Werk Heinrich Heines unter besonderer Berücksichtigung der "Reisebilder"* (Tübingen: Niemeyer, 2001), 72–90; here, 72–73. In a detailed interpretation, Hildebrand argues that Hegel's triadic model of history provides the conceptual frame of the *Bergidylle*.

[10] Heinrich Heine, *Historisch-kritische Gesamtausgabe der Werke*, ed. Manfred Windfuhr, 16 vols. (Hamburg: Hoffmann & Campe, 1973–97), 6:111. The page numbers of citations from this volume are given in the main body of the text. Citations from other volumes are indicated by successive Arabic numerals denoting the volume and page numbers respectively.

[11] Georg Wilhelm Friedrich Hegel, *Werke*, ed. Eva Moldenhauer and Karl Markus Michel, 20 vols. (Frankfurt am Main: Suhrkamp, 1969–71), 12:32.

[12] Ulrich Klein, *Die deutschsprachige Reisesatire im 18. Jahrhundert* (Heidelberg: Winter, 1997), esp. 9–33.

[13] Rebmann's satire *Empfindsame Reise nach Schilda* (1793) also parodies the classifying zeal and irrelevant eclecticism of contemporary travel journals: "*Querlequitsch*. Der Turm hat einen vergoldeten Knopf, und am Herrnhof ist eine Eule angenagelt. Getraut wurden in diesem Jahr fünf Paar. *Ypsilonshausen*. Wir kamen um ein Viertel nach zwölf Uhr an und fuhren um ein halb Uhr wieder ab. Die Regierungsform in dieser Residenz scheint oligarchisch zu sein. . . . Die Semmeln sind hierzulande eiförmig" (Rebmann, *Werke*, 1:177).

[14] The theory that systems of government are determined by climate appears in Montesquieu's *De l'esprit des lois* (1748). Herder, in the *Ideen zur Philosophie der Geschichte der Menschheit* (1784–91) goes further than Montesquieu in theorizing that climate — understood as a range of environmental factors prevailing in a particular region — is a determinant not only of constitutional forms but of a culture in its entirety.

[15] Klaus Pabel, *Heines "Reisebilder": Ästhetisches Bedürfnis und politisches Interesse am Ende der Kunstperiode* (Munich: Fink, 1977), 97–129; here, 97.

[16] There existed a considerable overlap between the *Turnbewegung* and the *Burschenschaften* in terms of both membership and ideology. For instance, Jahn, the founder of the athletics movement, had also been involved in establishing the patriotic student fraternities, and he played a key role in the 1817 Wartburg Festival, the largest political demonstration held by the student movement before its proscription.

[17] See Hildebrand for an account of the indirect references to *Heinrich von Ofterdingen* in the *Harzreise* (*Emanzipation und Versöhnung*, 49–54).

[18] Pabel, *Heines "Reisebilder,"* 99–100.

[19] Norbert Altenhofer, *Die verlorene Augensprache: Über Heinrich Heine* (Frankfurt am Main and Leipzig: Insel, 1993), 15.

[20] Hermand, *Der frühe Heine: Ein Kommentar zu den "Reisebildern"* (Munich: Winkler, 1976), 8–10.

[21] From the 1820s the panorama and the diorama became popular mass entertainments, foreshadowing the cinema in that they were exhibited in specially constructed buildings. The panorama created the illusion of an all-round view, usually from an elevation, by placing the viewer in front of a curved surface on which a landscape was depicted. In many cases the panorama took the form of a circular chamber completely surrounding the viewer. Dioramas, which positioned the observer in front of a chamber with a painted backdrop and side walls in which various objects were distributed, were especially suited to the representation of

interiors. While both panoramas and dioramas exploited the laws of perspective to create a three-dimensional view, the diorama introduced artificial illumination, which made it possible to simulate different lighting conditions, an innovation later used in panoramas. Günter Hess argues that the impact of these media in the nineteenth century contributed to a trivialization of modes of seeing. In this respect they had a similar effect to the mass-produced veduta in pre-structuring the experience of nature in wandering. See Hess, "Panorama und Denkmal: Erinnerung als Denkform zwischen Vormärz und Gründerzeit," in *Literatur in der sozialen Bewegung: Aufsätze und Forschungsberichte zum 19. Jahrhundert*, ed. Alberto Martino (Tübingen: Niemeyer, 1977), 130–206. See also Monika Wagner, "Ansichten ohne Ende — Oder das Ende der Ansicht — Umbrüche im Reisebild um 1830," in *Reisekultur: Von der Pilgerfahrt zum modernen Tourismus*, ed. Hermann Bausinger, Klaus Beyrer, and Gottfried Korff (Munich: Beck, 1991), 326–35.

[22] Friedrich Ludwig Jahn, *Deutsches Volkstum* (1810; repr., Leipzig: Reclam, [n.d.]), 249.

[23] Jahn, *Deutsches Volkstum*, 250.

[24] Hermand, *Der frühe Heine*, 46–47.

[25] The popularity of this ideal is reflected in the profusion of texts bearing the word "cosmopolitan" in the title circulating in the decade of the French Revolution and subsequently. The leading journal in the short-lived Mainz Republic was entitled the *Kosmopolitische Beobachter:* it appeared only in 1793. From this period until the March 1848 revolution several cosmopolitan travelogues appeared. Apart from Rebmann's *Kosmopolitische Wanderungen durch einen Theil Deutschlands*, Carl Feyerabend's *Kosmopolitische Wanderungen durch Preußen, Liefland, Litthauen, Vollhynien, Podolien, Galizien und Schlesien in den Jahren 1795 bis 1797*, in *Briefen an einen Freund*, 4 vols. (Danzig, 1798–1802) is representative of this sub-genre. In the pre-1848 period Franz Dingelstedt's *Lieder eines kosmopolitischen Nachtwächters* (1841; Leipzig: Klinckhardt & Biermann, 1923) enjoyed considerable success. Dingelstedt was also the author of a *Wanderbuch*, 2 vols. (Leipzig: Einhorn, 1839–43).

[26] Michael Werner, ed., *Begegnungen mit Heine: Berichte der Zeitgenossen*, 2 vols. (Hamburg: Hoffmann & Campe, 1973), 1:123.

[27] Ritchie Robertson, "Herr Peregrinus: Persona, Race and Gender in Heine's *Die Harzreise*," in *Brücken über dem Abgrund: Auseinandersetzungen mit jüdischen Leidenserfahrung, Antisemitismus und Exil*, ed. Amy Colin and Elisabeth Strenger, Festschrift für Harry Zohn (Munich: Fink, 1994).

[28] Letter to Moses Moser, 21 Jan. 1824, in Heine, *Säkularausgabe: Werke, Briefe, Lebenszeugnisse*, ed. Nationale Forschungs- und Gedenkstätten der klassischen deutschen Literatur and Centre National de la Recherche Scientifique (Paris and Berlin: Éditions du CNRS and Akademie, 1970–), 20:148.

[29] Thus the description of the mottoes inscribed in the Brocken visitors' book: "Hier wird des Sonnenaufgangs majestätische Pracht beschrieben, dort wird geklagt über schlechtes Wetter, über getäuschte Erwartungen, über den Nebel, der alle Aussicht sperrt. 'Benebelt herauf gekommen und benebelt hinunter gegangen!' ist ein stehender Witz, der hier von Hunderten nachgerissen wird" (128–29).

[30] Galley, *Heinrich Heines Werk im Urteil der Zeitgenossen*, 1:215.

[31] Norbert Altenhofer, *Die verlorene Augensprache*, 54.

[32] Hildebrand, *Emanzipation und Versöhnung*, 52.

[33] Constantin François Volney's work *Les ruines, ou méditations sur les révolutions des empires* (1791) was an important source for the early Romantic ruin cult.

[34] Friedrich Gottschalk, *Taschenbuch für Reisende in den Harz*, 3rd ed. (1806; repr., Magdeburg: Heinrichshofen, 1823,), 5.

[35] Johann Christoph Adelung, *Grammatisch-kritisches Wörterbuch der hochdeutschen Mundart*, 2nd ed., 4 vols. (Leipzig: Breitkopf & Härtel, 1798; repr., Hildesheim: Olms, 1970), vol. 3, col. 672; vol. 4, col. 978.

[36] Letter to an unnamed friend in Hamburg, Apr. 1833 (Heine, *Säkularausgabe*, 20:51). In the same letter Heine speaks of his "pacifike Mission, die Völker einander näher zu bringen," of his hope that "mit der Zerstörung der nationalen Vorurtheile, mit dem Vernichten des patriotischen Eigensinnigkeit schwindet ihr bestes Hülfsmittel der Unterdrückung" and styles himself as "der inkarnirte Kosmopolitismus."

[37] Hildebrand, *Emanzipation und Versöhnung*, 107–8.

[38] Jeffrey L. Sammons, *Heinrich Heine: The Elusive Poet* (New Haven, CT, and London: Yale, 1969), 13.

[39] T. J. Reed, "Number the Years," *Times Literary Supplement*, 22 July 2005, 7.

[40] Slobodan Grubacic, *Heines Erzählprosa: Versuch einer Analyse* (Stuttgart and Berlin: Kohlhammer, 1975), 68–72. Grubacic borrows the concept of carnivalization from Bakhtin's theory of the novel.

[41] Heine's avoidance of the term "Sehnsucht" in all its variants may stem from a perception that this term had become a cliché in narratives of wandering.

[42] Thus Sammons: "Heine has always figured as one of the most subjective of writers, without regard for propriety, humility or consistency." *Heinrich Heine*, 7.

[43] Hildebrand, *Emanzipation und Versöhnung*, 80.

[44] I follow Friedrich Sengle in using the term *Biedermeierzeit* to refer to the distinctive *cultural* epoch between the 1815 Congress of Vienna and the Revolution of March 1848. Friedrich Sengle, *Biedermeierzeit: deutsche Literatur im Spannungsfeld zwischen Restauration und Revolution, 1815–1848*, 3 vols. (Stuttgart: Metzler, 1971–80). However, it should be noted that political historians usually distinguish between the Restoration (1815–30) and the *Vormärz* (1830–48). I have used these latter terms where it is necessary to situate texts more precisely in their political contexts.

[45] The edition quoted throughout is Georg Büchner, *Werke und Briefe* (Münchner Ausgabe), ed. Karl Pörnbacher et al. (Munich: dtv, 2004), 135. References to this work will be given in the text using page numbers alone.

[46] Elisabetta Niccolini, *Der Spaziergang des Schriftstellers: "Lenz" von Georg Büchner, "Der Spaziergang" von Robert Walser, "Gehen" von Thomas Bernhard* (Stuttgart and Weimar: Metzler, 2000), 65–124; here, 76; Gerhard P. Knapp, *Georg Büchner*, 3rd ed. (Stuttgart and Weimar: Metzler, 2000), 139; Peter

Kubitschek, "Zur tödlichen Stille der verkehrten Welt: Zu Georg Büchners *Lenz*," in *Studien zu Georg Büchner*, ed. Hans-Georg Werner (Berlin: Aufbau, 1988), 86–104; here, 93.

[47] I will not enter into the debate (melancholia versus schizophrenia) about the categorical nature of the sufferings of the historical Jakob Michael Reinhold Lenz (1751–92), or of his counterpart in Büchner's story: Readers with diagnostic interests should refer to Harald Schmidt, "Schizophrenie oder Melancholie? Zur problematischen Differentialdiagnostik in Georg Büchners *Lenz*," *Zeitschrift für deutsche Philologie* 117 (1998): 516–42.

[48] For Albrecht the term *Wanderliteratur* is a "heuristischer Arbeitsbegriff" used to denote different kinds of texts: first, accounts of authentic experiences of wandering; second, autobiographical and literary texts in which wandering is a central motif; and, third, guides and handbooks. Albrecht, "Kultur und Physiologie des Wanderns: Einleitende Vorüberlegungen eines Germanisten zur interdisziplinären Erforschung der deutschsprachigen Wanderliteratur," in Albrecht and Kertscher, *Wanderzwang*, 1–12; here, 2.

[49] Albrecht bases his discussion on the analysis of two series of *Wanderbücher: Das malerische und romantische Deutschland*, 10 vols. and 4 supplements (1836–42) and *Die Wanderer um die Welt* in 6 vols. (1839–46). Both series were conceived with an informative function in mind: they were intended to provide readers with descriptions of landscapes in parts of Germany unfamiliar to them, and to encourage them to seek out those landscapes for themselves. See Wolfgang Albrecht, "Durchs 'malerische und romantische' Deutschland: Wanderliteratur der Biedermeier- und Vormärzepoche," in Albrecht and Kertscher, *Wanderzwang*, 215–38; here, 222.

[50] Wolfgang Albrecht, "Durchs 'malerische und romantische' Deutschland," 223.

[51] Friedrich Blumenhagen, *Wanderung durch den Harz: Mit 30 Stahlstichen* (Leipzig: Wigand, 1838; repr., Hildesheim and New York: Olms, 1972), from the series *Das malerische und romantische Deutschland.*

[52] Joachim Ritter, "Landschaft: Zur Funktion des ästhetischen in der modernen Gesellschaft," in *Subjektivität: Sechs Aufsätze*, 8th ed. (Frankfurt am Main: Suhrkamp, 1989), 150–51.

[53] Immanuel Kant, *Kritik der Urteilskraft* (1790), in *Werke*, 8:171–620, here 281.

[54] Wolfgang Riedel develops a compensatory model of the modern practice of the enjoyment of landscape based on his reading of Schiller's *Ueber naive und sentimentalische Dichtung* (1795–96) according to which the observer seeks to compensate himself for the defects in the moral world by contemplating the physical world. Riedel demonstrates that, for Schiller, external nature represents a system that is self-sufficient, at one with itself, governed by its own intrinsic laws, not subordinated to external purposes, and therefore capable of embodying the idea of freedom. See Riedel, *"Der Spaziergang": Ästhetik der Landschaft und Geschichtsphilosophie der Natur bei Schiller* (Würzburg: Königshausen & Neumann, 1989), 63–80.) This indicates a paradox at the heart of the aesthetic enjoyment of landscape as prescribed by German Idealism, whereby the contemplation of nature as a domain free from purpose became itself the purpose of recreational wandering.

[55] Wahrig defines the veduta as "sachgetreue Ansicht einer Stadt oder Landschaft (im Unterschied zum Prospekt mit geringer perspektiv. Wirkung)," *Wahrig Deutsches Wörterbuch* (Gütersloh: Bertelsmann, 1996).

[56] Gudrun König, *Eine Kulturgeschichte des Spazierganges: Spuren einer bürgerlichen Praktik, 1780–1850* (Vienna: Böhlau, 1996); On this topic see also Monika Wagner, "Ansichten ohne Ende", 326–35.

[57] Albrecht, "Durchs 'malerische und romantische' Deutschland," 230.

[58] Albrecht, "Durchs 'malerische und romantische' Deutschland," 237.

[59] See Günter Oesterle, "Die Schule minutiösen Sehens im Vormärz: Zur Raffinesse des Andeutens im Wechselspiel von Bild und Text," in *Vormärzliteratur in europäischer Perspektive*, ed. Helmut Koopmann and Martina Lauster, 3 vols. (Bielefeld: Aisthesis, 1996–2000), 1:293–305.

[60] "Das bürgerliche Selbstbewußtsein arbeitet sich an der Front dessen ab, was sich dem prätendierten Verfügungstitel 'Herr und Meister der Natur' (Descartes) als noch unbeherrscht scheinende Natur bisher entzieht. Solche Natur löst Angst aus, weil ihr gegenüber die humane Souveränität zu erliegen droht. Die Ästhetik des Erhabenen ist eine Konzeption, um sich in einer vor- und außertechnischen Dimension — nämlich dem Imaginären — mit dieser Angst auseinanderzusetzen und sie beherrschen zu lernen." Hartmut Böhme, "Das Steinerne: Anmerkungen zur Theorie des Erhabenen aus dem Blick des 'Menschenfremdesten,'" in *Das Erhabene: Zwischen Grenzerfahrung und Größenwahn*, ed. Christine Pries (Weinheim, Germany: VCH, Acta humaniora, 1989), 119–41; here, 123. Marjorie Hope Nicolson's *Mountain Gloom and Mountain Glory: The Development of the Aesthetics of the Infinite* (Seattle: U of Washington P, 1997) remains the standard text on the genesis of the aesthetics of the sublime.

[61] Friedrich Schiller, *Werke: Nationalausgabe*, ed. Julius Petersen et al. (Weimar: Böhlau, 1943–), 11:38–54; here, 41–42, 45.

[62] W. G. Sebald has given a pertinent description of the salient features of *Biedermeier* taste in landscapes: "Die Ruhe des Interieurs und die Ausdehnung einer befriedeten Häuslichkeit auf die Landschaft ringsum ist in der Malerei des Biedermeier eines der wiederkehrenden Motive. . . . Blickt man in diesen sicher umgrenzten Orbis Pictus eine Zeitlang hinein, dann könnte man meinen, hier habe einer das Uhrwerk angehalten und gesagt: so soll es jetzt bleiben für immer. Die imaginierte Welt des Biedermeier ist ein unter einen Glassturz gerücktes, vollendetes Miniaturarrangement." Sebald, *Logis in einem Landhaus: Über Gottfried Keller, Johann Peter Hebel, Robert Walser und andere*, 2nd ed. (Frankfurt am Main: Fischer, 2000), 80–81.

[63] Harald Schmidt, *Melancholie und Landschaft: Die psychotische und ästhetische Struktur der Landschaftsschilderungen in Georg Büchners Lenz* (Opladen: Westdeutscher Verlag, 1994), 286.

[64] "Das Rauschen eines Waldes, ein Bach, der vom Felsen fließt, eine Klippe, die im Tale aufspringt, es kann mich in einen Taumel versetzen, der fast an Wahnsinn grenzt." Ludwig Tieck to August Ferdinand Bernhardi and Sophie Tieck (late Jul./early Aug. 1793). (quoted from Wilhelm Heinrich Wackenroder, *Sämtliche Werke und Briefe: Historisch-kritische Ausgabe*, ed. Silvio Vietta and Richard

Littlejohns, 2 vols. [Heidelberg: Winter, 1991], 2:258). Ingrid Oesterle cites this passage from Tieck's account of his journey with Wackenroder through the Fichtelgebirge in May 1793 in support of her conclusion: "Statt der pantheistischen Vereinigungserfahrung einer bis ins Kleinste belebten Natur bei Goethe entdecken die Romantiker für die Kunst 'Einöde' und 'Wildnis' als jene Natur, die ein Gefühl von tiefer Trauer und Gottverlassenheit aufkommen läßt." Oesterle, "'Ach die Kunst — Ach die erbärmliche Wirklichkeit': Ästhetische Modellierung des Lebens und ihre Dekomposition in Georg Büchners *Lenz*," in *Ideologie und Utopie in der deutschen Literatur der Neuzeit*, ed. Bernhard Spies (Würzburg: Königshausen & Neumann, 1995), 58–67; here, 63–64.

[65] Peter Hasubek, "'Ruhe' und 'Bewegung' in Büchners *Lenz:* Versuch einer Stilanalyse," *Germanisch-Romanische Monatszeitschrift* 19 (1969): 33–59.

[66] Peter Hasubek, "'Ruhe' und 'Bewegung,'" 43.

[67] Schmidt, *Melancholie und Landschaft*, 400.

[68] Schmidt, *Melancholie und Landschaft*, 395.

[69] Schmidt, *Melancholie und Landschaft*, 397.

[70] For a detailed analysis of this construction see Inge Diersen, "Büchners *Lenz* im Kontext der Entwicklung von Erzählprosa im 19. Jahrhundert," *Georg-Büchner-Jahrbuch* 7 1988/89 (1991): 91–125; here, 114.

[71] "Seine Leiden konnte man, im eigentlichen Verstande, die *Leiden der Einbildungskraft* nennen — sie waren für ihn doch würkliche Leiden." Karl Philipp Moritz, *Anton Reiser: Ein psychologischer Roman*, ed. Horst Günther (Frankfurt am Main; Leipzig: Insel, 1998), 88.

[72] On this point see Georg Reuchlein, *Bürgerliche Gesellschaft, Psychiatrie und Literatur: Zur Entwicklung der Wahnsinnsthematik in der deutschen Literatur des späten 18. und frühen 19. Jahrhunderts* (Munich: Fink, 1986), 204–7.

[73] Reuchlein, *Bürgerliche Gesellschaft*, 383.

[74] In characterizing Oberlin as a representative of a repressive, judgmental patriarchy Sabine Kubick fails, in my view, to note the shift in the pastor's attitude from solicitude to suspicion, which was brought about by the arrival of Kaufmann. Kubick, *Krankheit und Medizin im literarischen Werk Georg Büchners* (Stuttgart: M&P, 1991).

[75] Götz Grossklaus, "Georg Büchners *Lenz:* Zum Verlust des sozialen Ortes," in *Recherches Germaniques* 12 (1982): 68–77.

[76] "Ich bin abgefallen, verdammt in Ewigkeit, ich bin der ewige Jude" (152). In *Dantons Tod*, Camille says "Die Welt ist der ewige Jude," evidence that Büchner, in common with the Romantics, sees parallels between the plight of the Wandering Jew and contemporary man (Büchner, *Werke*, 119).

[77] Manfred Frank, *Kaltes Herz — Unendliche Fahrt — Neue Mythologie* (Frankfurt am Main: Suhrkamp, 1989), 50–92; here, 68. Frank sees the rediscovery of the figure of the Wandering Jew in the context of the emergence in the modern era of the motif of the endless journey. See the discussion in chapter 2 of this study.

[78] Georg Lukács, *Die Theorie des Romans: Ein geschichtsphilosophischer Versuch über die Formen der großen Epik* (Berlin: Neuwied, 1963), 22–23, 35.

[79] Arthur Schopenhauer, *Gesammelte Werke*, ed. Arthur Hübscher, 6 vols. (Mannheim: Brockhaus, 1988) (based on the first edition of 1819), 2:416–17.

[80] Schopenhauer, *Die Welt als Wille und Vorstellung*, 240.

[81] Schopenhauer, *Die Welt als Wille und Vorstellung*, 230–31.

[82] Schopenhauer, *Die Welt als Wille und Vorstellung*, 209–11, and esp. 230–33.

[83] "Das ist der Fels des Atheismus. Das leiseste Zucken des Schmerzes und rege es sich nur in einem Atom, macht einen Riß in der Schöpfung von oben bis unten" (Büchner, *Werke*, 107).

[84] The phrase is Shaftesbury's, appearing in his polemic against atheism in Anthony Ashley Cooper (Third Earl of Shaftesbury), *An Inquiry Concerning Virtue, or Merit* (1699; Manchester, UK: Manchester UP, 1977), 43.

[85] Knapp, *Georg Büchner*, 37.

[86] "Man wird kaum fehlgehen, wenn man die entscheidenden Postulate des Monologs . . . als Ausdruck von Büchners eigener Ästhetik ansieht" (Knapp, *Georg Büchner*, 151).

[87] Niccolini, *Spaziergang des Schriftstellers*, 106–7.

[88] "Man versuche es einmal und senke sich in das Leben des Geringsten und gebe es wieder, in den Zuckungen, den Andeutungen, dem ganz feinen, kaum bemerkten Mienenspiel" (Niccolini, *Spaziergang des Schriftstellers*, 144).

[89] "Man muß die Menschheit lieben, um in das eigentümliche Wesen jedes einzudringen, es darf einem keiner zu gering, keiner zu häßlich sein, erst dann kann man sie verstehen" (Niccolini, *Spaziergang des Schriftstellers*, 145).

[90] "*Mein* Metier besteht darin, bis in alle Ewigkeit hinein 'Märkische Wanderungen' zu schreiben; alles andre wird nur gnädig mit in den Kauf genommen." 19 Jan. 1883, Fontane (quoted from Gotthard Erler, "Fontanes *Wanderungen* heute," *Fontane-Blätter* 3 [1975]: 353–68; here, 353).

[91] Peter J. Brenner, *Der Reisebericht in der deutschen Literatur*, 535–47. Walter Erhart, "'Alles wie erzählt': Fontanes Wanderungen durch die Mark Brandenburg," *Jahrbuch der deutschen Schillergesellschaft* 36 (1992): 229–54. Hubertus Fischer, "Märkische Bilder: Ein Versuch über Fontanes Wanderungen durch die Mark Brandenburg, ihre Bilder und ihre Bildlichkeit," *Fontane Blätter* 60 (1995): 117–42.

[92] Hanna Delf von Wolzogen, ed., *"Geschichte und Geschichten aus Mark Brandenburg": Fontanes Wanderungen durch die Mark Brandenburg im Kontext der europäischen Reiseliteratur* (Würzburg: Königshausen & Neumann, 2003).

[93] Anton von Etzel, *Die Ostsee und ihre Küstenländer, geographisch, naturwissenschaftlich und historisch geschildert* (Leipzig: Lorck, 1859).

[94] Fontane, Review of Anton von Etzel's *Die Ostsee und ihre Küstenländer, Preußische Zeitung*, 13 Jul. 1859; repr. in Theodor Fontane, *Werke, Schriften und Briefe*, ed. Walter Keitel and Helmuth Nürnberger, 20 vols. in four parts, 2nd ed. (Munich: Hanser, 1962–97), part 2, 3:813. Citations from this edition (the *Hanser-Ausgabe*) — based on the 1892 *Wohlfeile Ausgabe* — will be indicated in the text by numerals indicating the part, the volume number, and the page number (the citation above would be 2/3:813). Volume 1 of this edition contains the

text of *Die Grafschaft Ruppin* and *Das Oderland;* volume 2, *Havelland* and *Spreeland;* volume 3, *Fünf Schlösser* and the critical apparatus.

[95] "Mit den Rationalisten teilt der *Realist* Fontane den Glauben an die unproblematische Abbildbarkeit der Welt; wie sie weiß er sich im Besitz eines sicheren, das heißt *objektiven* Sehens, des klaren, von keiner subjektiven Verfärbung beeinträchtigen Auges." Erdmut Jost, "Das poetische Auge: Visuelle Programmatik in Theodor Fontanes Landschaftsbildern aus Schottland und der Mark Brandenburg," in Wolzogen, *"Geschichte und Geschichten aus Mark Brandenburg,"* 64–80; here, 68. Jost wrongly cites Fontane's letter to Hermann Wichmann of 7 July 1894 — "Dass die sentimentalen Seichbeuteleien, die zu Anfang des Jahrhunderts beliebt waren, jetzt ausser Mode gekommen sind, ist ein Glück." (4/4:372) —; as evidence of Fontane's self-distancing from early-nineteenth-century travel literature. In fact, the subject of Fontane's letter is not the travel literature but the epistolary culture of that period; however, Jost's main point about Fontane's concern to present himself as an objective observer — a concern shared by the historicists of his day — remains valid.

[96] "Das beste ist *fahren.* Mit offnen Augen vom Coupé, vom Wagen, vom Boot, vom Fiacre aus, die Dinge an sich vorüberziehen lassen, das ist das A & das O des Reisens." Letter to Emilie Fontane, 9 Aug. 1875, in Theodor Fontane and Emilie Fontane, *Der Ehebriefwechsel: Emilie und Theodor Fontane* (Große Brandenburger Ausgabe), ed. Gotthard Erler, 3 vols. (Berlin: Aufbau, 1998), 3:39.

[97] Fischer concludes that when Fontane began writing the *Wanderungen* few inhabitants of Berlin and Brandenburg possessed "Sinn für Landschaft" ("Märkische Bilder," 128). Given the popularity of domestic tourism in the Harz and elsewhere, it would perhaps be more correct to say that well-traveled Berliners had not yet learned to view their own surroundings as landscape. It is this aesthetic blindness *to the Mark* that Fontane's program aims to correct.

[98] However, the foreword to the second edition of *Die Grafschaft Ruppin*, which contains such admonitions as "Reisen in der Mark ist alles andre eher als billig." (2/1:13) may have led readers to confuse it with the Baedeker guides.

[99] This is one respect in which Fontane's work differs from *Wilhelm Meisters Wanderjahre*, which, it has been suggested, provided the kaleidoscopic structure on which the *Wanderungen* was modeled. See Wolfgang Albrecht, "Kulturgeschichtliche Perspektivierung und Literarisierung des Regionalen in den *Wanderungen durch die Mark Brandenburg*," in Wolzogen, *"Geschichte und Geschichten aus Mark Brandenburg,"* 109, n. 40. But despite some similarities — textual heterogeneity, multiple narrators, or, in Fontane's case, extensive citations from other narratives — Fontane's work differs from Goethe's in having a single, unified narrative perspective and a recognizable didactic tendency.

[100] Jost, "Das poetische Auge," 73 and 75.

[101] "Ja, vorfahren vor dem Krug und über die Kirchhofsmauer klettern, ein Storchennest bewundern oder einen Hagebuttenstrauch, einen Grabstein lesen oder sich einen Spinnstubengrusel erzählen lassen — *so* war die Sache geplant, und *so* wurde sie begonnen" (2/2:869). Despite this claim to spontaneity, Fontane's travels in the Mark were from the outset meticulously prepared and written up. Together with profuse notes made in the course of the excursions there exist tab-

ulated itineraries listing the places to be visited in a given area and the material likely to be found there.

[102] Theodor Fontane, *Der Stechlin* (1898), in *Werke, Schriften, Briefe*, 1/5:117.

[103] Gotthard Erler, "Fontanes *Wanderungen* heute," *Fontane-Blätter* 3 (1975): 353–68; here, 364.

[104] "Die zwei Bände, die bis jetzt erschienen sind, lassen das, worauf es mir ankommt, erst erraten: die Belebung des Lokalen, die Poetisierung des Geschehenen." Letter to Ernst von Pfuel, 18 Jan. 1864 (Fontane, *Werke, Schriften, Briefe*, 4/2:115).

[105] See Monika Wagner, "Ansichten ohne Ende," 326–35.

[106] Fontane adopts the term "Land und Leute" from the cultural historian Wilhelm Heinrich Riehl (1823–97) who published a *Wanderbuch* in 1869. Wilhelm Heinrich Riehl, *Wanderbuch: Als zweiter Theil zu "Land und Leute"* (Stuttgart: Cotta, 1869), vol. 4 of Riehl's *Die Naturgeschichte des Volkes als Grundlage einer deutschen Social-Politik*, 4 vols., 1854–69).

[107] Walter Erhart, "Die Wanderungen durch die Mark Brandenburg," in *Fontane Handbuch*, ed. Christian Grawe and Helmuth Nürnberger (Stuttgart: Kröner, 2000), 818–50; here, 842.

[108] "Das hart arbeitende Volk spielt in den *Wanderungen* allenfalls eine Statistenrolle, und hier unterscheidet sich Fontanes Reisen sehr deutlich von den politisch-republikanischen Traditionen der Reiseliteratur" (Erhart, "Die Wanderungen durch die Mark Brandenburg," 841).

[109] Albrecht, "Kulturgeschichtliche Perspektivierung," 103.

[110] Letter to Emilie Fontane, 20 May 1868 (*Ehebriefwechsel*, 2:323).

[111] "wie keine zweite das Blatt des sich zur Weltstadt entwickelnden Berlins." Hans-Heinrich Reuter, *Fontane*, 2 vols. (Munich: Nymphenburger, 1968), 1:357.

[112] Diary, 19 Aug. 1856 (Theodor Fontane, *Reise- und Tagebücher: Tagebücher 1852, 1855–1858*, ed. Gotthard Erler and Charlotte Jolles, 2 vols. (Berlin: Aufbau, 1995), 1:161.

[113] Letter from Fontane to Ernst Kossak, 16 Feb. 1864 (quoted from Jost Schillemeit, "Berlin und die Berliner," *Jahrbuch der deutschen Schillergesellschaft* 30 [1986]: 34–82; here, 58).

[114] Erhart, *"'Alles wie erzählt,'"* 243.

[115] Erhart, *"'Alles wie erzählt,'"* 244; Fischer, "Märkische Bilder," 125–26; Jost, "Das poetische Auge," 73–75.

[116] Hess, "Panorama und Denkmal," 130–206.

[117] "In diesem Werke hat sich der Verfasser auf den Sockel eines historischen Landschafters in der Literatur geschwungen." Albert Emil Brachvogel, *Wochenblatt der Johanniter-Ordens-Balley Brandenburg*, 11 Dec. 1861 (quoted in Fischer, "Märkische Bilder," 134).

[118] In the chapter "Karl Friedrich Schinkel" Fontane quotes a review of Schinkel's work for the diorama "Sieben Wunder der alten Welt," shown by Gropius in 1812. The review, by the art historian Franz Kugler, calls the exhibits "die geistreichsten

Restaurationen der Wunderbauten des Altertums" (2/1:114) —; the choice of citation can be taken as an indication of Fontane's admiration for Schinkel as *restorer.*

[119] "Der Sinn für Empirie und Realität im Geschichtsdenken und der Sinn für Realpolitik im Staatsdenken sind Erscheinungen dieser Epoche." Walter Müller-Seidel, *Theodor Fontane: Soziale Romankunst in Deutschland*, 2nd ed. (Stuttgart: Metzler, 1980), 61.

[120] Hess, "Panorama und Denkmal," 135.

[121] Hess, "Panorama und Denkmal," 154.

[122] Part of the attraction of dioramas and panoramas as mass entertainments derived from their status as substitutes for travel. This is especially clear from such innovations as the moving panorama which, incorporating the sound and lighting effects of the diorama, simulated the effect of movement through a landscape (pleoramas simulated the view seen by a boat passenger) by using a moving canvas backdrop. An early example was the *Pleorama des Rheins von Mainz bis St. Goar*, exhibited by Gropius in 1833. Since the Rhine was a favored destination for the patriotic tourism promoted by Jahn, Arndt, and others, a visit to the Rhine panorama was, in effect, a surrogate form of patriotic tourism, "vaterländische Wanderungen" in a virtual space.

[123] "Das Verfahren ist eine Art sprachliche *Kreisfigur*. Einige Verse leiten ein Kapitel ein, in der anschließenden Darstellung 'spielt' Fontane dann mit Versatzstücken aus diesen Versen, am Schluß folgt eine Zusammenfassung der 'Botschaft,' die zumeist wie eine Paraphrase des literarischen Mottos vom Beginn wirkt. Man kan dies sehr schön beim Abschnitt *Am Molchow- und Zermützelsee* und im Radensleben-Kapitel im ersten Band der *Wanderungen* nachvollziehen" (Jost, "Das poetische Auge," 76).

[124] Erler, "Fontanes *Wanderungen* heute," 361–62; Bodo Plachta refers to a "kritisches Potential" in the first volume. Plachta, "Preußens 'gesunder Kern': Zu Theodor Fontanes 'Wanderungen durch die Mark Brandenburg,'" *Germanisch-Romanische Monatsschrift* 44 (1994): 177–90; here, 184.

[125] "Bismarck ist der größte Prinzipienverächter gewesen, den es je gegeben hat." Letter to Mete Fontane 29 January 1894 (4:4.325–26). See Reuter, *Fontane*, 1:386–417, "Von Düppel bis Königgrätz und weiter," for a discussion of the war reportage. Eda Sagarra, while noting Fontane's admiration for Bismarck's "prägende Kraft," notes that his view of the chancellor becomes increasingly critical following the publication of *Vor dem Sturm* (1878). Sagarra, "Noch einmal: Fontane und Bismarck," *Fontane-Blätter* 53 (1992): 29–42; here, 42.

[126] Hegel, *Werke*, 15:332.

[127] Erhart, though noting the presence of "deutliche Anklänge an die ironische Reiseprosa des jungen Deutschland," concedes that moments of ironic reflection are rare ("'Alles wie erzählt,'" 233).

[128] Hugh Barr Nisbet, *Herder and the Philosophy and History of Science* (Cambridge: Modern Humanities Research Association, 1970), 226. See 223–31 on Herder's environmental determinism and 14, 48–54 on the use of the "Kraft" concept in the context of historiography.

129 Müller-Seidel, *Theodor Fontane*, 61. Chapter 1 of Müller-Seidel's study is entitled "Im Banne des Historismus."

130 "Mit diesem Werk zumal, mit den *Wanderungen*, bleibt Fontane den Traditionen des Historismus treu und nur zögernd geht er über sie hinaus" (Müller-Seidel, *Theodor Fontane*, 69).

131 Daniel Albrecht Thaer, *Grundsätze der rationellen Landwirtschaft*, 2nd ed. (Berlin: Reimer, 1821), 167.

132 Anne D. Wallace has discerned a similar connection between walking and cultivation in nineteenth-century English poetry, a connection first established by Wordsworth. Wallace sees Wordsworth's *Peter Bell* (1798) as inaugurating a new mode in English poetry, a mode she terms "peripatetic." This mode, Wallace avers, is an extension of the Virgilian georgic achieved "by placing the walker in the ideological space vacated by the farmer." *Walking, Literature and English Culture* (Oxford: Clarendon, 1993), 11. The rise of a mode of poetry that thematizes walking is thus seen as a reaction to "an era in which the culturally stabilizing capacity of agriculture seemed to have faded or failed" (149).

133 "die Belebung des Lokalen, die Poetisierung des Geschehenen." Letter to Ernst von Pfuel, 18 Jan. 1864 (Fontane, 4/2:115).

134 Erhart, "Die Wanderungen," 837, 847.

# 4: Wandering at the Margins: Journeymen and Vagabonds

It is a paradox of German nineteenth-century literature that the large-scale movements of people, which made that century so distinct from any that had gone before, find so little literary resonance. These movements fell into two categories: internal migration and emigration, each of which had what are termed their "push" and "pull" factors. On the "push" side the most important forces were, of course, population growth and concomitant pauperization (pre-1848). The prospect of improved material conditions, whether in the slowly emerging industrial centers of the German-speaking countries or overseas, especially in America, accounted for most of the "pull" factors; although the millenarian hopes of religious groups, such as the disciples of the Pietist theologian Albrecht Bengel, were by no means negligible.[1] Yet, despite the fact that over six million people would leave the German Confederation and the Reich in the period 1830–1913, the literary footprint of emigrant experience is a very small one. Of all the nineteenth-century emigration novels perhaps only Ferdinand Kürnberger's *Der Amerika-Müde* (1855) and Friedrich Spielhagen's *Deutsche Pioniere* (1871) are remembered today. Ernst Willkomm's *Die Europa-Müden* (1838, the phrase "Europa-müde" appears to be Heine's) is a tortuously plotted conspiracy novel (now barely readable) that ends just as the hero is about to take ship. I do not intend to open a discussion of emigration literature, inextricably linked though this is with the theme of wandering, but to make the point that that non-bourgeois wanderers occupy a marginal place in the period's literature, and this despite the fact that mobility touched the lives of the majority in the forms of internal migration and emigration. Such wanderers belong, to borrow Hans-Ulrich Wehler's term, to the "stumme Schichten"[2] of German literature — those classes whose history is insufficiently documented and thus obscure. This lack or absence motivates the choice of the two texts that will be discussed here: Jeremias Gotthelf's *Jakobs Wanderungen* (1846–47), and Karl von Holtei's bestselling first novel *Die Vagabunden* (1851). These works are unusual in that their wandering protagonists are young men — both orphans — from rural artisan backgrounds. Perhaps more significant are the realistic traits of both works: in Gotthelf's case these derive from research into the lives of journeymen, and in Holtei's from his lived experience as a strolling player and raconteur. In this respect the works stand apart from Eichendorff's *Aus dem*

*Leben eines Taugenichts* (1826), in which a lower-class wanderer serves as a vehicle for its aristocratic creator's critique of middle-class philistinism.

## Gotthelf's Jakobs des Handwerksgesellen Wanderungen durch die Schweiz (1846–47)

The relative neglect of the work of the Swiss author Jeremias Gotthelf (the *nom de plume* of Albert Bitzius) is nowhere more evident than in the case of this novel, although it was written when Gotthelf was arguably at the height of his powers, shortly before the composition of the mature works *Uli, der Pächter* (1849) and *Die Käserei in der Vehfreude* (1850). As recently as 1997, Hans-Peter Holl, a leading Gotthelf scholar, could refer to *Jakobs Wanderungen* as "ein unbekannter Roman."[3] The only recent substantial treatment of the work has been an article by Robert Godwin-Jones, which highlights its significance as a document of the socially and politically turbulent 1840s in Switzerland.[4] In view of the novel's obscurity I will provide a brief plot synopsis before moving on to consider the significance and implications of Gotthelf's narrative of the Swiss wanderings of a German *Geselle.*

Gotthelf's novel is structured along the lines of the *Gesellenreise.* Jakob is a youth who, orphaned in childhood by a cholera epidemic, is brought up by his grandmother in a German village. At her instigation he begins an apprenticeship in the trade (not specified by the narrator) practiced by his forefathers for three generations; on completing this and, again, prompted by his pious grandmother, he embarks on the *Wanderschaft* with the intention of acquiring trade skills and returning as an experienced *Meister.* On his departure his grandmother presents Jakob with a new haversack (rather than giving him one of the three proudly displayed in the family home), for the family observes a remarkable usage according to which the son is told at the outset of his journey that he is not to be trusted with the father's haversack but must make his own way in the world. The three haversacks are testimony to the successfully completed journeyman years; and they function as a symbol of the family honor, which is not heritable, but which must be renewed by the efforts of each succeeding generation.[5] During the *Wanderschaft* the haversack is intended to serve as "sein Tagebuch,"[6] a tangible reminder to the journeyman both of his origins and of his goal, which at journey's end is placed with the others as part of a "handwerkliche Familienregister" (16) — an enduring reminder of the obligations imposed by profession and social rank on following generations.

Jakob sets out with vague intentions of trying his luck in Switzerland before eventually proceeding to Paris. Right at the beginning of his journey, in Basel, the first station of his tour of Switzerland, a fateful pattern is set; having found work, the youth comes into contact with disillusioned journeymen, who exert a demoralizing influence upon him. To make matters worse, few of the various *Meister* in whose workshops he is employed provide an effective moral counterweight: while the *Meister* in Basel is a man of probity and — as *Ratsherr*— some standing, the opinions and lifestyles of several others represent a real danger to the youth (so much is made explicit by the narrator). Thus, in Zurich, the master and mistress are "Leute der neuen Zeit" (62), irreligious hedonists who rail against the prevailing order and especially against aristocrats and churchmen. Jakob proves increasingly receptive to the radical ideas circulating in the workshop, and eventually, goaded by his workmates over his habit of prayer, renounces his own beliefs. When the youth falls prey to drunkenness and insubordination in dissolute company, a colleague — "ein Brandenburger" — makes his first intervention, warning "Du dauerst mich, Junge. . . . Du gehst auf schlechten Wegen, gehst deinem Verderben entgegen" (80). This attempt to return the youth to the straight and narrow path fails and Jakob is forced to leave Zurich when his insubordination brings him into open conflict with his freethinking employer. A new position in Bern in the workshop of a "Mordiokerl von Philister und Spießbürger" (109) fails to check the descent into indiscipline. As Jakob's enthusiasm for the radical materialism of his colleagues grows, so also does his appetite for worldly pleasures. Bern is the scene of two dubious love affairs: here Jakob plumbs new depths by seducing and cynically abandoning the awkward Kathri. Lausanne sees his increasing entanglement in the activities of the radical artisans' clubs that maintain a strong presence in the journeymen's hostels. Inflamed by talk of an imminent upheaval in Geneva, he travels to that city, attending radical political gatherings before becoming swept up in the disastrous and abortive artisans' uprising, which began in the working-class district of St Gervais on 11 February 1843 and spread throughout the city, only to peter out in a matter of days. Along with the other foreigners, universally suspected of involvement in the unrest, Jakob is forced out of his post and his lodgings. Roaming the streets in distracted despair, he is saved from a plunge into a stormy Lake Geneva only by the providential intervention of the Brandenburger. The following chapter, located at the exact center of the novel, is also its turning point. Lying in a hospice bed, Jakob undergoes what Muret has called his "maladie éducatrice."[7] This, however, proves to be merely the beginning of a lengthy self-rehabilitation. Forced to leave Geneva — penniless, and without his haversack, the visible sign of a journeyman's *Ehrbarkeit*, and that which distinguishes him from a common vagabond[8] — the protagonist begins the grueling trek home through the French-speaking cantons. On the point of being turned away from an artisan dwelling, he is only saved from perishing in the wintry landscape by his involuntary utterance: "Mon dieu, mon dieu!" (229). Moved to pity, the pious artisan and his wife grant the wanderer shelter and provide him with work. Jakob, who has not yet relinquished his radical beliefs, attempts in vain to convert the elderly pair, thereby underestimating the *Meister*, who, far from being an ignorant provincial, has learned his trade in Paris. Nevertheless, their parting is an amicable one, the *Meister* giving the youth his own haversack for the onward journey.

The next station on the journey — the canton Waadt — was a major center for agitation in the 1840s: of the 28 workers' associations, or *Bildungsvereine*, set up in Switzerland and amalgamated to form the Leman League in 1842, some 10 were located here. Gotthelf provides a sharply satirical portrait of the patriotic demagoguery then associated with that region in the minds of his Swiss readers. Yet even in that canton a strongly pietistic strain of conservatism persists; and the household in which the wanderer finds work is symbolically divided between the radical *Meister* and his pious and reticent wife. When his employer is injured in a farcical accident following a drunken political meeting, Jakob is forced to manage the workshop during his lengthy convalescence. This experience as effective head of the household cures him of some of his illusions concerning radicals and their ideas.

In Hasletal, in the Bernese *Oberland*, Jakob comes under the tutelage of a *Meister* whose tolerance is born of service in Napoleon's *grande armée*. It is here, in the midst of a frugal, hard-working community, that the errant journeyman re-embraces Christianity, albeit initially with the ulterior motive of marrying the daughter of the house, Eiseli, who rebuffs his advances. The way to conversion had been paved by the revelation of his own nullity in the sublime Alpine landscape: "Er, der große Jakob, schien sich in dieser Bergmajestät kleiner als der kleinste Wurm, den je sein Fuß zertrat" (332). Rejection at the hands of Eiseli destroys the last traces of hubris, enabling Jakob to complete the process of spiritual rebirth, which he attains on Easter Day. Rebirth is accompanied by stirrings of conscience, which prompt a return to Bern and to the wronged Kathri, whom Jakob now intends to wed. Arriving in Bern, he learns that Kathri has since died — while bearing his child. The return phase of the journey thus involves a retracing of steps, a confrontation with the significant stations of past errancy, as part of a process of reform.

Toward the end of the novel, Gotthelf has his protagonist seek out the author Heinrich Zschokke in Aarau. The scene in which Jakob glimpses Zschokke out walking with Abraham Emanuel Fröhlich pays a deft compliment to both writers, while drawing the reader's attention to their morally improving works.[9] In Basel, a meeting with the formerly despised *Ratsherr* is followed by a reunion with the Brandenburger, who attempts to enlist Jakob for his mission to the journeymen. Jakob, however, is resolved to return to his grandmother and allows himself to be persuaded to complete his journey by rail, despite misgivings about the new mode of transport. In his home village Jakob is received joyously by his grandmother, who, having feared him dead, rejoices in his new-found capability and manliness. Moreover, he is reunited with his haversack, which had been in the possession of a disreputable journeyman. The narrative trajectory of a descent into dissolution followed by sickness and penury and an ultimate triumphant homecoming is obviously indebted to the Biblical parable of the prodigal son (Luke 15:11–32). Given this influence and the predominance of Christian ideas it would be easy to characterize Gotthelf's novel as a purely devotional work, a Swiss *Pilgrim's Progress*, perhaps. But that would be to overlook its topicality — the degree to which it grapples with the pressing social and political concerns of its day. It is these aspects that are likely to be of most interest to us today, not least because *Jakobs Wanderungen* is a document of that most agitated decade in modern Swiss history, the 1840s, which culminated in the *Sonderbundkrieg* and the liberal confederate constitution of 1848.

## Pauperization and the Crisis in Craft Manufacture

The idea of a novel based on the travels of a journeyman was not Gotthelf's own; rather it was suggested to him by Gotthilf Ferdinand Döhner of the Zwickau-based *Verein zur Verbreitung guter und wohlfeiler Volkschriften*, who was keen to get the Swiss author to contribute a book to his growing stock of improving popular literature. On 8 January 1844 Döhner wrote the following to Gotthelf: "Und was soll ich denn schreiben? fragen Sie jetzt vielleicht. Ich antworte: Was Sie wollen, Schweizerleben, Erfahrungen, Zustände, oder denken Sie sich einen deutschen Handwerksburschen, der die Schweiz durchwandert, oder geben Sie uns den Tell, damit unser schlechtes Geschlecht sich an seinem Anblick weide und ermanne."[10]

Döhner's proposal was a timely one; at the time of writing, craft manufacture had been in crisis for at least a decade. This crisis was connected with the wider phenomenon of pauperization, whose principal causes were rural overpopulation and economic recession. Following the lifting of the continental blockade in 1815, industries on the European mainland were exposed to competition from a highly industrialized Britain. The enduring effect of this competition was to depress prices and, with them, wages: as a result, artisans in the worst affected sectors — textile manufacturing — saw their earnings reduced to subsistence levels. The situation was exacerbated in Prussia by the fact that the Stein-Hardenberg reforms had already deregulated craft manufacture in 1810. At a stroke, this reform put an end to the guilds' ability to restrict the number of apprentices and journeymen. The ratio of journeymen to master-craftsmen increased dramatically, and as a consequence only a small proportion of *Gesellen* could hope eventually to become *Meister*. For those unwilling to accept an indefinite prolongation of their journeyman years, only the option of factory work remained — this usually entailed losing status to join the growing ranks of the industrial proletariat. Nor was the problem of a surplus of journeymen confined to Prussia; even those German states that retained guild structures were similarly affected, if to a lesser degree.[11] Given these circumstances, it is not surprising that contemporary sources are filled with complaints about the demoralization of journeymen. Conservatives were not alone in predicting the demise of craft manufacture in the 1840s: in the *Communist Manifesto* of February 1848 Marx and Engels speculated that advances in capitalist production would eventually bring about the extinction of the artisan class. But it was the conservatives who had particular reason to feel anxiety at the decline of the *Handwerkerstand*, since they viewed this class as the bedrock of the corporatist state.[12] The erosion of craft manufacture was not merely destabilizing in its own right; it also created a major reservoir of disaffection.[13] This was recognized by socialist groups like the Saint-Simonists and Fourierists, who recruited actively from among discontented tradesmen. Within the German Confederation, curbs on organizations and a virtual embargo on public meetings — partly the legacy of the Karlsbad Decrees of 1819 — made it difficult to recruit journeymen and mobilize them politically. In republican Switzerland, however, censorship and restrictions on public assembly were much less onerous, and radicals were able to operate more freely.

Switzerland thus found itself in a delicate position in the period of Restoration between 1830 and 1848. The country did not escape the economic gloom affecting the whole continent: rural population growth was driving the expansion of an underclass, just as it was in the German states. Moreover, because radical groups were able to operate with few restrictions, the radicalization of the proletariat must have seemed a more likely prospect in the Swiss cantons than elsewhere. To make matters worse, there existed the real possibility that Switzerland's neighbors might intervene in the case of any revolutionary upheaval. The major source of political instability, however, was not radical agitation but a simmering conflict between the mainly Protestant liberal cantons and the smaller, predominantly Catholic, conservative cantons.[14] The conservative cantons were resisting attempts by their larger neighbors to establish a centralized Swiss state, which, they feared, would be dominated by the liberals. In short, Switzerland was in the 1840s a house divided, where politically active foreigners could shelter with a degree of impunity — a situation eyed with concern from within the German Confederation.

German workers' associations began to appear simultaneously in Paris and in Switzerland in the turbulent early 1830s as state repression began to tighten in Germany. The most important of these was the *Deutscher Volksverein*, set up in Paris in 1832. While this group espoused a conventionally bourgeois democratic program (advocating a free press), what made it fundamentally new was its composition. For the first time, artisans and radical intellectuals were operating in the same political organization. In

1834 the French authorities followed the German Confederation in restricting the right of assembly, whereupon the *Volksverein* was replaced by a new and more secretive group. This was the *Bund der Geächteten*, whose structure was modeled on that of the Italian *Carbonari*. Four years later, however, the artisans rebelled against the obscurantism and secrecy favored by the intellectuals: the ensuing split gave rise to the less provocatively named *Bund der Gerechten*, which set up branches in London and Switzerland. The leaders of the new organization were Karl Schapper and Wilhelm Weitling: the latter's unsophisticated, religiously toned "Handwerkerkommunismus" was for a long time its official doctrine. The name chosen by Weitling for the branches of the organization in Switzerland — "Kommunistischer Bildungsverein" — marks the strategic importance of education to the workers' movement. Weitling's dominance ended when Karl Marx and Friedrich Engels joined the London branch of the *Bund der Gerechten* in February 1847, reforming it as the *Bund der Communisten* and injecting a new theoretical rigor. As Eric Hobsbawm has observed, the genealogy of these groups, steeped in the *compagnonnage* tradition, is of great interest, since it bears directly on the origins of organized Marxism.[15]

The Swiss workers' associations, too, underwent change in this period. Prior to 1836, when the *Tagsatzung* decreed the expulsion of German political refugees deemed to be involved in agitation, revolutionary societies had taken the form of highly popular artisans' singing clubs (*Handwerkergesangvereine*). Many of the expelled leaders succeeded in reentering the country to reconstitute these clubs as the *Bildungsvereine* mentioned previously. The first of these opened in Geneva in 1839; others were established in Zurich in 1840, and in Lausanne in 1842. Despite their innocuous appellation, the new entities proved more radical than their forebears, favoring the revolutionary communism of Weitling over the utopian socialist philosophies of Fourier and Saint-Simon.

The early 1840s thus marked an intensification of radical activity, and it is precisely this period in which Gotthelf has his protagonist travel through Switzerland. Significantly, the novel places Jakob in Zurich in 1841–42, at precisely the time Weitling was active in that city. Wilhelm Weitling (1808–71), who has been dubbed "der bedeutendste der deutschen Frühsozialisten des Vormärz,"[16] was in several respects a remarkable figure. Unlike most of the socialist leaders he was himself a tradesman, a journeyman tailor, an autodidact, and a prolific author who set out his ideas in numerous tracts: *Die Menschheit wie sie ist und wie sie sein sollte* (1838), *Garantien der Freiheit und Harmonie* (1842) and *Das Evangelium eines armen Sünders* (1845). Weitling saw revolutionary activity as a means to achieving a new social order which — strikingly and provocatively — he posited in terms of the redemption of mankind and the realization of Christ's teachings. Gotthelf was familiar with Weitling's ideas and activities from the Bluntschli report,[17] published shortly after the communist leader's expulsion from Zurich in 1843. Although in 1845 further police action resulted in the closure of the *Bildungsvereine* and the expulsion of their German leaders in most cantons, the sense of threat persisted even beyond the defeat of the 1848 rebellion in Germany.[18]

## Gotthelf and the Struggle over Artisanal Identity

It has already been remarked that revolutionary societies active in Switzerland, Paris, London, and Brussels were steeped in the traditions of the journeymen. There were a number of reasons for this. In the first place, most of the rank-and-file membership were themselves journeymen, and it was therefore natural that they should bring with them some of the usages of their guilds. Second, there were commonsense grounds for adopting such practices: they could be used to promote a sense of solidarity and to secure the societies against police infiltration; the *Wanderschaft* also provided ideal cover for the movements of activists from country to country. Finally, there was a not insignificant psychological factor in play. The exiled intellectuals who led these societies identified strongly with the journeymen, for theirs was also a highly nomadic existence — this becomes clear when we examine the biographies of Karl Marx, or of the radical poet Georg Weerth (1822–56), who moved frequently between the industrial centers of France, Belgium, and England. Moreover, the *Wanderschaft* spoke not only to the leaders' self-conception but also to their understanding of the current state and future role of the proletariat. It should be noted, however, that the symbolic appropriation of guild usages by the radicals was taking place at a time when such usages were in decline. Not only did the Stein-Hardenberg reforms in Prussia abolish compulsory guild membership, but the *Wanderpflicht* itself, the obligation on every artisan to spend a prescribed period (usually three years) acquiring skills on the road, was removed. These changes brought about a decline in the number of journeymen "auf der Walz," and those that persisted in the practice frequently found themselves regarded with suspicion by their counterparts in industrial manufacturing.[19]

The principal aim of the educational program of the *Bildungsvereine* was to counter this erosion of solidarity among artisans, and to instill in factory workers and artisans a sense that they belonged to the same social class, the proletariat. The *Bildungsvereine* occasionally succeeded in this aim: this is clear from the radicalization of the *Berliner Handwerkerverein* following its infiltration by activists from the *Bund der Gerechten*. By 1847, just three years after its establishment, its members were already referring to themselves as "Proletarier."[20] The hope of the radicals was that the traditions and professional ethos of the artisans would permeate this new class consciousness, invigorating demoralized factory workers and craftsmen alike. Of central importance was the tradition of the *Wanderschaft*, which provided a ready-made model of progress and self-improvement through work. But, beyond this, the *Wanderschaft* also offered a means of comprehending and getting to grips with a reality characterized by constant social and technological change, a world in which "Alles Ständische und Stehende verdampft,"[21] to use the words of the *Communist Manifesto*. For Marx and Engels held that the proletariat could fulfill its historical role as collective Messiah only if it first embraced the insecurity of modernity:

> Die Proletarier können sich die gesellschaftlichen Produktivkräfte nur erobern, indem sie ihre eigene bisherige Aneignungsweise und damit die ganze bisherige Aneignungsweise abschaffen. Die Proletarier haben nichts von dem Ihrigen zu sichern, sie haben alle bisherige Privatsicherheit und Privatversicherungen zu zerstören.[22]

Taken together with the famous pronouncement, "Die Arbeiter haben kein Vaterland. Man kann ihnen nicht nehmen, was sie nicht haben,"[23] this statement gestures toward the idea that the proletariat's ability to accede to power depends on its ability to assume a new cosmopolitan identity, predicated on constant mobility and change. As Wehler notes, one of the greatest difficulties in creating a new class consciousness lay in overcoming the sense of helplessness felt by workers.[24] One way of achieving this was by encouraging proletarians to see themselves, not as passive cogs in the industrial machinery, but as self-confident journeymen striving toward a new social dispensation.

The prominence of the image of the active, confident journeyman in the political poetry of Georg Weerth, whom Engels called "den ersten Dichter des deutschen Proletariats," is one indication of radical interest in the uses of artisanal identity.[25] Another is the resonance that Goethe's *Wanderjahre*, with its innovative handling of the journeyman theme, found with the socialist critics who were the first to attempt a serious interpretation of that work. The *Linkshegelianer*, Karl Rosenkranz, who first applied the term "Sozialroman" to the *Wanderjahre*, noted that the novel showed that "Das moderne Leben . . . zum Wanderleben geworden [ist]." His pupil, Ferdinand Gregorovious, found in Lenardo's *Wanderlied* "das Bewußtsein von der Weltbefreiung und Welterlösung überhaupt durch die Arbeit."[26]

If the radicals used artisanal traditions, including the *Wanderschaft*, as the basis of a new class-consciousness for the proletariat; the conservatives were convinced that the rehabilitation and depoliticization of the artisans was a prerequisite for the maintenance of social order. This is the task that Gotthelf sets himself in *Jakobs Wanderungen*. But rather than seeking "eine künstliche Stützung der agrarisch-handwerklichen Gesellschaft gegen die Industrie,"[27] the work focuses on the symbolic power of the *Wanderschaft* and is interested in exploiting it in the moral regeneration of the dissolute lower classes. In this respect, at least, Gotthelf resembles his opponents.

Moreover, Gotthelf — like Marx — sees man's essence as realized in labor, with the important distinction that for the Swiss parson work is never the means to temporal enjoyment, far less to a new social dispensation, but is a prophylactic against sin: "Heilmittel [der] sündigen Natur" (42). His attempts to instill a work ethic in the poor were not confined to the literary sphere but formed a vital part of his charitable activity. At the school for orphaned boys at Trachselwald, which Gotthelf was instrumental in setting up (described with great pathos in chapter 7 of the 1840 treatise *Die Armennot*), special emphasis was placed on the acquisition of trade skills. Like the educationalist Johann Heinrich Pestalozzi (1746–1827), whom he admired, Gotthelf regarded his literary output as an extension of his practical pedagogy. His attempts to communicate a work ethic and a sense of personal responsibility to his charges anticipate the sort of social engineering later proposed by the conservative theorist Wilhelm Heinrich Riehl,[28] with the important distinction that for his source of values Gotthelf looks not to the bourgeoisie but to the artisan class, with their regulated process of development, the *Wanderschaft:*

> Diese Lehrzeit des Wanderns ist von großer Bedeutsamkeit für den rechten Gesellen; er lernt daraus, Schritt um Schritt zu gehen mit Geduld, er erfährt, daß Schritt um Schritt zum Ziele führen so gut als Fliegen oder Rennen und sicherer noch obendrein, und diese Erfahrung, wenn sie praktisch angewendet wird, ist die Grundmauer des Handwerks. Jetzt fährt man auf Eisenbahnen für ein Lumpengeld hundert Stunden weit, aber wehe dem Gesellen, dem dieser Flug zu Kopfe steigt, der ihn übertragen möchte auf seinen Lebensweg, er kömmt von den rechten Schienen ab, gerät aus der Fahrbahn, kömmt nicht ans Ziel oder spät oder verstümmelt. (21–22)

In the above passage the *Wanderschaft* takes on a significance beyond that which it holds for artisans, becoming a model of gradual progress, of a painstaking and methodical mode of working undistracted by impatience. This entails renunciation, of course, the self-disciplined postponement of gratification that allows the steady accumulation of property; here "protestantische Ethik" and "Geist des Kapitalismus" combine in precisely the manner envisaged by Max Weber.[29] The railway, by contrast, is made to stand for the improvidence, acquisitiveness, and hubris that Gotthelf diagnoses in modern subjectivity. It is the symbol of what is elsewhere identified as the "Schwindeleien" (492) of the age, "a concept which blends a suggestion of the mendacity and ruthlessness of capitalism with the idea of vertiginous speed — at once the physical speed of the steam age and the impatience, desire for instant fulfillment and reward . . . which is the mood of the times."[30]

Gotthelf sets out to demonstrate the pedagogical value of the *Wanderschaft* by choosing as his protagonist not "den rechten Gesellen," but a credulous and suggestible youth, "ein Spielball von Welt und

Menschen" (418), who proves easy prey for proto-communist propaganda. The novel's strategy is to identify Jakob's moral failings as the source of his ills. To be sure, the economic and social forces bearing down on the artisan class are not neglected. Jakob experiences these at first hand in the expansion of workshops into factories. In these new establishments journeymen no longer break bread with the *Meister* but are paid an allowance for their food and lodgings. As a result, relations between *Meister* and *Geselle* become depersonalized, reduced to utilitarian considerations, and denuded of any pastoral element: "Die Handwerke steigerten sich zu Etablissements, das Fabrikartige, wo jeder Arbeiter nichts ist als der Zahn in einem großen Rade, ragte ins Handwerk hinüber, das christliche Band ward zerschnitten, das Benutzen ward die Hauptsache: der Meister benutzte die Gesellen, der Geselle den Meister" (32).

Despite acknowledging the difficulties posed for journeymen by industrialization, and hoping for the rehabilitation of the artisan class, Gotthelf holds a skeptical view of the possibilities of social change. Industrialization is to be regarded as "eine Sünde der Zeit" (255) which can no more be abolished than the root causes of poverty: "Es ordnen, daß es weder Arme noch Reiche mehr gibt, das vermag der Mensch nicht, denn 'die Armen habt ihr allezeit bei euch,' hat Christus gesagt" (249). In this perspective both the rational reform of society and violent revolution appear as futilities; Gotthelf sees the salvation of the age not in political terms but "in der Wiedergeburt des inneren Menschen" (250). To an unusual degree for a *Sozialroman*, the stress is on individual self-determination rather than on social environment, and herein lies both the work's strength and its weakness. Its strength, because the foregrounding of an individual existence provides us with a nuanced psychological portrait of the protagonist: Jakob's delusions of grandeur, his suggestibility, his vacillation and his incorrigibility are all brought out most convincingly. Its weakness, because its tendency to downplay the role of economic factors in the fates of individuals risks being read as insensitivity to the plight of industrial workers. Gotthelf persistently applies the categories of sin and free will to the analysis of that plight, suggesting, through Jakob's French-speaking *Meister*, that the workers themselves bear a measure of blame for the depredations of industrial manufacturing.

The author's preoccupation with the fate of a single soul is on one level a product of his Calvinism, but it is also integral to the novel's strategy of contesting the radical appropriation of artisan identity. For the socialists, the *Wanderschaft* was of symbolic value, not only because it connoted the mobility and boundless activity of the "Klasse, welche die Zukunft in ihren Händen trägt,"[31] but also because it offered a traditional model of solidarity. Notwithstanding their subaltern status, journeymen derived real power from the *compagnonnage* tradition. Guild membership made a degree of collective bargaining possible; the weapon of

*Gesellenverruf* (92) — a form of boycott — could, at least before wandering artisans became too numerous, be used to withhold skilled labor from an unscrupulous employer. In the bleak *Vormärz* period artisans continued to rely on the principle of solidarity, banding together to set up mutual funds that provided financial assistance to members' families in case of death or inability to work, and cash handouts to impoverished journeymen. These self-help groups were initially apolitical and remained so, for obvious reasons, in the German states.

In *Jakobs Wanderungen* Gotthelf seizes every opportunity to challenge the notion that true solidarity exists among politicized artisans. In the hostel at Basel, Jakob's companions exploit him out of naked self-interest. Astutely seeking out the weaknesses in his character, they use flattery and guile to loosen his purse strings. In Zurich, when the supposedly enlightened *Meister* pleads inability to pay, the *Gesellen* prove powerless; their lack of solidarity is blamed on the corrupting influence of radical politics: "Seit politische Vereine sind, ist das Handwerksband, das uralte, goldene, zerschnitten und kein Zusammenhalten mehr in dem, was zunächst im Kreise der Handwerker liegt. So sind fremde Gesellen in fremden Landen gegen unverschämte Meister, wenn auch nicht in Theorie, so doch in Praxis so viel als schutzlos" (93).

In general, however, the novel evinces suspicion of those aspects of the *Wanderschaft* — mobility and solidarity — that were attractive to the radicals. The state of wandering is not so much valued for its own sake as legitimized with reference to its end point: the stability conferred by the *Meisterschaft* and the acquisition of property. And, instead of emphasizing the comradely relationship between *Gesellen*, Gotthelf shifts the focus toward the state of relations between *Gesellen* and *Meister*, for he values the journeymen years primarily as a patriarchal mode of socialization.[32] So much is clear from the role played in Jakob's rescue by a French-speaking *Meister*, who in a series of dialogues successfully rebuts Jakob's radical ideas. To solidarity Gotthelf opposes an individualism informed by both a Christian conception of man as *homo viator* and a Hobbesian economic liberalism that views humanity in terms of contending interests. As was noted earlier, this individualism finds its symbolic expression in the new haversack presented to each youth at the outset of his wanderings.

## Realism, Satire and Fear in Gotthelf's "Genrebilder"

Wolfgang Menzel, a tireless partisan of Gotthelf's writings in Germany, was perhaps the first to use the term "Genrebilder" in the description of *Jakobs Wanderungen*.[33] The term is a particularly apt one to apply to the novel's mode of realism, with its fidelity to the detail of the pleasures and travails of the *Volk*. Indeed, the work does succeed to a large degree in reproducing something of the texture of the lives of tramping journeymen, and there are few literary works of the *Biedermeier* in which the laboriousness of such existences is evoked in such detail.[34] The exhaustion of laboring unter a heavy pack, footsoreness, backache; the misery of walking in winter, or on muddy roads — often with broken-down boots; the poor food, drunkenness, and violence in the hostelries: all are present. Nor is the psychic dimension neglected, the sense of desolation felt by the journeyman in foreign parts. The sense of viewing a series of genre pictures is enhanced by the episodic structure and the use of quasi-pictorial titles for each chapter — undoubtedly intended as *aides-memoires* for the relatively unsophisticated target readership. And, the designation "Genrebilder" also recalls the moralizing and socially normative functions of Dutch mass art, aspects that are always close at hand. Indeed, the tumultuous and chaotic tavern scenes, which the pastor of Lützelflüh sketches with considerable aplomb, have something of the atmosphere of Jan Steen's allegories of vice.

In the sense that it imagines the vicissitudes of a journeyman protagonist, Gotthelf's "Wanderbuch"[35] may be considered more deserving of the designation than Riehl's ethnographic study of the same name. In it, wandering has the status not of empirical method but of lived experience. That is not to deny that the work handles its protagonist "von oben herab,"[36] but despite the gulf separating the hapless "Esel" Jakob from the sermonizing narrator, a sustained effort is made to imagine the life of the *Volk* from the inside.

One of the key attributes of the genre form, whether in painting or in literature, is humor. And, in Gotthelf's hands, satiric humor is integral to his social commentary, a weapon to be deployed against German demagogues, Swiss liberals (referred to as "Radikale" throughout), and politicized artisans, as well as *Meistersleute* and servants with ideas above their station. Scenes such as that in which a cart overturns, spilling its load of drunken Waadtland patriots like "einen Kübel voll brüllender Frösche" (297) into the road are as sharply drawn as any in Gotthelf's *oeuvre*. Keenly observed, too, are the petty affectations of female servants on their Sundays off, careful to handle their wineglasses only with their fingertips. Gotthelf permits himself a slightly coarse tone at such junctures, one reminiscent of a *Volksbuch* like Grimmelshausen's *Simplicissimus*, and the text is liberally bestrewn with Lutherisms ("potz himmelsackerment"). The principal targets of the satire are radical intellectuals in the *Bildungsvereine* and elsewhere. Chapter 29 stages a confrontation in a tavern between a schoolmaster and a legal agent on the one side and a group of farmers and day laborers (representing the *Volk*) on the other. The progressive party is identified by its use of fashionable political slogans, "Fortschritt," "Zeitgeist," "Aufklärung" (447–48), which together with other shibboleths of the Young German literary movement, "Kultur" (117), "Zerrissenheit" (163), are derided throughout the novel. In this scene the farmers and day laborers put aside their differences, uniting in their rejection of the demagogues and their phrases. Here the

Swiss are *unter sich*, Jakob a mere observer: "So viel hatte er gelernt, daß man in fremde Verhältnisse hinein nur Dummes schwatze" (456). The implied message for the German artisans among the readership: stick to your last and keep out of Swiss affairs.

In his attack on socialism and communism Gotthelf invokes the anthropological categories of ingratitude and *ressentiment*.[37] The source of all social evil is the inability to accept one's place in the social order,[38] which is presented as God-given. Vain aspirations to social betterment cause individuals to neglect the roles assigned to them by birth. The consequences for social stability are evident at every stage of Jakob's journey through Switzerland: *Meister* neglect their patriarchal duties toward *Gesellen;* their wives shirk their domestic responsibilities and affect the manners of the bourgeoisie; and, most discouragingly: "Der Handwerksbursche wandert nicht mehr auf dem Handwerk, sondern bloß auf Ideen" (105). In view of this anthropological pessimism, Sengle's remark concerning Gotthelf's "übertriebenen Glauben an die Erziehbarkeit des Menschen"[39] should, perhaps, be qualified. As a Calvinist, though not a doctrinaire one, Gotthelf does indeed subscribe to the notion of human perfectibility; but one in which self-betterment is at all times threatened by a renewed fall into sinfulness. Accordingly, he harbors a deep suspicion of the bourgeois ideal of *Bildung* and its socialist variants, with their claims to perfect human nature. The diligent *Schulkommissär* who boasted about the number of new schools opened during his time in office sees school education divorced from Christian doctrine as undermining respect for age and authority:

> Die Griechen und Römer hatten großen Respekt vor grauen Häuptern; "vor einem grauen Haupte sollst du aufstehen und dich bücken!" steht geschrieben, und die Knaben, welche eines Propheten spotteten, fraßen die Bären. Nun ist es anders und altväterisch ist ein Spottname geworden, die Jugend hat das Szepter ergriffen. . . . Die Hauptschuld an diesem Übel trägt die Schule, denn sie ist es, welche den Jungen in den Kopf setzt, die Alten seien nichts. (245)

Essentially, Gotthelf is prepared to affirm schooling only insofar as this prepares the youth for a life within the class of their birth. Unlike the protagonist of Zschokke's *Meister Jordan*, who eventually rises to become an adviser to his prince, Jakob is not permitted to transcend class horizons. The author's understanding of the uses and limits of education is reflected in the novel's implicit evaluation of the *Wanderschaft*. As previously noted, this is ratified only with regard to the *terminus ad quem* of property and the settled life. It is not, however, presented as a means to unlimited social advancement and self-improvement.

This apparent reluctance to embrace the *Wanderschaft* for its own sake is perhaps why, for Muret, the protagonist seems "un produit d'importation étrangère."[40] It is tempting to seek an explanation for this queasiness in the author's biography. Gotthelf's life was, after all, a settled one: apart from a semester at Göttingen in 1821 followed by a brief tour of northern Germany, he seldom left the confines of the Emmental, far less the Canton of Bern.[41] The title of chapter 18 may be adduced as evidence of discomfort with the notion of a life of wandering: "Ein zweites Erwachen, diesmal ein freudiges; hinter der Türe hat ihm Gott eine bleibende Stätte bereitet und zwar eine warme, gesunde für Leib und Seele." The affirmation of the "bleibende Stätte," the patriarchal space of the workshop where the errant journeyman's rehabilitation begins, takes place via the implicit identification of the space of the *Wanderschaft* as an insalubrious one for body and soul.

Aware that the sharpness of the satire in *Jakobs Wanderungen* might cause him to be represented in Germany as a defender of aristocratic privilege, Gotthelf sets out his republican credentials in the foreword to *Jakobs Wanderungen:* "Da dieses Büchlein aber möglicherweise in Kreise kommt, wo weder der Verfasser noch seine früheren Schriften bekannt sind, so glaubt er bemerken zu sollen, er sei ein Republikaner, liebe das ganze Volk, nicht bloß einige Glieder desselben, und diese Liebe sei die Quelle seiner Schriften" (6).

Doubtless such protestations do not exclude the possibility of a subliminal "Fear of the *Volk*" (Perraudin) expressed in the flood and disease metaphors that abound in Gotthelf's writings. But the thesis that the pastor of Lützelflüh feared the Swiss people, or, more specifically, the disenfranchised and unpropertied proletariat, must be weighed against the part he played in establishing and running the school at Trachselwald. Such commitment surely went far beyond the call of duty. A stronger case can perhaps be made, however, for Gotthelf's fear of those threatening foreigners, the German journeymen and intellectuals who sought to turn his homeland into "einer Festung der Propaganda . . ., aus welcher Festung Tore in aller Herren Länder führen" (279).

Naturally, the prime targets of the novel's at times virulent rhetoric are "die Verführer . . . die Apostel der verruchten Lehren," that is, the intellectual ringleaders: "Schlingel, welche durch eigene Schuld die Heimat verloren und nun die ganze Welt anstecken möchten, damit niemand mehr eine Heimat habe" (474–75). In demonizing these the novel is careful to express sympathy for the gullible journeymen who fall into their clutches. But the criterion on the basis of which the enemy is discredited, exile or homelessness, applies in full measure to many of the *Gesellen* themselves. In *Die Armennot*, which is not addressed to an artisan readership, the distinction between leaders and led is not so carefully observed:

> Es gibt noch eine Klasse, welche wenigstens ebenso versunken ist als das Proletariat und zu dessen Verdorbenheit jetzt mehr noch beiträgt als die obern Stände. Es ist das große Regiment von Taugenichtsen. . . . Sie sind

> die Kneipenpfaffen, die Mönche der Kaffeehäuser, denn sie verlassen sie selten, sie sind die Theaterengel, sie sind die Hetzer der Hefe des Volkes, die Schreiber der schlechtesten Blätter, die Missionäre des Unglaubens und der Zerrüttung, als: Flüchtlinge, Handlungsreisende, Hausierer, wandernde Pädagogen, Handwerksbursche und sonstige Landstreicher.[42]

Here a whole range of socially undesirable elements are brought together and linked by the defining attribute of homelessness or vagrancy. Their non-settled status marks members of the social categories listed as work-shy "Taugenichtse," whose presence is an enduring source of instability. To the extent that it voices suspicions about the non-settled life, *Jakobs Wanderungen* also implicitly participates in the anathemization of the very journeymen who are ostensibly the focus of its charitable concern. Gotthelf's unsparing condemnation of those unwilling or unable to work recalls the great confinement of persons in those categories underway in Europe since the mid-sixteenth century, described so vividly by Foucault.[43]

In truth, Swiss conservatives had much to fear from the potential threat posed by German artisans and their associations. The institution of the *Wanderschaft* long eluded official attempts to bring it under control: individual police actions (the expulsions of 1836 and 1845) offered little more than short-term success. Such actions were primarily aimed at the ringleaders; the rank and file journeymen were, for the most part, little affected by them. Similarly, the *Wanderverbot* of 1835, which prohibited journeymen in the German Confederation from traveling to states where they might be influenced by radical ideas, seems to have been ineffective. In any event, the Swiss cantons, then in the early stages of industrialization, could ill afford to dispense with the technical know-how of German artisans. Still more worrying was the fact that the workers' associations had made great strides in educating and disciplining their members, who, as an 1850 report of the new Swiss *Bundestag* noted, exhibited none of the dissolution formerly associated with artisans.[44]

By the early 1850s, however, it was clear that the threat to the Swiss Confederation had been averted. The 1852 *Kommunistenprozess* in Cologne broke the power of the *Bund der Kommunisten* and the German workers' associations abroad went into decline. Pauperization, too, quickly vanished from the political agenda as industrialization gathered momentum in Germany and Switzerland. The new industries absorbed the majority of artisans, who became depoliticized as their material conditions improved. Official concern about the subversive potential of the journeyman class, a group whose traditional mobility made its members, for a time, ideal conduits for political ideas, gradually ebbed away. Nevertheless, the radicalization of the *Gesellen* and the attempts to counter it in *Volksschriften* may have created an abiding association in the popular mind between vagrancy and political insubordination, fostering the idea of a contrast between the settled "Biedermann" and wandering "Brandstifter."

Such anxieties would again become virulent in Germany in the 1880s, when internal migration became a truly mass phenomenon. Then, many of the themes and preoccupations that we find already in Gotthelf's novel would resurface in the debate on the so-called *Vagabundenfrage*. I will return to this debate below, arguing that it consolidates a new "ideology of the settled life" in Wilhelmine Germany, and that the rise of that ideology is reflected in a general decline in narratives of wandering.

## Holtei's *Die Vagabunden* (1851)

### Holtei's Novel as "Trivialliteratur"

The second work on which I will base my discussion of socially marginal wanderers in German literature is Karl von Holtei's "zu Unrecht vergessener Roman" *Die Vagabunden*.[45] This work differs markedly from Gotthelf's *Jakob* in that its *raison d'être* is entertainment rather than moral didactics, yet both works were intended for and succeeded in reaching a mass readership (*Die Vagabunden* achieving ten editions by 1909). Since Karl von Holtei (1798–1880) is now an almost entirely forgotten figure of nineteenth-century literature, it will be necessary to provide some biographical detail before attending more closely to the work itself.

Although Holtei's family belonged to the minor nobility of Silesia (his father was an officer of the hussars), his childhood was by no means secure: his mother died soon after bearing him, and he was brought up by a great-aunt, without ever being formally adopted. The passion for the theater that would mark Holtei throughout his adult life appears to have been kindled by a production of *Die Räuber* he saw in Breslau when he was thirteen. Throughout his legal studies he maintained contact with theatrical circles in Breslau; 1819 saw his debut in that city both as an actor and as a dramatic author. There followed a career as prolific actor, author, and director in numerous cities and towns throughout the German Confederation. His repeated attempts to secure a long-term position at a German theater met with little success; instead Holtei and his first and second wives (both actresses) had to content themselves with guest roles, short-term and seasonal engagements. The year 1847 marks an important caesura: in that year Holtei went to live with his daughter in Graz. Having resigned his last directorial post in 1844, he began to concentrate on giving public recitations and composing a series of novels. In this latter, more sedentary, phase of his life, Holtei had for the first time a permanent home in Graz (and later in Breslau), although he continued to travel widely, giving readings in Berlin, Vienna, and elsewhere. It is for his role as reader and *raconteur* that Holtei was perhaps best known in his own lifetime; indeed, in this capacity his fame was surpassed only by that of Ludwig Tieck.

Holtei's *Vagabunden*, his first novel, is the product of this more settled phase, and its immediate precursor is the sprawling memoir *Vierzig Jahre*, which appeared in eight volumes between 1843 and 1850. This is significant, because the novel can be seen as embodying the organizing theme of the biography, that of a vagabond life in German theater. To be sure, the milieu of the novel is the world of wandering artistes, circus entertainers and the like, and not primarily the theater, but the parallels are evident. Taken together with the memoir, it appears that *Die Vagabunden* is intended as a memorial to a past phase of existence, one that Holtei perhaps felt he had overcome, or that he even desired to consign to the past. Its historical setting corresponds closely to Holtei's young manhood: excluding the epilogue, the narrated time spans a seven-year period ending approximately in the mid-1820s — Goethe is still alive, and the railways have not yet made an appearance. Thus the work could be said to fulfill a need felt by its author; indeed it seems to serve in some respects as an attempt to come to terms with a vivid past and to ground some of its more chaotic energies.

This, however, is only one aspect of a composition that is designed in the first instance to appeal to a wide readership, satisfying its needs and garnering for its author a significant income. For there can be no doubt that *Die Vagabunden* is the product of commercial calculation; it is an attempt by Holtei to package the essence of his theatrical life in a more saleable form than that of his more cumbrous memoirs. This observation brings us to the question of the possible status of the work as *Trivialliteratur*, a category to which it has long been assigned.[46] It will become apparent that Holtei's narrative of wandering exhibits some of the characteristics of trivial fiction, but first a brief exposition of the plot of this forgotten novel is required.

*Die Vagabunden* is the story of the seventeen-year-old orphan Anton Hahn, brought up by his maternal grandmother, a Lutheran cantor's widow, in Liebenau, a Silesian village. It is a poor household, dependent on the income from Anton's basket weaving. The idyll is disturbed when the youth is finally enlightened about the circumstances of his birth, out of wedlock, and the subsequent disappearance of his mother, an actress who had been seduced by a nobleman. More unsettling events follow when the Baron of Liebenau dies and the territory becomes the property of a speculator, Theodor van der Helfft. But the real impetus for departure comes with the death of grandmother Hahn, when house and workshop fall into the hands of a trustee, a rival craftsman. At a stroke, Anton is dispossessed. Too young to assume control of the business, and unwilling to become the ward of his rival, he departs Liebenau in haste, spurred by the memory of a company of strolling players. His career as a wandering entertainer begins when the youth is engaged by a traveling menagerie — and acquires the documents and alias necessary for further travel. With Madame Amelot the youthful protagonist begins the first of the *affaires* that accompany his subsequent career. Nor is she the first object of erotic interest: in Liebenau the youth's attention was divided between Ottilie, the baron's daughter, and a gypsy-girl, "die braune Bärbel." From the menagerie Anton makes the transition to the circus, where he is engaged as a trick rider. In this milieu of petty jealousies and intrigues his affections are soon transferred to a novice *artiste*, distinguished from the others by her purity and naiveté. When Anton is injured in a fall, this paragon supervises his care; but there is no further consummation, for in contrast to other female figures Adele embodies the ideals of renunciation and of "heilige, reine Liebe" (199).[47] Nevertheless the pursuit of her provides the *movens* for Anton's subsequent journey to Paris. During his convalescence Anton conceives a passion for the theater, but he is dissuaded from pursuing a stage career by Ludwig Devrient, a contemporary of Holtei's. Later, discovering that Adele has left the Guillaumes' circus, Anton breaks his own engagement and resolves to follow her to Paris. In the company of the giant Schkramprl, the hero tours the fair at Leipzig, where all manner of wandering entertainers have foregathered. An opportunity to travel to Paris presents itself in the company of Herr Blämert and his cabinet of waxworks, and, inevitably, Anton becomes the object of Frau Blämert's attentions.

The Paris episode renews the focus on the question of Anton's origins; the past resurfaces in a series of mysterious encounters: with "die braune Bärbel," now the mistress of van der Helfft, and with the tragic Madame Carina (Anton's mother, whom he believed dead), who disappears almost as soon as she appears. In this episode Holtei gives free reign to the erotic and melodramatic elements in the description of Anton's seduction at the hands of Bärbel, a *Grand Guignol*[48] confrontation at the opera, and Bärbel's violent death. None of the requisites of melodrama are omitted: police spies, a tantalizingly unreadable letter, catastrophe, and rescue at the hands of a pious woman (Adele). The letter directs the young vagabond — chastened by his experiences in Paris — to Pisa, where he hopes to learn his mother's fate. On the way he falls in with Theodor, now a broken and dying man, who promises to install Anton as his heir and the new sovereign of Liebenau. Predictably, however, Theodor dies before he can draft his testament, and the prospect of a solution to the mystery of the youth's origins recedes as Madame Carina departs for Vienna.

Anton's gradual return to his homeland sees him taking on a series of new roles: first as a camel-driver in the pay of a member of the *Carbonari*, later (and still in his assumed French role) as a dancing-master, before stumbling on a puppet-theater performance of *Der verlorene Sohn* (!) in Erfurt. Something of his earlier enthusiasm for the theater is rekindled by this performance, and he succeeds in entering the employment of Herr Dreher and his reticent and ailing wife. Madame Dreher is none other than Anton's mother, the late Madame Carina. Silenced by her shame at abandoning her son she succeeds in suppressing her true identity, devoting herself to smoothing the path toward an eventual union between Anton and the conventionally pure Hedwig. It is only with the death of "Madame Dreher" and the reading of her testament that the mystery of her identity and of her vagabond life subsequent to parting from her infant son is elucidated. The testament becomes the *deus ex machina* guiding the wanderer back to Silesia and to a confrontation with his natural father, Count Guido. The latter embraces the revenant but is prevented from making restitution to him by his ingrate son and heir, an antagonist who has crossed Anton's path on previous occasions. It is another mark of the novel's pastiche quality that it culminates in a *Bruderzwist* reminiscent of *Die Räuber*. With the sudden deaths of the count and his legitimate son the way is clear for the count's widow — aided by the giant Schkramprl — to make amends by installing Anton as the sovereign of Liebenau. Not Ottilie, a spinster who has kept Anton's home as a shrine, but Hedwig then becomes his bride: the provisions of his mother's testament fulfilled, Anton's wanderings, and his homelessness, are at an end.

It will already be apparent from this highly schematic résumé that *Die Vagabunden* meets some of the specifications for trivial fiction, not least in its highly convoluted plot. This becomes even more evident when we apply some of the standard criteria for *Trivialliteratur*. The *Reallexikon der deutschen Literaturwissenschaft* sees literature of this category as an attempt to satisfy three basic needs of its readers, who are assumed to include those less educated than the traditional constituency for the novel:[49]

1. The need for rapid and easy orientation within the fictional world. This is achieved *inter alia* by a simple typology of characters who are readily classified as "good" or "bad." Reading becomes a source of intellectual unburdening against the background of pressure on individuals to process and assimilate ever-increasing amounts of information, a tendency present even in the mid-nineteenth century.
2. The reader's need to see confessional, regional, or class norms confirmed and upheld. The protagonists of trivial fictions continue to uphold generally accepted social norms even where they transcend the experiential horizon of the reader (for example, in the happy ending).
3. The need for emotional participation by the reader. This need is usually explained in terms of a trend toward the stripping away of the affective side of social intercourse. Trivial texts provide compensatory emotional stimulation by alternately building up and dissipating affective tension.

With regard to the first, *Die Vagabunden* makes a virtue of simplicity, both by providing figures that correspond to recognizable types and by employing a uncomplicated style: note, for example, the predominance of character speech over authorial narration. Moreover, the work presents a world that is inherently ordered: mysteries and uncertainties of identity abound; but there are none that are not, at last, resolved. Separations are always balanced by reunions, and some final settling of accounts is always permitted before death supervenes. Interestingly, and unexpectedly, the metropolis, that milieu where Holtei's contemporaries experienced most acutely the atomized state of the individual, is the very place where all the threads of past life combine. Paris is banalized, imagined as a Silesian village, and thus rendered harmless for the readership.

Holtei's novel, although treating the vagabond life with warmth, essentially ratifies the canon of conventional bourgeois values. This is especially clear from the figures with whom female readers are tacitly invited to identify: Ottilie, Adele, and Hedwig. All are exemplars of *the* salient behavioral value in Restoration society, which may be glossed as "Entsagung" or "Geduld." It is significant that for all these figures renunciation entails some degree of sexual abstinence. Hedwig, who eventually marries, is above reproach because she shows herself to be willing to renounce Anton when commanded to do so by the ailing father to whom she owes her first loyalty. The conclusion sees even the *picaro*, Anton, firmly contained within moral bounds of which even relatively censorious readers might approve, and this despite his fairy-tale elevation to the status of squire of Liebenau.

Finally, with regard to the third need, the novel stages a number of dramatic shifts of fortune that permit the reader a measure of emotional participation. The vicarious concern felt in viewing Anton's accident in the ring — or his degradation in a Parisian *demi-monde* of gamblers and courtesans — ebbs away in relief at the sight of his rescue (on both occasions) at the hands of the chaste Adele. This simple pattern of triumph and reversal is kept up throughout. In addition, the narrator caters to the perceived need for emotional reassurance in numerous apparently heartfelt apostrophes of the reader.[50] In these, and in the pronounced sentimentality of the various deathbed scenes, we see the hand of the dramaturge, skilled in the production of sentimental comedies (*Rührstücke*).

## The End of "Bildung": Wandering, Heteronomy, and Epigonentum

Toward the end of the novel, Holtei's garrulous narrator once again apostrophizes the reader about the intentions underlying the story:

> Wie oft, mein gütiger Leser, haben wir in diesem Büchlein unseren Helden schon beobachtet, wenn er wieder zu wandern begann. Ich wage nicht zu behaupten, aber ich wünsche, daß es mir gelungen wäre, deutlich darzustellen, wie er von Jahr zu Jahr an Einsicht und Verstande reifer,

> aus vielen Prüfungen immer besser, aus mancherlei unsauberen Verhältnissen und Umgebungen immer gereinigter hervorging. So wollt' ich ihn an dir, mein Leser, vorüberführen; doch, wie gesagt, ich weiß nicht, ob ich es vermocht habe. (422)

With these words the classical paradigm of the *Bildungsreise* is invoked. But the expressed doubts about the extent to which the protagonist has actually undergone some form of development are all too justified. It is worth recalling Friedrich Sengle's remarks on this passage: "'Bunte Schicksale,' einen etwas modernisierten Abenteuerroman erzählt Karl von Holtei in den *Vagabunden*. . . . Ab und zu ist von Bildung und Besserung die Rede. Der Erzähler behauptet einmal, er wolle solches Höherwachsen zeigen. Im ganzen aber liegt die Bewegung auf der Horizontalen, Gutes und Böses, Glück und Unglück mischen sich ständig."[51] Continuing, Sengle notes the absence of "irgendein Bildungsziel." The problem seems to be that the work is conceived with two conflicting guiding principles in mind: first, it seeks to show a process of maturation or learning and second, it seeks to affirm that the protagonist is as faithful to some "essence" of character at the end as he is at the outset. Thus in her testament Antonie is at pains to assert of her son: "Er hat in unsteten Wanderungen, in Torheiten und Irrtümern ein reines Herz bewahrt" (425). And Anton draws the following balance of his vagrant career: "Ich hab' vielerlei erlebt, Gutes und Schlimmes; hab' vielerlei getan — leider mehr Schlimmes als Gutes . . . aber im Herzen bin ich eigentlich unverändert geblieben; bin immer noch der Anton von damals" (462).

It is not easy to take seriously Anton's claim to have remained unaltered, that he has remained true to some essence. Fidelity to an inner essence, or growth impelled by it, are the attributes of the heroes of early Romanticism. But Anton does not undergo "growth," nor can he be said to have been true to a "natural" essence, unless that essence be changeability itself. Moreover the initial trigger for his wandering is not metaphysical but material: the death of his grandmother dispossesses him. Freedom, in the novel's terms, rather than having anything to do with adherence to a self-created set of ideals — as it would have done for the Romantics — is invariably bound up with the possession of money and the right papers.

*Die Vagabunden* celebrates tactical ability over strategic commitment. Although lip service is paid to Romantic-Platonic notions of elective affinities (Anton — Adele), the area of love relations is dominated by a series of short-lived liaisons. This is true also of the professional sphere, where survival requires adaptability, the ability to seize fleeting opportunities, to improvise. Among the guild of vagabonds there is no place for false pride; what is instead required is willingness to don the "Affengarderobe" (346) and to come to terms with one's second rate status. Nevertheless, the invocations of the topos of the "reines Herz" lead us to suspect that Holtei is unable to embrace the actorly ideal of mutability without some qualms. In his biography, *Vierzig Jahre*, Holtei cleaves to the Romantic notion of being born to the role of actor, and he is inclined to blame setbacks on his lack of fidelity to his natural talent. His lived existence, however, gives the lie to notions of an essence to which one need only be true to succeed. This contradiction between the ideal of loyalty to one's gift and the actorly ideal of adaptability is reflected in the novel, whose idyllic ending requires that the hero be shown as unscathed, uncompromised by his "Vagabundenleben." But Anton's essential quality is his "Wanderlust," whose reappearance briefly threatens the idyllic situation, and therein lies the paradox: what Anton is ultimately loyal to is the principle of mutability.

The novel's inability to operate convincingly within the paradigm of *Bildung* is connected with contemporary developments in the theater with which Holtei would have been all too familiar. The main tendency of the *Biedermeier* period was the steady decline of the idealistic bourgeois theater with its educative program and the rise of a theater predicated largely on the entertainment function. This process was accompanied by an erosion of the status of the author within the theater hierarchy, and an increasing emphasis on music, dance, and spectacle. As Sengle observes, "Man braucht dabei nicht gleich an den dressierten Hund zu denken, den Goethe zum Anlaß für seinen Rücktritt von der Theaterleitung nahm (1817),"[52] but this affair was then considered symptomatic of the changes taking place, and it is surely significant that Holtei makes explicit reference to it in chapter 52 of his novel. There Holtei reflects — ironically, and perhaps ruefully — on the ousting of the author by the vagabonds of the new theater, represented by Anton. In doing so, he reflects also on his own role in the destruction of the theater as an educational institution. For Holtei had, in his capacities as author and director, sought to satisfy the growing demand for inconsequential entertainments, in part with his attempts to introduce a new genre, the one-act *Liederspiel*, based on the French *vaudeville* form.[53] In common with other authors of his generation (Immermann: *Die Epigonen*) Holtei is haunted by the sense of his own *Epigonentum*, of living in the shadow of Weimar Classicism. Indeed, the shadow of *Wilhelm Meister* lies over his debut novel: at one point an "Anton Hahns Wanderjahre" is playfully imagined (353). It is characteristic of Holtei's awareness of the diminution of dramatic art that Anton makes the journey from the stage proper to the puppet-theater: the reverse of Wilhelm Meister's progress.

Wandering is in Holtei's novel no longer the expression of creative sovereignty that it had been for Novalis or Tieck, but a metaphor for the artist's absolute dependency, his exposure to the play of market forces and to the jealousies and intrigues of his colleagues. This becomes especially clear when we read the novel in conjunction with *Vierzig Jahre*. There Holtei's wanderings are an index of powerlessness, the result of persistent efforts to secure a long-term engagement. In them we discern not the progressive unfolding of a unique essence but a struggle for survival; not self-determination but wandering as heteronomy. Art of the kind practiced by Holtei's generation is not "die auch in ihrem Zwecke wie in ihren Mitteln *freie* Kunst," which Hegel deems the only fitting object of an aesthetics, but the "nicht unabhängige, nicht freie, sondern *dienende* Kunst," which, though serving its purpose, is incapable of giving expression to "die tiefsten Interessen des Menschen."[54] Holtei's use of the term "Vagabunden" to refer to artists of his generation indicates a sense not only of the lack of seriousness of his profession but also of aesthetic homelessness, of exile from the homeland of classical art, identified with Weimar.

The fullest expression of Holtei's views on the heteronomy of the artist are to be found in the speech given to Ludwig Devrient in chapter 30. Devrient berates Anton for wanting to throw over his budding career as a circus artiste in favor of the stage, defining "ein großer Schauspieler" as

> ein Mensch, der, ein Spielball seiner eigenen Nerven, keine Gewalt mehr hat über sich selbst[,] keine moralische Kraft, sich zu beherrschen; der sich mit Beifall überschüttet hört, wenn er an sich selbst zweifelt; den sie kalt vorübergehen lassen, wenn er den Gott in sich fühlt; der um Beifall buhlen muß, welchen er verachtet — ohne welchen er doch nicht leben könnte, weil er nur aus ihm Lebenslust atmet! (209)

For the *Biedermeier* artist the theater no longer holds out any real prospect of "ästhetische Erziehung," a sentiment these lines powerfully express, but the novel seems to go beyond this to cast doubt, if implicitly, on the possibility of *Bildung* in any social domain. In Anton it presents a personality incapable of steady development over an extended period. This is a "modern," evanescent personality type for which Eduard von Bauernfeld, a dramatist and contemporary of Holtei's, found apposite words: "Man ändert sich nicht in Jahren, nicht in Tagen, sondern in Minuten."[55] Given that not only the ideal of *Bildung* but also the institution of a vocation appears in a dubious light, it is not surprising that the value of the "reines Herz" is invoked with such fervor. It is here alone that Holtei perceives something like a guarantee of authenticity, and of enduring personality.

## Die Vagabunden and the Ideology of the Settled Life

Holtei cannot escape the reigning assumptions concerning the lives of actors and, more generally, nomadic existences. Moreover, he effectively reproduces such assumptions in his memoir and in *Die Vagabunden. Vierzig Jahre* attests not only to the persistent awareness of *Epigonentum* that afflicted Holtei's generation but also to a deeper sense of unease about the actor's life. This is what Holtei has to say about his decision to pursue a stage career after seeing Ludwig Devrient play Franz Moor at Breslau in 1811: "Am nächsten Tag machte ich in der Klasse bekannt, ich würde

Schauspieler werden! Nun gute Nacht, Fleiß, Ausdauer, Bestreben, Ehrgeiz, und wie die Stacheln heißen mögen, die den begabten Schüler durch die staubige Bahn des Schulschlendrians der klaren Morgenröte heiterer Wissenschaft entgegenführen."[56] To be sure, these remarks are written in the spirit of ironic self-deprecation with which the memoir is imbued. Yet it is difficult to escape the conclusion that Holtei suffered under the stigma that marked his chosen profession. On occasions he represents himself as divided — torn between "halb wahnsinnige Theaterlust" and "Sehnsucht nach stillem, waldumrauschten Landleben."[57] Dilettantism, inconstancy, improvidence, dissolution: these were the components of the stigma with which Holtei had to contend in his lifetime. Unable to transcend them, he reproduces these categories in his retrospective self-evaluation. Indeed, the degree to which Holtei concurs with contemporary and later descriptions of his life is remarkable.[58] Gustav Freytag's assessment is the archetypal one: "Holtei hatte ein langes Wanderleben hinter sich und in dem unsteten Treiben wohl manche Einbuße erlitten. Aber in allen Beziehungen zu seinen literarischen Bekannten war er ein feinfühliger Mann von Ehre geblieben."[59] This "aber" is important: it points to Freytag's conviction, symptomatic of the time, that a nomadic lifestyle implied a defective personality, or a lack of that which, in the epoch of bourgeois realism, was termed "character." The notion that nomadism was incompatible with the standard repertoire of secondary virtues — diligence, order, constancy — emerges most strongly from Freytag's *Bilder aus der deutschen Vergangenheit* (1859–67). The second volume "Aus dem Jahrhundert der Reformation" contains a pen-portrait of "ein fahrender Schüler," one Thomas Platter, whose rise from humble origins as a shepherd to become a distinguished publisher in Basel seems the model of a successfully completed *Bildungsweg*. Freytag, however, draws a sobering conclusion: "Nicht ohne Einfluß blieb das unstäte Leben der Kinderzeit auf die Seele des Mannes: wie tüchtig er war, die stäte Ausdauer und frohe Kraft fehlte seinen Unternehmungen."[60] (Incidentally, Platter's adventurous autobiography would become a canonical text of the *Wandervogel* youth movement founded at the end of the century.[61]) On numerous occasions *Bilder aus der deutschen Vergangenheit*, whose status as popular historiography makes it a valuable source of information on prevailing social values — values that it in turn served to mold and propagate — brings the categories of disease and delinquency to bear on its discussions of the lives of itinerant scholars, strolling players, and other nomads. The significant amount of space given over to such discussions is itself eloquent: it is as if the work wishes to record a mode of existence in the moment of its dying.

The prominence given to nomadism in Freytag's history becomes less remarkable when we consider the hold exerted on the popular imagination of a single pair of antonyms: "Ruhe" and "Bewegung." This influence went far beyond the political discourse of the *Vormärz* period in which that contrast first became productive.[62] Toward the beginning of the 1840s the term *Arbeiterbewegung* made its first appearance; coined by conservatives, the term carried an exclusively pejorative charge until its successful appropriation and revaluation by the workers' associations. (I have discussed the symbolic role of the *Wanderschaft* in this process above.) In the period leading up to and following the foundation of the Wilhelmine *Reich* in 1871, historians taking stock of the previous century frequently cast it in terms of movement or revolution. For Jakob Burckhardt (1871/72) the previous hundred years were best summed up as "lauter Revolutionszeitalter"; it had been an epoch stirred by "Bewegung . . ., die im Gegensatz zu aller bekannten Vergangenheit unseres Globus steht."[63] What the historians were saying around the time of the *Reichsgründung*, namely that the signal feature of their age had been "Bewegung," had already been a commonly held view in the *Vormärz* period. By "Bewegung" contemporaries understood a whole range of processes that they saw as interconnected: the advent of the railways, emigration, and large scale movements of people within the German lands, but also urbanization and political unrest.

The association in the collective consciousness of "Bewegung" with radical politics was cemented by the symbolic use of the railway in the journalism and literary offerings of the Young German writers. Stokers and engineers were regularly apostrophized as the harbingers of an era in which technology would set men free; characteristically, one of the most widely circulating illustrated newspapers of the left bore the title *Die Lokomotive* (it was suppressed in 1843). But the railway was more than a symbol seized upon by political radicals: in March 1848 it became an instrument of effective mass protest when, in the duchy of Nassau, some 30,000 farmers used it to converge on Wiesbaden, forcing the capitulation of the Prince of Orange.[64] Such events helped to forge the conceptual link between the ideas of "Bewegung" and "Revolution."

The psychological correlate of the diagnosis that the condition of the age was fundamentally one of movement and revolution was a longing for order, peace, and stability. Such a mood was not confined to historians and the political elite, of course, but it found its most potent expression in the writings of the *Historische Schule*, the theoreticians of what I have called "the ideology of the settled life." Here is Freytag again, in a dedication to his publisher, S. Hirzel, written in 1866, which forms the preface to the *Bilder aus der deutschen Vergangenheit:* "Seit dem Staufen Friedrich dem I. haben neunzehn Geschlechter unserer Ahnen den Segen eines großen und machtvollen deutschen Reiches entbehrt, im zwanzigsten Menschenalter gewinnen die Deutschen durch Preußen und den Sieg der Hohenzollern zurück, was vielen so fremd geworden ist wie Völkerwanderung und Kreuzzüge: ihren Staat."[65]

For Freytag, as for many of his contemporaries, German history viewed in retrospect takes on the appearance of the wanderings of Ahasver, a long and disconsolate straying, the end of which is now in sight, thanks to establishment of the *Reich*. As I have shown in the discussion of Fontane's *Wanderungen*, members of the *historische Schule* interpreted that event as "the end of history." That view had the epistemological status of wish-dream; in the cited passage history is written using the trope of homecoming. It is scarcely surprising, then, to find this trope already present in Holtei's novel. Not only does Anton Hahn return to Liebenau; he takes possession of the "Heimat" as feudal lord. The vagabond artist is reintegrated under the conditions of feudal absolutism. It is remarkable that this conclusion is imagined so soon after the 1848 revolution, which had shattered that order beyond any real hope of restoration. Anton's embrace of his birthplace amounts to acquiescence in a principle that finds ironic formulation in the title of a contemporary novel by Willibald Alexis: "Ruhe ist die erste Bürgerpflicht." If Holtei's ending were so banal it would be of no further interest; but Anton's return precipitates an emotional crisis. With the onset of spring his old wanderlust reasserts itself: "Was sollen mir die Boten der Freiheit? Ich bin nicht mehr frei" (492). Evidently the return to the "Idiotie des Landlebens" (Marx) from an existence lived out in the towns and fairgrounds of Europe exacts a similarly high price in terms of repression as did bourgeois participation in civil society after 1848. The novel's solution is to have the revenant's new wife give him *carte blanche* to resume the vagabond life at will: the mere possession of that warrant is then sufficient for him. From this contrived ending we may conclude that Holtei, although ultimately upholding the ideology of the settled life, cannot do so without at least a rueful backward glance at the rough-and-ready liberties of the vagabond. Of course, as we have seen, at another level — perhaps below that of the author's consciousness — the text unmasks the heteronomy of that life.

In truth, Holtei was never entirely comfortable with the ideal of *Heimat*, a fact that was connected with the painful circumstances of his fosterage: "O Gott, ihr preiset die Tage eurer Kindheit, eurer Jugend; den goldenen Frieden eurer Heimat! Die Liebe zu euren Eltern! ihr Glücklichen! wohl euch, die ihr Eltern, Heimat, Kindheit und Jugend hattet! *Meine* Kindheit war ein Fegefeuer und meine Jugend eine Hölle."[66]

But, as is known, Holtei's political convictions were conservative, and these led him inexorably to an affirmation of the home-place, even as the bitter memories of his own childhood made it impossible for him wholly to embrace such idealizations. Holtei's dilemma is that his conservatism prevents him from repudiating the ideal completely, just as it makes him unable to transcend the stigma attaching to his own "Vagabundenleben." Thus Holtei accords with his contemporaries in linking nomadism with the category of sickness:

> Glücklich die Völker, die nicht eine Hauptstadt haben! Wann soll die Zeit wiederkehren, wo Städte von etwa 10.000 Einwohnern sich selbst genügend, ein angenehmes Dasein kannten? . . . Da wir Deutsche glücklicherweise nicht eine "Capitale" gehabt haben, könnt' es bei uns so schlimm nicht werden. Schlimm genug ist's aber doch schon geworden, mit den oft albernen Vergleichen zwischen Wien, Berlin, Hamburg etc. und minder großen Städten; mit den unerfüllbaren Ansprüchen und Forderungen, die sich an jene dummen Vergleiche knüpfen; mit der daraus entspringenden Unruhe, Unzufriedenheit, krankhaften Reisewuth. Das kann leider auch nicht mehr besser werden . . . man müßte denn Mittel finden, die Eisenbahnen abzuschaffen. Und das geht nun doch einmal nicht mehr.[67]

"Unruhe, Unzufriedenheit" and "krankhafte Reisewuth" are conventionally represented as the symptoms of the malady of the age whose root causes lie in the expansion of the railways and the concomitant phenomenon of urbanization. Set against these symptoms are the ideally bounded horizons of the home town, whose population has not grown to the point where it is no longer possible for the individual to experience it as an integrated whole, and which continues to exist in something like a state of autarky. From these lines the sense emerges powerfully that *Heimat*, specified in these terms, has vanished forever. It is also notable that Holtei connects the symptom of "Reisewuth" with the conditions of German particularism — the long absence of a capital city that could serve as a focus for ambitious provincials like himself. Given that the German people had indeed acquired a capital, Berlin, at the time of writing, these lines at least imply that the end of particularism will usher in a more settled epoch of the kind hoped for by the writers of the *historische Schule*.

Holtei is not alone in possessing a troubled conception of *Heimat:* the feeling of homelessness was even more pronounced among those at the opposite end of the political spectrum, the bourgeois revolutionaries of 1848. Many had been forced into exile by the time *Die Vagabunden* had emerged: for those who remained, their homeland had come to resemble a dungeon, like that described in Hermann Kurz's novel *Sonnenwirt* (1855), a retelling of the life of Friedrich Schwan, the subject of Schiller's *Der Verbrecher aus verlorener Ehre* (1786). Holtei's choice of a socially marginal protagonist, though perhaps dictated by the success of the *Sozialroman* genre, itself draws our attention to the connection between the problematic status of *Heimat* in the post-1848 period, the phenomenon of pauperism, and the legislative responses to it. The trouble with the *Heimat* had been its inability to sustain its people in the face of population growth; it was the structural crisis in the agrarian economy that had been the prime motor of emigration, the first major wave of which occurred in the decade 1846–56.[68] The legislative responses to the pauperism crisis in Prussia (legislation which would later and under different circumstances be applied throughout the *Reich*) if anything made it easier to leave one's home parish. In addition, those responses brought about a diminution in the legal status of the previously independent home towns and municipalities (*Gemeinden*), which eroded their status as a stable point of orientation. But the idea of *Heimat* as an ultimate refuge, "the place where they have to take you in" to borrow Mack Walker's phrase,[69] was also threatened by political developments, by the growth of the centralized state apparatus, including such bodies as the *Polizeiverein*, which operated from 1848–66 throughout the German Confederation.

How did the legislative response to pauperism contribute to increased population mobility in the Prussian states, including Holtei's Silesia?[70] In the winter of 1842–43 a package of three laws was enacted, laws that represented an attempt to resolve the pauperism crisis by applying the principles of economic liberalism. The essential idea was to enable those without an income to move more easily within the Prussian territories to areas where a demand for labor existed. The first law obliged each municipality to undertake the care of the poor in its own area, a function previously fulfilled by private individuals and charities. Further provisions were more fundamentally connected with the principle of freedom of movement: in the first place every adult Prussian citizen gained the right to *Freizügigkeit*, that is, to settle, conduct business, and marry, anywhere in the Prussian states. The *Unterstützungswohnsitz* provision meant that the migrant became entitled to financial assistance from the host municipality in the event of sickness or other distress after one year, provided that he or she remained in employment. After three years' residence the migrant acquired full right of domicile (*Wohnsitzrecht*); conversely, right of domicile in the home municipality was deemed to have lapsed after an absence of three years. In some respects these laws can be seen as the logical culmination of the economic liberalism that had made itself felt in Prussia since the modernizing Stein-Hardenberg reforms, which had abolished both guild privileges and hereditary serfhood.

Apart from creating the legal conditions for increased internal migration, these changes represented a reduction in the legal status of individual parishes and towns, which had hitherto been self-legislating to a considerable degree. No longer did these entities have the ultimate say as to who might settle within them. Moreover, they were now answerable to Berlin for the provision they made for the vagrant poor. Thus, *Heimat*, understood as a legal entity, had been effectively reduced to a branch of the Prussian state. This decisive shift in the balance of power away from *Heimat* to the state was replicated throughout the *Reich* after 1871, when the Prussian approach became the model for Imperial poor law. The provisions outlined above became the object of vigorous debate, attacked by conservatives and defended by liberals, during the early 1880s, when internal migration, foreshadowing the later large-scale population transfers from the Prussian states east of the Elbe to the expanding industrial centers of the Rhine and Ruhr, gave rise to renewed debate about the so-called *Vagabundenfrage*. The liberals, whose viewpoint carried the day, argued that the increased visibility of vagrancy following the unification of Germany was a temporary phenomenon that would eventually disappear "mit der steigenden Kultur-Entwickelung," in the words of the economist, Karl Braun.[71] In this they concurred substantively with historians like Gustav Freytag, who also viewed nomadism as an anachronistic mode of existence, a symptom of war and disorder that would eventually wither away in the "eternal peace" of the *Reich*.[72]

In the preceding discussion I first sought to show how an ideology of the settled life grew up in the period following the 1848 revolution (especially following the establishment of the *Reich*) and that it was propagated in popular historiography. Second, I indicated that this ideology came into being despite, or perhaps as a result of, the declining objective political and economic importance of local municipalities, and thus of *Heimat* itself. Third, I suggested that migration and nomadism, though portrayed as phenomena of more agitated eras, were actually no less prevalent after 1871 than they had been at any other time in the previous century. In fact, internal migration would reach unprecedented levels in the period from the foundation of the Second Empire until the outbreak of the Great War.[73] Nevertheless, and despite its increasing divergence from empirical reality, the ideology of the settled life was powerfully normative: so much is evident from the fact that Karl von Holtei felt compelled to conform to it.

Yet this is not the only option that Holtei might have taken in *Die Vagabunden*. He might, for example, have taken a cue from Goethe's *Wanderjahre* and broken with the orthodoxy that affirmed the settled life over his own peripatetic existence. In a prologue written to mark the opening of the theater in Riga (1837) Holtei apparently comes close to embracing the vagrant life of the artist:

> Man pflegt zu sagen, daß kein Vaterland
> Der Künstler habe. — Welch ein traurig Wort! —
> Und dennoch ist's gewissermaßen wahr:
> Ihn treibt ein pilgernd Leben durch die Welt.
> Da muß er sich ein Vaterland erschaffen,
> Er muß es suchen, wo die Pflicht ihn fesselt,
> Er wird es finden, wo die Bildung wohnt.
> Hier oder nirgends ist dies Vaterland.
> Ja, nehmt uns auf! Gönnt uns das Bürgerrecht
> In Euren Herzen und in Euerem Geist![74]

The fundamental tone is one of resigned acceptance: far from roaming freely, the artist is driven by "ein pilgernd Leben" through the world. Nevertheless, the capacity of the artist to create a fatherland is asserted: one notes the Goethean echo in "Hier oder nirgends ist dies Vaterland," which paraphrases Lothario's motto in *Wilhelm Meisters Lehrjahre*. Although we find in *Die Vagabunden* parallels between the fragile lives of vagabond players and the shocks, contingencies, and discontinuities experienced by many in the post-1848 era as the most visible processes of modernity, industrialization and urbanization, gathered pace — setting ever more people in motion through the attendant phenomena of migration and emigration — Holtei does not attain the insight that the philosophical stance articulated in these lines might have an application beyond the actors' world. He fails to draw the conclusion that suggests itself, namely that the actor's ideals of mobility and mutability might actually be more appropriate to the objective requirements of the age than an ideology that stigmatizes wanderlust as a symptom of dissolution and incapacity.

Instead of recognizing the untimeliness of that ideology, Holtei remains discomfited by the awareness of his own deviation from it, reproducing in the novel and in his biography the prevailing association of wandering with fecklessness and unproductiveness. It is perhaps an unintended irony when he has an actor (Ludwig Devrient) attempt to dissuade Anton from giving up the career of a circus rider to take to the stage:

> Wir Franzosen sagen: embrasser un métier. Das ist ein schöner Ausdruck; man soll, was man nun einmal zum Beruf gewählt, fest umhalten, ans Herz drücken wie eine Geliebte; nicht loslassen, nicht wechseln, nicht von einem aufs andere äugeln. Folglich bleib' im Stalle, in deiner Reitbahn. Dort blühen auch Röschen, wenn keine Rosen — und Dornen stechen überall. (213)

Here Devrient appeals to the notion of "Beruf" in the Lutheran sense of a lifetime calling that both commands unwavering loyalty and imparts a strong sense of identity. However, at the time of writing "Beruf" was arguably an ideal diminishing in importance, as adaptability and the ability to uproot oneself in search of work began to supplant older professional values.

## Raabe's *Abu Telfan oder Die Heimkehr vom Mondgebirge* (1867)

### Abu Telfan as Faustian Novel

We have in Wilhelm Raabe's novel, the product of the North German writer's exile to the "Deutsches Ausland"[75] of Stuttgart, a narrative constructed on a special case of the wanderer motif: the revenant, the *Heimkehrer*. Naturally the revenant has maintained a presence in the Western literary canon since the *Odyssey*, an epic that, as Adorno and Horkheimer have argued, reflects in exemplary fashion upon the genesis of modern subjectivity and the "dialectic of enlightenment."[76] In *Abu Telfan*, too, the motif of homecoming is used to develop a critique of the process of civilization that grasps the dialectical nature of that process. Previously I have concentrated on one side of this dialectic: on the emergence of an "ideology of the settled life," on the concomitant marginalization of nomadism, and on the emergence in historiography — especially after the *Reichsgründung* — of narratives in which the Germans reassured themselves that they had come to rest at last after centuries wandering in a wilderness. But, as I have suggested, the process of civilization in the post-1848 period was not experienced only in terms of stabilization, whether political or material. Certainly, the process of civilization meant for many a gain in security in the form of improved living standards, a gain purchased at the price of a new monotony in everyday life as individuals became increasingly subject to the constraints of the discipline and standardization that had made material progress possible. On the other hand, however, the period from 1848 to, say, the economic crisis of 1873 was one of restless activity, manifested on the economic level in the rapid expansion of the railway network and in a spate of company formations. This was what Hobsbawm has called the "Blütezeit des Kapitals,"[77] the age of the dynamic venture capitalist, a type who finds his literary apotheosis in Anton Wohlfart, the hero of Gustav Freytag's bestselling novel *Soll und Haben* (1855), a fiction that uniquely captures the expansive mood of German capitalism in those years. Added to this dynamism was an underlying sense of insecurity, experienced most acutely by those forced to emigrate — and emigration did continue unabated despite the economic growth — but also more subtly as an erosion of traditional institutions and forms of life by the majority who remained.

The society of post-1848 Germany was thus characterized by apparently conflicting aspirations: a longing for stillness and seclusion in the *Heimat*, and a restless actionism of a kind we saw foreshadowed in the Romantic movement, but which now had become the defining characteristic of pioneer capitalists of the kind represented by Freytag's hero. In fact, these two aspirations were dialectically interconnected: the thirst for mastery through unceasing labor calling forth its corresponding quietive, a desire for enduring peace. What made the new species of actionism different from the Romantic variety was its dissociation from the idea of mobility — while the early Romantics had taken the wanderer as the ideal type of man in action, settled status was now held to be the prerequisite for productive activity. In literature, one consequence of the new insistence on the settled life as the bedrock of bourgeois striving was a diminution in the importance of the wanderer motif, which appeared in ever fewer fictions. Nowhere was the assertion of a stay-at-home philistinism more apparent than in those fictions that sought to exert a normative influence, especially *Soll und Haben*, which played a key role in popularizing bourgeois ideology.[78] Its protagonist, Anton Wohlfart, displays in exemplary fashion the required attitude of loyalty to the native soil when he declines an invitation to emigrate, quoting the proverbial advice of his father: "Bleibe im Lande und nähre dich redlich."[79]

In Raabe's *Abu Telfan*, by contrast, the wanderer motif gets something of a reprieve, becoming a significant element of composition. One of my tasks in the following discussion will be to establish why Raabe opts to rehabilitate a motif that had become so uncontemporary. I will advance the argument that Raabe enlists the motif as part of a critique of the pervasive actionism of the time, and as a binding element connecting the novel both to Goethe's oeuvre and to the Romantics. Perhaps the strongest literary testimony to the value placed on action, striving, and the uncompromising assertion of the individual will in the period in question is to be found in the contemporary reception of Goethe's *Faust*. Monika Yvonne Stein has shown that the shadow of Goethe's epic looms large over *Abu Telfan*, which she has gone so far as to characterize as a "Faust-Kontrafaktur."[80] Stein distinguishes three phases in the modern reception of the Faust saga prior to the composition of Raabe's second Stuttgart novel, beginning with Lessing, who interprets Faust for the Enlightenment as a *philosophe* driven by a thirst for knowledge. More influential is Goethe's *Faust*, who becomes for contemporaries the "*Vorbild des rastlos strebenden Menschen*."[81] The final phase — of which the representative text is Ferdinand Stolte's sprawling epic, *Faust* (1859–69) — involves a national turn, with Faust now viewed as a specifically German type rather than as the general embodiment of modern striving man. In her analysis Stein shows convincingly that the principal figures in *Abu Telfan* all possess to some degree the Faustian traits of restlessness and striving, most notably the protagonist Leonhard Hagebucher, but also Nikola von Einstein, the animal trader Cornelius van Mook (who liberates Hagebucher from his African captivity), and — in a comically mild form — Lieutenant von Bumsdorf, a secondary figure.[82] What links Hagebucher (and the others) with Faust at the level of motivation is their "Streben nach Welterfahrung, Selbsterkenntnis und Selbstverwirklichung."[83] Each of these figures can be said to have entered into a pact of some sort: Nikola accepts an arranged marriage for the sake of a quiet life; Hagebucher persuades the uncanny Lieutenant Kind to postpone his revenge upon Baron von Glimmern. The pact motif is of no further interest here, and I cite it only in order to demonstrate that the case for *Abu Telfan* as a Faust novel is a strong one. This brings us to Stein's main thesis concerning the relationship between the novel and the contemporary discourse on Goethe's *Faust*. Stein construes *Abu Telfan* as a critical and corrective response to that discourse, or, more specifically, to a contradiction at the heart of the reigning Faust cult, which she expresses as follows: "Dieser *Widerspruch in der nationalen Faust-Verehrung des Nachmärz*, den zur größtmöglichen Selbstverwirklichung sogar zum Teufelsbündler werdenden Faust einerseits zu verehren und andererseits die Selbstverwirklichung von weniger übermenschlichen Individuen zu behindern, wird von Raabe in seinem Faust-Roman *angeprangert*" (226).

From this point of view, Raabe's engagement with the Faust theme is an attempt to expose the hypocrisy of a society that reveres a figure who stands for unfettered self-realization, while at the same time curtailing the personal and political freedoms of its members. The thesis is compelling because it forges a link between the Faust material and the undeniable socially critical thrust of Raabe's fictions. By rejecting or marginalizing the Faustian figures Leonhard Hagebucher and Nikola von Einstein, the argument runs, society is repressing the very ideal of individual striving and self-realization it professes to esteem.[84] But is that really the total extent of the part played by the Faust myth in the criticism of contemporary social conditions? Is it really just a case of criticizing the hypocritical worship of a titanic individualism on the part of a society that denies its members the possibility of full self-realization? What is tacitly presupposed by Stein's thesis is that Raabe shares the prevailing view of the Faust figure as "Identifikationsfigur aller Deutschen," and that in doing so he takes Goethe's *Faust* to be an essentially affirmative myth. But even if contemporary critics were blind to Goethe's highly problematic presentation of Faust's titanism, as seems to have been the case, there is no reason to suppose that Raabe's vision was similarly clouded.[85] I will argue here that Raabe, far from merely taking his society to task for curbing individualism, also engages in a critique of the dominant ethic of voluntarism and actionism. In order to conduct that critique he enlists the wanderer motif.

"Der Wanderer *Leonhard* wird mit dem Wanderer *Faust identifiziert*," Stein remarks, without, however, considering the semantic ramifications of the motif connecting the two figures.[86] Goethe portrays Faust as a wanderer the better to evoke his energy, his restless striving — expressed in the image of the waterfall[87] — but also his acute sense of homelessness:

> Bin ich der Flüchtling nicht? Der Unbehauste?
> Der Unmensch ohne Zweck und Ruh',
> Der wie ein Wassersturz von Fels zu Felsen brauste,
> Begierig wütend nach dem Abgrund zu?[88]
> (*Faust I*, 3348–3351).

This homelessness is the bitter fruit of Faust's impious *curiositas*, the scholar's willingness to discard the moral precepts of Christianity in an uncompromising pursuit of knowledge. Faust is thus a type familiar to us from the chapter on Romanticism — the scientist as wanderer. Moreover, by casting Faust as wanderer, Goethe reactivates the motif in all the ambivalence it possessed for the Romantics, who used it both to affirm and to reflect critically upon artistic and scientific autonomy.[89] As we have seen, contemporaries were not alert to this ambivalence, and to the tragic consequences of Faust's will to power — a litany of crimes ranging from his seduction of Gretchen to his ruinous misadventures in engineering and science (*homunculus*). Bearing these in mind, it is a striking illustration of critical blindness that Heinrich Düntzer found it possible to praise in Faust not only "deutsche Ausdauer und Tatkraft" but "deutsche Begeisterung für wahre Menschenwürde"![90] It would fall to a later generation of critics to explicate the vein of anti-actionism in Goethe's epic and to recognize it as a "Tragödie der unbedingten Tätigkeit."[91]

The most obvious embodiment of the dictum "es irrt der Mensch, so lang' er strebt" (*Faust I*, 317) in *Abu Telfan* is Hagebucher's rescuer, Viktor von Fehleysen, whose name is uniquely evocative of protracted erring with its blend of "fehlen" and "Felleisen" (haversack). Fehleysen's reaction to the disgrace and sudden death of his father, the result of an intrigue, is panicked flight. Abandoning his mother, Klaudine, he flees to the Orient, where he reinvents himself as Cornelius van Mook, a trader in exotic animals, in a despairing attempt to evade ruin and dishonor. In his new incarnation Fehleysen proves to be an exemplary capitalist, "ein sehr praktischer, kühler, scharfer Rechner,"[92] but his incessant activity, crossing and recrossing the continent of Africa in pursuit of business, is primarily the means by which he hopes to efface guilt-laden memory. The parallels with Ahasver, as well as with Faust, are evident. Like Ahasver, Fehleysen is condemned to wander because he has failed to seize his opportunity for salvation, represented by Nikola von Einstein, with whom he had carried on a blameful and inconsequential affair. The sense of a shipwrecked, goalless existence, like that of the protagonist of Müller's *Winterreise*, emerges from Fehleysen's self-description as "der verwilderte, störrige Landstreicher, der Mann ohne Heimat, ohne Ehre, ohne Namen" (218).

Hagebucher's attempt to make his own way in the world has every appearance of a Faustian project, and not only because he too abandons the study of theology and the city of Leipzig. The journey, first to Italy, then to Egypt to take part in the Suez canal project (itself an exercise in hubris of the national variety), and thereafter into the African interior in the company of a disreputable Italian merchant, represents a series of uncompromising attempts at self-realization. In a sense, Hagebucher's departure results not from a rejection of his society's values but from a willingness to take them too literally. Instead of seeing that the general affirmation of individualism in the repressive environment of post-1848 Germany is necessarily hollow, and trimming his sails accordingly, the "relegierter Studiosus der Theologie" (23) goes abroad because he is unable to relinquish the idea that his will is the prime determinant of his future. This insistence on the primacy of his own will leads, in the ironic logic of the narrative, to captivity, enslavement, and abjection.

Hagebucher's project foreshadows that of another character of Raabe's whose attempts to bend the world to his own will end in defeat: Velten

Andres in *Die Akten des Vogelsangs* (1895). In this late work an irresistible will meets an immovable object in the form of Helene Trotzendorff — yet another of Raabe's eloquently named figures. Velten's life becomes a relentless pursuit of Helene, the daughter of an emigrant who had returned to the suburb of Vogelsang. His unwillingness to substitute another life-goal for her, and his deluded belief that winning her is merely a matter of persistence, are suggestive of the destructive potential of the much-vaunted bourgeois attributes of fixity of purpose and resoluteness.[93] The uncompromising pursuit of his goal turns Velten into "ein Wanderer im Leben"(19:326), and — as that goal recedes into unattainable distance — an embittered renunciant whose maxim is the cynical lines of Goethe's *Third Ode to Behrisch:* "Sei gefühllos! / Ein leichtbewegtes Herz / Ist ein elend Gut / Auf der wankenden Erde"(19:352). Following the disappointment of his hopes, Velten Andres returns to Vogelsang and to his mother, who persists in believing that her son has "die Welt durch seine Tatkraft überwunden"(19:351). There, the dark side of his actionism, his uncompromising will, which had remained hidden, reveals itself as nihilism. After his mother's death Velten stages a shocking "Autodafé" (19:371), systematically burning and destroying every scrap of paper, every memento, every heirloom that connects him with his past. With the work of destruction complete he is characterized as: "der eigentumsmüde Mann, der freie Weltwanderer"(19:383). What is striking about Velten's autodafé — surely one of the most unsettling episodes in nineteenth-century German fiction — is the reaction it elicits from a minority. Although most of the inhabitants of Vogelsang regard Velten as simply mad, a few, evidently the elite, find words of approval for his actions. A senior manager speaks of him in the following terms: "Ein drolliger Patron; aber unter Umständen eigentlich zu beneiden und nachahmenswert!"(19:374). The uncompromising ethic of striving and the destructive potential contained in it are thus identified not merely with an "outsider" but subtly with the ruling class itself. The Faustian moment emerges more starkly in Velten Andres than in any of Raabe's previous figures, no doubt because Raabe uses this figure to pass his final verdict on the spirit of the *Gründerzeit*, an epoch whose restless expansionism (including, after 1880,[94] colonialism) surpassed that of the 1850s.[95] No other German author, with the possible exception of Nietzsche, reveals in such stark terms the dream of destruction that haunts the bourgeois will to power.[96]

## The Wanderer Motif as Goethean Element in Abu Telfan

Raabe is perhaps unique among prose writers of his generation for the prominence of wanderers in his fictions, a feature that is likely attributable to the enduring influence of Goethe and Jean Paul. These figures have more usually been classified as "Sonderlinge" or "Außenseiter,"[97] but it would appear that considering them as wanderers is more revealing of their function as intertextual elements. In particular, the wanderer motif seems to function as a ligature binding Raabe thematically to Goethe. For instance, Raabe frequently uses the motif as a vehicle for the theme of renunciation, just as Goethe does in *Wilhelm Meisters Lehrjahre*, but above all in the *Wanderjahre.* I have just cited the most extreme Raabean embodiment of that theme in the figure of Velten Andres, "der Wanderer auf der wankenden Erde." This and other epithets can only have put attentive contemporary readers in mind of Goethe's League of Wanderers, the association that seeks to master unremitting change, to achieve "Dauer im Wechsel," through renunciation and cooperative activity. In the *Wanderjahre* Goethe postulates a stance adequate to modernity, one characterized by adaptability, flexibility, and circumspection — and a certain indifference to fixity. Velten's "Eigentumsmüdigkeit" is especially reminiscent of the *Wandererbund*'s preference for portable over fixed assets, for intellectual over material capital. Of course, Velten's renunciation differs from that of the *Wandererbund* in that it is absolute and in no way subordinated to any collective interest. That is why he comes to grief. Moreover, his case is an object lesson in the risks of making maxims — even those of such an authority as Goethe — the basis for the practice of life.

So numerous are the wanderers in *Abu Telfan*, so strongly does each wandering figure exemplify some possibility of acting in the world, that one is tempted to suggest that Goethe's *Wanderjahre* is as important a pretext for Raabe as is *Faust.* In fact, every one of the principal characters is in some sense uprooted, set in motion by larger forces. That is as true of Nikola von Einstein, who is forced to flee the *Residenz* for the refuge of the Katzenmühle following the destruction of her marriage of convenience, as it is of her husband, the scheming Baron von Glimmern. The latter, a well-connected courtier, seems utterly in control of his destiny until nemesis overtakes him in the shape of Lieutenant Kind. Kind's revenge explodes like a mortar-bomb in the midst of the Baron's settled, privileged existence (318); at a stroke the Baron is unhoused and put to flight, eventually dying at the hands of his antagonist in a squalid London boarding-house. Then there is the painful odyssey of Viktor von Fehleysen, who must relinquish his sanctuary in the Katzenmühle to make way for the twice-wronged Nikola von Einstein, and who thereupon resumes his wandering, initially with the object of tracking down Kind in order to prevent him from murdering Glimmern. Having failed in this effort to prevent bloodshed, he takes ship for the United States to die in the service of General Grant at the battle of Richmond.

What more evidence of the importance of the wanderer motif to *Abu Telfan* can we adduce, before looking more closely at its intertextual function? The motif occurs also in two other as yet unmentioned figures: Hagebucher's uncle Wassertreter, and his neighbor in the Residence, Felix Zölestin Täubrich (a name that hints at narcosis or numbness). Both are wanderers: the elderly bachelor Wassertreter on account of his function as "Wegebauinspektor," and the tailor Täubrich by virtue of his travels in the Near East. They are, on the face of it, socially marginal figures: Wassertreter inhabits the highways and byways of the Grand Duchy; Täubrich is marginal by virtue of his ascetic unworldliness. But the customary application of such terms as "Außenseiter" to these and other figures in Raabe's novels arguably obscures more than it reveals. It should be clear from the foregoing that *all* of the figures in *Abu Telfan* might be so described. In a sense Raabe's fictional model of society is all periphery — there is no stable center. Consider *Steuerinspektor* Hagebucher, who, one might think, represents the center; a figure whose unsentimental philistinism makes him apparently ideally adapted to his prosaic circumstances. Yet not even he, who is ruthless enough to exclude his revenant son as a "Rechnungsfehler" (102), is able to control the destabilizing consequences of the homecoming. He too is exiled, if only from the male society at the inn, by the innuendo and scorn of his erstwhile companions. By the example of *Steuerinspektor* Hagebucher, Raabe not only denounces bourgeois ideology, including the ideology of the settled life, for its hypocrisy and latent violence[98] and its complacency,[99] but also reveals unsparingly its inadequacy to cope with the instability it has created. This last is demonstrated in the case of Nikola von Einstein, who decides to adapt to the social pressures bearing down upon her by acquiescing in an arranged marriage to Baron von Glimmern. She describes the decision in these terms: "Mein Herz habe ich begraben und die Welt angenommen, wie sie ist; ich habe das Buch meiner Hoffnungen und Träume abgeschlossen und mich in das Unabänderliche ergeben!" (106). Nikola opts for stillness, for immobility in the widest sense; she decides to play by the rules of a bourgeois ideology that envisages for women the maximum restriction of freedom of movement. However, even this highly conformist strategy of playing dead — "sich 'totzustellen' in der Hand des Fatums" (113) — proves in the light of subsequent events to afford no protection.

In the discussion of the *Wanderjahre* it was argued that wandering is there associated with activity *per se*, and that the various wanderers in the novellas provide examples of different kinds of behavior: constructive or destructive, insightful or deluded. And I have remarked above that each of the wanderers in *Abu Telfan* seems similarly to exemplify some possibility of acting in the world. In the case of Viktor von Fehleysen we have flight, including flight from the self, through feverish action. Hagebucher's journey to Africa is the expression of uncompromising will, but under the tutelage of Vetter Wassertreter his wanderings — his movements back and forth between Nippenburg, the Katzenmühle and the *Residenz* — acquire a different quality. Further possibilities are embodied by Felix Zölestin Täubrich and Vetter Wassertreter, two figures that merit closer attention.

Täubrich, the journeyman tailor, whose strayings once took him "weit über Constantinopel," is, like Hagebucher, a revenant. In him we encounter wandering as flight from the world: his adventures in Palestine are followed upon his return by episodes of inner journeying, reveries in which the Orient again becomes vividly present to him. The oriental journey is no mere fantasy, for although Täubrich has no memory of his return, and a visit from "der große Alexander von Humboldt" (140) is no more than a rumor, he is able to produce his *Wanderbuch*, inscribed by those who had helped him on his way back to Europe.[100] Nevertheless, Täubrich's absent-minded travel and his inner journeying resemble the fugue states that were to so preoccupy psychiatry in the latter decades of the century.[101] His strategy for coping with inhospitable surroundings involves withdrawal: taking refuge in memory and imagination and minimizing commerce with the external world.

If Täubrich's fuguelike daydreaming stands for the option of withdrawal from the social sphere and its onerous responsibilities, Wassertreter's wandering represents action in the public interest. In Wassertreter the wanderer motif expresses an ethical stance similar to that articulated in the *Wanderjahre*. Indeed, Wassertreter is explicitly identified as a devotee of Goethe, although he can claim only to have glimpsed the great man "von hinten" (157). It is from the person and works of Goethe that the roads inspector, a former corps-student who had fallen foul of the Karlsbad Decrees, draws the practical philosophy that enables him to "tread water," to preserve his dignity in the face of Nippenburg's contempt. From the sub-chapter on the *Wanderjahre* we recall that Goethe uses the wanderer motif to illustrate an ethical stance that involves adaptability, knowing and accepting the constraints on the individual's capacity for knowledge and action, subordinating individual interests to the common good, striving for constancy in the midst of change, and eschewing all forms of longing and impatience in favor of sustained activity in the present: in short, an active form of renunciation. Wassertreter, though marginal in the esteem of Nippenburg's philistines, is actually central to the life of the Grand Duchy he serves: it is he who keeps the roads open by his ceaseless tours of inspection, and he acts as Samaritan to those who fall by the wayside (Klaudine, Hagebucher).[102] He belongs to those whose task it is "der Menschheit die Wege offen[zu]halten" (65), and he does so on behalf of the widow Klaudine (mediating between her and her at times hostile surroundings), Hagebucher junior (for whom he secures a post as assistant to Professor Reihenschlager), and Hagebucher senior (whom he reconciles with his drinking companions). In Wassertreter the wanderer motif is used to instantiate not unconditional activity, action for the sake of action, as in the cases of Viktor Fehleysen or Velten Andres, but a renunciative activity directed toward common ends. The motif thus functions as an intertextual link, connecting *Abu Telfan* both to Goethe's *Faust* (and via that text to Romanticism's fictions of striving man) and, if we accept the foregoing, to the *Wanderjahre*.

Wassertreter's tuition enables Hagebucher to make the transition from one mode of wandering to the other, from the Faustian mode with its intolerance of limits, to mobility determined by the interests of others. Under his uncle's supervision Hagebucher begins his "Häutungsprozeß" (122), the onerous acquisition of the knowledge and behaviors expected of a "civilized" man.[103] Much of this knowledge is of questionable value; the revenant must work his way through the "Konversationslexikon" (122) and "Makulaturberge" (156), gleaning in the process a host of forgotten "facts" from the journalistic offerings of the previous decade. All this dryness is, however, alleviated by the works of Goethe, interpreted enthusiastically by his mentor. The exclusion of the African adventures from the main narrative is thus more than a deliberate attempt to reduce the level of drama in the work: it is intended to show that the actual work of homecoming takes place after the physical return to Europe. The *Heimkehr* of the title refers to a painful process of assimilation to the norms of German civil society at the end of a period (1849–66) in which the German bourgeoisie was itself giving up its dream of democratic self-assertion and was trying to "come home." That is perhaps a useful working thesis to adopt with regard to Raabe's novel.

By his mobility and adaptability, Wassertreter provides a model for survival that Hagebucher can emulate, showing that it is possible even for an outsider to create a role for himself. Following this example, Hagebucher becomes a wanderer, an emissary on behalf of others, undertaking two rescue missions that set him in motion back and forth between the novel's key locations. First, he succeeds in freeing the errant Viktor von Fehleysen from the malign influence of Lieutenant Kind, reuniting him with his mother, Klaudine. Subsequently he is able to bring Nikola von Einstein to the refuge of the Katzenmühle, shielding her from the effects of her husband's disgrace. The repeated references to Hagebucher as "der Wanderer" during the first of these missions (233, 234, 236) indicate more than his strenuous march: the epithet summons up the Goethean nexus of activity and renunciation, as is apparent from the following: "'Dem Manne ein Schwert, dem Weibe das schwarze Brot der Frau Klaudine!' murmelte der Wanderer, dessen Pfad sich durch so viele Trümmer und Täuschungen wand" (233).

## "Vagabondage und Unreelität": A Note on Raabe's Realism

"Ich bitte ganz gehorsamst, weder den Ort Abu Telfan noch das Tumurkieland auf der Karte von Afrika zu suchen." With this remark in the introduction to the first edition of *Abu Telfan*, Raabe distances himself humorously from the dominant literary orthodoxy of realism, a movement whose exemplary text was Freytag's *Soll und Haben*. Even if Raabe had been content to swim in the realist mainstream at the outset of his career

— the first of the three Stuttgart novels, *Der Hungerpastor*, is a fairly conventional *Bildungsroman* in this mode — it is clear that he had a more sophisticated grasp of the possibilities of realism by the time *Abu Telfan* was in the making. By no means does he aspire, as Freytag does, to affirming and reconciling readers to contemporary social and political horizons; nor do his fictions fulfill a reassuring or compensatory function, setting aesthetic totality against the experience of contingency. On first acquaintance, *Abu Telfan* does indeed appear to demonstrate a Hegelian "Erziehung des Individuums an der vorhandenen Wirklichkeit,"[104] with Hagebucher reaching an uneasy accommodation with Nippenburg. After all, the last description of the hero finds him decked out with the pipe, dressing-gown, and philistine mien of his tax-inspector father, a portrait that has caused much irritation to those critics minded to read *Abu Telfan* as a straightforward piece of social criticism.[105] Well might Müller say in conclusion: "Der Weg Leonhards aus dem subjektivistischen Schmollen mündet in einem von sozialer Moralität getragenen Lebensrealismus,"[106] but that does not tell us a great deal about the nature of Raabe's realism; indeed, it conveys the false impression that Raabe had written a thoroughly conventional novel of a kind that thronged the presses at the time, one in which the protagonist gives up his youthful velleities and capitulates to objective social reality. To read the novel in this reductive way is to do an injustice to the epistemological subtlety of Raabe's work. How then does Raabe's realism differ from that of the contemporary mainstream?

The most important difference concerns Raabe's conception of reality. Whether or not they truly believed in an ordered reality, governed by unchanging laws of causation, programmatic realists like Freytag went to considerable lengths to represent the world in such terms in their fictions. These realists understood their task as stripping away the dross of contingency to arrive at some essence of reality.[107] The protagonists of their novels face a similar problem: recognizing the true nature of reality and submitting to it. The fundamental assumption is that there exists a unified reality, a stable and logically consistent set of circumstances, the "feste, sichere Ordnung der bürgerlichen Gesellschaft und des Staats" that Hegel sees as the objective manifestation of reason.[108] Raabe does not share in this optimism. Far from subscribing to a unified reality, which it is the duty of the artist to make visible so that others may embrace it in its incontrovertible logic, Raabe holds the Schopenhauerian view of the world as a great ferment of contending wills. Human existence is, for him, "der ägyptische Proteus, das Leben" (380), something irreducibly complex, multifarious, and fluid, and thus something from which it is not possible to distil some sort of essence. This sense emerges from *Abu Telfan*, especially from Hagebucher's monologue in the final chapter. We recall the scene: a carefree summer's day; on the hilltop the young lieutenant is flirting with Lina Hagebucher, while below the Professor and Vetter Wassertreter are intent on unearthing the stone that supposedly proves Bumsdorf's Roman origins. Meanwhile Hagebucher is trying to console Täubrich, whose enjoyment of the moment is clouded by belated agonizing over the difficulty of distinguishing dreams from reality. Turning his back on Täubrich, Hagebucher addresses the following to the surrounding woods:

> Wer weiß von der Welt in der er lebt und von sich selber mehr als dieser Kamerad hier hinter mir? Da lachen sie im Sonnenschein und treiben ihre Spiele, solange sie jung sind; da wühlen sie alte, versunkene Steine, einen Traum im Traum, hervor, und alle glauben sie an ihr Spielzeug, nur dieser kluge Gesell hinter mir will nicht an das seinige glauben und nennt sich einen Narren! . . . es ist auch unter jenen nicht einer, der mit Sicherheit sagen kann, ob er in seinen Gedanken, Wünschen und Handlungen wahrhaftig in der Wirklichkeit wandle. (380)

What emerges from these lines is not only a certain epistemological skepticism — the notion that knowing the world in which one lives is a far from straightforward matter — but also perspectivism, the idea that the world is apprehended in different ways by different people. It is apparent that an author who holds views of this kind cannot in his fictions go along with the Hegelian schema of correcting a wayward subjectivity to the "objective spirit" manifested in the social institutions of the day.[109] His is a realism of a different order, one that insists on the primacy and unrepeatability of individual experience.

How does Raabe's use of the wanderer motif relate to his peculiar species of Realism? At the family council convened to determine the fate of the returned Hagebucher, Aunt Schnödler demands that the returnee abandon "Vagabondage und Unreelität und sonstige Phantasterei" (41) and take concrete steps to integrate himself into the Bumsdorf milieu. In doing so she makes the standard, pejorative, equation between vagabondage and the life of the imagination, implicitly contrasted with the settled life dominated by principles of pragmatism. Raabe appears to subscribe to this opposition to some degree: in his works wandering is frequently used to connote a mode of existence distinct from but not necessarily wholly incompatible with bourgeois philistinism. *Abu Telfan* attempts to reconcile the two spheres: to give pragmatic thinking its due, while upholding the claims of fantasy and imagination. To achieve this Raabe reaches for a motif — the wanderer motif — that had previously been used to assert an essential opposition between the philistine or well-adapted burgher and the artist (in Eichendorff's *Taugenichts*, but also in Heine's *Harzreise*). Raabe blurs the distinction between the two poles of this opposition, asserting on the one hand that "Wohin wir blicken, zieht stets und überall der germanische Genius ein Drittel seiner Kraft aus dem Philistertum" (357), while using the wanderer motif to illustrate the creative role of the subject in adapting to circumstances inhospitable to individuality. The motif is used to present a range of such creative responses. First, there is the attempt at the unconditional assertion of the will, manifested in the journey to the Near East: this is Hagebucher's attempt to establish himself on his own terms, when the terms available in Restoration Germany prove unfavorable. Second, there is the aesthetic life option, suggested to the revenant by Nikola von Einstein: "Uns eine Drehorgel kaufen und unsere eigene Geschichte auf eine Leinwand malen lassen und ein Lied davon machen und es absingen auf allen Gassen des Vaterlandes!" (55). Although this breathless proposal is perhaps less a viable plan than an expression of Nikola's desire to flee her impending marriage, it is seconded by Klaudine Fehleysen. An artistic career briefly appears as one way of bringing the otherwise incommensurable experience of Africa "auf den Markt" (75). From this proposal stems Hagebucher's lecture, a failed attempt to make his outlandish experiences the raw material of profitable aesthetic production. Third, there is the course represented by Wassertreter, who, despite his apparent peripherality, manages to maneuver himself into some sort of center on the strength of his activities on behalf of others.

Finally, the motif is used to suggest the possibility of renewal in the midst of prosaic routine, of creating "grüne Stellen,"[110] oases in the "erbärmliche, langweilige Routine des europäischen Alltagslebens" (31). This function is fulfilled in the final chapter's account of Professor Reihenschlager's "Fußreise" in the company of Täubrich from the ducal capital to Nippenburg. The pretext for this undertaking is a quixotic attempt to prove the Roman origins of Nippenburg, a faintly ludicrous notion, but the pilgrimage provides the basis for the cautiously optimistic conclusion. Prior to setting out on the journey the Professor had been sunk in despondency because of the departure of his daughter, Serena, who has herself succumbed to wanderlust. In this episode the wanderer motif establishes an intertextual connection, not with any one specific text, but with the tradition of Romanticism, and, more specifically, with the culture of the *Burschenschaften*. When the Professor dusts off his "Kommersbuch" and his "Ziegenhainer," he is not only renewing his acquaintance with his student fraternity days but is also recalling to the reader's mind the spirit of optimism and good fellowship in the face of shared adversity that represented what was best about the patriotic student movement.[111]

In common with the Romantics, Raabe regards reality not as monolithic but as process, flux and transition, which, though baffling comprehension, is at times amenable to being grasped and molded. He shares in the view that there is no *rerum natura*, no immutable order of things, and that man is called upon to create his own values and goals.[112] Raabe's use of the wanderer motif coincides with that of the Romantics in this respect: it signifies man acting to change his circumstances rather than submitting to them. The Professor's quixotic expedition is just such a creative response to uncongenial circumstances, if a modest one. The whole undertaking is based on a fiction, that of the milestone that will supposedly prove

Bumsdorf's status as part of the Roman *urbs*. In fact, Wassertreter is convinced that the stone is one of his own, but he is prepared to sustain the illusion for the sake of a friendship forged in the comradely student wanderings of the *Burschenschaften*. The moments of fiction, play, and fantasy are the dominant ones in the final chapter; through them a utopian space, something resembling *Heimat*, is created, if only for a brief interval. *Heimat* is itself no less a fiction than are Bumsdorf's Roman origins; it is a construct born of play, of the collective will to aestheticize one's surroundings; it is, as Brenner rightly observes, "das Ideal, das der Realität entgegengestellt wird; und als Postulat behält er seine kritische Potenz."[113]

Beauty as construct, rather than as essence inhering in reality, and the modest capacity of the individual to create aesthetically pleasing islands of order: these are the basic tenets of Raabe's realism. For such ideas he is likely indebted to the aesthetics of Friedrich Theodor Vischer, whom he befriended during his years in Stuttgart (1862–70) and whose *Faust* parody is, as Stein notes, another important pre-text for *Abu Telfan*.[114] The Vischer I have in mind here is not the author of the Hegelian *Ästhetik oder Wissenschaft des Schönen* of 1847–58 but the Vischer of *Kritik meiner Ästhetik* (1866), who renounces the notion of "das Real-Schöne" in favor of a new emphasis on the primacy of the subject in aesthetic perception and production:

> Die Ästhetik muß den Schein, es gebe ein Schönes ohne Zutun . . . des anschauenden Subjekts schon auf ihrem ersten Schritte vernichten. . . . Das Schöne ist nicht einfach ein Gegenstand, das Schöne wird erst im Anschauen, es ist Kontakt eines Gegenstandes und eines umfassenden Subjekts, und da das wahrhaft Tätige in diesem Kontakte das Subjekt ist, so ist es ein Akt. Kurz das Schöne ist einfach eine bestimmte Art der Anschauung.[115]

Vischer's subjective turn is summarized in the observation: "Die ideale Anschauung schaut in das Objekt hinein, was nicht in ihm ist." The wanderer motif as it appears in *Abu Telfan* plays its part in communicating this aesthetics by receiving meaning from Romanticism, in which the wanderer appears — among other functions — as the maker of his own reality. For Raabe, belief in the human capacity to make the world habitable is always tempered by an awareness of the resistance — institutional and political — working against it: that is the nature of his realism.

## Notes

[1] See Hans Schimpf-Reinhardt, "'Ein besseres Los zu suchen und zu finden': Deutsche Auswanderer," in Hermann Bausinger, Klaus Beyrer, and Wolfgang Griep, eds., *Reisekultur: Von der Pilgerfahrt zum modernen Tourismus* (Munich: Beck, 1991), 108–14. Albrecht Bengel (1687–1752) predicted that the advent of the "tausendjähriges Reich" would take place in 1836.

[2] Hans-Ulrich Wehler, *Deutsche Gesellschaftsgeschichte*, 4 vols. (Munich: Beck, 1987–2003), vol. 1 (2nd ed., 1989), 74. Wehler refers here to the problems of writing an adequate history of agriculture in view of the lack of records left by farmers.

[3] Hans-Peter Holl, "*Jakobs Wanderungen:* Ein unbekannter Roman von Jeremias Gotthelf," *Alpenhorn-Kalender* 72 (1997): 88–92. The most comprehensive recent bibliography of literature on Gotthelf is to be found in Walter Pape, Hellmut Thomke, and Silvia Serena Tschopp, eds., *Erzählkunst und Volkserziehung: Das literarische Werk des Jeremias Gotthelf* (Tübingen: Niemeyer, 1999), 345–88.

[4] Robert Godwin-Jones, "Soziale und politische Modelle in George Sands 'Le compagnon du tour de France' und Gotthelfs 'Jakobs des Handwerksgesellen Wanderungen durch die Schweiz,'" in Pape, Thomke, and Tschopp, *Erzählkunst und Volkserziehung*, 267–88. Friedrich Sengle's analysis of Gotthelf's *oeuvre* remains unrivalled for its breadth: Sengle, *Biedermeierzeit: Deutsche Literatur im Spannungsfeld zwischen Restauration und Revolution, 1815–1848*, 3 vols. (Stuttgart: Metzler, 1971–80), 3:888–951; on *Jakobs Wanderungen*, 902 and esp. 904–6.

[5] The theme of a family honor that must be vigilantly protected and renewed from generation to generation occurs also in the novella *Die schwarze Spinne* (1842): "Um das Haus lag ein sonntäglicher Glanz, den man mit einigen Besenstrichen, angebracht Samstag abends zwischen Tag und Nacht, nicht zu erzeugen vermag, der ein Zeugnis ist des köstlichen Erbgutes angestammter Reinlichkeit, die alle Tage gepflegt werden muß, der Familienehre gleich, welcher eine einzige unbewachte Stunde Flecken bringen kann, die Blutflecken gleich unauslöschlich bleiben von Geschlecht zu Geschlecht, jeder Tünche spottend." Jeremias Gotthelf (Albert Bitzius), *Sämtliche Werke in 24 Bänden* [and 18 *Ergänzungsbände*], ed. Rudolf Hunziker und Hans Bloesch (Zurich: Rentsch, 1921–77), 17:6. Citations from other volumes in this edition will be indicated by volume and page number. Citations from the *Ergänzungsbände* will be indicated by the abbreviation *EB*.

[6] Gotthelf, *Sämtliche Werke*, vol. 9: *Jakobs des Handwerksgesellen Wanderungen durch die Schweiz* (1937), 15. Further references to this volume are indicated in the text by the page number alone.

[7] Gabriel Muret, *Jéremie Gotthelf: Sa vie et ses oeuvres* (Paris: Gap, 1913), 295.

[8] Jakob's grandmother warns him on his departure: "Solange du ein Felleisen trägst, bist du ein ehrenwerter Geselle; trägst du die Trümmer deiner Habe in einem Nastuche herum, dann bist du ein Vagabund und Bettler, und vor solchem Zustande möge Gott dich bewahren!" (18).

[9] I refer here to Fröhlich's satirical pamphlet *Der junge Deutsch-Michel* (1843), and Zschokke's *Meister Jordan oder Handwerk hat goldenen Boden* (1845). Like *Jakobs Wanderungen*, these works can be classed as conservative *Tendenzliteratur* on the journeyman theme.

[10] Gotthelf, *Sämtliche Werke*, 6:16.

[11] Wolfgang Hardtwig, *Vormärz: Der monarchische Staat und das Bürgertum*, 4th ed. (Munich: dtv, 1998), 84–88; here, 87. See also Wehler, *Deutsche Gesellschaftsgeschichte*, 2:54–64, for an account of the situation of craft manufacture in the *Vormärz* period.

[12] A speech made by Bismarck in October 1849 that referred to the continued survival of the artisan class as essential to the life of the state ushers in the conservative political concept of the *Mittelstand* as a force for social stability and cohesion: see Hardtwig, *Vormärz*, 88.

[13] Ultimately, the almost universal predictions of the downfall of the artisan class proved unfounded. Although industrialization spelled the end for some trades (e.g. coachmakers, dyers), others — especially those trades related to construction — were able to profit from the economic upturn of the 1850s.

[14] This conflict manifested itself in liberal anxiety about Jesuit influence on the government in the Canton of Lucerne. When, in 1847, the *Tagsatzung* (the consultative council of the Swiss confederation) issued an ultimatum instructing the Canton of Lucerne to expel Jesuit priests, the result was a brief civil war between the liberal and conservative factions, the *Sonderbundkrieg*. This ended with the defeat of the secessionist Catholic *Sonderbund*.

[15] Eric John Hobsbawm, *Primitive Rebels: Studies in Archaic Forms of Social Protest in the 19th and 20th Centuries* (New York: Norton, 1965), 168–69. For a concise overview of the beginnings of the German workers' movement see Hardtwig, *Vormärz*, 153–60.

[16] Gerhard A. Ritter, *Arbeiter, Arbeiterbewegung und soziale Ideen in Deutschland: Beiträge zur Geschichte des 19. und 20. Jahrhunderts* (Munich: Beck, 1996), 32.

[17] Johann Caspar Bluntschli, *Die Kommunisten in der Schweiz nach den bei Weitling vorgefundenen Papieren* (Zurich: Orell & Füssli, 1843).

[18] As late as 24 December 1846, after the publication of the first part of the novel, Gotthelf wrote to Joseph Burkhalter: "Die Leute taumeln in einem schweren Rausche, und da ist nicht zuzusprechen, nicht abzuwehren, so wenig als besoffenen Nachtbuben; da wird man ausgelacht, verhöhnt, daß man längs Stück nicht weiß, soll man weinen oder dreinschlagen; denn schweigen, wenn es doch das klügste wäre, ist doch gegen die Pflicht" (Gotthelf, *Sämtliche Werke, EB* 6:333–34).

[19] Frank Möbus and Anne Bohnenkamp cite the case of the tanner Johann Eberhard Dewald, who in the memoir of his journey in the years 1836–38 notes the extent to which guild practices had fallen into desuetude among factory-based artisans. Möbus and Bohnenkamp, *Mit Gunst und Verlaub! Wandernde Handwerker: Tradition und Alternative*, 5th ed. (Göttingen: Wallstein, 2001), 41–42.

[20] Wehler, *Deutsche Gesellschaftsgeschichte*, 2:275–76.

[21] Karl Marx, *Manifest der Kommunistischen Partei*, in *Frühe Schriften*, ed. Hans-Joachim Lieber and Peter Furth, 6 vols. (Darmstadt: Wissenschaftliche Buchgesellschaft, 1975–81), 2:813–58; here, 821.

[22] Marx, *Manifest*, 831.

[23] Marx, *Manifest*, 839.

[24] Wehler, *Deutsche Gesellschaftsgeschichte*, 3:150.

[25] Admittedly, the early optimism of Weerth's poems *Deutscher und Ire* (with its theme of solidarity among workers across the boundaries of language and

nationality), *Im grünen Walde*, and *Drei schönen Handwerksburschen* yields to the pessimism of the later *Es war ein armer Schneider*. See Florian Vaßen, *Georg Weerth: Ein politischer Dichter des Vormärz und der Revolution von 1848/49* (Stuttgart: Metzler, 1971), 60, 71.

[26] Gille, *Goethes Wilhelm Meister: Zur Rezeptionsgeschichte der Lehr- und Wanderjahre* (Königstein im Taunus: Athenäum, 1979), 153–58; here, 156; and 159–63; here, 162. The excerpts are taken from Karl Rosenkranz, *Göthe und seine Werke* (1847) and Ferdinand Gregorovius, *Goethes Wilhelm Meister in seinen socialistischen Elementen entwickelt* (1849).

[27] Ritter, *Arbeiter, Arbeiterbewegung und soziale Ideen*, 23.

[28] Wilhelm Heinrich Riehl, *Die deutsche Arbeit* (Stuttgart: Cotta, 1861). Riehl held that orientation toward the profit motive had a demoralizing effect on the working classes and hindered their betterment. He argued that the only effective way for this group to overcome its misery and deprivation was by assimilating to bourgeois values, in particular, the principle of success. This, in Riehl's view, would enable these classes to embrace the idea of education. Riehl knew and approved of Gotthelf's *Volksschriften*, referring to the Swiss writer in *Die deutsche Familie* (Stuttgart: Cotta, 1861) as "Shakespeare als Dorfpfarrer im Emmental" (quoted from Tschopp, *Erzählkunst und Volkserziehung*, 7).

[29] "Die guten Bursche [*sic*] dachten nicht daran, daß das Gut der meisten Reichen durch hartes Schaffen bei spärlichem Essen erworben worden, daß eben das die gerechte Ordnung Gottes sei, daß was einer erworben, er behalten dürfe, seinen Kindern hinterlassen könne, so daß also, wenn sie hart schafften und sparsam lebten, auch ihre Kinder oder Kindeskinder gut essen und in der Kutsche fahren könnten, wenn es ihnen beliebe. Dieses Entbehren auf die Zukunft hinaus, dieses Tüchtigsein in der Gegenwart, damit man sich ein Haus erbaue in der Zukunft, daß man eines habe, wenn diese arme Hütte bricht, ist die wohlweise Ordnung Gottes" (Gotthelf, *Sämtliche Werke*, 9:58).

[30] Michael Perraudin, *Literature, the* Volk *and Revolution in 19th Century Germany* (Oxford: Berghahn, 2000), 65–100; here, 81. I would, however, dissent from Perraudin's thesis concerning Gotthelf's alleged anti-capitalism.

[31] Marx, *Manifest*, 829.

[32] "Im Hausvater liegt eine ganz eigene Kraft und Macht, auf dem Hausvatertum ruht das Deutschtum und das Christentum, vom Hausvater aus geht die erziehende Kraft und die väterliche Liebe; er ist die sichtbare Vorsehung, nimmt Anteil an den Freuden und Leiden des Leibes, vermittelt der Jugend übersprudelnde Lust mit dem christlichen Fortschritt, kümmert sich um das Heil der Seelen und um die Ehre seines Hauses, welche vom Betragen aller abhängt" (31). *Die Armennot* recommends that the community should take on the role otherwise fulfilled by godparents — "Gotte und Götti sein dem kleinen Christenkinde" (Gotthelf, *Sämtliche Werke*, 15:150) — toward children orphaned or born out of wedlock; Paternalistic socialization plays an important part in the novel *Uli, der Knecht, und wie er glücklich wird* (1842).

[33] Menzel wrote two brief reviews of the novel in his *Literaturblatt* (a supplement to Cotta's *Morgenblatt für gebildete Leser*): no. 37, 22 May 1847, 146–47, and no.76, 23 Oct. 1847, 302–4. See Gotthelf, *Samtliche Werke*, 9:522.

34 Möbus, *Mit Gunst und Verlaub!* draws on sparse autobiographical materials dating from the seventeenth to the twentieth centuries to provide a useful account of the privations faced by journeymen (27–42). One of the rare autobiographical accounts from the wandering underclass in the early nineteenth century owes its publication to Goethe's interest in the early life of his servant J.C. Sachse: Sachse, *Der deutsche Gilblaß eingeführt von Goethe: Oder Leben, Wanderungen und Schicksale Johann Christoph Sachses, eines Thüringers; von ihm selbst verfaßt* (Stuttgart, Tübingen: Cotta, 1822). Goethe remarks in the foreword: "Man dürfte es die Bibel der Bedienten und Handwerksbursche nennen" (iv).

35 Adolf Bartels, *Jeremias Gotthelf, Leben und Schriften* (Leipzig: Meyer, 1902), 109–17. In the *Deutsches Wörterbuch* the primary definition of the term *Wanderbuch* is "das buch das früher die wandernden handwerksburschen bei sich tragen muszten und in das zeugnisse und polizeiliche bescheinigungen geschrieben wurden," and its secondary definition is "reisebuch, reiseführer" vol. 12, col. 1648.

36 Sengle, *Biedermeierzeit*, 3:898.

37 See Gotthelf, *Sämtliche Werke:* Jakob views his Meister in Basel with "ein kurioses Gemisch von Verachtung und Respekt" (9:31 and 34); "gelb angelaufene Gesellen mit düstern Augen" in Basel, "Diese grollen der Welt, denn in der Welt haben sie nichts davongebracht als einen finstern Sinn" (9:41); Jakob and his companions cast envious glances at the wealthy guests at the spa in Baden: "Ob sie eigentlich bloß neidisch wurden oder zornig oder vielleicht sich schämten, wir wissen es nicht, wir hörten bloß, daß sie weidlich schimpften über das vornehme, hochmütige Gesindel, welches täte, als sei es vom Herrgott apart erschaffen" (9:61).

38 Gotthelf, *Sämtliche Werke*, 9:63: "Wer über seinem Stande steht, der schwebt in der Luft, und wer in der Luft schwebt, sehe zu, daß er nicht falle und zwar tief! Die Hauptsache ist die, daß einer in seinem Stande feststehe, daß er im kleinen getreu sein kann."

39 Sengle, *Biedermeierzeit*, 3:903.

40 Muret, *Gotthelf*, 284–98 (quoted from Gotthelf, *Sämtliche Werke*, 9:527).

41 In this context it is notable that Gottfried Keller ironizes the pastor's preoccupation with the domestic sphere, accusing him of treating "die Interessen von Küche und Speisekammer" "mit breiter Geschwätzigkeit" and parading "seine genaue Kenntnis der Milchtöpfe, der Hühner- und Schweineställe" in an effort to curry favor with female readers. Keller, *Sämtliche Werke*, ed. Carl Helbling, 22 vols. (Zurich: Benteli, 1926–48), 22:99. Less acerbically, but in a similar vein, Ernst Bloch has contrasted "Gotthelf der Bodenständige" with Johann Peter Hebel "der wandernde, weit Aufgeschlossene" in his 1926 essay "Hebel, Gotthelf und bäurisches Tao," in *Gesamtausgabe*, 9:365–84; here, 383.

42 Gotthelf, *Sämtliche Werke*, 15:266.

43 Michel Foucault, *Madness and Civilization* (London: Routledge, 2002): "Confinement was required by something quite different from any concern with curing the sick. What made it necessary was an imperative of labor. Our philanthropy prefers to recognize the signs of a benevolence toward sickness where there is only a condemnation of idleness" (43). For Foucault the establishment of the carceral system of the *hôpitaux généraux* (and their equivalents in Germany and

England) is attributable to "a new sensibility to poverty and to the duties of assistance, new forms of reaction to the economic problems of unemployment and idleness, a new ethic of work, and also the dream of a city where moral obligation was joined to civil law, within the authoritarian forms of constraint" (42). The delay in establishing an equivalent system of confinement in Switzerland was due to the fact that poverty only became an acute political issue there during the pauperization crisis of the 1830s.

[44] See Wermuth and Stieber, *Die Communisten-Verschwörungen des neunzehnten Jahrhunderts: Im amtlichen Auftrage zur Benutzung der Polizei-Behörden der sämmtlichen deutschen Bundesstaaten*, 2 vols. (Berlin: Hayn, 1853–54; repr., Hildesheim: Olms, 1969), 1:158.

[45] Sengle, *Biedermeierzeit*, 2:895.

[46] Paul Landau, *Karl von Holteis Romane: Ein Beitrag zur Geschichte der deutschen Unterhaltungs-Literatur* (Leipzig: Hesse, 1904). The most recent research on Holtei is contained in Christian Andree and Jürgen Hein, *Karl von Holtei (1798–1880): Ein schlesischer Dichter zwischen Biedermeier und Realismus* (Würzburg: Korn, 2005), which includes a select bibliography (403–8).

[47] Karl von Holtei, *Die Vagabunden von Karl von Holtei*, ed. and with a postscript by Hans Körnchen (Berlin: Wegweiser, [n.d.]). Subsequent references to this volume are given in the text using page numbers alone.

[48] Theater in Montmartre, Paris, that put on dramatic entertainments featuring the gruesome or horrible.

[49] Jan-Dirk Müller et al., *Reallexikon der deutschen Literaturwissenschaft*, 3 vols. (Berlin and New York: de Gruyter, 1997–2003), 3:691–95; here, 691. See also Rolf Grimminger, *Hanser Sozialgeschichte der deutschen Literatur, 16. Jh. bis zur Gegenwart* (Munich: Hanser, 1980–), 5:313–38, esp. 325–30. It will be understood that the identification of Holtei's novel with trivial literature in no way implies a disavowal of the work's literary worth or stylistic merits. In the view of no less an authority than Friedrich Sengle the story is told "mit einer so großen Leichtigkeit und Liebenswürdigkeit, daß wir an große Beispiele der Erzähldichtung, etwa an den rokokohaft gewordenen Schelmenroman des Lesage (*Gil Blas* 1715) erinnert werden" (Sengle, *Biedermeierzeit*, 2:911).

[50] Thus, as a preface to the Paris episode: "Es ist dem Verfasser, der Anton liebt, schmerzlich und peinvoll, diese finsterste Periode im Leben des Wanderers umständlich zu behandeln" (293).

[51] Sengle, *Biedermeierzeit*, 2:911.

[52] Sengle, *Biedermeierzeit*, 2:336.

[53] Sengle, *Biedermeierzeit*, 2:397.

[54] Georg Wilhelm Friedrich Hegel, *Werke*, ed. Eva Moldenhauer and Karl Markus Michel, 20 vols. (Frankfurt am Main: Suhrkamp, 1969–71), 13:20–21.

[55] Eduard von Bauernfeld, *Das letzte Abenteuer*, in *Gesammelte Schriften*, 12 vols. (Vienna: Braumüller, 1871–73), 2:96–97.

[56] Karl von Holtei, *Mit dem Thespiskarren durch die Lande: Karl von Holtei — Vierzig Jahre*, ed. Norbert Hopster (Heidenheim: Verlagsanstalt, 1971), 21.

[57] Holtei, *Mit dem Thespiskarren*, 51–52.

[58] Recalling Friedrich Hebbel's description of Holtei's life as a "krause Pilgerfahrt," Norbert Hopster rehearses the topos of the wandering dilettante in the foreword to his edition of excerpts from *Vierzig Jahre;* see Holtei, *Auf dem Thespiskarren*, 12.

[59] Karl von Holtei, *Jugend in Breslau*, ed. Helmut Koopman (Berlin: Nicolai, 1988), 137.

[60] Gustav Freytag, *Gesammelte Werke*, 2nd ed. (Leipzig: Hirzel, 1898–1910), 19:33.

[61] See John Neubauer, "Romantische Wandervögel," in *Jugend — ein romantisches Konzept?* ed. Günter Oesterle (Würzburg: Königshausen & Neumann, 1997), 333–48; here, 343.

[62] See Hardtwig, *Vormärz*, 115; Wehler, *Deutsche Gesellschaftsgeschichte*, 2:273.

[63] Quoted from Hardtwig, *Vormärz*, 7.

[64] Wehler, *Deutsche Gesellschaftsgeschichte*, 2:710.

[65] Gustav Freytag, *Gesammelte Werke*, vol. 17, n.p. (preface).

[66] Holtei, *Mit dem Thespiskarren*, 27.

[67] Karl von Holtei, *Simmelsammelsurium aus Briefen, aus dem Leben und aus ihm selbst*, vol. 1 (Breslau, 1872), 91 (quoted from Andree and Hein, *Karl von Holtei (1798–1880)*, 39).

[68] Wehler, *Deutsche Gesellschaftsgeschichte*, 3:543.

[69] Mack Walker, *German Home Towns: Community, State, and General Estate, 1648–1817*, 2nd ed. (Ithaca, NY and London: Cornell, 1998), 323.

[70] See Wehler, *Deutsche Gesellschaftsgeschichte*, 2:281–96.

[71] Karl Braun, *Die Vagabundenfrage* (Berlin: Simion, 1883), 33.

[72] Gustav Freytag, *Gesammelte Werke*, 2nd ed. (Leipzig: Hirzel, 1898–1910, 20:457–77 In this chapter, "Gauner und Abenteuerer," Freytag claims that the lawlessness and destruction of the Thirty Years' War led to a rise in vagrancy in subsequent years: "So geschah es, daß nach dem Frieden das Treiben der Glücksritter, Abenteurer und Betrüger eine sehr große Ausdehnung erhielt. Es ist bezeichnend für die folgenden hundert Jahre der Schwäche und Rohheit, ein Gegensatz zu dem dürftig verkümmerten Familienleben, in welchem sich das Gemüth des deutschen Bürgers zusammenzog" (461).

[73] "Zwischen 1860/70 und 1914 hat die deutsche Binnenwanderung fünfzehn bis sechszehn Millionen grenzüberschreitende Wanderer erfaßt; diese Zahl übertraf um das Dreifache der gesamten deutschen Auswanderung in 19. Jahrhundert" (Wehler, *Deutsche Gesellschaftsgeschichte*, 3:504).

[74] Quoted from Holtei, *Karl von Holtei*, 88–89.

[75] Horst Denkler, *Wilhelm Raabe: Legende — Leben — Literatur* (Tübingen: Niemeyer, 1989), 85.

[76] Theodor W. Adorno and Max Horkheimer, *Dialectic of Enlightenment* (London: Verso, 1997).

[77] Eric J. Hobsbawm, *Die Blütezeit des Kapitals: Eine Kulturgeschichte der Jahre 1848–1875* (Frankfurt am Main: Fischer, 1980).

[78] Freytag's stigmatization of nomadic existences as incompatible with bourgeois values in his *Bilder aus der deutschen Vergangenheit* has already been discussed in the sub-chapter on Karl von Holtei.

[79] Gustav Freytag, *Soll und Haben* (Leipzig: Manuscriptum, 2002), 312.

[80] Monika-Yvonne Stein, *Im Mantel Goethes und Faust auf der Fährte: Wilhelm Raabes* Faust- *und Goethe-Rezeption in seinem Roman Abu Telfan oder Die Heimkehr vom Mondgebirge* (Frankfurt am Main: Peter Lang, 2005), 113. Stein furnishes evidence of Raabe's intensive engagement with the Faust saga in the period immediately preceding the composition of *Abu Telfan*, including extensive annotations made by Raabe to his copy of Karl Rosenkranz's monograph, *Göthe und seine Werke* (1847).

[81] Stein, *Im Mantel Goethes*, 112. Emphasis in original. On the Faust reception see also Karl Robert Mandelkow, *Goethe in Deutschland: Rezeptionsgeschichte eines Klassikers*, 2 vols. (Munich: C. H. Beck, 1980–89), 1:240–61. Mandelkow draws out several distinct aspects of the "Identifikationsangebot" that the Faust figure held for the academic youth in the *Vormärz* era (241–42).

[82] Stein characterizes Viktor von Fehleysen *alias* Cornelius van Mook as "der rastlose Faust" (Stein, *Im Mantel Goethes*, 208).

[83] Stein, *Im Mantel Goethes*, 190.

[84] "*Der Autor stellt* nicht nur die Ausgrenzung irgendwelcher Personen durch die Philister und Adel eines deutschen Kleinstaates *dar*, sondern *die Ablehnung Fausts, d.h. . . . der Identifikationsfigur aller Deutschen* in ihrem Streben nach Wissen und Wahrheit schlechthin" (Stein, *Im Mantel Goethes*, 226).

[85] It is here that the absence of an interpretation of Goethe's *Faust* as pre-text, and of a survey of the *Faust* research, make themselves most keenly felt as a lacuna in Stein's intertextual analysis. Raabe's position is closer to that of Jean Paul, who opined in 1810 that *Faust I* had been "gegen die Titanenfrechheit geschrieben" (see Mandelkow, *Goethe in Deutschland*, 1:250).

[86] Stein, *Im Mantel Goethes*, 136. Stein locates the source for the following description of Hagebucher's unease: "Aber dem Unbehagen wuchsen doch täglich mehr züngelnde, saugende Polypenarme, mit welchen es die Seele des müden Wanderers immer fester umschlang" (136); cf. *Faust I*, 3894–3900: "Und die Wurzeln, wie die Schlangen, / Winden sich aus Fels und Sande, / Strecken wunderliche Bande, / Uns zu schrecken, uns zu fangen; / Aus belebten derben Masern / Strecken sie Polypenfasern / Nach dem *Wanderer*."

[87] See also scene 1, "Anmutige Gegend," of part 2 of Goethe's epic, in which Faust interprets the waterfall as a symbol of striving: "Der spiegelt ab das menschliche Bestreben" (line 4725).

[88] Goethe, *Faust I*, 3348–3351.

[89] This ambivalence is reflected in the fact that despite the troubling aspects of the character contemporary scientists, among them Carl Gustav Carus, were capable of identifying wholeheartedly with Faust. See Witte et al., *Goethe-Handbuch*, 4 vols.

(Stuttgart: Metzler, 1996–98), 2:483. Hans-Jürgen Schings, among others, has argued that Faust is constructed so as to embody values that are the antithesis of Goethe's philosophy of life, "'Gedenke zu leben': Goethes Lebenskunst," in Helmut Fuhrmann, *Wilhelm Meister und seine Nachfahren: Vorträge des 4. Kasseler Goetheseminars* (Kassel: Wenderoth, 2000), 36–39. The incautious adoption of Faust as an identification figure by many contemporaries in some respects resembles the *Werther* cult, which Goethe deplored.

90 Heinrich Düntzer, *Goethes Faust* (1850), 2nd ed. (Leipzig, 1857) (quoted from Witte, *Goethe-Handbuch*, 2:485).

91 Karl Jaspers, "Goethes Menschlichkeit," *Basler Universitätsreden* 26 (1949): 11–33; here, 16 (quoted from Witte, *Goethe-Handbuch*, 2:491).

92 Wilhelm Raabe, *Abu Telfan oder die Heimkehr vom Mondgebirge*, ed. Werner Röpke, vol. 7 of *Sämtliche Werke*, ed. Karl Hoppe et al. (Freiburg im Breisgau: Klemm: Vandenhoeck & Ruprecht, 1951–94), 89. References to this volume will be given in the text using page numbers alone. References to other volumes of this edition will be indicated usingvolume and page numbers.

93 Velten Andres's "Weltfahrten" (Raabe, 19:311) are imbued with an obvious actionism. Of his failure to gain the hand of Helene, whom he has pursued to America, he writes: "Ich habe das Meinige getan, durch Stunden, Tage, Wochen, Monate und Jahre, bei Tag und Nacht, bei allem, was ich getan, überdacht und gedacht habe, den schönen Schmetterling für mich . . . festzuhalten" (325). The narrator Karl Krumhardt remarks of his late friend's unbending will: "An meinem armen Velten habe ich erst als Neunzigjährige gelernt, daß es eine Dummheit ist, wenn man sagt: Der Mensch braucht nur zu wollen" (396).

94 This date after A. Adu Boahen, *African Perspectives on Colonialism*, 4th ed. (Baltimore: Johns Hopkins, 1992), 1.

95 In this respect Velten Andres perhaps fulfills a culturally diagnostic function similar to that of Hauke Haien, the protagonist of Theodor Storm's novella *Der Schimmelreiter* (1888).

96 "Die moderne Unruhe: . . . Aus Mangel an Ruhe läuft unsere Civilisation in eine neue Barbarei aus. Zu keiner Zeit haben die Thätigen, das heisst die Ruhelosen, mehr gegolten. Es gehört deshalb zu den nothwendigen Correkturen, welche man am Charakter der Menschheit vornehmen muss, das beschauliche Element in grossem Maasse zu verstärken" (Nietzsche, *Menschliches — Allzumenschliches*, 1:285; quoted from Nietzsche, *Kritische Studienausgabe*, 2:232).

97 Hans Mayer rightly criticizes the unreflected use of these terms as one of the unproductive commonplaces of Raabe research. Mayer, "Wilhelm Raabe: *Abu Telfan oder die Heimkehr vom Mondgebirge*," in *Wilhelm Raabe: Studien zu seinem Leben und Werk*, ed. Leo A. Lensing and Hans-Werner Peter (Braunschweig: pp-Verlag, 1981), 128–32; here, 128. Representative of the research on outsiders in Raabe's fictions is Hermann Meyer, *Der Sonderling in der deutschen Dichtung* (Munich: Hanser, 1963). See also Dieter Kafitz, "Die Appelfunktion der Außenseitergestalten: Zur näheren Bestimmung des Realismus der mittlerern und späteren Romane Raabes," in Lensing and Peter, *Wilhelm Raabe: Studien zu seinem Leben und Werk*, 51–76.

[98] "Über der Pforte stand der biblische Spruch: Gesegnet sei dein Eingang und Ausgang — und hinter der Tür stand der dicke Knüppel für unverschämte Bettelleute, Handwerksgesellen und fremde Hunde; denn das Haus des Steuerinspektors war dicht an der Landstraße gelegen, und seine Küchenfenster waren nur durch einen Graben von derselben getrennt" (15).

[99] "Das germanische Spießbürgertum fühlte sich dieser fabelhaften, zerfahrenen, aus Rand und Band gekommenen, dieser entgleisten, entwurzelten, quer über den Weg geworfenen Existenz gegenüber in seiner ganzen Staats- und Kommunalsteuer zahlenden, Kirchstuhl gemietet habenden, von der Polizei bewachten und von sämtlichen fürstlichen Behörden überwachten, gloriosen Sicherheit" (42).

[100] Raabe uses the *Wanderbuch* motif to look askance at the tightening net of police controls in Europe, and the growing pressure on travelers to prove their bona fides: Täubrich's book lacks "kein Stempel und keine Polizeikralle" (145), and it is humorously suggested that Alexander von Humboldt "auch sein Wanderbuch aufzuweisen hatte" (140).

[101] See Ian Hacking, *Mad Travelers: Reflections on the Reality of Transient Mental Illnesses* (Cambridge, MA: Harvard, 1998).

[102] "Tag und Nacht keine Ruhe — Herr Inspektor vorn, Herr Inspektor hinten" (65). Stein notes that Wassertreter combines patience with the Goethean precept of restless activity on behalf of humanity. Stein, *Im Mantel Goethes*, 251.

[103] "Erstaunlich häufig verwendet Raabe in *Abu Telfan* schon den Begriff 'Zivilisation' in kritischer Akzentuierung zur Kennzeichnung der aktuellen Verhältnisse. Dieser Begriff ist noch nicht mit jenem ideologischen Potential befrachtet, das ihm im späteren 19. Jahrhundert zu einem Schlüsselwort des konservativen Geschichtspessimismus werden läßt, aber er trägt schon deutlich negative Konnotationen." Peter Brenner, "Die Einheit der Welt: Zur Entzauberung der Fremde und Verfremdung der Heimat in Raabes 'Abu Telfan,'" *Jahrbuch der Raabe-Gesellschaft* 1989: 45–62; here, 53.

[104] Hegel, *Werke*, 14:220. Christian Müller is the most recent critic to read *Abu Telfan* in this way. Christian Müller, "Subjektkonstituierung in einer kontingenten Welt: Erfahrungen zweier Afrika-Heimkehrer — Gottfried Kellers 'Pankraz, der Schmoller' und Wilhelm Raabes 'Abu Telfan,'" *Jahrbuch der Raabe-Gesellschaft* 2002: 82–110.

[105] Barker Fairley, *Wilhelm Raabe: An Introduction to His Novels* (Oxford: Clarendon, 1961), 169–71.

[106] Müller, "Subjektkonstituierung," 110.

[107] Gerhard Plumpe provides invaluable theoretical background on the aesthetics of realism in "Das Reale und die Kunst: Ästhetische Theorie im 19. Jahrhundert," in Grimminger, *Hanser Sozialgeschichte*, 6:242–307. See also Martin Swales, *Epochenbuch Realismus: Romane und Erzählungen* (Berlin: Schmidt, 1997).

[108] Hegel, *Werke*, 14:219.

[109] It is worth noting that Hagebucher, in the account of his instruction at the hands of Wassertreter, refers sarcastically to Hegel's *Identitätsphilosophie:* "Bei allen Meistern, Lehrern und Propheten diesseits und jenseits der fünf Sinnen des

Menschen, ohne den trefflichen schwarzen Kaffee des Vetters Wassertreter, ohne die Frau Klaudine und ohne den Mantel des alten Goethe säße ich jetzt sicher im Landesirrenhaus und zählte an den Fingern: a) der subjektive Geist — b) der objektive Geist — c) der absolute Geist" (156–57).

110 The phrase is from F. T. Vischer's *Ästhetik oder Wissenschaft des Schönen*, ed. Robert Vischer (Hildesheim: Olms, 1996), 177.

111 The "Kommersbuch" was the name given to any anthology of student *Wanderlieder.* A "Ziegenhainer" was a coarse walking stick named for the village of Ziegenhain near Jena, where the *Urburschenschaft* was founded in 1815.

112 The two key principles of Romanticism, according to Isaiah Berlin, *The Roots of Romanticism*, ed. Henry Hardy and Roger Hausherr (London: Pimlico, 1998), 114, 119 and elsewhere.

113 Brenner, "Die Einheit der Welt," 60.

114 Friedrich Theodor Vischer, *Faust: Der Tragödie dritter Theil* (Tübingen: Laupp, 1862; repr., Stuttgart: Reclam, 1994).

115 Friedrich Theodor Vischer, *Kritische Gänge*, ed. Robert Vischer, 2nd ed., 6 vols. (Munich: Meyer & Jessen, 1920–1922), 4:229.

# Conclusion

In the introduction I justified assigning texts to different thematic categories on the grounds that casting the discursive net as widely as possible would help to grasp the full functional range of the wanderer motif. However, given the capacity of narrative to integrate the various discourses of its era, one should acknowledge that each text might well have been discussed from a different point of view. For example, in Heine's *Harzreise* political and anthropological discourses are intertwined, with the motif functioning as a point of contact between them. Thus, the protagonist's wandering in the *Harzreise* foregrounds the appetitive and sensual aspects of the individual as part of a critique of the ideology of renunciation.[1] Although in each analysis I have placed the emphasis on a different discourse, the wanderers in the fictions studied here appear always as individuals at the focal point of intersecting discourses — aesthetic, ethical, philosophical, economic, and so on.

This is perhaps a useful point of departure to take in attempting to synthesize the findings of the foregoing study. Generalizing from the separate interpretations, we might say that the main role of the wanderer motif has been to reflect upon the vicissitudes of individuality in the nineteenth century, on the individual's possibilities for self-realization, on his (and here we have to do primarily — but not exclusively — with male, bourgeois individuality) hopes and fears, the social, economic, and institutional forces impinging on him, and his responses to them. If there is a semantic strain that is always present in the motif, and for which it has a natural affinity, it is the strain of emancipation. For Goethe, as for his colleague in the project of Enlightenment, Karl Philipp Moritz, the wanderer is the conceptual figure of an empirical practice aimed at liberty, whether through an emphatic turn to the outside world (in Goethe's case) or through self-scrutiny (in Moritz's *Anton Reiser*). In the case of the Romantics, the motif becomes the emblem both of intellectual and creative freedom and of the terrors engendered by the separation from traditional intellectual models, such as the idea of a providential order, or of the "great chain of being." Out of the metaphysical idea of a world in flux and the insecure and frequently nomadic nature of their lives grew the tendency of the Romantics to conceive of themselves as wanderers, a self-conception that uniquely captured their orientation toward new knowledge and the future.

The Young German writers, especially Heine, who among them had the profoundest understanding of Romanticism, appropriate the motif with a view not only to intellectual freedom but also to press the claims of material emancipation. The *Harzreise* asserts pleasure as the birthright of the individual, thereby opposing the tendencies of nationalism and Hegelian political philosophy to subordinate the interests of the individual to the collective process of history. In *Lenz* (which seems in certain respects like an anti-*Harzreise*) pain, not pleasure, is the guarantee of the ineluctability of individuality, which here seems more of a cage. Büchner constructs his wanderer in such a way as to deny that the contemplation of nature can provide healing or transcendence in a society dominated by the *principium individuationis* that divides men from men. What Heine's and Büchner's wanderers have in common is that they allow the adverse conditions of an age (*Vormärz*) to be represented by showing how they impress themselves on the body as physical sensations. The motif thus becomes an organon for registering the characteristic emotional climate of an historical age.

It was this capacity to apprehend man as unity of body and mind, as *commercium mentis et corporis*, that caused the wanderer to be adopted in the first place as the symbol of Enlightenment *par excellence*. The symbol acquired special importance in late Enlightenment anthropology with its program of rehabilitating the corporeal and sensual aspects of man. For Herder, upright gait, which made possible the free and unencumbered view and the ability to grasp and use tools, was evidence of man's vocation to reason. Literature, especially Moritz's *Anton Reiser*, played a key role in communicating the new anthropological perspective to the public imagination, propagating walking as a technique of bringing mind and body into balance, and as a specifically bourgeois habitus symbolizing emancipation.

Considered as a cultural symbol, the wanderer motif derives its potency from its capacity to be embodied. That is to say, conceiving of oneself as wanderer summons up certain kinds of corporeal feeling by means of which certain ethical and philosophical contents can be conveyed. The readily imagined physical sensations of uprightness, alertness, and rapid pace lend themselves to the idea of a dynamic, striving individuality. In other contexts, however, for example by association with the historical practice of artisanal wandering, the motif communicates ideas of collective striving and progress, of solidarity in the face of adversity. The motif was thus capable as functioning as the linchpin of both individual and group identity. Certainly this was the case for an academic elite who imagined themselves both individually and collectively as wanderers, and whose whole corporate culture was founded on vacation wanderings on which friendships were forged.[2] If the university was the crucible of a national and democratic consciousness, uniting students across the barriers of social origin and particularism, then the walking tours prescribed as a constructive use of lecture-free time intensified that process. This activity was literarily mediated to a high degree: novels whetted the appetite for travel; *Wanderlieder*, sung or recited, were used to foster a sense of *esprit de corps; Wanderberichte* and guidebooks exerted a normative influence, setting the itinerary and providing an ideological context for the perception of landscape. Although such wanderings were above all occasions of avid literary consumption, the moment of production was also significant. The vacation walking tour was a veritable school for the aesthetic sensibility of young writers, while the travel journals they kept served as valuable exercises in style.

As I noted earlier, the motif displays a double valency as far back as in the fictions of the Romantics, being used not only to validate the individualizing tendencies of the age but also to give expression to anxieties surrounding them. Thus from the outset the motif is always available as a vehicle for the theme of homelessness, be it in the sense of the loss of a "transzendentales Obdach"[3] or of the separation from artistic and other traditions. This sense emerges powerfully from Karl von Holtei's characterization of his generation of actors as *Vagabunden*, as exiles from the *Heimat* of Weimar Classicism. There, too, wandering appears not as development in accordance with an internal essence, as it does for some Romantics and in the *Bildungsroman*, but as the motor of perpetual difference. Apart from serving as a symbolic promoter of individualism, then, the wanderer motif also enables the diagnosis of the toll taken on the individual as that ideology tightened its grip in the course of the century.

Despite the affinity of the motif for the theme of homelessness, it seems scarcely ever to be applied in direct treatments of precisely those forms of uprootedness that touched the lives of the majority. In vain one searches for wanderers caught up in the traumas of mass migration or in the great internal movements of workers within the *Reich* in the 1880s (such as the great migration from the Prussian provinces to the *Ruhrgebiet*). Frustratingly for the literary historian, such matters appear simply not to have been *salonfähig*. Apparently the only major work to connect the motif to the matter of emigration is Goethe's *Wanderjahre*, and there the manner of the connection is hypothetical, or prophetic, rather than historically descriptive.

Although the emancipatory strain of the motif is drastically curtailed in this latter novel, it is thoroughly preoccupied with the fate of the individual in modernity. On one level that work seeks to answer the question: on what terms can the individual expect to survive in a modernity that greatly limits the possibilities of self-determination? While the *Wanderjahre* is too elliptical and too scrupulous to be in any way prescriptive, Goethe's "merkwürdige Verlassenschaft"[4] gestures toward the idea that the appropriate attitude to cultivate toward a populous modernity is a nomadic one.

Survival in this setting requires renunciation, in the sense both of submitting to the principle of the division of labor, and of being willing to give up essentialist notions of a bond between blood and soil in favor of a pragmatic conception of *Heimat*. The two strands of mobility and renunciation considered as a technique of survival come together in what I have called "pragmatic cosmopolitanism." What is truly radical about the *Wanderjahre* is that it imagines homelessness, understood as an indifference to natural origins, as a good thing.

Later, in the period between the upheavals of 1830 and 1848, mobility and cosmopolitanism would indeed be propagated as part of a response to an age in which venerable social, economic, and ideological institutions were diminishing in importance. The innovators in this context were the *Linkshegelianer*, who seized on the valuation of labor and what they saw as the advocacy of mobility in the *Wanderjahre*, making these ideas available to the socialist radicals, who would put them at the heart of their ideological program. In this sense it might be said that the wanderer motif gets transferred from the literary to the political text. In their attempt to forge a new proletarian identity, and thereby unite the victims of pauperization, the radicals drew also on artisanal traditions, including the *Wanderschaft*. This served as a ready-made model of progress through work and education and likely helped to foster the impression of an interim phase of privation and struggle culminating in social revolution. Gotthelf's novel *Jakob* is interesting precisely because it combats this symbolic appropriation of artisanal traditions by "die Apostel der verruchten Lehren."[5] It does so by representing the *Wanderschaft* in terms rather different from those of the workers' associations, casting it as a Pilgrim's Progress, an individual struggle to distinguish revealed truth from the world's blandishments, rather than as an occasion of solidarity or comradeship. It is in this effort to reclaim the artisan's wandering as a model of individual rather than collective striving that Gotthelf's argument is strongest. That argument is, however, vitiated by a detectable suspicion of nomadic existences, and a certain queasiness in the handling of the subject matter of journeymen and their wanderings.

It is notable that the rise of the wanderer motif takes place against the background both of the emerging practice of bourgeois recreational wandering and the decline of more traditional forms of mobility, especially that of artisans. The awareness of this decline may have been something of a spur to the symbolic appropriation of the *Wanderschaft* by Tieck (whose father was an artisan), and to the subsequent attempts to revive artisanal traditions referred to above. In Tieck's *Franz Sternbalds Wanderungen*, and to an extent in Gotthelf's *Jakob*, the motif operates partly as a vehicle of cultural memory, preserving certain ideal features of the artisan's life, and partly as a site of innovation. This is especially evident in Tieck's novel, which reinterprets the journeyman years, not as an interim phase in an otherwise settled existence, but as an initiation into the permanent threshold state characteristic of the Romantic artist's existence.

In his *Wanderungen durch die Mark Brandenburg* Tieck uses the motif to keep alive uncontemporary meaning in a manner consistent with his program of reviving conservative Prussian values. Semantic traces from the late Enlightenment and Romanticism are present in the appeal to "jenem stolzen Wandergefühl, das sich nach Strapazen sehnt":[6] the wanderer once again appears as the paragon of an effortful and purposeful existence. Although Fontane is by no means an opponent of industrial and technological developments, he invokes wandering to promote the idea of deceleration, in the aesthetic sense of renewed attention to the fine detail of landscape, and in the political sense of damping the pace of change. In its advocacy of localized wandering as a means of kindling patriotic sentiment, Fontane's program is closer in spirit to the "vaterländische Wanderungen" pioneered by Jahn and practiced by the *Burschenschaften* than to the "kosmopolitische Wanderungen" of the late Enlightenment. Other authors employ the wanderer motif in more direct criticism of the depredations of modernity, and especially of the acceleration brought on by the advent of the railways with all its supposedly deleterious effects on the moral and perceptual economy of the individual. This moment of cultural criticism is pronounced in Eichendorff's autobiographical fragment *Erlebtes*, which opposes "die unbestimmte Abenteuerlichkeit des altmodischen Wanderlebens" to the "fliegender Salon" and the "große Eilfertigkeit" of the railway stations, whose proliferation is viewed as the symptom of an increasingly pervasive rationality and uniformity.[7] Of course, Eichendorff's best-known reckoning with the bourgeoisification taking place all around him comes in *Aus dem Leben eines Taugenichts* (1826), whose wandering protagonist asserts the rights of spontaneity and pleasure in the face of calculating philistinism.

In several of the texts already mentioned it has been possible to see how the motif functions as an intertextual link, either between literary texts or between a non-literary pre-text and a literary work. Frequently the non-literary pretext is the artisans' *Wanderschaft*, but aesthetically formed texts also connect via the motif with the cultural practice of student wandering. One text to engage with student wandering as a contemporary practice, simultaneously celebrating it and deploring its appropriation by Jahn's demagogues, is Heine's *Harzreise*. Heine's text derives some of the freshness that so appealed to his contemporaries from the fact that it interprets student wandering against the grain of contemporary ideology, using it to debunk rather than buttress key nationalist assumptions by restoring to it the critical potential of the Enlightenment travelogue. In Raabe's *Abu Telfan* the practice is invoked not as something contemporary but as a slightly outmoded institution. By the time Raabe composed the novel, the sense was growing that individualism was the signature trait of the age:

thus, when Jakob Burckhardt writes in *Die Cultur der Renaissance in Italien* (1860) that the Italian Renaissance witnessed the birth of the individual, we feel that, whether he is aware of it or not, he is framing the experience of his own time. Raabe uses the wanderer motif to reflect critically on the hegemony of individualism: he exploits the negative potential of the motif known to the Romantics to indicate unbridled, restless striving; he summons up student wandering to imagine bourgeois solidarity; and he establishes an intertextual link with the *Wanderjahre*, in which wandering is a figure for renunciative activity directed toward common ends. Of course, like Goethe, Raabe is a writer with strongly individualistic leanings, and it is these that attract him to the wanderer motif in the first place. Not individualism *per se*, but its worst excesses: an exaggerated belief in the power of the human will, social Darwinism, and titanism — trends increasingly apparent in the ruthlessly competitive *Gründerzeit* — are what stimulate his concern. It is interesting to note, however, that as the *Gründerzeit* progresses, Raabe is no longer able to associate the wanderer motif with a positive individuality; indeed, in the figure of Velten Andres the motif reaches a maximum of negative potential.

The persistence of the motif in Raabe's work is untypical: from mid-century onward we are confronted by a dearth of fictional wanderers in German literature, a state of affairs that demands some manner of explanation from the literary historian. Partly in an attempt to provide such an explanation I have advanced the hypothesis that the period post-1848 saw the rise of an "ideology of the settled life," which had its origins in the perception that the previous half-century had been a period of exceptional turmoil and instability. Out of this perception grew a general longing for order, continuity, and predictability. There was a narrowing of horizons, and a preoccupation with what was close at hand. Realism became the dominant mode, in literature and politics alike: and the long-standing association of the wanderer motif with the idealisms of the late Enlightenment and of Romanticism may have made the exponents of realism reluctant to adopt it. Moreover, to this group of writers, many of them disillusioned by the defeat of national-liberal hopes in 1848, nomadic existences were anathema, since they seemed like a shabby evasion of the difficult task they had set themselves of adapting to the new reality. It bears repeating that this anti-nomadic ideology was being propagated in literature and popular historiography at precisely the time that emigration — and, after 1871, internal migration — was reaching unheard-of levels. Nevertheless, it strengthened the stigma that played a part in the objective decline of such traditional forms of non-settled life as the *Wanderschaft* or the peregrinations of itinerant players.

One is struck by the number of references to the opposition "Ruhe" *versus* "Bewegung" in the historiography and political discourse of the German nineteenth century. So frequently does it occur that it is difficult to escape the conclusion that the dialectic of rest and motion was a central figure of thought in this era. After 1871 historians have regular recourse to this antinomy, putting it at the service of a narrative that represents the foundation of the Second Empire as the emergence of order from chaos. But the grip this opposition exerted on the collective consciousness may itself explain the prominence of the wanderer motif in the first half of the century and its subsequent decline. For as long as the sense persisted that the age was characterized, for good or ill, by movement of whatever kind, social, political, or economic, writers appear to have been willing to employ the motif to lend expression to the mood of dynamism. However, as soon as history was no longer felt to be in the making but was viewed as a process that had reached some sort of end point with the establishment of the Second Empire, the figure of the wanderer seems to have fallen into disuse. An exception in this regard is Fontane's *Wanderungen*, which, I have argued, sustains the notion of historical progress beyond the horizon of the present, thereby differing from a mainstream historicism that sought to legitimize the *status quo*. The wanderer motif plays its part in dynamizing the conception of history in Fontane's work, whereas in Freytag's *Bilder aus der deutschen Vergangenheit* it serves only to illustrate a turbulent and uncomfortable past.

This study would not be complete without referring to a particular species of literary wanderer long regarded as absent from the German cultural landscape: the *flâneur*.[8] The nineteenth century, which in its early stages was marked by the dissolution of age-old institutions, was not only a period of burgeoning individualism. Other forces were present, forces that had their source in the unprecedented growth in population that Europe had been experiencing since the mid-eighteenth century, and as the century wore on, they acted powerfully to curtail expressions of individuality. They were various but may be summarized under the headings of the emergence of mass societies, industrialization, and urbanization. Of all the processes of modernity, the creation of a mass urban society was experienced as putting the greatest pressure on the individual. To be sure, the city as place of venality has been a topos of cultural criticism since classical times, but it is not until the nineteenth century that the fear of the de-differentiating effects of metropolitan life emerges in literature. This fear, of being swamped or submerged, finds its expression in the oceanic metaphors then being applied to the urban mass[9] and first acquired a clear outline in the literature of the nineteenth century, in Poe's *The Man of the Crowd* (1840), and Grillparzer's *Der arme Spielmann* (1848). What does this have to do with the wanderer motif? It is generally held that the experience of the crushing of individuality in the metropolis gave rise to a species of urban wanderer, the *flâneur*, who sought to mitigate what Simmel has called "die Atrophie der individuellen durch die Hypertrophie der kollektiven Kultur"[10] by a demonstrative idling, spectating at the business of production, and especially, of consumption. For Walter

Benjamin the wanderings of the *flâneur* through the streets and arcades are an extravagant non-participation in the anonymous processes of the metropolis; as movement, physical and mental, undertaken for its own sake, the habitus of the *flâneur* is a quixotic assertion of individual freedom. Quixotic, because the *flâneur* is a transitional figure of modernity whose demise Benjamin blames on the reconfiguration of urban space, specifically, on the advent of the department store.

Since Benjamin the prevailing view has been that this figure emerged in Paris in the latter part of the nineteenth century, and that it essentially has no counterpart in German culture. In fact this view is doubly wrong, for the *flâneur* was already an established sociological and literary type in Paris by the 1820s, and the type was well-known in German-speaking cities, especially Vienna. As Martina Lauster has shown, the neglect of the strolling observer of urban life by literary historians is due ultimately to the privileging of canonical prose narratives over other, more discursive, text types.[11] What Lauster has in mind is the genre of the urban sketch, the long neglect of which is due to its accessibility and ephemerality, traits that have led interpreters mistakenly to deny the genre any capacity to reflect upon and interpret the complexities of urban modernity. Yet not only does the urban sketch undeniably possess such a capacity, but it is founded on an empirical practice whose very embodiment is the mobile urban *observateur*.

At the outset I had hoped to find texts in which urban wandering was thematized. However, the perusal of material ranging from the travel writing of the Young German authors Börne, Gutzkow, and Heine, to the feuilletons of Daniel Spitzer, yielded little in the way of sustained reflection on the specifics of movement in urban spaces and how they are perceived. Thus, while Ludwig Börne treats us to the following remark — "Ein aufgeschlagenes Buch ist Paris zu nennen, durch seine Straßen wandern heißt lesen. In diesem lehrreichen und ergötzlichen Werke, mit naturtreuen Abbildungen so reichlich ausgestattet, blättere ich täglich einige Stunden lang" — any reader expecting him to elaborate on the problems of moving in and reading the urban space is soon disappointed.[12] If the *flâneur* is not especially prominent in *Vormärz* travel writing, it is almost completely absent from the narrative fictions that are the principal object of interest in this study. German authors are familiar with the type, but they seem to regard it as primarily journalistic, and thus it is to the urban sketches of Ignaz Castelli, Adalbert Stifter, and others that we must turn to find German *flâneurs*.[13]

It might have been expected that toward the end of the century the wanderer would be interpreted in the direction of a Nietzschean vitalism. But Zarathustran wanderers, striding out of the city, the dwelling place of the herd, and into the mountain fastnesses, do not make their appearance in literature until well after the establishment of the *Wandervogelbewegung* in Berlin in 1896. This youth movement, whose members were predominantly students of the Gymnasium, was profoundly influenced by Romanticism, sharing its urban base and its inclination to cultural criticism. The students of the *Wandervogel* would have to wait for the turn of the century to acquire an original literature they could call their own. Hermann Hesse, the first author to lend a voice to this restless youth,[14] who felt stifled by the high-pressure atmosphere of the conformist educational system, also belonged, with Thomas Mann, to the first generation of writers to make productive use of Nietzsche's ideas. (Nietzsche had remained virtually unknown until Georg Brandes rebuked Germany for her ignorance of the thinker in his Copenhagen lectures of 1888.) However, in his themes and preoccupations Hesse is a writer of the twentieth century, and is therefore best excluded from this study.

Any continuation of this survey would have to attend to the function of the wanderer motif in Hesse's fictions, in particular to its role as a conduit for Nietzschean vitalism, and to ask to what extent such ideas shaped the ideology of the *Wandervogel.* Another desideratum would be an examination of wanderers in the literature of Expressionism, which is likely to have had a considerable affinity for the motif, given its antipathy toward bourgeois civilization, expressed in a championing of the non-bourgeois existence of beggars, strolling players, gypsies, and vagabonds. It would be something of an irony to find that what had originally been the paramount symbol of bourgeois identity had for a time become part of the iconography of the struggle against that identity. An irony, but hardly a surprising one when we recall that this possibility, too, had already been exploited in the nineteenth century, in Eichendorff's *Taugenichts.* Indeed, it is this very amenability to being appropriated and reinterpreted, while simultaneously carrying over residues of meaning from previous interpretations, that is a compelling indication of the versatility of a cultural symbol which I believe ranks above all others whenever the claims of the individual are asserted in the German nineteenth century.

## Notes

[1] Heine's critique of renunciation is reflected in his characterization of the literature of Restoration Germany as "Entsagungsromane" in *Französische Zustände* (1833) (Heine, Historisch-kritische Gesamtausgabe, 12/1:113). See also the reference in *Deutschland: Ein Wintermärchen* (1844) to: "das alte Entsagungslied, / Das Eyapopeya vom Himmel, / Womit man einlullt, wenn es greint; / Das Volk, den großen Lümmel" (ibid., 4:91, Caput I).

[2] Student wandering of this kind as a specifically German cultural phenomenon is affectionately parodied in Thomas Mann's *Doktor Faustus*, chapter 14.

[3] Georg Lukács, *Die Theorie des Romans: Ein geschichtsphilosophischer Versuch über die Formen der großen Epik* (Neuwied; Berlin, 1963), 22–23, 35.

[4] This phrase from book 3, chapter 7 of the *Wanderjahre, HA* 8:376.

[5] Jeremias Gotthelf, *Sämtliche Werke in 24 Bänden, ed. Rudolf Hunziker and Hans Bloesch*, 24 vols. and 18 supplementary vols. (Zurich: Rentsch, 1921–77), 9:474.

[6] Fontane, *Werke, Schriften und Briefe*, ed. Walter Keitel and Helmuth Hürnberger, 20 vols. in 4 parts, 2nd ed. (Munich: Hanser, 1969–97), 2/2:607.

[7] Joseph Eichendorff, *Werke*, 5 vols. (Munich: Winkler, 1976–88), 1:895–96.

[8] "Die müßige Flanerie durch das turbulent bewegte Leben der modernen Großstadt hingegen ist der deutschen Literatur fremd geblieben." Angelika Wellmann, *Der Spaziergang: Stationen eines poetischen Codes* (Würzburg: Königshausen & Neumann, 1991), 151. Wellmann follows Benjamin in concluding that the *flâneur* is a type absent from German literature.

[9] Oceanic metaphors have been a staple of descriptions of urban masses from Fontane ("Der Zauber Londons ist — seine *Massenhaftigkeit.* Wenn Neapel durch seinen Golf und Himmel, Moskau durch seine funkelnden Kuppeln, Rom durch seine Erinnerungen, Venedig durch den Zauber seiner meerentstiegenen Schönheit wirkt, so ist es beim Anblick Londons das Gefühl des Unendlichen, was uns überwältigt — dasselbe Gefühl, was uns beim ersten Anschauen des Meeres durchschauert" [Fontane, *Werke, Schriften und Briefe*, 3/3:10]) to Canetti, whose use of the metaphor in *Masse und Macht* (1960) no longer contains any suggestion of the sublime but emphasises the destructive force latent in such masses.

[10] Georg Simmel, "Die Großstädte und das Geistesleben" (1903), in *Brücke und Tür: Essays des Philosophen zur Geschichte, Religion, Kunst, und Gesellschaft* (Stuttgart: Koehler, 1957), 227–42; here, 241.

[11] Martina Lauster, "Walter Benjamin's Myth of the *Flâneur*," *Modern Language Review* 102 (2007): 139–56. By the same author, *Sketches of the Nineteenth Century: European Journalism and its "Physiologies" (1830–50)* (Basingstoke, UK: Palgrave Macmillan, 2007).

[12] Ludwig Börne, *Werke in zwei Bänden*, ed. Helmut Bock and Walter Dietze (Berlin and Weimar: Aufbau, 1986), 1:225.

[13] Karl Johann Braun von Braunthal, *Antithesen oder Herrn Humors Wanderungen durch Wien und Berlin* (1834); Ignaz Franz Castelli, *Wiener Lebensbilder* (1835); August Schilling's *Spaziergänge eines Wiener Humoristen* (1842). Kai Kauffmann provides an excellent survey of these sketches; see *"Es ist nur ein Wien!" Stadtbeschreibungen von Wien, 1700 bis 1873: Geschichte eines literarischen Genres* (Vienna, Cologne, Weimar: Böhlau, 1994).

[14] See Christian E. Völpel, *Hermann Hesse und die deutsche Jugendbewegung* (Bonn: Bouvier, 1977).

# Works Cited

## Primary Sources


Adelung, Johann Christoph. *Grammatisch-kritisches Wörterbuch der hochdeutschen Mundart.* 2nd ed. 4 vols. Leipzig: Breitkopf & Härtel, 1798. Reprint, Hildesheim: Olms, 1970.

Bauernfeld, Eduard von. *Gesammelte Schriften.* 12 vols. Vienna: Braumüller, 1871–73.

Bloch, Ernst. *Gesamtausgabe.* Frankfurt am Main: Suhrkamp, 1959–.

Blumenhagen, Friedrich. *Wanderung durch den Harz: Mit 30 Stahlstichen.* Leipzig: Wigand, 1838. Reprint, Hildesheim: Olms, 1972. Vol. 5 of *Das malerische und romantische Deutschland.*

Börne, Ludwig. *Werke in zwei Bänden.* Edited by Helmut Bock and Walter Dietze. Berlin and Weimar: Aufbau, 1986.

Büchner, Georg. *Werke und Briefe.* Edited by Karl Pörnbacher, Gerhard Schaub, Hans-Joachim Simm, and Edda Ziegler. Munich and Vienna: Hanser, 1988 (= Münchner Ausgabe).

Byron (George Gordon). *The Major Works.* Edited by Jerome J. McGann. Oxford: Oxford UP, 2000.

Chamisso, Adelbert von. *Peter Schlemihls wundersame Geschichte.* Nuremberg: Schrag, 1814. Reprint, Munich: dtv, 2003.

Eichendorff, Joseph. *Werke.* 5 vols. Munich: Winkler, 1976–88.

Etzel, Anton von. *Die Ostsee und ihre Küstenländer, geographisch, naturwissenschaftlich und historisch geschildert.* Leipzig: Lorck, 1859.

Fontane, Theodor. *Tagebücher.* Edited by Gotthard Erler and Charlotte Jolles. 2 vols. Berlin: Aufbau, 1995 (= Große Brandenburger Ausgabe).

———. *Werke, Schriften und Briefe.* Edited by Walter Keitel and Helmuth Nürnberger. 20 vols. in 4 parts. 2nd ed. Munich: Hanser, 1962–97.

Fontane, Theodor, and Emilie Fontane. *Der Ehebriefwechsel.* Edited by Gotthard Erler. 3 vols. Berlin: Aufbau, 1998 (= Große Brandenburger Ausgabe).

Forster, Georg. *Werke in vier Bänden.* Edited by Gerhard Steiner. Frankfurt am Main: Insel, 1967–70.

Freytag, Gustav. *Gesammelte Werke.* 2nd ed. Leipzig: Hirzel, 1898–1910.

———. *Soll und Haben.* Leipzig: Manuscriptum, 2002.

Goethe, Johann Wolfgang von. *Gedenkausgabe der Werke, Briefe und Gespräche.* Edited by Ernst Beutler. 24 vols. Zurich: Artemis, 1948–54 (=Artemis Gedenkausgabe).

Goethe, Johann Wolfgang von. *Goethes Gespräche: Gesamtausgabe.* Edited by Flodoard Biedermann et al. 2nd ed. 5 vols. Leipzig: Biedermann, 1909–11.

———. *Sämtliche Werke, Briefe, Tagebücher und Gespräche.* 40 vols. Edited by Hendrik Birus, Dietrich Borchmeyer, Karl Eibl, and Wilhelm Voßkamp. Frankfurt am Main: Deutscher Klassiker Verlag, 1985–2003 (=Frankfurter Ausgabe).

———. *Die Schriften zur Naturwissenschaft: Im Auftrage der Deutschen Akademie der Naturforscher (Leopoldina) zu Halle.* Edited by Wolf von Engelhardt and Dorothea Kuhn. Weimar: Hermann Böhlaus Nachfolger, 1947– (= Leopoldina Ausgabe).

———. *Werke.* Edited by Erich Trunz. 14 vols. Hamburg: Wegner, 1948–60 (= Hamburger Ausgabe). Cited as *HA*.

———. *Werke.* Edited by Gustav von Loeper, Erich Schmidt, et al., im Auftrage der Großherzogin Sophie von Sachsen. 4 parts, 133 vols. Weimar: Böhlau, 1887–1919 (= Weimarer Ausgabe). Cited as *WA*.

Gotthelf, Jeremias (Albert Bitzius). *Sämtliche Werke in 24 Bänden.* Edited by Rudolf Hunziker and Hans Bloesch. 24 vols. and 18 supplementary vols. Zurich: Rentsch, 1921–77.

Gottschalk, Friedrich. *Taschenbuch für Reisende in den Harz.* 3rd ed. Magdeburg: Heinrichshofen, 1823.

Gutzkow, Karl. *Die Ritter vom Geiste* (1850). http://gutenberg.spiegel.de/gutzkow/ritter/ritt0011.htm (accessed 18 Aug. 2006).

Hardenberg, Friedrich von. *See* Novalis.

Hegel, Georg Wilhelm Friedrich. *Werke.* Edited by Eva Moldenhauer and Karl Markus Michel. 20 vols. Frankfurt am Main: Suhrkamp, 1969–71.

Heine, Heinrich. *Historisch-kritische Gesamtausgabe der Werke.* Edited by Manfred Windfuhr. 16 vols. Hamburg: Hoffmann & Campe, 1973–97.

———. *Säkularausgabe: Werke, Briefe, Lebenszeugnisse.* Edited by Nationale Forschungs- und Gedenkstätten der klassischen deutschen Literatur and Centre National de la Recherche Scientifique. Paris and Berlin: Éditions du CNRS and Akademie, 1970–.

Herder, Johann Gottfried. *Ausgewählte Werke in Einzelausgaben.* Edited by Heinz Stolpe. Berlin and Weimar: Aufbau, 1965–.

———. *Ideen zur Philosophie der Geschichte der Menschheit.* Riga: Hartknoch, 1784–91.

Holtei, Karl von. *Karl von Holtei: Jugend in Breslau.* Edited by Helmut Koopmann. Berlin: Nicolai, 1988.

———. *Mit dem Thespiskarren durch die Lande: Karl von Holtei — Vierzig Jahre.* Edited by Norbert Hopster. Heidenheim: Verlagsanstalt, 1971.

———. *Die Vagabunden von Karl von Holtei.* Edited by Hans Körnchen. Berlin: Wegweiser, n.d.

Humboldt, Alexander von. *Kosmos für die Gegenwart.* Edited by Hanno Beck. Stuttgart: Brockhaus, 1978.

Jahn, Friedrich Ludwig. *Deutsches Volkstum.* Leipzig: Reclam, n.d.

Kant, Immanuel. *Beantwortung der Frage: Was ist Aufklärung?* In *Schriften zur Anthropologie, Geschichtsphilosophie, Politik und Pädagogik 1*, vol. 9 of *Werke*, 53 and 54.

———. *Kritik der Urteilskraft.* In vol. 8 of *Werke*, 171–620.

———. *Werke.* 10 vols. Darmstadt: Wissenschaftliche Buchgesellschaft, 1975.

Keller, Gottfried. *Sämtliche Werke.* Edited by Carl Helbling. 22 vols. Zurich: Benteli, 1926–48.

Marx, Karl. *Frühe Schriften.* Edited by Hans-Joachim Lieber and Peter Furth. 6 vols. Darmstadt: Wissenschaftliche Buchgesellschaft, 1975–81.

Marx, Karl, and Friedrich Engels. *Manifest der Kommunistischen Partei.* In Marx, *Frühe Schriften*, 813–58.

Moritz, Karl Philipp. *Anton Reiser: Ein psychologischer Roman.* Edited by Horst Günther. Frankfurt am Main and Leipzig: Insel, 1998.

Mozart, Wolfgang Amadeus. *Songs for Solo Voice and Piano.* Mineola, NY: Dover, 1973.

Müller, Wilhelm, and Franz Schubert. *Die schöne Müllerin: Die Winterreise.* Stuttgart: Reclam, 2001.

Nietzsche, Friedrich. *Kritische Studienausgabe.* Edited by Giorgio Colli and Mazzino Montinari. 15 vols. Munich: Deutscher Taschenbuch Verlag, 1999.

———. *Menschliches: Allzumenschliches I*, no. 285, in *Kritische Studienausgabe*, 2:232.

———. *Menschliches: Allzumenschliches I*, no. 638, in *Kritische Studienausgabe*, 2:362–63.

Novalis. *Schriften: Die Werke Friedrich von Hardenbergs.* Edited by Paul Kluckhohn and Richard Samuel. Stuttgart: Kohlhammer, 1977– (= Historisch-kritische Ausgabe).

Raabe, Wilhelm. *Sämtliche Werke.* Edited by Karl Hoppe, with Hans-Werner Peter and Jost Schillemeit. Freiburg im Breisgau: Klemm, 1951–94 (= Braunschweiger Ausgabe).

Rebmann, Georg Friedrich. *Werke und Briefe.* Edited by Wolfgang Ritschel. 3 vols. Berlin: Rütten & Loening, 1990.

Riehl, Wilhelm Heinrich. *Die deutsche Arbeit.* Stuttgart: Cotta, 1861.

———. *Die deutsche Familie.* Stuttgart: Cotta, 1861.

———. *Die Naturgeschichte des Volkes als Grundlage einer deutschen Social-Politik.* 4 vols. Stuttgart: Cotta, 1854–69. Vol. 4, *Wanderbuch: Als zweiter Theil zu "Land und Leute."*

Sachse, Johann Christoph. *Der deutsche Gilblaß eingeführt von Goethe: oder Leben, Wanderungen und Schicksale Johann Christoph Sachses, eines Thüringers; Von ihm selbst verfaßt.* Stuttgart and Tübingen: Cotta, 1822.

Schiller, Friedrich. *Sämtliche Werke.* Edited by Peter-André Alt, Albert Meier, and Wolfgang Riedel. 5 vols. Munich and Vienna: dtv, 2004.

———. *Schillers Werke.* Edited by Lieselotte Blumenthal, Julius Petersen, and Norbert Oellers. Weimar: Böhlau, 1943– (= Nationalausgabe).

Schlegel, August Wilhelm, and Friedrich Schlegel, eds. *Athenäum*. Berlin: n.p., 1798–1800. Reprint, Stuttgart: Cotta, 1960.

Schopenhauer, Arthur. *Gesammelte Werke*. Edited by Arthur Hübscher. 6 vols. Mannheim: Brockhaus, 1988.

Seume, Johann Gottfried. *Werke in zwei Bänden*. Edited by Jörg Drews. 2 vols. Frankfurt am Main: Deutscher Klassiker Verlag, 1993.

Steffens, Henrik. *Was ich erlebte: Aus der Erinnerung niedergeschrieben*. 10 vols. Breslau: Josef Max, 1840–44.

Sulzer, Johann Georg. *Unterredungen über die Schönheit der Natur*. Berlin: Haude, 1750.

Thaer, Daniel Albrecht. *Grundsätze der rationellen Landwirtschaft*. 2nd ed. Berlin: Reimer, 1821.

Tieck, Ludwig. *Franz Sternbalds Wanderungen* (Studienausgabe). Edited by Alfred Anger. 2nd ed. Stuttgart: Reclam, 1994.

———. *Werke in vier Bänden*. Edited by Marianne Thalmann. 4 vols. Darmstadt: Wissenschaftliche Buchgesellschaft, 1972.

Vischer, Friedrich Theodor. *Ästhetik oder Wissenschaft des Schönen*. Hildesheim: Olms, 1996.

———. *Faust: Der Tragödie dritter Theil*. Tübingen: Laupp, 1862. Reprint, Stuttgart: Reclam, 1994.

———. *Kritische Gänge*. Edited by Robert Vischer. 2nd ed. 6 vols. Munich: Meyer & Jessen, 1920–22.

Wackenroder, Wilhelm Heinrich. *Sämtliche Werke und Briefe: Historisch-kritische Ausgabe*. Edited by Silvio Vietta and Richard Littlejohns. 2 vols. Heidelberg: Winter, 1991.

## Secondary Sources

Adelung, Johann Christoph. *Grammatisch-kritisches Wörterbuch der hochdeutschen Mundart*. 2nd ed. 4 vols. Leipzig: Breitkopf & Härtel, 1798. Reprint, Hildesheim: Olms, 1970.

Adorno, Theodor W., and Max Horkheimer. *Dialectic of Enlightenment*. London: Verso, 1997.

Albrecht, Wolfgang. "Durchs 'malerische und romantische' Deutschland: Wanderliteratur der Biedermeier- und Vormärzepoche." In Albrecht and Kertscher, *Wanderzwang*, 215–38.

———. "Kultur und Physiologie des Wanderns: Einleitende Vorüberlegungen eines Germanisten zur interdisziplinären Erforschung der deutschsprachigen Wanderliteratur." In Albrecht and Kertscher, *Wanderzwang*, 1–12.

———. "Kulturgeschichtliche Perspektivierung und Literarisierung des Regionalen in den *Wanderungen durch die Mark Brandenburg*." In Wolzogen, *"Geschichte und Geschichten aus Mark Brandenburg,"* 95–110.

Albrecht, Wolfgang, and Hans-Joachim Kertscher, eds. *Wanderzwang — Wanderlust: Formen der Raum und Sozialerfahrung zwischen Aufklärung und Frühindustrialisierung.* Tübingen: Niemeyer, 1999.

Altenhofer, Norbert. *Die verlorene Augensprache: Über Heinrich Heine.* Frankfurt am Main and Leipzig: Insel, 1993.

Althaus, Hans-Joachim. "Bürgerliche Wanderlust: Anmerkungen zur Entstehung eines Kultur- und Bewegungsmusters." In Albrecht and Kertscher, *Wanderzwang*, 25–43.

Andree, Christian, and Jürgen Hein, eds. *Karl von Holtei (1798–1880): Ein schlesischer Dichter zwischen Biedermeier und Realismus.* Würzburg: Korn, 2005.

Assmann, Jan. *Das kulturelle Gedächtnis: Schrift, Erinnerung und politische Identität in frühen Hochkulturen.* 5th ed. Munich: C. H. Beck, 2005.

Bachmann-Medick, Doris. *Kultur als Text: Die anthropologische Wende in der Kulturwissenschaft.* Frankfurt am Main: Fischer, 1996.

———. "Kulturelle Spielräume: Drama und Theater im Licht ethnologischer Ritualforschung," in *Kultur als Text*, 98–121; here, 103.

Bahr, Erhard, ed. *Johann Wolfgang Goethe: Wilhelm Meisters Lehrjahre: Erläuterungen und Dokumente.* Stuttgart: Reclam, 1982.

———. *The Novel as Archive: The Genesis, Reception, and Criticism of Goethe's* Wilhelm Meisters Wanderjahre. Columbia, SC: Camden House, 1998.

———. "Wilhelm Meisters Wanderjahre oder die Entsagenden." In Witte, *Goethe-Handbuch*, 3:186–231.

Barkhoff, Jürgen. "Theatricality in Goethe's *Wilhelm Meisters Lehrjahre*." In *Goethe and Schubert: Across the Divide* (Proceedings of the Conference "Goethe and Schubert in Perspective and Performance," Trinity College Dublin, 4–5 Apr. 2003), edited by Lorraine Byrne and Dan Farrelly, 90–101. Dublin: Carysfort, 2004.

Barkhoff, Jürgen, and Eda Sagarra, eds. *Anthropologie und Literatur um 1800.* Munich: Iudicium, 1992.

Bartels, Adolf. *Jeremias Gotthelf: Leben und Schriften.* Leipzig: Meyer, 1902.

Bausinger, Hermann, Klaus Beyrer, and Wolfgang Griep, eds. *Reisekultur: Von der Pilgerfahrt zum modernen Tourismus.* Munich: Beck, 1991.

Bayertz, Kurt. "Der aufrechte Gang: Ursprung der Kultur und des Denkens; Eine anthropologische Debatte im Anschluß an Helvétius' *De L'Esprit*." In *Zwischen Empirisierung und Konstruktionsleistung: Anthropologie im 18. Jahrhundert*, edited by Jörn Garber and Heinz Thoma, 59–75. Tübingen: Niemeyer, 2004.

Becker, Carolyn. "From the Jacobins to the Young Germans: The Liberal Travel Literature from 1785 to 1840." Ph.D. diss., U of Wisconsin, 1974.

Berlin, Isaiah. "Herder and the Enlightenment." In *The Proper Study of Mankind: An Anthology of Essays*, edited by Henry Hardy and Roger Hausheer, 359–435. London: Pimlico, 1998.

———. *The Roots of Romanticism.* Edited by Henry Hardy. London: Pimlico, 2000.

Berman, Marshall. *All That Is Solid Melts into Air: The Experience of Modernity.* New York: Simon & Schuster, 1982.

Blackbourn, David. *The History of Germany, 1780–1918: The Long Nineteenth Century.* Oxford: Blackwell, 2003.

Blessin, Stefan. *Die Romane Goethes.* Königstein im Taunus: Athenäum, 1979.

Bloch, Ernst. "Hebel, Gotthelf und bäurisches Tao." In Bloch, *Gesamtausgabe*, 9:365–84; here, 383. Frankfurt am Main: Suhrkamp, 1959–.

Bluntschli, Johann Caspar. *Die Kommunisten in der Schweiz nach den bei Weitling vorgefundenen Papieren.* Zurich: Orell & Füssli, 1843.

Boahen, A. Adu. *African Perspectives on Colonialism.* 4th ed. Baltimore: Johns Hopkins, 1992.

Böhme, Hartmut. *Natur und Subjekt.* Frankfurt am Main: Suhrkamp, 1988.

———. "Das Steinerne: Anmerkungen zur Theorie des Erhabenen aus dem Blick des 'Menschenfremdesten.'" In Pries, *Das Erhabene*, 119–41.

Borchmeyer, Dieter. *Höfische Gesellschaft und französische Revolution: Adliges und bürgerliches Wertsystem im Urteil der Weimarer Klassik.* Kronberg im Taunus: Athenäum, 1977.

Bosse, Heinrich. "Zur Sozialgeschichte des Wanderliedes." In Albrecht and Kertscher, *Wanderzwang*, 135–58.

Bourdieu, Pierre. *Distinction: A Social Critique of the Judgement of Taste.* London: Routledge, 1986.

———. *Language and Symbolic Power.* Cambridge: Polity, 1991.

Boyle, Nicholas. *Goethe: The Poet and the Age.* Oxford: Oxford UP, 1992–.

Brannigan, John. *New Historicism and Cultural Materialism.* London: Macmillan, 1998.

Braun, Karl. *Die Vagabundenfrage.* Berlin: Simion, 1883.

Braungart, Wolfgang. *Ritual und Literatur.* Tübingen: Niemeyer, 1996.

Brenner, Peter J. "Die Einheit der Welt: Zur Entzauberung der Fremde und Verfremdung der Heimat in Raabes 'Abu Telfan.'" *Jahrbuch der Raabe-Gesellschaft* 1989: 45–62.

———. *Der Reisebericht in der deutschen Literatur: Ein Forschungsüberblick als Vorstudie zu einer Gattungsgeschichte.* Tübingen: Niemeyer, 1990.

Brinkmann, Richard, and Waltraud Wiethölter, eds. *Dichter über ihre Dichtungen: Theodor Fontane.* 2 vols. Munich: Heimeran, 1973.

Bruford, Walter Horace. *The German Tradition of Self-Cultivation: 'Bildung' from Humboldt to Thomas Mann.* Cambridge: Cambridge UP, 1975.

Chernaik, Judith. "No resting could he find: The Mariner, the Dutchman and the Wandering Jew." *Times Literary Supplement*, 24 Jan. 2003.

Colin, Amy, and Elisabeth Strenger, eds. *Brücken über dem Abgrund: Auseinandersetzungen mit jüdischen Leidenserfahrung, Antisemitismus und Exil.* Festschrift für Harry Zohn. Munich: Fink, 1994.

Cooper, Anthony Ashley (Third Earl of Shaftesbury). *An Inquiry Concerning Virtue, or Merit* 1699. Reprint, Manchester, UK: Manchester UP, 1977.

Cozic, Alain, Françoise Knopper, and Alain Ruiz, eds. *Heine voyageur.* Toulouse: Mirail, 1999.

Craig, Edward, ed. *Routledge Encyclopaedia of Philosophy.* 10 vols. London: Routledge, 1998.

Degering, Thomas. *Das Elend der Entsagung: Goethes Wilhelm Meisters Wanderjahre.* Bonn: Bouvier, 1982.

Denkler, Horst. *Wilhelm Raabe: Legende — Leben — Literatur.* Tübingen: Niemeyer, 1989.

Derrida, Jacques. "Avoir l'oreille de la philosophie." In *Écarts: Quatre essais à propos de Jacques Derrida*, edited by Lucette Finas, 301–12. Paris: Fayard, 1973.

Diersen, Inge. "Büchners *Lenz* im Kontext der Entwicklung von Erzählprosa im 19. Jahrhundert." *Georg-Büchner-Jahrbuch* 7 1988/89 (1991): 91–125.

Dingelstedt, Franz. *Lieder eines kosmopolitischen Nachtwächters.* 1841. Reprint, Leipzig: Klinckhardt & Biermann, 1923.

———. *Wanderbuch.* 2 vols. Leipzig: Einhorn, 1839–43.

*Duden: Das große Wörterbuch der deutschen Sprache.* 6 vols. Mannheim: Bibliographisches Institut, 1976–81.

Düntzer, Heinrich. *Goethes Faust.* 1850. 2nd ed., Leipzig: Dyk, 1857.

Erhart, Walter. "'Alles wie erzählt': Fontanes Wanderungen durch die Mark Brandenburg." *Jahrbuch der deutschen Schillergesellschaft* 36 (1992): 229–54.

———. "Die Wanderungen durch die Mark Brandenburg." In Grawe and Nürnberger, *Fontane Handbuch*, 818–50.

Erler, Gotthard. "Fontanes *Wanderungen* heute." *Fontane-Blätter* 3 (1975): 353–68.

Fairley, Barker. *Wilhelm Raabe: An Introduction to His Novels.* Oxford: Clarendon, 1961.

Fambach, Oscar. *Goethe und seine Kritiker.* Düsseldorf: Ehlermann, 1953.

Feyerabend, Carl. *Kosmopolitische Wanderungen durch Preußen, Liefland, Litthauen, Vollhynien, Podolien, Galizien und Schlesien in den Jahren 1795 bis 1797.* In *Briefen an einen Freund.* 4 vols. Danzig, 1798–1802.

Fischer, Hubertus. "Märkische Bilder: Ein Versuch über Fontanes Wanderungen durch die Mark Brandenburg, ihre Bilder und ihre Bildlichkeit." *Fontane Blätter* 60 (1995): 117–42.

Fontius, Martin, and Annaliese Klingenberg, eds. *Karl Philipp Moritz und das 18. Jahrhundert: Bestandaufnahmen — Korrekturen — Neuansätze.* Tübingen: Niemeyer, 1995.

Foucault, Michel. *Madness and Civilization.* London: Routledge, 2002.

———. *The Order of Things.* London: Routledge, 1994.

Frank, Manfred. *Kaltes Herz — Unendliche Fahrt — Neue Mythologie.* Frankfurt am Main: Suhrkamp, 1989.

———. *Die unendliche Fahrt: Die Geschichte des fliegenden Holländers und verwandter Motive.* Leipzig: Reclam, 1995.

———. *Die Unhintergehbarkeit von Individualität: Reflexionen über Subjekt, Person und Individuum aus Anlaß ihrer 'postmodernen' Toterklärung.* Frankfurt am Main: Suhrkamp, 1986.

Frenzel, Elisabeth. *Stoff- Motiv- und Symbolforschung.* 3rd ed. Stuttgart: Metzler, 1970.

Fricke, Harald, Georg Braungart, Klaus Grubmüller, Jan-Dirk Müller, Friedrich Vollhardt, and Klaus Weimar, eds. *Reallexikon der deutschen Literaturwissenschaft.* 3rd ed. 3 vols. Berlin: DeGruyter, 1997–2003.

Fuhrmann, Helmut, ed. *Wilhelm Meister und seine Nachfahren: Vorträge des 4. Kasseler Goetheseminars.* Kassel: Wenderoth, 2000.

Galley, Eberhard, et al., eds. *Heinrich Heines Werk im Urteil der Zeitgenossen.* 13 vols. Hamburg: Hoffmann & Campe, 1981–2006.

Geertz, Clifford. *The Interpretation of Cultures.* New York: Basic Books, 2000.

Gersch, Hubert, and Stefan Schmalhaus. "Quellenmaterialien und 'reproduktive Phantasie': Untersuchungen zur Schreibmethode Georg Büchners; Seine Verwertung von Paul Merlins Trivialisierung des Lenz-Stoffs und von anderen Vorlagen." *Georg Büchner Jahrbuch* 8 (1990–94): 69–103.

Gerth, Klaus. " 'Das Wechselspiel des Lebens': Ein Versuch 'Wilhelm Meisters Lehrjahre' (wieder) einmal anders zu lesen." In Fuhrmann, *Wilhelm Meister und seine Nachfahren*, 12–32.

Gille, Klaus F. "Der Berg und die Seele: Überlegungen zu Tieck: 'Der Runenberg.' " *Neophilologus* 77 (1993): 611–23.

———, ed. *Goethes Wilhelm Meister: Zur Rezeptionsgeschichte der Lehr- und Wanderjahre.* Königstein im Taunus: Athenäum, 1979.

Godwin-Jones, Robert. "Soziale und politische Modelle in George Sands 'Le compagnon du tour de France' und Gotthelfs 'Jakobs des Handwerksgesellen Wanderungen durch die Schweiz.' " In Pape, Thomke, and Tschopp, *Erzählkunst und Volkserziehung*, 267–88.

Graham, Ilse. *Goethe: Portrait of the Artist.* Berlin and New York: Walter de Gruyter, 1977.

Grawe, Christian, and Helmuth Nürnberger, eds. *Fontane Handbuch.* Stuttgart: Kröner, 2000.

Greenblatt, Stephen. "Introduction: The Forms of Power." *Genre* 7 (1982): 3–6.

———. "Invisible Bullets: Renaissance Authority and Its Subversion, Henry IV and Henry V." In *Political Shakespeare: Essays in Cultural Materialism*, edited by Jonathon Dollimore and Alan Sinfield, 18–47. 2nd ed. Manchester: Manchester UP, 1994.

———. *Renaissance Self-Fashioning.* Chicago, IL and London: U of Chicago P, 1980.

Gregorovius, Ferdinand. *Goethes Wilhelm Meister in seinen socialistischen Elementen entwickelt.* Königsberg: n.p., 1849.

Grimm, Jacob, and Wilhelm Grimm. *Deutsches Wörterbuch.* 33 vols. Leipzig: Hirzel, 1854–1971.

Grimminger, Rolf, et al., eds. *Hanser Sozialgeschichte der deutschen Literatur, 16. Jh. bis zur Gegenwart.* Munich: Hanser, 1980–.

Groppe, Sabine. *Das Ich am Ende des Schreibens.* Würzburg: Königshausen & Neumann, 1990.

Grosche, Stefan. *"Zarten Seelen ist gar viel gegönnt.": Naturwissenschaft und Kunst im Briefwechsel zwischen C. G. Carus und Goethe.* Göttingen: Wallstein, 2001.

Grossklaus, Götz. "Georg Büchners *Lenz:* Zum Verlust des sozialen Ortes." *Recherches Germaniques* 12 (1982): 68–77.

Grubacic, Slobodan. *Heines Erzählprosa: Versuch einer Analyse.* Stuttgart: Kohlhammer, 1975.

Haas, Rosemarie. *Die Turmgesellschaft in "Wilhelm Meisters Lehrjahren": Zur Geschichte des Geheimbundromans und der Romantheorie im 18. Jahrhundert.* Frankfurt am Main: Peter Lang, 1975.

Hacking, Ian. *Mad Travelers: Reflections on the Reality of Transient Mental Illnesses.* Cambridge, MA: Harvard, 1998.

Hardtwig, Wolfgang. *Vormärz: Der monarchische Staat und das Bürgertum.* 4th ed. Munich: dtv, 1998.

Haslinger, Josef. *Die Ästhetik des Novalis.* Königstein im Taunus: Hain, 1981.

Hasubek, Peter. "'Ruhe' und 'Bewegung' in Büchners *Lenz:* Versuch einer Stilanalyse." *Germanisch-Romanische Monatszeitschrift* 19 (1969): 33–59.

Henkel, Arthur. *Entsagung: Eine Studie zu Goethes Altersroman.* 1954. 2nd ed., Tübingen: Niemeyer, 1964.

Hermand, Jost. *Der frühe Heine: Ein Kommentar zu den "Reisebildern."* Munich: Winkler, 1976.

———. *Das junge Deutschland: Texte und Dokumente.* Stuttgart: Reclam, 1966.

Herwig, Henriette. *Das ewig Männliche zieht uns hinab: Wilhelm Meisters Wanderjahre; Geschlechterdifferenz, Sozialer Wandel, Historische Anthropologie.* Tübingen and Basel: Francke, 1997.

Hess, Günter. "Panorama und Denkmal: Erinnerung als Denkform zwischen Vormärz und Gründerzeit." In Martino, *Literatur in der sozialen Bewegung,* 130–206.

Hildebrand, Olaf. *Emanzipation und Versöhnung: Aspekte des Sensualismus im Werk Heinrich Heines unter besonderer Berücksichtigung der "Reisebilder."* Tübingen: Niemeyer, 2001.

Hobsbawm, Eric John. *Die Blütezeit des Kapitals: Eine Kulturgeschichte der Jahre 1848–1875.* Frankfurt am Main: Fischer, 1980.

———. *Primitive Rebels: Studies in Archaic Forms of Social Protest in the 19th and 20th Centuries.* New York: Norton, 1965.

Holl, Hans-Peter. "*Jakobs Wanderungen:* Ein unbekannter Roman von Jeremias Gotthelf." *Alpenhorn-Kalender* 72 (1997): 88–92.

Hoppe-Sailer, Richard. "Genesis und Prozeß: Elemente der Goethe Rezeption bei Carl Gustav Carus, Paul Klee und Joseph Beuys." In Matussek, *Goethe und die Verzeitlichung der Natur*, 276–300.

Hotho, Heinrich Gustav. Review of Goethe's *Wanderjahre.* 2nd ed. In *Jahrbücher für wissenschaftliche Kritik*, Dec. 1829 and Mar. 1830.

Jantsch, Erich. *Die Selbstorganisation des Universum: Vom Urknall zum menschlichen Geist.* Munich: dtv, 1979.

Jaspers, Karl. "Goethes Menschlichkeit." *Basler Universitätsreden* 26 (1949): 11–33.

Jauss, Hans Robert, ed. *Die nicht mehr schönen Künste: Grenzphänomene des Ästhetischen.* Munich: Fink, 1968.

Jost, Erdmut. "Das poetische Auge: Visuelle Programmatik in Theodor Fontanes Landschaftsbildern aus Schottland und der Mark Brandenburg." In Wolzogen, *"Geschichte und Geschichten aus Mark Brandenburg,"* 64–80.

Kafitz, Dieter. "Die Appelfunktion der Außenseitergestalten: Zur näheren Bestimmung des Realismus der mittlerern und späteren Romane Raabes." In Lensing and Peter, *Wilhelm Raabe*, 51–76.

Kauffman, Kai. *"Es ist nur ein Wien!" Stadtbeschreibungen von Wien, 1700 bis 1873: Geschichte eines literarischen Genres.* Vienna, Cologne, and Weimar: Böhlau, 1994.

Kehn, Wolfgang. "Die Schönheiten der Natur gemeinschaftlich betrachten: Zum Zusammenhang von Freundschaft, ästhetischer Naturerfahrung und 'Gartenrevolution' in der Spätaufklärung." In Mauser and Becker-Cantarino, *Frauenfreundschaft-Männerfreundschaft*, 167–93.

Kermode, Frank. *The Sense of an Ending: Studies in the Theory of Fiction.* New York: Oxford UP, 1967.

Klein, Ulrich. *Die deutschsprachige Reisesatire im 18. Jahrhundert.* Heidelberg: Winter, 1997.

———. "Reiseliteraturforschung im deutschsprachigen Raum." *Euphorion* 87 (1993): 286–318.

Knapp, Gerhard P. *Georg Büchner*, 3rd ed. Stuttgart and Weimar: Metzler, 2000.

Knopper, Françoise. "Heine et la tradition des chroniques de voyage." In Cozic, Knopper, and Ruiz, *Heine voyageur*, 99–111.

Komar, Kathleen L. "The Structure of Heine's *Harzreise:* Should We Take the Narrator at His Word?" *Germanic Review* 56 (1981): 128–33.

König, Gudrun. *Eine Kulturgeschichte des Spazierganges: Spuren einer bürgerlichen Praktik, 1780–1850.* Vienna: Böhlau, 1996.

Köpke, Rudolf. *Ludwig Tieck: Erinnerungen aus dem Leben des Dichters nach dessen mündlichen und schriftlichen Mitteilungen.* Leipzig: Brockhaus, 1855. Reprint, Darmstadt: Wissenschaftliche Buchgesellschaft, 1970.

Korff, Hermann August. *Geist der Goethezeit: Versuch einer ideelen Entwicklung der klassisch-romantischen Literaturgeschichte.* 3rd ed. 5 vols. Leipzig: Koehler & Amelang, 1957.

Kremer, Detlef. *Prosa der Romantik.* Stuttgart: Metzler, 1996.

Kristeva, Julia. *Sémeoitiké: Recherches pour une sémanalyse.* Paris: Éditions du Seuil, 1969.

Kubik, Sabine. *Krankheit und Medizin im literarischen Werk Georg Büchners.* Stuttgart: M&P, 1991.

Kubitschek, Peter. "Zur tödlichen Stille der verkehrten Welt: Zu Georg Büchners *Lenz.*" In Hans-Georg Werner, *Studien zu Georg Büchner*, 86–104.

Landau, Paul. *Karl von Holteis Romane: Ein Beitrag zur Geschichte der deutschen Unterhaltungs-Literatur.* Leipzig: Hesse, 1904.

Lauster, Martina. *Sketches of the Nineteenth Century: European Journalism and Its "Physiologies" (1830–50).* Basingstoke, UK: Palgrave Macmillan, 2007.

———. "Walter Benjamin's Myth of the *Flâneur.*" *Modern Language Review* 102 (2007): 139–56.

Leistner, Bernd, ed. *Deutsche Erzählprosa der frühen Restaurationszeit.* Tübingen: Niemeyer, 1995.

———. "Heinrich Heine: Die Harzreise." In *Deutsche Erzählprosa der frühen Restaurationszeit*, 272–315.

Lensing, Leo A., and Hans-Werner Peter, eds. *Wilhelm Raabe: Studien zu seinem Leben und Werk.* Braunschweig: pp-Verlag, 1981.

Lepenies, Wolf. *Das Ende der Naturgeschichte: Wandel kultureller Selbstverständlichkeiten in den Wissenschaften des 18. und 19. Jahrhunderts.* Munich and Vienna: Hanser, 1976.

Lovejoy, Arthur Oncken. *The Great Chain of Being: A Study of the History of an Idea.* Cambridge, MA: Harvard, 1998.

Lukács, Georg. *Die Theorie des Romans: Ein geschichtsphilosophischer Versuch über die Formen der großen Epik.* Berlin: Neuwied, 1963.

Lützeler, Paul Michael, ed. *Romane und Erzählungen zwischen Romantik und Realismus: Neue Interpretationen.* Stuttgart: Reclam, 1983.

Mähl, Hans-Joachim. *Die Idee des goldenen Zeitalters im Werk des Novalis: Studien zur Wesensbestimmung der frühromantischen Utopie und zu ihren ideengeschichtlichen Voraussetzungen.* Heidelberg: Winter, 1965.

Mahoney, Dennis F. *Friedrich von Hardenberg (Novalis).* Stuttgart and Weimar: Metzler, 2001.

Maierhofer, Waltraud. *"Wilhelm Meisters Wanderjahre" und der Roman des Nebeneinander.* Bielefeld: Aisthesis, 1990.

Mandelkow, Karl Robert, ed. *Briefe an Goethe.* 2 vols. Hamburg: Wegner, 1982.

———. *Goethe im Urteil seiner Kritiker.* 4 vols. Munich: C. H. Beck, 1977–84.

Mandelkow, Karl Robert, ed. *Goethe in Deutschland: Rezeptionsgeschichte eines Klassikers.* 2 vols. Munich, Beck, 1980–89.

———. *Goethes Briefe.* 4 vols. Hamburg: Wegner, 1962–76.

Mann, Thomas. "Die Kunst des Romans." In *Gesammelte Werke.* 13 vols. 2nd ed. Frankfurt am Main: S. Fischer, 1974.

Marquard, Odo. "Anthropologie." In Ritter and Gründer, *Historisches Wörterbuch der Philosophie*, vol. 1, cols. 362–74.

Martini, Fritz. "Bildungsroman: Zur Geschichte des Wortes und der Theorie." *Deutsche Vierteljahresschrift* 35 (1961): 44–63.

Martino, Alberto, ed. *Literatur in der sozialen Bewegung: Aufsätze und Forschungsberichte zum 19. Jahrhundert.* Tübingen: Niemeyer, 1977.

Matussek, Peter, ed. *Goethe und die Verzeitlichung der Natur.* Munich: Beck, 1998.

Mauser, Wolfram, and Barbara Becker-Cantarino, eds. *Frauenfreundschaft-Männerfreundschaft: Literarische Diskurse im 18. Jahrhundert.* Tübingen: Niemeyer, 1991.

May, Kurt. "'Wilhelm Meisters Lehrjahre,' ein Bildungsroman?" *Deutsche Vierteljahresschrift* 31 (1957), 1–37.

Mayer, Hans. "Wilhelm Raabe: *Abu Telfan oder die Heimkehr vom Mondgebirge.*" In Lensing and Peter, *Wilhelm Raabe*, 128–32.

———. *Zur deutschen Klassik und Romantik.* Pfullingen, Germany: Neske, 1963.

Meuthen, Erich. "'. . . denn er selbst war hier anders': Zum Problem des Identitätsverlusts in Ludwig Tiecks 'Sternbald'-Roman." *Jahrbuch der deutschen Schiller-Gesellschaft* 30 (1986): 383–403.

Meyer, Hermann. *Der Sonderling in der deutschen Dichtung.* Munich: Hanser, 1963.

Miller, J. Hillis. *Theory Now and Then.* Hemel Hempstead, UK: Harvester Wheatsheaf, 1991.

Miller, Norbert. *Der Wanderer: Goethe in Italien.* Munich: Hanser, 2002.

Möbus, Frank, and Anne Bohnenkamp. *Mit Gunst und Verlaub! Wandernde Handwerker: Tradition und Alternative.* 5th ed. Göttingen: Wallstein, 2001.

Morgenstern, Karl. "Über das Wesen des Bildungsromans." *Inländisches Museum* 1, no. 3 (1820): 13–27.

Müller, Christian. "Subjektkonstituierung in einer kontingenten Welt: Erfahrungen zweier Afrika-Heimkehrer — Gottfried Kellers 'Pankraz, der Schmoller' und Wilhelm Raabes 'Abu Telfan.'" *Jahrbuch der Raabe-Gesellschaft* 2002, 82–110.

Müller, Jan-Dirk, et al., eds. *Reallexikon der deutschen Literaturwissenschaft.* 3 vols. Berlin and New York: Walter de Gruyter, 1997–2003.

Müller-Seidel, Walter. *Theodor Fontane: Soziale Romankunst in Deutschland.* 2nd ed. Stuttgart: Metzler, 1980.

Müller-Seidel, Walter, and Wolfgang Riedel, eds. *Die Weimarer Klassik und ihre Geheimbünde.* Würzburg: Königshausen & Neumann, 2003.

Mundt, Theodor. Review of the *Wanderjahre.* 2nd ed. *Blätter für literarische Unterhaltung.* Leipzig. 1830, no. 266ff.

Muret, Gabriel. *Jéremie Gotthelf: Sa vie et ses oeuvres.* Paris: Gap, 1913.

Muschg, Adolf. *Goethe als Emigrant: Auf der Suche nach dem Grünem bei einem alten Dichter.* Frankfurt: Suhrkamp, 1986.

Neubauer, John. "Romantische Wandervögel." In Oesterle, *Jugend*, 333–48.

Neuhaus, Volker. "Die Archivfiktion in *Wilhelm Meisters Wanderjahren.*" *Euphorion* 62 (1968): 13–27.

Neumann, Gerhard, and Sigrid Weigel, eds. *Lesbarkeit der Kultur: Literaturwissenschaften zwischen Kulturtechnik und Ethnographie.* Munich: Fink, 2000.

Niccolini, Elisabetta. *Der Spaziergang des Schriftstellers: "Lenz" von Georg Büchner, "Der Spaziergang" von Robert Walser, "Gehen" von Thomas Bernhard.* Stuttgart and Weimar: Metzler, 2000.

Nicolson, Marjorie Hope. *Mountain Gloom and Mountain Glory: The Development of the Aesthetics of the Infinite.* Seattle, WA: U of Washington P, 1997.

Nisbet, Hugh Barr. *Herder and the Philosophy and History of Science.* Cambridge: Modern Humanities Research Association, 1970.

———. "Naturgeschichte und Humangeschichte bei Goethe, Herder und Kant." In Matussek, *Goethe und die Verzeitlichung der Natur*, 15–43.

Oesterle, Günter, ed. *Jugend — ein romantisches Konzept?* Würzburg: Königshausen & Neumann, 1997.

———. "Die Schule minutiösen Sehens im Vormärz: Zur Raffinesse des Andeutens im Wechselspiel von Bild und Text." In *Vormärzliteratur in europäischer Perspektive*, ed. Helmut Koopmann and Martina Lauster, 3 vols., 1:293–305. Bielefeld: Aisthesis, 1996–2000.

Oesterle, Ingrid. "'Ach die Kunst — Ach die erbärmliche Wirklichkeit': Ästhetische Modellierung des Lebens und ihre Dekomposition in Georg Büchners *Lenz.*" In Spies, *Ideologie und Utopie in der deutschen Literatur der Neuzeit*, 58–67.

Osols-Wehden, Irmgard. *Pilgerfahrt und Narrenreise: Der Einfluß der Dichtungen Dantes und Ariosts auf den frühromantischen Roman in Deutschland.* Hildesheim: Weidmann, 1998.

*Oxford English Dictionary.* 2nd ed. 20 vols. Oxford: Oxford UP, 1989.

Pabel, Klaus. *Heines "Reisebilder": Ästhetisches Bedürfnis und politisches Interesse am Ende der Kunstperiode.* Munich: Fink, 1977.

Pape, Walter, Hellmut Thomke, and Silvia Serena Tschopp, eds. *Erzählkunst und Volkserziehung: Das literarische Werk des Jeremias Gotthelf.* Tübingen: Niemeyer, 1999.

Paulin, Roger. *Ludwig Tieck.* Stuttgart: Metzler, 1987.

Perraudin, Michael. *Literature, the* Volk *and Revolution in 19th Century Germany.* Oxford: Berghahn, 2000.

Pfister, Manfred. "Konzepte der Intertextualität." In *Intertextualität: Formen, Funktionen, anglistische Fallstudien*, edited by Ulrich Broich and Manfred Pfister, 1–30. Tübingen: Niemeyer, 1985.

Plachta, Bodo. "Preußens 'gesunder Kern': Zu Theodor Fontanes 'Wanderungen durch die Mark Brandenburg.'" *Germanisch-Romanische Monatsschrift* 44 (1994): 177–90.

Plumpe, Gerhard. "Das Reale und die Kunst: Ästhetische Theorie im 19. Jahrhundert." in Grimminger, *Hanser*, 6:242–307.

Preisendanz, Wolfgang. "Der Funktionsübergang von Dichtung und Publizistik bei Heine." In Jauss, *Die nicht mehr schönen Künste*, 343–74.

Pries, Christine, ed. *Das Erhabene: Zwischen Grenzerfahrung und Größenwahn.* Weinheim, Germany: VCH, Acta humaniora, 1989.

Reed, T. J. "Number the Years." *Times Literary Supplement*, 22 Jul. 2005, 7.

Reuchlein, Georg. *Bürgerliche Gesellschaft, Psychiatrie und Literatur: Zur Entwicklung der Wahnsinnsthematik in der deutschen Literatur des späten 18. und frühen 19. Jahrhunderts.* Munich: Fink, 1986.

Reuter, Hans-Heinrich. *Fontane*, 2 vols. Munich: Nymphenburger, 1968.

Richards, Robert J. *The Romantic Conception of Life.* Chicago and London: U of Chicago P, 2002.

Riedel, Wolfgang. "Anthropologie und Literatur in der deutschen Spätaufklärung: Skizze einer Forschungslandschaft." *Internationales Archiv für Sozialgeschichte der deutschen Literatur* 6 (1994): 93–157.

———. "Literarische Anthropologie: Eine Unterscheidung." In *Wahrnehmen und Handeln: Perspektiven einer Literaturanthropologie*, edited by Wolfgang Braungart, Klaus Ridder, and Friedmar Apel, 337–66. Bielefeld: Aisthesis, 2004.

———. *"Der Spaziergang": Ästhetik der Landschaft und Geschichtsphilosophie der Natur bei Schiller.* Würzburg: Königshausen & Neumann, 1989.

Ritter, Gerhard A. *Arbeiter, Arbeiterbewegung und soziale Ideen in Deutschland: Beiträge zur Geschichte des 19. und 20. Jahrhunderts.* Munich: Beck, 1996.

Ritter, Joachim. "Landschaft: Zur Funktion des ästhetischen in der modernen Gesellschaft." In *Subjektivität: Sechs Aufsätze*, 150–51.

———. *Subjektivität: Sechs Aufsätze.* 8th ed. Frankfurt am Main: Suhrkamp, 1989.

Ritter, Joachim, and Karlfried Gründer, eds. *Historisches Wörterbuch der Philosophie.* 12 vols. Basel: Schwabe, 1971–2004.

Robertson, Ritchie. "Herr Peregrinus: Persona, Race and Gender in Heine's *Die Harzreise.*" In Colin and Strenger, *Brücken über dem Abgrund*, 145–57.

Rosenkranz, Karl. *Göthe und seine Werke.* Königsberg: Bornträger, 1847.

Ryan, Kiernan, ed. *New Historicism and Cultural Materialism: A Reader.* London: Arnold, 1996.

Sagarra, Eda. "Noch einmal: Fontane und Bismarck." *Fontane-Blätter* 53 (1992): 29–42.

Sammons, Jeffrey L. *Heinrich Heine: The Elusive Poet.* New Haven, CT, and London: Yale UP, 1969.

Sauerland, Karol. "Heinrich Heines *Reisebilder* — ein besonderes literarisches Genre?" In *Heinrich Heine: Streitbarer Humanist und volksverbundener Dichter; Internationale wissenschaftliche Konferenz aus Anlaß des 175. Geburtstages von Heinrich Heine vom 6. zum 9. Dezember 1972 in Weimar*, 145–58 and 472–74.

Schillemeit, Jost. "Berlin und die Berliner." *Jahrbuch der deutschen Schillergesellschaft* 30 (1986): 34–82.

Schimpf-Reinhardt, Hans. "'Ein besseres Los zu suchen und zu finden': Deutsche Auswanderer." In Bausinger, Beyrer and Griep, *Reisekultur*, 108–14.

Schings, Hans-Jürgen. "Agathon — Anton Reiser — Wilhelm Meister: Zur Pathogenese des modernen Subjekts im Bildungsroman." In Wittkowski, *Goethe im Kontext*, 42–68.

———. "'Gedenke zu leben': Goethes Lebenskunst." In Fuhrmann, *Wilhelm Meister und seine Nachfahren*, 33–52.

———. *Melancholie und Aufklärung: Melancholiker und ihre Kritiker in Erfahrungsseelenkunde und Literatur des 18. Jahrhunderts.* Stuttgart: Metzler, 1977.

———. "'Wilhelm Meister' und das Erbe der Illuminaten." In Müller-Seidel and Riedel, *Die Weimarer Klassik und ihre Geheimbünde*, 177–203.

Schlaffer, Heinz. "Exoterik und Esoterik in Goethes Romanen." *Goethe-Jahrbuch* 95 (1978): 212–17.

Schlechta, Karl. *Goethes Wilhelm Meister.* Frankfurt am Main: Suhrkamp, 1985.

Schmidlin, Bruno. *Das Motiv des Wanderns bei Goethe.* Ph.D. diss., University of Bern, 1953. Reprint, Winterthur, Switzerland: Keller, 1963.

Schmidt, Harald. *Melancholie und Landschaft: Die psychotische und ästhetische Struktur der Landschaftsschilderungen in Georg Büchners Lenz.* Opladen: Westdeutscher Verlag, 1994.

———. "Schizophrenie oder Melancholie?: Zur problematischen Differentialdiagnostik in Georg Büchners *Lenz*." *Zeitschrift für deutsche Philologie* 117 (1998): 516–42.

Schmidt, Thomas E. *Die Geschichtlichkeit des frühromantischen Romans: Literarische Reaktionen auf Erfahrungen eines kulturellen Wandels.* Tübingen: Niemeyer, 1989.

Schößler, Franziska. *Goethes Lehr- und Wanderjahre: Eine Kulturgeschichte der Moderne.* Tübingen and Basel: Francke, 2002.

Schutjer, Karin. "Beyond the Wandering Jew: Anti-Semitism und Narrative Supersession in Goethe's *Wilhelm Meisters Wanderjahre*." *German Quarterly* 77 (2004): 389–407.

Schweikert, Uwe, ed. *Dichter über ihre Dichtungen: Ludwig Tieck.* 3 vols. Munich: Heimeran, 1971.

Sebald, Winfried G. *Logis in einem Landhaus: Über Gottfried Keller, Johann Peter Hebel, Robert Walser und andere*, 2nd ed. Frankfurt am Main: Fischer, 2000.

Selbmann, Rolf. *Der deutsche Bildungsroman.* Stuttgart: Metzler, 1984.

Sengle, Friedrich. *Biedermeierzeit: Deutsche Literatur im Spannungsfeld zwischen Restauration und Revolution, 1815–1848.* 3 vols. Stuttgart: Metzler, 1971–80.

Siebers, Winfried. "Ungleiche Lehrfahrten: Kavaliere und Gelehrten." In Bausinger, Beyrer, and Griep, *Reisekultur*, 47–57.

Simmel, Georg. "Die Großstädte und das Geistesleben." 1903. In *Brücke und Tür: Essays des Philosophen zur Geschichte, Religion, Kunst und Gesellschaft*, 227–42. Stuttgart: Koehler, 1957.

Skorna, Hans-Jürgen. *Das Wandermotiv im Roman der Goethezeit.* Ph.D. diss., University of Cologne, 1961.

Spies, Bernhard. ed. *Ideologie und Utopie in der deutschen Literatur der Neuzeit.* Würzburg: Königshausen & Neumann, 1995.

Stadler, Ulrich. "Wilhelm Meisters unterlassene Revolte: Individuelle Geschichte und Gesellschaftsgeschichte in Goethes *Lehrjahren.*" *Euphorion* 74 (1980): 360–74.

Stein, Monika-Yvonne. *Im Mantel Goethes und Faust auf der Fährte: Wilhelm Raabes* Faust- *und Goethe-Rezeption in seinem Roman Abu Telfan oder Die Heimkehr vom Mondgebirge.* Frankfurt am Main: Peter Lang, 2005.

Swales, Martin. *Epochenbuch Realismus: Romane und Erzählungen.* Berlin: Schmidt, 1997.

Taylor, Charles. *Sources of the Self: The Making of the Modern Identity.* Cambridge: Cambridge UP, 1989.

Turner, Victor. *From Ritual to Theatre: The Human Seriousness of Play.* New York: PAJ, 1982.

———. "Liminal to Liminoid in Play, Flow, Ritual: An Essay in Comparative Symbolology," in *From Ritual to Theatre*, 20–60.

Ueding, Gert. "Klassik und Romantik im Zeitalter der französischen Revolution." In Grimminger, *Hanser Sozialgeschichte der deutschen Literatur vom 16. Jh. bis zur Gegenwart*, 4:461–80.

Uerlings, Herbert. *Friedrich von Hardenberg genannt Novalis: Werk und Forschung.* Stuttgart: Metzler, 1991.

———. "Novalis in Freiberg: Die Romantisierung des Bergbaus — mit einem Blick auf Tiecks *Runenberg* und E. T. A. Hoffmanns *Bergwerke zu Falun.*" *Aurora* 56 (1996): 57–77.

Vaget, Hans Rudolf. "Johann Wolfgang Goethe: Wilhelm Meisters Wanderjahre (1829)." In Lützeler, *Romane und Erzählungen zwischen Romantik und Realismus*, 136–64.

Vaßen, Florian. *Georg Weerth: Ein politischer Dichter des Vormärz und der Revolution von 1848/49.* Stuttgart: Metzler, 1971.

Veeser, Harold Aram. *The New Historicism Reader.* London: Routledge, 1994.

Vischer, F. T. *Ästhetik oder Wissenschaft des Schönen.* Edited by Robert Vischer. Hildesheim: Olms, 1996.

Völpel, Christian E. *Hermann Hesse und die deutsche Jugendbewegung.* Bonn: Bouvier, 1977.

Wagner, Monika. "Ansichten ohne Ende — oder das Ende der Ansicht: Umbrüche im Reisebild um 1830." In Bausinger, Beyrer, and Griep, *Reisekultur*, 326–35.

Walker, Mack. *German Home Towns: Community, State, and General Estate, 1648–1817.* 2nd ed. Ithaca, NY and London: Cornell, 1998.

Wallace, Anne D. *Walking, Literature and English Culture.* Oxford: Clarendon, 1993.

Wehler, Hans-Ulrich. *Deutsche Gesellschaftsgeschichte.* 4 vols. Munich: C. H. Beck, 1987–2003.

Wellmann, Angelika. *Der Spaziergang: Stationen eines poetischen Codes.* Wurzburg: Königshausen & Neumann, 1991.

Wermuth and Stieber. *Die Communisten-Verschwörungen des neunzehnten Jahrhunderts: Im amtlichen Auftrage zur Benutzung der Polizei-Behörden der sämmtlichen deutschen Bundesstaaten.* 2 vols. Berlin: Hayn, 1853–54. Reprint, Hildesheim: Olms, 1969.

Werner, Hans-Georg, ed. *Studien zu Georg Büchner.* Berlin: Aufbau, 1988.

Werner, Michael, ed. *Begegnungen mit Heine: Berichte der Zeitgenossen.* 2 vols. Hamburg: Hoffmann & Campe, 1973.

Werner, Petra. *Himmel und Erde: Alexander von Humboldt und sein Kosmos.* Berlin: Akademie, 2004.

Williams, Raymond. *Problems in Materialism and Culture.* London: Verso, 1980.

Wilson, Richard, and Richard Dutton, eds. *New Historicism and Renaissance Drama.* Harlow. UK: Longman, 1992.

Witte, Bernd, Theo Buck, Hans Dahnke, Regine Otto, and Peter Schmidt, eds. *Goethe-Handbuch.* 4 vols. Stuttgart: Metzler, 1996–98.

Wittkowski, Wolfgang, ed. *Goethe im Kontext: Kunst und Humanität, Naturwissenschaft und Politik von der Aufklärung bis zur Restauration.* Tübingen: Niemeyer, 1984.

Wolzogen, Hanna Delf von, ed. *"Geschichte und Geschichten aus Mark Brandenburg": Fontanes Wanderungen durch die Mark Brandenburg im Kontext der europäischen Reiseliteratur.* Würzburg: Königshausen & Neumann, 2003.

Wundt, Max. *Goethes Wilhelm Meister und die Entwicklung des modernen Lebensideals.* Berlin and Leipzig: Göschen, 1913.

Ziolkowski, Theodore. *German Romanticism and Its Institutions.* Princeton: Princeton UP, 1990.

# Index